CONVERSATIONS WITH BLACKS IN EVANSTON, ILLINOIS

An Evaluation of
African-American Progress in
this Suburb of Chicago

George W. Williams

American Literary Press, Inc.
Five Star Special Edition
Baltimore, Maryland

EVANSTON PUBLIC LIBRARY
1703 ORRINGTON AVENUE
EVANSTON, ILLINOIS 60201

CONVERSATIONS WITH BLACKS
IN EVANSTON, ILLINOIS

Copyright © 1998 George W. Williams

All rights reserved under International and Pan-American copyright conventions. No part of this book may be reproduced, stored in a retrieval system, or transmitted in any form, electronic, mechanical, or other means, now known or hereafter invented, without written permission of the publisher. Address all inquiries to the publisher.

Library of Congress
Cataloging in Publication Data
ISBN 1-56167-437-0

Library of Congress Card Catalog Number:
98-85765

Published by

American Literary Press, Inc.
Five Star Special Edition
8019 Belair Road, Suite 10
Baltimore, Maryland 21236

Manufactured in the United States of America

977.32 Convers

Conversations with Blacks
in Evanston, Illinois

Acknowledgments

I would like to acknowledge with gratitude the help from members of the Association for the Preservation of African American Culture and History in Evanston for providing me with names of more than one hundred prospects for interviews. Also, I am indebted to Mr. Prentis Bryson who provided me with the names of the ministers of the Black Ministers Alliance of Evanston. Mr. Bryson accompanied me when we interviewed Reverend John Norwood, pastor of Mt. Zion Missionary Baptist Church, Reverend Terrell Jackson, pastor of New Hope M.E. Church, and Reverend Larry W. Edwards, United Faith Missionary Church

I am grateful to Mr. Thomas Garnett for his material on Second Baptist Church and Nathan Branch.

For the material on the history of Ebenezer AME Church, I thank Mrs. Geraldine Cooper, Riverdale, Georgia. Her family goes back a long way in the history of Ebenezer.

Willie Higgins presented a great comprehensive history of the activities of the Twentieth Century Golf Club of Evanston. Many thanks to her.

Thanks to the Fleetwood-Jourdain Art Guild publication, "Shaping of Black Evanston," for material used.

Thanks to Yvonne Davis and the Unity publication, June 25, 1995, Community Scholarship Recognition Reception for timely materials.

Thanks to Bob and Dorothy Hancock for the Tech Sgt. William Benjamin Snell Post No. 7186 of the Veterans of Foreign Wars materials.

Thanks to Beulah Avery for her report on the history of the North Shore, Illinois LINKS.

Thanks to all of my Evanston friends who encouraged me in this project and contributed interesting and valuable information to make it a success.

Thanks to Barbara Redmond for her assistance in typing and arranging my manuscript.

Thanks to Betty, my wife, for contributing ideas and helpful hints for my writing.

Finally, I thank the people who agreed to be interviewed. They exceeded my expectations in their responses to the questions they were asked. All were generous with their comments and appeared to be eager to express them. I hope they will be happy when they see their words in print.

Table of Contents

Introduction 1
Interview Questions 7
Mrs. Ruby Alexander 10
Beulah M. Avery 14
The Bess Family 26
Lillian Cannon 41
Geraldine Franklin Cooper 51
Mrs. Helen Cooper 55
Reverend Larry W. Edwards 66
Rachel Graves 79
Bob and Dorothy Hancock 85
Dr. Avery Hill 93
Reverend Dr. Ndung'u Ikenye 112
The Reverend Terrell Jackson 122
Mrs. Anest R. Marshall 131
Louis Moseley 145
Reverend John Norwood 159
Dan Phillips 170
Albert Price 186
Allen Price 197
Edna Summers 210
Mrs. Martha Walker 214
Evelyn Williams 223
Dr. Donald Lawson 230
Mr. Spencer Jourdain 241
Bill Logan 247
Bill Saulsbury 263
Epilogue 270
Appendices 275
Appendix A 277
   New Hope Christian
Methodist Episcopal Church 282
   St. Andrew's Episcopal Church 284
   Mt. Zion Missionary Baptist Church 285
Appendix B 289
Appendix C 295
   Community Hospital of Evanston 296

Appendix D 299
    Alpha Kappa Alpha Sorority 300
Appendix E 303
    The History of the North Shore Illinois Links 304
    Twentieth Century Golf Club, Evanston Illinois 314
Appendix F 323
Appendix G 333
    Snell Post History 335
    Snell Post Commanders 337
    Youth Programs 338
    Snell Auxiliary Past Presidents 341
Appendix H 343
    History of the Alpha Phi Alpha Fraternity, Inc. 344
    Report from the 57th Anniversary Convention of
    the Alpha Phi Alpha Fraternity, Inc. 350
Appendix I 357
    The Jack-Roller
    Juvenile Delinquency: A Group Tradition

Introduction

Symbolic of blacks who left their homes in the South to seek freedom and opportunities for progress that they did not have there, was a man named Nathan Branch.

According to an article which appeared in the *Evanston News Index* in 1896, Nathan Branch was a slave who refused to be whipped. When his master threatened to whip him, he ran away, but was caught and promised a whipping by his master. Nathan promised himself that he would kill his master if his master did not kill him first. But one day his master got drunk and fell off his horse and was killed, so Nathan never got his whipping.

Eventually Nathan became tired of living conditions in the South, and he went North and joined the Army. When he was mustered out in the fall of 1864, he came to Evanston, where he worked at various jobs and finally at the post office. Nathan married and became the father of four children, moving his family to Evanston, Illinois. He purchased a house on the corner of Lake Street and Dewey Avenue.

Nathan and his wife, Ellen, were among the founders of the Second Baptist Church of Evanston.

Considering Nathan's quality of life in the South, his upward mobility in Evanston, financially and socially, was remarkable.

Like Nathan Branch, most of the blacks in Evanston belong to families which have left their homelands to escape persecution and discrimination and to obtain better opportunities to achieve at least middle class status. Other black families have moved to Evanston to enjoy the excellent features of the northern suburban city, such as the attractive shores of Lake Michigan on the eastern border, the proximity to Chicago on the southern border, easy and efficient access to western suburbs, and upscale neighborhoods on the northern border.

Evanston has benefitted from the political, educational, and social contributions of a large number of upper and upper-middle class residents who provided employment, guidance, and welfare assistance to immigrants who were in need of help.

Many blacks who worked in the homes of the upper class whites became skilled in the social graces practiced by their employers and adopted these skills for their own personal use. Consequently, many elaborate affairs, such as dinner parties and banquets were given by blacks who had worked for upper class whites. Black chauffeurs, housekeepers, and gardeners, and butlers enjoyed steady employment by wealthy whites in the years before the income tax structure changed so that income which previously had been available to them was reduced by taxation.

So blacks who had previously held jobs where their employers could give them assistance in adjusting to the requirements of living in this city had to look elsewhere for jobs, and usually found them where their relationships with bosses or employers were less personal and the employers were indifferent to the environmental adjustments required by their employees.

Some blacks who were able to spend years in employment with wealthy whites became social and cultural leaders in the black community and often they became the spokespersons for the community.

Although the dependency of blacks on the assistance of whites was helpful to blacks during the period of racial separation and discrimination, it, in many cases, resulted in creating a patronizing attitude of many whites toward blacks. They found it difficult to accept the fact that some blacks were capable of making appropriate decisions for themselves. Also, there were blacks who had become so used to their white benefactors making their decisions that they became reluctant to accept black leadership.

This attitude of blacks has lessened during the past years because of the emergence of black leaders who have gained the confidence and respect of most of the residents of the city.

My parents came to Evanston in 1914 from Greenville, South Carolina. Why they chose to live in Evanston, I don't know, but I think it was because there were so many of their friends who had moved from Greenville to Evanston and liked it here. I have never heard a word of criticism of Evanston from my parents as long as they lived.

At the time my parents came to Evanston, employment for blacks was limited. Many blacks worked as servants for affluent whites. Some became employees of government agencies. Some worked in factories located within or outside of Evanston. A few worked as caretakers of shops or other properties. A few provided professional services as medical doctors, dentists, lawyers, optometrists, ministers, and teachers.

Also, there were several stores owned by blacks which served the black community. Most of the black business and professional people prospered because blacks felt more comfortable with their own people and to avoid the embarrassment of being rejected by white business or professional people.

My father chose the building trades for his occupation. Dad was six feet tall and weighed over two hundred pounds. His hands were large and scarred from handling heavy materials. When he took his shirt off, the muscles of his arms seemed to "jump up" at you. Any heavy object to be lifted became a challenge for him which he accepted willingly. Dad needed all of the strength that he had to do his job as a hod carrier. A hod carrier in the building trades loads cement or brick on a V-shaped wooden platform with a long handle. The hod carrier would place the loaded hod on his shoulders and take it to a place where the plasterer or brick layer was working. Sometimes it required carrying the one hundred plus pound loaded hod two or three stories up the ladder. It took a pretty strong man to do this eight or more hours a day.

But Dad loved this work. He often laughed with his friends about how a man would get on the ladder with a load and find it too heavy, so Dad would have to go and help him. Dad was proud of his Hod Carriers Union card.

Dad worked with men of different nationalities. As he talked to some of his friends about his work he would sometimes speak in the dialect of a Swede, or an Italian, or an Irishman. He had no problems with people of other races. That was probably because he was sure of himself. He was unafraid and unpretending. You took him just for what he was. He had to apologize for nothing.

Dad worked for plastering contractors. He worked for several different ones, but I think his favorite contractor was Hugh Orr who lived on Central Street in Evanston. Hugh Orr had a son named Jack who went to Haven School when I was a student there.

I remember Dad coming home from work, opening the front door, walking down the hall, dressed in overalls covered with lime and cement, and smoking his pipe, in a jolly mood. He would kiss my sister and me, proceed to the kitchen where my mother was cooking supper, pat her on the fanny and kiss her. Mamma always responded as though she had been waiting for this moment.

If you are wondering how Dad got the strength to handle his job you have to know what Mamma was feeding us. We had a stove which was fired by coal on one side and gas burners on the other side. Mamma always cooked dinner on the coal fire side. Of course, it was my job to make the fires and bring up coal from the basement.

Some of our menu consisted of mustard greens, collard greens, cabbage, string beans, lima beans, baked beans, pigs' feet, pig tails, corn bread, biscuits, and rolls. On Sunday we had chicken or ham and some kind of cake or pie for dessert.

Dad ate like there was no tomorrow. Mamma didn't even sit at the table. She sat to the side on her little stool, ready to serve anything to us she thought we wanted. Dad sat at one end of the table. Next to him I sat. My sister, Edna, sat next to me, and Aunt Lula, Dad's sister sat at the other end of the table. The back of the table was against the wall under a window, which gave us a view of the Hunter property next door.

After supper, Dad would retire to his bedroom, take off his shoes, smoke his pipe for a while, then retire so he would be ready for the next day.

Mamma supervised the cleaning, of the kitchen, which was done by my sister and me. Then she reminded us to get at our homework. Before she went to bed she checked our homework assignments to see that they were completed. When Edna and I were students at Haven School and Evanston Township High School, Mamma impressed us with the fact that we must compete with others in everything we did— our studies, athletics, conduct, projects—to expect no favors, and not to be discouraged if others seemed to get the breaks and we did not. Her important message was that we should persevere, no matter how difficult the circumstances might be.

Mamma was a fire ball and a fighter. I remember an occasion when I was in the fifth grade at Foster School. Three other boys and I were in disagreement about something, and when we reached a vacant lot at the corner of Dewey Avenue and Emerson Street, they jumped me. My house was in the middle of the block at 1715 Emerson Street, between Darrow and Dewey Avenues. Mamma just happened to be on the porch and saw these boys giving it to me on the corner. Mamma always wore a long skirt and a short apron. Well, you should have seen her lift up that skirt and apron and dash down to the corner with a big stick and light into those boys. They didn't waste any time getting out of there. But both Mamma and I knew that I would be playing with those boys the next day. That's the way it was then. Kids had bloody fist fights one day, and the next day they were pals again.

It has been said that "it takes a village to rear a child." Sociologists express that in a different way. They say that a child should have the advantage of an "extended family." Simply, it means that others are involved in transmitting cultural traits to the child in such a manner that the child can identify with others who care about him.

My parents had purchased, in 1928, a large two flat stucco house with basement and attic, a three car garage, and grounds which contained three cherry trees, three apple trees, and a pear tree. We rented the second floor apartment, which contained six rooms and a bath. The address is 1715 Emerson Street.

In our first floor apartment lived my parents, my sister, my aunt, my grandmother and step-grandfather, and I.

Usually, the tenants were friendly with us and we did some socializing. This meant that my conduct was always under scrutiny of this household.

This brief description of my formative years in Evanston is to convey my interest in Evanston and my appreciation for all the advantages and opportunities I had in this city. Whatever achievements I have made, I owe to my family and other Evanstonians who have assisted me.

Since 1980, my wife and I have lived in the Dearborn Park development on the near South Side of Chicago. There was a time in our lives when we felt in need of a new life style. All of the family I have mentioned had passed, and it seemed that the ties that had bound us to this city were weakened considerably. But, we do make occasional trips back to Evanston to visit friends and for me to attend monthly meetings of my college fraternity, Alpha Phi Alpha. Perhaps, my most regular visit is to Woody's Barber Shop on Emerson Street. I am always delighted to talk to Woody and familiar customers who are waiting to be served. This seems to be where I get the latest news about Evanston, and particularly black life in Evanston.

Most of the comments I hear are positive about the progress of many blacks in Evanston, but there seems to be a consensus among them that the quality of black life in Evanston is deteriorating

In order to obtain a consensus of the attitudes of blacks in Evanston about their city, I prepared a list of questions which concern events, conditions, and activities that have or are still affecting their lives in Evanston today.

Volunteers were asked to be interviewed for information which would be tape recorded and published in book form. Most of the volunteers are over the age of sixty. One lady is 101, and one girl is twenty-six. All interviewees were asked the same questions.

Comments of the volunteers were quite frank, and expressions were very colorful. To convey the candor of the interviewees, their comments were not too closely edited. What was heard is what I have printed.

At the end of each interview a list of questions is provided to encourage discussion of the interview.

I hope you have as much fun reading your neighbors' comments about Evanston as I did.

Interview Questions

The following is a copy of the letter I forwarded to many of my interviewees before the actual interviews took place.

Dear   :

    Thank you for consenting to participate in my research project.

    In order to prepare you for your interview, I have outlined the questions you will be asked. You may say as much as you want to in discussing the questions asked, and I hope you will express yourself freely as though you are in conversation with a personal friend.

    To gather the important information for my research, I have designed the questions to cover the major subjects which affect the lives of African-American residents of Evanston.

Survey Questions

1. Describe, as well as you can, your family's settlement in Evanston. Tell where they came from, why they settled in Evanston, and the number of residential changes they have made since they have been here.
2. Discuss, if you can, how your neighbors have organized to promote fellowship and improve life and property where they live.
3. Comment on African-Americans who have served the community as business or professional people. For example, grocers, druggists, dentists, medical doctors, optometrists, podiatrists, etc.
4. Describe the types of jobs you and others in your family have held in Evanston. Be sure to mention your duties and employer-employee relationships.
5. Describe your education in Evanston. Mention where you went to school, your attitude toward the teachers, the teachers' attitude toward you, opportunities to participate in all of the

school activities, etc.

6. What is your interest in politics in Evanston? Are you a party member? Do you feel that you are well represented? Can you name some of your local political heroes? How do you think politics has changed in Evanston over the years?

7. If you attend church, tell us about it. What do you enjoy the most in your service? Who are some of the historical people in your church? How do you think the church can be helpful in making the community a safe and happy place in which to live?

8. Do you attend the YMCA or YWCA? If not, why not? If you do, tell about your participation in activities there. If you remember attending the YMCA when it was located at 1014 Emerson Street, tell us about you experiences there. Mention as many names as you can.

9. If you were a participant in sports or a sports fan, tell us about your experiences as a fan or an athlete, or both. Mention Foster Field, Mason Park, ETHS, YMCA, or Northwestern University. Also mention as many names as you can.

10. Discuss the kinds of entertainment you have enjoyed in Evanston, and where they took place. Example: Foster School, YMCA, Masonic Temple, house parties, churches, plays, dances, gambling, after hours clubs, policy wheels, etc.

11. If you belong to a social club, describe your activities, your goals, interesting personalities. If you belong to a fraternity or sorority, describe your goals, activities, interesting personalities, how long your chapter has been active in Evanston, etc.

12. If you or someone in your family is a lodge member, name the lodge and tell us as much as you can about the lodge and how it may be different from other lodges.

13. If you or someone in your family has served in the military, describe this service and mention as many interesting stories about the service as you can think of.

14. Describe, as much as your experiences will permit you, the medical facilities including hospitals and clinics that provide medical services to African-Americans in Evanston.

15. Discuss your relationship with the various arms of the government, such as the mayor, alderman, health department, police department, etc. What are some improvements you would like to see in these relationships?

16. Describe the social environment in regards to conditions which threaten the peaceful, progressive lives of African-Americans and other citizens of Evanston.

You will be given at least a week to examine these questions, before an appointment will be made for the interview. Your conversation will be tape recorded.
I look forward to a great visit with you.
Sincerely,
George W. Williams

Mrs. Ruby Alexander

Well, my family came from Abbeville, South Carolina, as a lot of Evanstonians did. My father died when I was about three years and six months old, so my mother came North. We had some relatives up here. Of course, at that time they had a lot of prejudice and incidents in the South. My grandparents were sharecroppers, and they lived out on a farm. Every Saturday people would get their wagons and go into town and get their supplies and stuff like that. Once there was an incident where a black man got "smart." He was Annabelle Crawford's grandfather. I think you have heard about that incident. At first they put him in jail then they let him out, and then they killed him and took his body and tied it to a wagon and dragged it through the street. It was a horrible thing. So my mother said that all of the blacks who could get train fare caught the first train North. So that is why, of course she had relatives in Evanston, we came to live here.

The first place we lived was right on the corner of West Railroad and Payne Streets. There was a little house there. Then we moved to a house on Jackson Avenue, a while later we lived in the 1800 block of Brown Avenue. Finally we moved to this house, 1935 Brown Avenue. We have been here ever since, even when I was in high school.

We have a block club. I can't say that I go to all of the meetings, but I did go to a meeting last month. They have a meeting every third Wednesday. Elsa LaVelle Cleveland organized the club quite a few years ago. She is a very good worker, and I wish I did as well. The club does a lot of good things, like paving our alleys, getting lights put in the alleys, and working with the police department to try to keep the place clean.

Business and Professional People

Well, you know Watkins, Small, Griffin, Fleming. They are all gone now.

We don't know whether integration had anything to do with it, or just what the reason is. Now we just feel that we don't have anything.

Back in those days we had the Community Hospital, it's gone. The YMCA, that was our old haunt, and it's all gone. There are very few blacks who have businesses here. At Fleming's place they have some foreigners now. Even right here on the corner where the cleaners were, I can't think of the owner's name, but he used to play the organ at Friendship Church, that place is now run by some Asians. I don't know whether it's our indifferences, or what, but it just looks like we have sort of lost everything. Others just seem to come in and take over. Maybe it's because they are more industrious than we are. It has changed. It wasn't that way when we were growing up.

Jobs Ruby and Family Held

You know, I didn't go any further than high school. My main job that I held for twenty-nine years and retired from was a nurses aide at St. Francis Hospital. Del had different factory jobs. He worked a lot on those games and things that he designed, and stuff like that, but he could never get anything going, because, I was talking to Les Brownlee not too long ago, and you know they were close friends, and he said that Del was just before his time. It just wasn't time for us. Maybe if things had been different, he could have made it with his games. He had a baseball game, a bowling game. In fact, my son took some of the stuff and he still fools around with it.

What is Your Interest in Politics in Evanston?

Not very much. I vote every time election day comes around. I will vote, but I attend very few political meetings. I pay my dues to the NAACP, and I should work more with them, but that's about the size of it.

We have a black mayor who is a beautiful person and I think she is doing as much as she can. I really do.

We were discussing our alderman in a recent block club meeting last month. They were saying that they call him, but he doesn't return the calls. I guess he is doing something, but he should be in closer contact with the people of his ward.

Do You Attend Church, Ruby?

All the time. I grew up in Ebenezer, but we had four children, and it was so hard to get they kids to Sunday School, because at the time we didn't have a car, so I started sending them right here to Bethel Church. So, I thought that rather than uproot the kids, I would also go to Bethel. It's a nice little church I go to every Sunday. I work with the Missionary

Society, a lay organization, and a visitation and concerns committee. That's about three that I work with, but I do go to church faithfully. I think that helps me quite a bit.

Our minister is Reverend Baldwick. He's been there about ten years.

YMCA

That's where we had to go. We had our proms there. We couldn't have them at the high school.

I remember Mr. Hummons and Mr. Bouyer, who was also at Foster School. He was quite a guy,.also, Mr. Pyant, who lived right across the street from me.

Sports

My husband Del played with the Pike's Pals football team, so I had to attend their games. Some of his teammates were Julius Sutton, Babe Cooper, Pike Powell, Gordon Gunn, Leon "Bennie" Price, Charlie Whitside, Chuck Glass.

Social Clubs

I still have a group of girls, some are my friends from high school, with whom I still meet, like Helen Glass, Marian Mitchell Dawson, Ruby Taylor. We get together a couple of times a month. We don't do anything but get together and talk about people and eat and play cards, like bridge. You know you have to have some kind of outlet.

Community Hospital

I worked with the hospital auxiliary. The hospital seemed to run very well as long as Dr. Hill was there. Then they started getting new doctors in there and they started to do all kinds of underhanded things. They would bring people in there with supposed accident cases, suing people when there really was no reason and stuff like that. So the hospital just went down.

I miss the hospital, but after they started letting blacks go to Evanston Hospital and St. Francis Hospital, and all those places, I think that is the thing that really killed the Community Hospital. You know how we are. If we could afford it, we went to the bigger hospital. It seems that we don't have anything in the neighborhoods anymore.

Neighborhood Problems

The world is so different these days. These kids are not raised the way we were. Maybe the parents are too busy, because it takes so much to live now that they are trying to make a living. They do the best they can, but you can only do so much. Sometimes we talk about that at the block club meetings and people say, "What can I do?" I don't know, and no one can tell you what you can do. All they do is say, "You should become involved."

Discussion Questions

1. Describe the conditions in Abbeville, South Carolina which caused Ruby's family and other blacks to move North? Why did Ruby's family come to Evanston?
2. What are some of the accomplishments of Ruby's block club?
3. Why does Ruby feel that the blacks of Evanston do not have the contact with each other that they used to have?
4. How does Ruby feel about her political representation in Evanston?
5. What does Ruby say about the neighborhood problems?
6. When did Ruby feel that the Community Hospital was running well?

About Ruby Alexander

When we were growing up in Evanston, I knew Ruby as Ruby Cater. She was a grade a head of me in school, and in my sister Edna's class. Edna always spoke of her with high regard, and said that she was very quiet.

Ruby married Delbert Alexander. "Del was about three years older than I, and I considered him a role model. Del was intelligent, an excellent athlete, an inspirational leader, and carried all of these attributes in a modest, quiet way. You should have seen him in action as the left-handed quarter back of the Pike's Pals football team, which played its home games at Foster Field.

Del was also an inventor. He designed some electronic sports games which should have been marketed. Maybe if Del had been less modest and more "pushy" his games would have been promoted. Anyway, Del was my role model.

I was delighted to be welcomed into Ruby's home to talk to her about her experiences in Evanston, and I think she enjoyed reminiscing.

Beulah M. Avery

I came to Evanston because I met James Avery in college in Langston, Oklahoma. We were married on June 28, 1939 in Pueblo, Colorado, which was my home, and I came to live in Evanston after that marriage.

We worked here for two years, and when World War II came along, we moved to Detroit. James was looking for some defense work. We were there for two years when Uncle Sam called him to go into the service. I came back to Evanston in July, and he was sent overseas in December. Then I went back to Colorado and lived with my family until he returned from the war.

Then we came to Evanston and went into business. We took over the Fleming Grocery Store and ran that business for a while until the Flemings came back.

After that we moved to 2304 Emerson Street and we lived there for twenty-nine years. Then we moved to 4520 Madison Street, Skokie, Illinois, where we reside now.

Our first address in Evanston, after we got married was 2117 Emerson Street in an apartment over Mrs. Flournoy. The two years that we lived there were wonderful. I met a lot of people in Evanston who are still my good friends. It hasn't changed. We had a lot of fun. We didn't have any money, but we had a lot of fun.

Neighborhood Organizations

Strangely enough, I have never lived anyplace where they had an active block club. But, I have been a member of organizations that worked for the betterment of the community, local and national. And so did James. We both worked in scouting. You know we have three children. Jim Jr. was born in Detroit. Arlene and Marsha were born in Evanston, but as they grew up we belonged to organizations that involved the children. We devoted a lot of time to that, and I think it paid off well for our children.

After they outgrew scouting, then we joined Jack and Jill, which was a family organization. When they outgrew that, then James and I went into adult organizations. He went back into the lodge, the Masons, the Shriners, and in later years, the 33rd Degree Mason organization. I became active again in Delta Sigma Theta Sorority. Then I joined the Links. All of these are service organizations. I never wanted to belong to an organization that was not a service organization but was purely social.

Business & Professional People

I think of Mr. and Mrs. John Fleming, who were grocers at that time, and also Mr. and Mrs. Watkins who had Watkins Grocery Store. Then there were Ezell and Chlotel Griffin who had a grocery store on Emerson Street near Dodge Avenue.

The druggist was Dr. Morrison.

Some of the physicians were Dr. Hill who delivered Arlene, and Dr. Gatlin who delivered Marsha.

Dr. Penn was my mother-in-law's doctor for years and years. In fact, one of my brothers-in-law, Rudy, is named Abelard for Dr. Penn.

Dr. Avery Hill was the optometrist. Dr. Alvin Keith was the podiatrist. He grew up with James' brother, Joseph. My mother-in-law took care of him while his mother worked. They lived on Ridge Avenue, and the Avery family lived on Clark Street. Their back doors were kind of close, and my mother-in-law took care of Alvin for years.

Then, there were teachers; for instance, Mr. Bouyer. He was at Foster School. We have known him as one who kept order rather than teach. Then Joseph Hill came to Evanston. He grew up in Evanston also. He became a P.E. teacher at Foster Elementary School, which my children attended. I became very friendly with him because I would go over and volunteer at Foster in the lunch program. He was assigned by the principal to also be there to help with the lunch program. I did that for years. Then he became the principal of Foster School. Then he later received several promotions, until finally he became superintendent of District Sixty-Five. Through those years, we became very close friends and remain so to this day.

He said that when he would come to school in the morning, he was having some family problems, and two little girls would come and run to him and take hold of his hands, and that helped him to make his day. One little girl was Marsha Avery and the other little girl was Tyrona Anderson. They are still friends, too.

Employment

James did not want me to work until the children were up to a certain age. I stayed home with the kids until Marsha, the youngest was going to school full time.

I went to employment agencies, etc. The first thing they said was "Well, Beulah, you know you're colored." Then I finally went out to the Fair Store, which was in Old Orchard at that time. They told me that they did not hire black people to sell. They didn't have that policy yet. They took all of my history and everything and in the mean time, I did volunteer work up at Haven School. I would go up there at the noon hour and relieve the secretary so she could go to lunch. When that job became available, I applied. Nothing happened, so I went down to the Board of Education and Dr. Anderson, who was the personnel director at that time, told me that job was filled, but asked me to fill out an application because they were going to hire some secretaries in the elementary schools in September. I didn't bother. I threw out the applications because I didn't believe anything he said. I went back to the Fair because they called me to go to work. In the beginning they told me all these tests I would have to take, such as a TB test and all that kind of stuff. And then they told me to come to work the next day. I couldn't understand that.

Well, they put me in the marking room. I stayed there for a little while, and the manager called me into his office and said, "I've been looking at your application and I think I have a job that you can do." Well, they were having trouble with the clerk on the cash register. At night he had to balance everything out and then take it to the downtown store. Many cash registers would have a lot of overages, and some shortages. So he set a table up in his office and put me in there and showed me how to find these mistakes.

The next day he would go down to the manager of the department of the clerk who made the mistake. You see, I couldn't work as a clerk, but I could get behind the scenes and find those dumb mistakes those clerks were making.

In the meantime, Dr. Anderson called and said that he got my telephone number from Dr. Clem, who was principal of Foster School. I had not filled out the application, so I went down and he said that he wanted me to start at Dawes School.

I worked there a couple of years. The principal always gave me good evaluations, so when a job became available in the personnel office, to work for Dr. Anderson, who was the personnel director, I went for an interview. There was one other girl who was also a secretary in the district elementary schools who was interviewed. Well, I didn't get that job, but he told me that it wasn't because I wasn't qualified, or anything like that. It was just his choice. He just chose the other girl. So, I went back to my old school. I hadn't been there but about two weeks and they called me to go back to Dr. Anderson. The girl didn't last but two weeks. So, I got the job.

I worked in the personnel office for twenty years. I was there when Joe Hill became personnel director, before he left to be superintendent.

I worked for the district for twenty-three years. I had very good relations with my employers and the employees. I was very fortunate that I didn't have to leave Evanston. When I was at the elementary school, I had the same time off that the kids had off, so I was there with my children. When I went to working a full year, when the kids were older, it worked out well.

Education in Evanston

My kids were educated in Evanston. A lot of their little friends' parents took them out of Foster School and put them in private schools, etc., and they didn't do any better than my kids. We worked with the kids, and we worked with the teachers. We let the teachers know that we were interested in our children, and if there was any problem, they were to let us know and we would be there and see about it and take care of it. We were always available.

They did have problems. One teacher didn't give Marsha the grade that she thought she should have received. We went out to the school, and we told our kids, "We will be out there, but you had better be right, too." So, I talked to the teacher, and she said, "Well, if she were going to college, that would be different." Oh, James hit the ceiling. He said, "I'll buy every damn book in this school. That girl is going to college." She had prejudged. But that's what we did all through high school, for all three children.

The same thing happened to Arlene in high school. James told the teacher, "You know what? You were out here when I was in high school, you've been here too long." But it was always a case of black kids being slighted.

There were three kinds working on the same project, and our child got a lower grade. We wanted to know why our child, if there were three of them working on the same project, would get a lower grade. So, those are the things we had to fight, and we did. I even went out there and one teacher said, "I'm not sure that she knows the material, because she doesn't talk." Well, they had an assignment and Arlene got a straight A on that, so whether she talked on or not, she knew the work. Lo and behold, Arlene did her student teaching at Evanston Township High School, and then got a job out there and taught next door to the same teacher who had said, "I don't know if she knows the material . . ." So, those are the things we had to go through and laugh at, but it paid off because the kids were serious about their work.

Politics

We have belonged to the Fifth Ward Republican Club for many years. James worked in that and it paid off because when he came back from the service, for some reason I can't remember exactly, he didn't get the service pay that all the soldiers were getting. When he contacted Margaret Stitt Church, she got right on that one. Whatever it was that he was supposed to get and was entitled to, came through.

The last job James had was with the State of Illinois. He worked there for many years on the state trucks, but he wasn't as active as before in politics.

Some of my political heroes were Mr. Jourdain, and I guess everybody knows Dr. Fischer, Leon Robinson, and Josephine Robinson.

Church

I attend Ebenezer AME Church. I have been an AME all my life. I enjoy church.

Church and schools. Everybody has to do a little bit more about the community to try to make it safer and happier. We should get the children into the church, because they are our next leaders, etc. If they don't learn now, and I think they are having a big problem with that, they need to be taught the fundamentals of living with people, growing up together and sharing, helping each other, being responsible for their own actions, and not being led by someone else who is leading them down the wrong path. There are so many things that need to be done. And I guess the churches are trying, but getting leaders, that's another problem.

Church Programs for Children and Youths
They have the Sunday School and they have started, in June, the Frances Bell Literacy Program. It is a summer school program named for Mrs. Bell about historical people in Ebenezer. They have the choir for the children. We have quite a few children in, and we have a group called the Contemporaries. They're out of school, but they are young people, and they still need some direction. They are very active in the church.

YMCA
The YMCA, before I came to Evanston, was quite active. It was the place my husband, James, attended. He went to conferences and so forth. His friends were members and they learned quite a lot there. The Y was *the* place to go.

Sports
When Jim Jr., was in high school, we went to everything that he was in. He ran track. We were there all the time. But we didn't let our kids go to Mason Park and Foster Field that much We felt that we didn't need that facility, so they did not go over there that much. Then, too, we weren't close by those parks. There was always someone at home to direct them.

Marsha's boys learned to swim at the Evanston Y. I would go with them on Sundays and watch them.

Sororities
I belong to the Delta Sigma Theta Sorority, and have been a member of the Evanston chapter since 1939.

I joined at Langston University, but I was inactive for a few years when I was trying to bring my children up and I just didn't have the money. James was working all these many jobs so that I could stay home, and so I didn't get out a lot at night. But when I got to the time when I could, I became active because it is a service organization it's not a social organization.

In later years, I joined the Links. This is another service organization. I joined the Eastern Star in Colorado. I joined under my brother because James was not a member at that time. He was overseas. When I came back to Evanston, I never rejoined.

Both the sorority and the Links are very active and they give scholarships. They have health fairs, and all of their energies are directed toward helping someone else. The programs don't have to be right here in Evanston they can be overseas. We give money to the African Water Wells, and all that sort of thing.

James belonged to the house which was here in Evanston, and it was called Mt. Moriah. He was a past worthy master of that. He worked hard in that organization. He loved it. Later he joined the Council of Deliberation, but the chapter is located in Waukegan. He also joined the Shriners, and that is located in Waukegan. As long as he could, he went up there to meetings. He went to national meetings, and so on. He loved those organizations. They were very nice to him, and very nice to me during his illness and when he was deceased. As a matter of fact, one of the members from the Waukegan chapter paid for my Mother's Day breakfast that Mr. Moriah give this year, 1995.

Military

James Senior went into the military and became a boatswain's mate. That was something new when he first joined the Navy. He knew he had to go into the service, but he preferred the Army because they would give him three weeks to get ready to leave home. But when he went down, they put him into the Navy, because they needed men. So, he had one week to get ready.

I was in Colorado with my first born, showing him off to my dad, and I had to come back real fast because James only had a week He moved me back to Evanston, and then he was gone for two years.

He told me of a lot of interesting experiences in the Navy. He said he was glad that he did go into the Navy, but he never went any further than Hawaii. He was eating steaks, fried in butter, while here we were scuffling to get some beans because everything was rationed. He was living the life out there. He always told me not to send him any care packages. I never could understand, but he couldn't put it in a letter, because the letters were so highly censored. When he came home he said he was eating good food and everything. He never had to sleep in a hammock. He slept in a bed all the time.

But he was overseas, and he got into some situations which could have been fatal. The good Lord just took care of him. He was over a group of men, and they were going down into this hold, which was on a ship that was sunken, and bring out these bodies, or whatever was down there.

The men rebelled. They said they weren't going down there anymore. The next night that whole ship blew up. There was an explosion. He could have been in there. The Good Lord was with him.

Then there was a time when they had a mutiny because, when the entertainers would come over there, the black sailors couldn't attend the affairs. Then there would be black entertainers. They had to stand outside the fence. They didn't like that, and they didn't like the idea that when the Navy went into town to bring the entertainment to the base, they thought maybe some of the blacks should go too. But no, they wouldn't allow that.

One night they had that black unit that was stationed there in Hawaii, so they went up there and got those guys and brought them down to their place. Those guys were armed. After that, they broke that division up. They sent some of them to Olkinawa, and all around. They didn't want those black boys with ammunition. They got rid of them real fast.

I wish Jim were here to tell you all of this because he had some weird tales.

It was hard, even though it wasn't as hard as sleeping in hammocks and not getting the best food. But it was harder for two years.

While he was gone, I saved everything I could. He used to send me extra money. Where did he get that money? I don't know. I think he was gambling myself. He sent that money home and we saved it, and when he came back we had saved enough for a down payment to buy the grocery store from his uncle and aunt, Mr. and Mrs. John Fleming.

Then we started saving all over again for the house, and we bought the house.

I remember my dad saying when I got the letter that Jim was coming home, "Now you can prepare to live." I had never thought about it any other way, you know, that he would never come back. Some things you just remember, and I remember my dad saying that.

I kept the pictures of him in front of my little boy, so he would know his daddy when he came back. Of course, he came back to Great Lakes because that is where he went originally. I was in Colorado. They didn't give him any train fare to Colorado. He just got a quarter to go to Evanston.

So he came out to Colorado to get us and he rode the train, the Zephyr. The train went to Denver, and he had to change trains to come down to Pueblo. He found out that he had a long wait for another train, but he could get a bus and come down much faster, so he got the bus. When he got to Colorado Springs, the bus stopped and he got off like everybody else and went into this little restaurant. Now Colorado Springs is just forty miles from Pueblo. Don't you know they didn't want to serve him. He said, "I'm just here waiting on the bus." They called the police. The police came by and put him in the police car and drove him around Colorado Springs for what they called a "cooling off period," but when he got back to the bus station, the bus was gone.

Well, when the bus arrived at Pueblo, I was looking for James, and the bus driver said, "You looking for a colored guy?" and threw his bags to me. The bag had his discharge papers in there, everything of importance, everything that he had, and you know the world is full of "colored guys." I didn't have to be the wife. No name. He just threw them off.

James came down on the next bus. Let me tell you. He was mad. He was mad. I won't say he was angry because he was mad. At that time, I was working at the Girl Scout headquarters, and that was the first time they had ever had a black employee. So we came down there and got a street car. Jim didn't want a white person to touch him. The street car would be crowded, but he was so angry he didn't want a white person to touch him. He was a mess. He was just angry. Mad. To have been overseas trying to do something for this country and then to come home and be treated like that. Oh! He was angry, it took him a long time to get over that, too. But he finally did.

Now, I said that I was the first black employee at Girl Scout Headquarters and when I came to Evanston, the first job I got, I was the first black secretary in School District 65. Also, I was the first black secretary to go into the administration building. Now, Mr. Lanton had worked in the building, but after he got his doctorate degree, they couldn't put him back over there at Foster School, so they gave him some research project and that sort of thing.

Well, it was a mess. They were going to hire a black woman and Dr. Anderson told the people who were working in the building, "We are going to hire a black woman." So, I was told that this woman who was head bookkeeper was enraged that a black person was going to work there. But she turned out to be one of my best friends. She was just as nice and friendly, so I broke that color line. After that, they hired a lot of blacks. More black teachers were hired and so on.

Dr. Gordon Anderson was instrumental in starting to hire black teachers.

He used to talk with me. He had a lot of applicants, and would say, "Mrs. Avery, you know I talked with him. He knows his work, but the man's English is terrible. I can't hire him because those kids out there at the junior high school would tear him up, laughing, and he wouldn't be able to control a class. But he knows his work. He knows his subject matter." But we have come a long way from that now. People are speaking better English.

Vera Brownlee and I used to talk about that. She was trying to help some of the black teachers in speaking English.

It's too bad she had to die so early, because she was interested in helping children and the black teachers as they came along.

Medical Facilities

When my children were born, they had the clinic and it was at Foster School. You could take a baby over there, so I took my children. I don't remember taking Marsha, but I guess I did I remember taking Arlene and Jim.

The Links conduct a health fair every March in North Chicago. At that fair they give shots or vaccinations or whatever is needed, and a led poisoning screen, and that is sponsored by our chapter of the Links (North Shore Illinois Chapter of the Links).

Community Hospital

Arlene and Marsha, both, were born at the Community Hospital.

When Marsha was born, they still had that elevator where you had to pull the ropes down, and I had rushed over there with Marsha and I think Jewel and Ben pulled those ropes.

I had very good treatment there.

I have been in the Evanston Hospital with my back.

Relations with Governmental Agencies

The Mayor, Lorainne Morton, is one of my good friends. Alderman, Gene Beck, we had a good relationship with him when he was alderman. Mr. Jourdain was alderman before I moved here, so I don't know about him.

My husband's mother had a lot of problems with police, because when they had something happen in Evanston they would start looking for a nice looking young man, black young man, they would always pick up Joe or James. She was tired of it. She told them "Don't put your foot on my porch anymore." They were looking for her sons, but they weren't the ones in trouble. But that is what they would always do until she got them told. They didn't bother her anymore.

Social Environment

At this point, I think not only Evanston, I believe all over the world we are going backward. Because young people are not interested in values. Of course, we have the drug problem. And that is not helping. It is hindering. The way they dress and these hair styles. It is not conducive to good thinking, good living, in my opinion.

The movies. The violence on TV. They say that isn't hurting the kids, but I believe it is. I can't help but believe that, the way these kids see too much and they know too much, too young. If you could see some of these programs on the air.

A mother and her sixteen-year-old daughter were not getting along because she wanted the sixteen-year-old daughter to have sex, and the girl didn't want it. But she had convinced her thirteen-year-old daughter to have sex. The thirteen-year-old girl now is sexually active. Now, what can you do at thirteen? They don't even know what love is.

So, they get so many things that are going on that are not healthy. I think our people ought to get hold of things. If black people don't help black people, white people certainly are not going to do it. You are not going to get anywhere if you don't have the skills that are needed, and our kids are not staying in school. The skills used to be handling a broom, but that's not it anymore. They have a computer to handle the broom. People have fought computers for a long time, but everything is on computers now.

Discussion Questions

1. What were the residential changes of the James Avery family from the time of their marriage until this date? What made the changes necessary?
2. James and Beulah participated in several organizations which worked for the betterment of the community. Describe some of their activities.
3. How did Beulah help the Foster School program? Why did she give this service? With which member of the faculty was she the most impressed?
4. Why was Beulah's entry to the work force delayed?

5. What examples of racial discrimination did Beulah face in throughout her career?
6. How did the Averys respond to instances where high school teachers or administration had been unfair or prejudiced in the evaluation of the work of the Avery children?
7. How did political involvement benefit the Averys?
8. Describe the Avery social and civic affiliations.
9. Describe Jim's difficult experiences while he was in the Navy.
10. What experience did Jim have in Colorado Springs that made him angry and disgusted with the authorities?
11. How did Beulah "break the color line" in District 65?
12. What is Beulah's opinion of the social environment in Evanston?

About Beulah "Boots" Avery

My wife, Betty, and I visited the home of the Averys, who now live in Skokie, and sat around a familiar table in their kitchen. We reflected on the days when so many delicious items were being prepared and served from this room. There was, also, a tone of sadness, too, because Jim, Boots' husband was no longer with us. He had passed about two years before. All of us miss him tremendously.

Betty recalls that one of Jim's classmates at Langston University, which both Jim and Boots attended, said that when Jim got there he wanted to meet the "finest chick on the campus." Well, it turned out to be Boots, and he got his wish.

Beulah and Jim, Betty and I, and three other couples formed a social club. This group carried us through the depression and early war years with humor, cooperation and care. If I do say so, when Betty and Boots walked down the street wearing shorts, heads turned.

Sadly, the war and family situation changes, plus the loss of some of the members ended the Couples Club as we knew it. But we still remember.

Boots' cooperation in giving us this interview revives those old memories and brings us up to date on her life since the "good old days" when we were young.

The Bess Family

Mrs. Evelyn Bess, mother
Ted Bess, son
Hugh Bess, son
Reva, daughter

Evelyn: Well, I came from Jamaica. *James also came here before us. He came in 1967. I came over in 1968. I arranged for the children to come in 1969. I found that the biggest problem here in Evanston was the housing. We lived in a "cracker box" with one room until the children came. We eventually found an apartment, but it wasn't that good. We soon had to get another one. Finally, we moved here where we have been ever since.

The children went through school here without any problems. Reva attended college, but Hugh said he didn't want to go. He wanted to go into the service, so he joined the Marines.

Question: Why did you leave Jamaica?

Evelyn: I didn't want to come, but James had come here before me and he wanted me to come to see how things were. So I came in and I promised to go home in August. The girl had a scholarship in Jamaica, and if she should leave that scholarship she would not get it back. He knew the head mistress over there and he told her that the girl was here. When I received the letter from Jamaica, I was surprised because I didn't know he had done that because I was planning to go home in August. But we were doing pretty good in Jamaica.

Question: When you came here, did you find employment? Where?

Evelyn: Yes. The first place was at the Belmont Hotel in health care. Mr. Bess was working at the Hyatt Regency Hotel.

Question: How are your neighbors?

*James: Mr. Bess, father of the family.

Evelyn: We don't have any problems around here. Everybody around here helps. We have good relationships. There is one neighbor who is nosey, but he is all right because he watches the place when we're away. This is a mixed neighborhood. We have meetings sometimes, but I don't go.

Reva: I have been to some meetings, but basically it's just about getting along with each other and about what is happening, such as crime and property damage. As my mom said, the old neighbors had kids, but most of the new neighbors did not have kids that we grew up with. So we did not have a close relationship.

Evelyn (on professional and business people): I remember a doctor whose office was on Pitner Street. His name was Dr. Spencer.

Hugh: I had a few odd jobs before going into the service. I had a job with Mr. Dougherty, right down the street. I used to do gardening for him on weekends. I used to have a friend of Mom's, Mrs. Sherman, who lived in Winnetka. I used to go up there and do a little gardening work. I had a paper route, and worked in a bake shop over here.

    I went to Nichols Junior High School and Evanston Township High School. I did my elementary work back in Jamaica. Nichols School was rough for the first few months because of coming in with the black Americans looking at me and thinking I speak funny. I used to get in a lot of fights, so I tended to stick more with the whites. They were more interested in my country and my culture and everything. I used sit around and talk with them. When the first snow fall came, they were more excited than I was because, like, "Gosh! Is this the first time you have seen snow?" I used to get excited. It was just the experience of seeing and touching it for the first time.

    After the years went by I still had problems and was getting into fights because I was being called "Uncle Tom" and "Whitey Lover" and things like that by other blacks. Finally, one day this guy came to me and we fought and after that, it was like a totally different ball game. Everyone accepted me then.

    In high school I played soccer for three years. When we came here from Jamaica, I was older than the rest of the kids. The American School system is different from the one we had in Jamaica, so they sent me back one grade. That is why I had to go to junior high school. When I got to high school, I was a freshmen at sixteen years old. I was the only freshman who had a driver's license. But I played soccer and basketball. I played soccer until my junior year. In my senior year I couldn't play because I was ineligible because of my age. The year before that we had formed a soccer league. We went to Sweden and England. We played over there for the summer. The following year I joined the services.

I did go out for the basketball team in high school. I made second string for a little while, then I moved up to "A" string. I didn't get much playing time, but it was good just to have the prestige of being out there on the court.

The coach wanted me to run track, too. Ted and Reva went through high school before I did, and they were into track, especially Reva.

Reva: When I was there, they didn't have a girls track team. We just had to go out with the guys, but I didn't do much in athletics in high school at all. Actually, high school, for me, was an experience. Unlike them, I did not go the junior high school here. I went straight into high school as a freshman when I came here from Jamaica, so that was a cultural shock. I wanted to go back home. I felt like a fish out of water. You know, in Jamaica you would hear how big and great America is and you would be looking forward to so much, but when I got here, I was so disappointed. It was really a cultural shock. You know, we came here in August and started school right away in September. Can you imagine?

We had the same experience with black Americans. They weren't very receptive. I found that the white kids were more friendly and receptive to us than the black kids. I don't know why. Maybe it was they way we spoke. The black kids would sort of pick on you and tease and all that kind of stuff, but the white kids would ask you more about your home, what it is like, and things like that. One thing that really made my experience at the high school tolerable was my counselor, Mrs. Pierce. As a matter of fact, the teachers were really, really nice. I had really good experiences with my teachers. I found we hung out more with other kids from the islands.

Ted: Over the years in high school, you know, after the black Americans and the Jamaicans started to get along, they said they didn't understand what we were talking about. They thought we were talking about them, so they said, "OK, they are talking about us, so we are going to beat them up." Their attitudes began to change once they came to know us.

There were some who persisted in teasing us, but the majority of the kids were OK.

Question: Has the attitude of American blacks changed any?

Reva: Somewhat, but I think there still is some kind of polarization. It is not bad because we are accepting the fact that we are all one black family.

Like I said, in high school there was so much going on that I was not aware of. My academics were not so bad because a lot of things that we started in my freshman year I had already done in Jamaica. That helped out, so most of my energy could be put into more social things. From my junior year, or maybe sophomore year, we had a glee club that we joined. We helped the boys to do time laps. I would have loved to have done track, but at that time they did not have a girls track team.

My teachers in high school were wonderful. I felt free to join any activity which was offered by the high school—the French Club, the Spanish club, etc.

When I left high school, I went to Loyola University. My experiences here were much different from in high school. I felt more accepted. I knew the ropes. I had no problems making friends. I went to the Lakeshore campus. I graduated with a bachelor's degree in psychology.

I have a daughter who is eleven. She goes to the Washington School. We go to PTA meetings, and there is just a handful of black parents there. The school is one-third black, one-third white, and one-third Hispanic. The kids play around in the playground, but the socialization after school is not there.

We are not integrated, and I think what has to be done is to integrate the neighborhoods.

Ted: I was the youngest, so the culture attack wasn't as serious. I started at Dewey School. There was a good mix of African-Americans and Caucasians there. I guess I find the assimilation was more with the white kids in the neighborhood we grew up in, like my next door neighbor. Mom said we grew up together. He was like my closet friend. The teasing was there, and I think, for me, as I was growing up, it came to be more that I didn't know where I belonged. I hung around with the white kids and got teased by the black kids, so I grew up with that sort of back and forth, and later on it got to the point where I had to decide for myself, Am I a Jamaican? Am I an American? Am I white, or am I black? I had all of that to deal with in my later years when I started going to school. But school was pretty uneventful. Being at a younger age, I was able to fit in a lot easier. My accent in language was not as noticeable as my oldest sibling. Then in sports I was able to excel through school. And that, again, brought acceptance by the students. Having most of my friends white, I was also exposed to a lot more than the average African-American as far as getting into the Boy Scouts, the camping trips, the YMCA, the after-school clubs, football and basketball teams. It wasn't unusual for me to sleep over at the house of one of my friends who lived down by the lake. Or he might be over here. I just had a pleasant childhood growing up here. I went to Southern Illinois University after I left high school, where I had excelled in sports, played football and track all four years and lettered. I went down state in track in my junior and senior years. I turned down a scholarship to run at Northern, but went to Southern Illinois and played football down there for a year. When I went to Southern I saw a different mixture of some of the inner city kids who came from places like East St. Louis, or the city schools of Chicago.

So that was, again, a rude awakening to see their life-styles and how they grew up, and the experiences that they were unable to do, and just how the polarization was there between the whites and the blacks. I guess that was when the appearance of racism or separatism started setting in. In most of my twenties I had that struggle to find out where I really belonged, as I started venturing into the city and seeing some of the inner city kids and the different things that go on there. I tried to redefine who I am. You could say I'm a Jamaican boy, and I should be proud of that and that history and heritage, because, for the longest, I tried to not associate myself with Jamaica, because of the connotation that it brought a lot of the black kids. A lot of times I would say I was born here, in England, because Jamaica was an English colony. There was that struggle I had to deal with so as not to go through the harassment and stuff like that. I found later on that it caused me a great deal of trouble trying to figure it out and accept myself for who I am.

But, overall, I think growing up in Evanston was a blessing to have the experience. It did open up a lot more culture than we would have had in the inner city. I think it also gave us maybe a false sense of the real world because everyone sort of grew up here at high school and played on the same teams and interacted with each other. When I left this, I look back and say, "Now this is the real world."

Hugh: Although we grew up here, Evanston is divided. You come South past Church Street, you know, you get into the better neighborhoods. You go North, then you are into the rough and tough. Here we are basically in the middle. We go a little further toward Howard Street and we are back in the rough and tough, so we sit here in the middle, in order to get some knowledge of how the inner city is.

Ted (on track): I pretty much ran the quarter mile run. I didn't really like track, but my natural ability and talent made it possible for me to excel. So I didn't put my mind to it. And to this day I can hear my coach, Willie May, say, "Bess, if you could get your mind in the shape that your body is in, there would be no stopping you." But I just couldn't make the connection at that time. I really loved football. That was my passion. Up until my senior year, I played both ways. In my freshman year, I returned punts and kickoffs, played defensive end, tight end, pretty much tight end and defensive end as sophomore and junior. I didn't pick up the weight, so defense was a little more of a struggle and I went to the tight end and wide receiver. I walked on at Southern Illinois University and played for a year down there. Since, I was a "walk-on" they didn't have scholarships, etc. So I decided to hang up my cleats.

For track I did the triple jump, the hundred yard dash; occasionally, two hundred, four hundred, but basically the four hundred and anchor on the relay team. It was something that came naturally to me.

Reva: I think being in sports insulated me from a lot of other things which could have caused me problems.

At Loyola they didn't have a woman's track team. In my second year, they had intramural sports they called the "turkey trot." We went out for that, and the coach spotted me. So we formed a track club, and in my senior year they gave me an extra year, and we started a girls track team from then on. My specialty was the quarter mile. I hated running it, but I did. I also ran the two hundred. My daughter is in the track club at high school.

Ted: Growing up I did everything from cutting grass for the neighbors, a paper route, worked in a bakery, shoveled snow, and whatever. That was one thing that Mom always instilled in us, that if you wanted something, you had to go out and earn it. She would buy me K-Mark gym shoes, and those weren't cool. So, if I wanted a more popular brand, I had to supplement the cost from my income.

I grew up with that type of work ethic. I did whatever was needed to bring income to the family. In the summer time I worked for the park district in Evanston for a couple of years.

Question: Why aren't more young men availing themselves to these opportunities to earn money?

Evelyn: Nowadays nobody wants their children to do that. Their parents give them everything they want. They don't teach them to go out and do summer work.

Hugh: You have black and white people who get hooked up into fast money. They see their next door neighbor, maybe he is only eighteen or nineteen, but he's driving a Mercedes Benz or a BMW. So he might say "Why should I go out there and sweat when I could just sit back and make money? Over the years, that attitude takes effect and people just don't work to appreciate what they get nowadays. There's one thing I can say from the way Mom's bringing us up. She didn't let us grow up and run wild, but she gave us enough rope to go out there and experience life. When we made a mistake, she would pull us back and talk to us or chastise us. Now, looking back on that, the thing that I do have and do accumulate in life is life experience and appreciation that keeps me going. You know, being in the service, you run into a whole lot of different racial backgrounds or whatever you want to call it, and people coming into our unit may be smarter, but when it comes down to toiling in a sweating job, nobody wants to do it.

It's a change in the service now. That's why I'm on my way out. It is not the same anymore. I have another year and ten months in the Marines.

The Marine Corps was the last branch of service to accept blacks.

When I leave the Marine Corps, I plan to go into the security program of the California Prison System. They have a good program in the food service department. Or I would like to work in the postal system or some other federal employment.

I didn't go to college. When I was in high school, I enjoyed it, but coming to my senior year, I said if I go to college I would just be wasting their money, so I decided to go into the service.

Question: Ted, you said you work at Ameritech. What do you do there?

Ted: Besides sales, I am a customer consultant. I pretty much take care of wireless data. I answer the phone. I spent about ten years traveling in retail management with Osco and in Cincinnati at Super X, which was bought out by Wesco. I spent a good part of my adulthood in retail management. It got to the point where I was working a hundred hours and getting paid for forty hours. The equation was getting way out of proportion. I just recently made the switch over to Ameritech where I am compensated for what I produce plus a basic salary, which is a little bit better now. I have always had entrepreneurial aspirations. I dabbled in real estate, etc. I guess my passion right now is to really put a strong distributorship with the Amway Corporation together. The lessons I have learned from the people who are associated with the corporation have taught me more than a lot of my formal education, as far as how business works, having a goal or a plan that you can work and achieve, instead of just working day in and day out and not really looking ahead forty or fifty years down the road. So, from that aspect, I am really excited and enthusiastic about working that plan and making sure that my kids have a solid foundation. It really started showing me the family values that anything that you want or achieve in life, you are going to have a put some effort into it. I was getting into that mode where I just wanted to sit back and have things happen, think the good life was just going to fall into my lap. I didn't know I would have to go out there and make it happen. So, being involved with the Amway Distributorship has really taught me how to become successful.

Question: How do you feel that the church has helped you in growing up in your spiritual or educational life?

Ted: Well, like Mom said, we grew up in the church It has always been a part of our lives. I think as young adults, you get to that point where maybe education or stupidity takes over and you start saying, "I'm doing this on my own." It is probably over the last six years where I personally accepted the Lord Jesus Christ as my savior and was working to grow in His word and to run my family according to His word. But the church has always been there, and we have always used it, as they say, as a "spare tire." Whenever we need it, we go grab that tire and throw it on the car and run with it for a while, and then we put it back in the trunk.

Some of the experiences I have gone through have made me stop and say "Thank you, Lord, because I would not have been here if it wasn't for your guidance." So, I am trying more to get involved in His word and teachings and pass that on to my kids. I see more importance in that now than when Mom was teaching us that many years ago.

Hugh: Back in Jamaica we were in church every Sunday, and when we got here growing up it was the same. It's not that I hated it or anything like that I guess, in a away it was like we were being forced to go there.

Reva: Church has always been a part of my life. It's sort of automatic. It's sort of taken for granted. I personally feel that we don't have to go to church, but I just automatically get up and go. Of course Mom tries to make me feel guilty, if I don't go, until this day. But I guess that is a part of her life. It's something she has always done. On Sunday you go to church. I have a daughter, and she goes to church. Even if I am not going, I make sure that she goes.

Question: Reva, do you feel that the church has done its job in helping the people to get along with each other in the community?

Reva: In a way, lately, I find a lot of that. I can only speak for my church. Outreach is more prevalent than it was when I was younger. We have things like neighborhood bake sales, we have marched around the neighborhood and tried get people to come to our special services. We sponsor car washes. Like I said, I see that more now than I did when I was younger.

But right down the street there is another church, Springfield Baptist. I don't see that much interaction with them. We also find there is sort of a polarization because somehow St. Andrew's has sort of evolved into a Caribbean church, because so many of our members are from the West Indies.

Hugh: I went to church in California. I guess it just turned me off because, to me, the church is more commercialized. What I mean by that is the preacher is like, you will be there for an hour a half and they send the plate around four or five times. It is better to give than receive. But when you are giving to the preacher, and he is out there driving a Cadillac, and everybody else is struggling, what's the sense in going to church? That's why I don't go much.

Reva: I always looked at church as being special, since I came over here. I always looked at church as being the last bastion where everything that's wrong with the world is outside, and when you go to church, it's all over, but I found that it doesn't work that way. It's actually in there. That was kind of a rude awakening. You always think of church as being the last place where everything that's ill with the world stays outside the church, but it's smack dab, right in there. That's when you learn that it's not really the churches, it's the people.

Ted: We are at a CME in Cincinnati, Ohio. My family is in sort of a division now because my wife started going to another fellowship, where I don't feel comfortable going because it's, sort of like he was saying more commercial, like a church where they got into talking in tongues, which is fine, it's in the Bible, but coming from an Episcopal background, it was a little bit too much for me.

And then the money that is being raised and how it is used, and they are trying to branch out and have branches here and there, to me, that was a big turn off. I didn't feel comfortable in that type of surroundings. The church where we are is a smaller congregation, much like St. Andrew's, with older patrons on down to little kids. I have found that is important, where you get that history and knowledge and that sense of family in the church. If we are missed, and I go back next Sunday, it's like "Where were you? We missed you guys." All of the parishioners know my kids.

Right now, in my family it's a big struggle because my wife prefers this other church and the kids and I are still down at our church. It's hard to say who is right.

For a long time, I was not involved actively, but I do try to get up every morning and take the kids down to church. They want me to become more involved, but working retail, and my schedule like it is, it is hard to really get a lot of things done on the outside.

Dangers to the Community and the City

Reva: I think it's a lack of true integration. If the neighborhoods were truly integrated, I think we would see a lot more difference in the interaction with each other. Because, you talk about desegregation, if you go to North Evanston, like Central Street toward Wilmette, I really came face to face with that through the PTA, seeing where the kids came from and how they played together at school. And then they go home to their separate little corners, but I see some changes.

Right in this neighborhood, whites are coming back. Some are buying old houses and redoing them and moving back into them.

Ted: That's because it's affordable to them. A lot of the African-Americans have reached middle class status, but they don't have the resources to get two hundred or more thousand dollars, where even a young middle class white couple would have more of an advantage of getting a loan for the same amount of money, so they can easily move back or get a house in a black neighborhood for pretty much nil compared to what they would have to pay in Wilmette or some place like that, and enjoy the same benefits that Evanston provides. I think that is the big disparity or the big gap in socio-economics between the blacks and whites. That's where racism really kicks in. If my family is making forty or fifty thousand dollars a year, that forty or fifty thousand dollars a year is probably half the value of a white couple who has the same income. It takes a lot more money to get the same things done as far as finding loans, and usually your credit histories are not as clean as your white counterparts' may be. One of the things I think is lacking in the African-American family is that those things are addressed. You know, once you get going, what kind of money are you going to have to put aside to get a home and stuff like that?

It's hard to bridge the middle class gap and go further. It's hard to say what is the answer. I think it is a lot of things, like community involvement, getting involved with the different community activities, especially having seminars or different kinds of programs to educate the African-American family in some of business, things they need to be in tune with to take the next step up.

Threats to the Safety of Evanston Black Communities

Hugh: I would say our own race, because it seems as if that attitude of OK he's my neighbor and he goes out there and, you know, busts his guts to achieve his property and make it what he want to make it. I am envious of him and start degrading him. I think what we need to do is to start educating our own people. They keep saying that the white man is doing this, the white man is doing that. Yes, the white man has his hand in it, but we are the ones that are doing it to our ourselves. We can get away from that, I think the black race will come together and unite. Look at the Asian people that come here. They come here and live in a one room shack. They make enough money, then the oldest son goes and buys a house and gets married and brings Mom in to live there and soon they will have a full community and live in harmony. I think if blacks stop envying one another and bringing each other down, we will survive.

Evelyn: Yes. This fence we have here was broken down and I paid 1,900 dollars to have the man restore the iron work. I went out there one day early in the spring. There was somebody who just drove his car across the lawn and through the fence. Nobody stopped to say anything. I wasn't here to see who it was. So we had to spend some money to fix it again. He could have stopped and said something. If he had insurance it would have paid for the damage.

Ted: That shows the lack of respect for ownership that the black community shows for each other. When you look at Evanston, you go down to the Church and Dodge area and you still have nice structures there, but then the clientele are not responsible enough to value ownership, and if economic factors or resources are not here to keep the properties up, the property will deteriorate. But then, there are youth who don't respect property or anything and they will walk by and throw stuff on your property or deface it and never think about it.

Evelyn: Like last summer, I went to church, and the whole block Darrow Avenue, someone went around with something and flattened the automobile tires. Almost every car had a tire that was flattened

One day I went out and saw a nice looking young fellow coming along with a policeman who had put handcuffs on the young man's hands. You had to cry that day. Such a good looking fellow should be out there working or doing something good. Any time you hear of something bad that happens on the news, you look for one of us. Why? Why does this have to happen?

Hugh: Because of stereotype. Then the blacks are doing the dirty work for the white guy. The white guys are up in Wilmette and Winnetka, and places like that, and reap the big money, while the younger guys are these guys who want to make fast money.

Ted: I also feel that a small community like Evanston is probably more equipped to attack a problem or cancer than when you start looking at Chicago. Evanston has the resources to do it. Also, as important properties become scarcer for your Caucasian partner, Church and Dodge won't exist anymore. That area will be cleaned up, renovated, and become valuable property if the demand exists. But right now it just sits there festering and dying. We have seen that in other communities. Look at Cabrini Green in the city. Whereas Rush Street became more prominent and more of the yuppies started working in the city. That became a valuable piece of property. So, now, instead of the crime wave, you could probably go outside and sleep without police support. I think it comes from an institution in the community saying what they are willing to accept.

Right now, it's an acceptable part of doing business in this community, by keeping that part of the city in stagnation. I believe that the community of Evanston should pull together and say, "Hey, we are not going to tolerate this."

Question: A building is boarded up and closed, because of dope traffic. What do you think of this plan to stop the narcotics traffic in Evanston?

Ted: That is a valid program, if you are going to use your property for ill use. But, it should not go back into a big corporation. Instead, the average guy should be able to buy it. Maybe a first time buyer who may be having difficulty getting a mortgage. I think the property should roll back into that kind of a program. They should try to get some quality buyer in the community.

But a lot of time what happens is that those houses go to auctions and the people who know about those auctions, such as Caucasian corporations, have the money go and buy the property and reap the benefits of programs like that.

I think that if there is to be any kind of eradication, it should be rolled over into some type of minority owned or minority construction company who can go in and redo the property and get responsible families back in the neighborhoods.

Questions for Discussion:
1. Who in the Bess family was motivated to come to Evanston first?
2. What was the attitude of Mrs. Bess toward coming to Evanston?
3. What kind of employment did Mr. and Mrs. Bess have in Evanston or Chicago?
4. How did Hugh get along with his classmates at Nichols Junior High School? Why did Hugh enter high school at age sixteen, instead of 13 or fourteen?
5. Why did Reva feel the cultural shock of coming to Evanston? How was she treated by the black and white students in Evanston?
6. What was Reva's suggestion for improved race relations in Evanston?
7. Describe Ted's problem with self identification when he was in high school.
8. What did Hugh mean when he said, "Evanston was divided when he grew up"?
9. What did Ted mean when he said, "I think being in sports insulated me from a lot of other things which could have caused me problems?
10. What were some of the things Ted has learned from his association with the Amway Company?
11. What were the differences in the attitudes of the Bess children toward the church?
12. What is Hugh's criticism of African-Americans in Evanston?
13. What is Ted's recommendation for dealing with property where there is dope traffic?

About the Bess Family

The Bess family is one of many families which have emigrated from the islands in the Caribbean to Evanston. Their family has been prominent in the activities and services at St. Andrew's Episcopal Church. My experiences have been primarily with Mrs. Evelyn Bess and her husband, James, who were quite active in the church. At that time, the children were very young, and I had little contact with them. In the years after I lost contact with them, James, the father left the family and one of the daughters passed, so the family now consists of Evelyn, Ted and family, Hugh, and Reva and her family.

We were fortunate to get the Bess family together because Ted was returning to Cincinnati, Ohio to his work and his family, and Hugh was on his way back to the Marine barracks to complete his tour of duty.

We appreciate the frank expressions of the Bess family about the people of Evanston and realize that other residents from the Caribbean may have similar feelings.

Lillian Cannon

When woman first got into politics, I voted Republican. I had come from the South and I knew that everybody there was a Democrat and I didn't want to be what they were.

I worked on the polls there in Evanston. Everybody in Evanston was a Republican. The only Democrat in the Fifth Ward was Mr. E. J. Coffey, who lived at 1703 Emerson Street near your father, Mr. John L. Williams. The Fifth Ward went all the way down Emerson Street to Niles Center.

People just didn't walk over there to Niles Center. If you wanted to go over there, you had to come down Dempster Street and go west and over the bridge of the canal.

People went to Dempster Street to see Duke Ellington and others who were playing at road houses on Dempster Street. That was where they had road houses and ditches on both sides of the street. You could see white folks dancing and having a good time. Some of my friends, like Norman White and Irena, used to walk out there and stand by the ditch just to hear the music. I never had time to do it and never loved music that well to stand out there and listen to it.

Where I lived we had very good neighbors. There was Mr. Kelsch, who became a policeman, and Mr. Sanford, who was our city treasurer. Mr. Kelsh married Lillian Wieland and lived over there in a big house. They also had a green house.

They didn't have radios and television then, but Charles, my husband, and his friends got together and had a thing they called a crystal set. They put that in their barbershop window and laid it down among the plants and things they kept there. They were trying to get Del Rio, Texas or some other station with their crystal set, and if they got just a little squeak, that was like hearing from London.

Sometimes people would come down Asbury Avenue or Ridge Avenue and get lost. But, they would see a light in the shop where Charlie and his friends were operating their crystal set and they would stop and ask for directions to the road houses to see Duke Ellington or some other orchestra. So Charlie would tell them to go South to Dempster Street, then turn right and go west on Dempster across the canal bridge to Niles Center. At that time there was a parkway in the middle of Dempster Street.

Early Church Life in the South

I never was much on church because my great-aunt, who raised me in the South, didn't go to church at all. She would let me go where they thought I could sing.

Hattie Reese, up on the corner, could play the piano. She was older, and she played the piano over at her church. His mother was a great AME Zion member, and when Hattie grew up, she sent her to school in Saulsbury, N.C.

Hattie would always let me have a solo, but I couldn't carry a tune. My aunt thought it was great that I was in a church where they would let me sing.

When they brought me up and wanted me to go to a kindergarten, they didn't have a kindergarten in my home. That seemed to be something "snooty." I had some cousins who are now in Chicago but were then living in Birmingham, Alabama. They attended an Episcopal church on Avenue C and Eighteenth Street The church took up the whole block. There they had a kindergarten, the priest's home, and the church. So, I started going, with my cousin, to kindergarten. After I got out of kindergarten, I went back home and started going to grade school.

Church in Evanston

A girl would pick me up and take me to Ebenezer. Well, the preacher up there was preaching and telling you to "come up front." I think they must have had me signed up before I knew it. So, I never went back anymore.

But I would go up there and help them in the kitchen. They did some remodeling and put in all nice things. We started making flowers and decorated the church.

If you had a canary bird, you would take it to the church and hang it up there on Easter. I had canary birds, but none of my birds ever went But I would help them at church.

I became so busy working that I forgot the church. I would go to anybody's funeral, but when they started having funerals at night, I was working and didn't have a chance to go to many funerals.

Catholic Church

When I was a little girl in Birmingham, my mother wanted me to be Catholic. At that time, there was a Catholic church in town. Since I was my own boss, I didn't have to go to church if I didn't want to, and my aunt didn't go to church at all. I guess they would call her a sinner! But she was nice to me. They say she confessed to religion while I was in Evanston, but I don't know. I did have a preacher read over her.

My mother was a "dyed in the wool," and wanted me to be, Catholic. In Birmingham in my neighborhood was the Hillman Hospital in a park with a big iron fence. We kids used to play around it and look in there and see the priests with little hats on. The would be reading the offices of the day. The other kids would say, "They're getting ready to put you in the pot and cook you." I kind of thought it was the truth. I was scared to death.

I got along with the church all right, so I joined the Catholic church and still go to church. I pay my dues. I mail them to my church, St. Mary's. I am loaded with church bulletins.

Evanston Memories

I remember Mr. Adam P. Perry. My husband used to run with Adam. He lived right down the alley from St. Mary's Church where they built the country club. You know, then Mrs. Perry and her family lived in the little house near the alley, in back of the YMCA. The Y used to be over there on Sherman Avenue near where I used to go to pay my telephone bills. We'd go through a little park there to reach the post office. In the park was a log cabin. The Evanston Y used to be in a building which was bought by Lords Store.

The telephone office was also in this building. We always had trouble with a lady in the office. She would say, "You owe me ten cents more." At that time all three of us were staying in the same house and had private telephones. We were paying three dollars each for our phones. If you had a party line, you could get it for $2.50. But all of us were big shots in those days. We paid three dollars for our phones. If I owed $3.10, I would give exactly three one dollar bills and one dime, because if I paid $3.50, the clerk would say I owed forty cents more and refuse to give me my change.

Emerson Street Y and Neighborhood

Charles and I used to give Albert Carter a membership. I think it cost ten dollars a year.

You know, Albert is dead now.

The Tuskegee boys came up here and built the stable that Mr. Butler owned on Emerson Street, next to the Y. We used to keep our car in there.

Mr. Russell had a garage in there. They would deliver the car to us over at 1309 Emerson. We paid him fifteen dollars a month.

Dr. Cotton used to live in a building across the street from the Y. He used to wear celluloid collars. I bought my birds from a Mr. Bell who lived in the same chain of brick houses where Dr. Cotton lived.

Lillian's Employers and Friends on the North Shore

Do you know where the Hahn Building was? Well, he had a bank. I used to go around and serve weddings when the workers in his bank got married, all up on Noyes Street. That was kind of a poor folk's job, you know. When you got to working for Don Mercer, the loan company people, and Mr. Compton, the encyclopedia people, all on the North Shore, you called a job like Mr. Hahn's people a poor man's job. But we took them all.

Mr. Ingraham used to ask me how I was feeling. He was mayor at that time. Eddie Bell, I knew him. I remember when Peter Jans got elected alderman. He used to send us a big picture.

I know Dick Fishl, a dentist, who, with his wife, sent me large plants every Christmas. She would come here and spend a whole day with me. She lives up in Deerfield now. One of her boys, Paul, is down here, now where you buy airplane tickets, where Sergeants is located. He and his family have it now. I hear from all of them. I have some of their family pictures. She was here last year. It was snowing, and she had boots on. I remember I got my house shoes for her, which she put on and she stayed here all day with me. I gave her a cup and saucer to take to Cathy at her house in Naperville.

They had, let me see, a son Michael who's married and is living down in Florida. That's their oldest boy. They were friends with the Meigs boys. Mr. Meigs is who Meigs Field is named after. He came out of Evanston. He got mad with his wife and left her with the boys. The Fischl boys and the Meigs boys grew up together. I knew Mrs. Meigs, and I knew she was worrying. I worked for the Cradle, and she belonged to that group. I was a good friend of hers, and she was a good friend of Mrs. Fischl, and Mrs. Fischl was a good friend of mine at the church.

Cannon's Barbershop

Well, the First World War is breaking up and George Cannon was living down on 1111 Forest Avenue, in the rear of Mr. S. F. Wilson's place, rent free. George had a brother who was supposed to be coming back from the Army, 169th Regiment, and he had been gassed. Well, George and his brothers decided that they would go in and establish a business so their brother would have something to come back to. Now, that is the way it started out to be.

So, there was a Creole man here, and he had a bakery down on Emerson Street, where a colored drug store had been on the corner. That fellow used to go with Lurleen Perrin. That was before my time.

I don't know how long it lasted, but that went out. Then there was a man next door whose name was Caruso. He was from New Orleans, foreign like, and wasn't just an average colored man. This Caruso was selling out his bakery, so the Cannons bought it and put in this barbershop for Don, their brother, to have.

It didn't work out right because Don came back and was the Don that the folks knew, unstable, so they had to carry him along all the time, but said nothing about it.

Now, when George Cannon died, some of the women who played cards around—and I could call their names because I knew them well and something about pretty well all of them, but I am not going to tell, because it was none of my business—told Ethel, George's wife, to get rid of everything she had. Now George Cannon had worked hard all of his life. He saw only one movie: *Mr. Smith Goes to Washington*. We took him to see that.

Well George Cannon had accumulated a little. He owned, with Mr. Charlie Jackson, some property right across the street, where the Jewel Store is down there on Chicago Avenue.

You see, they were buying little things and also buying cars together. I know the first time Charlie and I had it out. They had a Hudson car. You could go down to Chicago and park at Grant Park. You pay about twenty-five cents to park Then you walk over to the loop and shop. One night Harriet had taken me downtown. You see, my husband owned half of the car, and her husband owned one half. We weren't coming back to Evanston on Lake Shore Drive then. They didn't have all of that. We had to come through Clarington Beach. It was kind of a rainy night, and we got a flat tire near Clarington Beach, so I was late coming home and Charlie didn't know why I didn't call him. But it didn't dawn on me to try to get out in that neighborhood. Harriet had to leave me locked up in the car to go back to Broadway to get somebody to come to see about us. You see, she was older than I was and knew more about what to do in this kind of a situation. I wouldn't even drive. What would I look like trying to find a telephone to call him? You didn't have all these things like you've got now. So we got home and Charlie got mad. But, he could just swell up as much as he wanted to. I didn't care.

Now, back to the barbershop.

Mr. Winters built this building and encouraged the Cannons to open up a pool room. That's what started it. They started it. They were cutting hair for people like Harry and Dower Griffin for twenty-five cents, and providing pool for those who wanted to play. They charged ten cents a game.

Charlie would bring home his money. George didn't have nothing to do with it, but he was putting money in it, and everybody knew it.

We used to go up to Mr. Winters on Fourth Street in Wilmette and ask Mr. Winters why did he own so much property. Mr. Winter's brother owned the Arrow Market. The Winters also owned the lot across the street from Woody's Barbershop.

I met Mrs. Winters and her children. All of their property was called L. A. Winters, but that wasn't Mr. Winters' name at all. That was his wife's name. I don't know what Mr. Winters' first name was. He was the brother of George Winters who owned the grocery store on Davis Street. They did not speak to each other.

Mr. Winters said that property in Wilmette was cheaper, and they were living up there for that reason But he offered to sell to Charlie, and ever since, we have been right here in this house. He sent George Corcoran, before he died, to try to make Charlie buy all that property down there. But it was a big mortgage, and all that we had we were getting out of the hole and getting cash. I said, "No, indeed." I didn't like mortgages, but when I moved in this house, I had a mortgage. As I told you, Ethel was buying things, trying to spend the money they had accumulated on Emerson Street.

I was away with a woman I knew, a white woman, Mrs. Thorkhill, working in New York and Martha's Vineyard. She and I would read letters together. She knew Ethel, too, because Ethel had worked for her. I'd bring in mail and read letters with Mrs. Thorkhill. She would say, "Oh, Lillian, you sent Ethel a blouse." I had sent it from New York because I could get it without paying any taxes on it.

I couldn't tell all of this if they were living, but I can tell it now because I've got nobody to kick back at me.

But I wouldn't even tell it if Donald was living. They were George's brothers. He's gone. These old women were out trying to make everyone think that Ethel was rich and had plenty of sense cause she had all of that schooling, you know, and everything.

Ethel was doing dumb things. She was spending every nickel cause they told her the government was going to pass Social Security and they were talking about everything they were going to get free.

Charlie said, "Don't you ever have a diary and don't you ever get in these clubs and things where they are going to do a whole lot of mouthing and talking about your business."

I never had time for that, but John Griffin and all of them over there had her in five bridge clubs. She got to the place she couldn't entertain them, and they would entertain and they would get the money she would pay them.

Martha's Vineyard

Now, I am down East with Mrs. Thorkill. How did I happen to go there? I just bummed my way in there.

I know every town there. I've been around the island many times. I've been out to Nantucket. This was in the 1960s. I've been over to Oak Bluffs for the big shindig they have, singing, you know, and visiting the little cottage all around. I've got pictures of it.

Mrs. Thorkill had me moving around in a little foreign car. I can't remember the name of it now.

When she would take me up to Johnny's she would say, "Lillian, we don't want to stay up here in the county in New Hampshire."

She would take me all around and say, "See that lady over there? This is Exeter College. That's Mrs. Saltonstall. Her husband was a great senator." Or, "That's where the water turns from salty to fresh."

She gave me a ticket to go to Boston. She said, "You meet me at the Plaza Hotel at nine o'clock Monday. I will be there. "Well we would have breakfast, then head for Woods Hole. She paid my expenses everywhere we went.

Once in Woods Hole, we took the ferry to Martha's Vineyard. She drove our car right down to the ferry. And I said to her, "I think we are moving." She said, "I've got news for you. We are there. I didn't want to tell you 'cause you might get seasick."

It got to the place when she would ask me, "Lillian, do you want to go over to New Bedford? We've still got to make that boat, you know."

I lived in Edgartown. Her house was called Starfield.

I would get up on Sunday morning and go to the Catholic Church in Edgartown.

We lived right on Eal Pond. Folks would be out there getting clams every morning. When the tide came in, it came up under our kitchen. We were so close to the water.

We also visited Menemsha. I've been all around the island. She would take me to see a woman from Canada who lived around on the upper end, and we would pass Jimmy Cagney's cottage. There were places like East Chop and West Chop.

We went to the art galleries. They were just barns. I know all about Chappaquidick and about Kennedy and that girl. It was only ten cents to go to Chappaquidick.

I had more time off than I had on, so I went all around, even to the cemetery and rummage sales, just to be going.

Then you go down to the fish house and eat all the raw fish you want. But I didn't want any raw fish.

She would take me to the art gallery, and we would take a chance on a picture. We never won anything. We just put twenty-five cents on this one or that one, but we never won a picture. She just did the paying, I would just look silly and say, "I think we're leaving." And she would say, "Drop everything and come one."

She even went to Boston one time and left her pocketbook. I looked down on the floor and there was Mrs. Thorkhill's pocketbook. "I'm staying home," I said. I wondered how she got on that boat. She borrowed the money from the man who runs the boat, and even had the nerve to bring me a present. I've got some of the stuff and some I gave away to friends.

Trip to Canada

I worked that day and came home. At night Isma Bacon and I got it in our heads, and I don't know why, but they were going to Pittsburgh for six-dollar round trip. They used to have all kinds of things that you could go to and made it pleasant. I went to Niagra Falls, and even went under the falls. We put on rubber suits and everything and didn't get wet. I tried to make Charlie go, but he wouldn't even go on the United States side. But he did stand on the bridge, and I showed him all of Canada, because I had been there before.

Question: What was the property where the Cannon Barbershop is located now?

That was a school, before it was turned into a business block. Mr. and Mrs. Anderson went in there and opened a store. They had a grocery store and an old dog named Laddie. The name of the school was the Emerson Street School. I think the building was built in 1907.

The Masonic Temple was built on ground that used to be used as picnic grounds. Dr. Bess went in there and build that. He was a dentist around here, too.

Dick Lee and his brother bought 1923 Asbury and made it the Lee Hotel. I spent a night in the Lee Hotel counting votes.

The Lees were the first colored to get over there. People thought they were white when they sold it to them years ago. You see, there were no Negroes over there then. After that block went colored, whites bought the two end houses.

They have a children's school right across from Woody's Barber Shop. The entrance is on Asbury.

In the 1800 block on Asbury, there was a bungalow on the east side of the street, which was owned by Mr. Bixby. He was the head of the Evanston YMCA.

People in the 1800 block had chauffeurs like Mr. Gus Williams and Flat Foot Floogie. Also, Waverly Curry's brother, who went with Esther Sanders, was a chauffeur.

The Pagewoods lived on the corner of Asbury and Lyons Streets. Josephine Robinson's boys got the Pagewood sister's house in back of the Pagewood house.

Questions for Discussion
1. What was Mrs. Cannon's attitude toward the Democratic Party?
2. If you were a black in Evanston in Lillian's day and wanted to hear Duke Ellington's band play in a tavern in Niles Center, which way would you go there? Could you buy a ticket?
3. How did Lillian's attitude toward church change as she became older?
4. What are some of Lillian's memories of the downtown Evanston area?

5. Name two prominent Evanstonians who lived or had businesses in the Emerson Y neighborhood?
6. When Lillian worked as a waitress and caterer for people on the North Shore, how did she classify her employers?
7. What are the names of some of her prominent employers?
8. What was the reason for establishing the first Cannon Barbershop?
9. How was Charlie Cannon able to acquire an expensive item like an automobile?
10. What other activity took place in the Cannon Brothers Barbershop?
11. There is a barbershop called Cannon's Barbershop in the 1300 block of Emerson street. What was this building used for when it was first built?
12. Describe Lillian's travel experiences with her employers.

About Lillian Cannon

Woody Cannon, proprietor of Cannon's Barbershop introduced me to Mrs. Lillian Cannon, no kin to Woody, at her home, 1400 Florence Avenue. Mrs. Cannon is small in stature, fair in complexion, has silver hair, is full of energy and has a sparking personality. Once she started talking and relating her many life experiences, she seemed to become more energized and the words kept flowing.

She had just returned from a trip to Alabama on her first airplane flight. She said the crew learned that it was her one hundredth birthday and celebrated it by announcing it to the passengers and giving her a cake. The celebration somewhat eased the tension of her first airplane ride.

Mrs. Cannon had much to say about everything in Evanston, but we tried to limit her story to her employment, family business, and social life in Evanston. She is still a popular neighbor in the Florence Avenue and Greenwood Streets area. She attends St. Mary's Catholic Church when she is able to do so.

Lillian is the widow of Charles Cannon, a prominent businessman in Evanston who worked with his brothers, Donald and George.

Geraldine Franklin Cooper

Horace and Carrie Franklin arrived in Evanston in 1910 from South Carolina. They were born in Lawrence County. With them was their daughter, Wilma, who was a young girl at that time. Horace had been a delivery man for a grocery store in Greenwood. Both he and Carrie had been born on farms. My father was one of fourteen children born to John and Dolly Franklin. There were three girls and eleven boys. My father said they had enough players for their own baseball team. Three of the brothers and the three sisters eventually followed him to Evanston, as he had followed some of his friends.

Their first home was on West Railroad Avenue, now called Greenbay Road. Later they moved to 1859 East Railroad, which was on the corner of Emerson and East Railroad Avenue. They lived on the second floor, and this is where I was born in 1918.

They joined Ebenezer AME Church, which was across the street. They found a very active North and South Carolina Club in the church. Many of the members were from the same area in South Carolina they had left, which made the transition much easier.

My mother was appointed a stewardess and later was consecrated a deaconess. Wilma attended Sunday School and was also a member of the choir. She was nineteen years older than I and married soon after I was born. Her husband, Clarence Hudson, served in World War I as a Sergeant Major. They lived with us several years, and moved to 1029 Ayers Place, a three story brick house owned by the Edens family.

Clarence was a purchasing clerk for the Chicago Board of Education and it was his responsibility to buy the coal for all of the Chicago schools. He was very active in the Thomas Garnett Post of the American Legion.

During the time we lived on East Railroad, there were many shops on the first floor of the building. Link Johnson had a tire shop there. Outside was an air pump, and it was used more often for bicycles than automobiles. One afternoon, an overzealous attempt to fill a bicycle tire with air caused the tire to explode.

Another tenant there was Percy Baker, who had a restaurant there. Many years later, Mr. Baker operated a restaurant in the lower level of the Emerson Street YMCA, and I was employed as a waitress my senior year in high school. His customers were men who lived in the YMCA and black students attending Northwestern University who were not allowed to live in the dormitories there. Some lived in the Y, and others lived in the homes of other black families who had bedrooms to rent.

Each Christmas, Mr. Baker cooked a hog's head for my father. I don't remember eating or even seeing it, but there was a lot of conversation about it between my father, relatives, and his friends about this delicacy.

The owner of this building was "Old Man Sam Taggart." He also owned the building next door on East Railroad. That building had a basement apartment, and his relatives lived on both floors with him. We never saw him dressed in anything but overalls and a work shirt, which was usually well worn, and I remember hearing the adults in the neighborhood discuss his stinginess.

Our neighbors on Emerson Street were Mr. and Mrs. Lorenzo Griffin and their sons, Harry, Dower, and George. They had a beautiful daughter, Gladys, who died in her teens. Her casket was placed in the window of their living room. It made quite an impression on the younger children in the block.

There were two Jewish families in the block. The Lapidas family lived in the middle. Their daughter, Ruth, was my age, and there was an older brother.

Then the Crost family had a "secondhand" store closer to Maple Avenue. It was a source of furniture for many people.

In 1930 our two families built a house at 1846 Ashland Avenue. Wilma and Clarence thought we were moving into the Dewey School district, but the boundary had been moved to the alley between Ashland and Wesley. This would reduce the number of black students attending Dewey School.

Our house was in the Foster School district. The white families in our block were German, and they attended Bethlehem Lutheran. The white children across the street attended Dewey School. For some reason, although they knew I no longer lived at 1859 East Railroad Avenue, I was allowed to continue attending Noyes School through the sixth grade, when all students were sent to Haven School for seventh and eighth grades.

It was in the sixth grade that I first noticed that black students were being treated differently. The teacher, Miss Wheeler, assigned each of the black children to the last desk in each row, and when Conklin

Smith couldn't sing the notes in a song, her comment was that she had never heard of a colored person who couldn't sing.

ETHS, the only public high school, was very racist, with the approval of the principal and most of the staff. The desks in each of the homerooms were in pairs and a black student and a white student were never appointed seat-mates. The swimming team, which practiced at the Grove St. YMCA, had no black members. There were no black members of the Glee Club until Melvin Smith prevailed. There were no black players on the basketball team until Jesse Peak was chosen in his senior year. He was the tallest player they had.

The senior prom was organized by individual parents and held at the Evanston Club, to which no black students were invited. We (the black seniors) had our prom at the Emerson Street YMCA (the Black Y).

We sat in the balcony of the local movie houses and did not eat or shop in the better stores or restaurants. We had to stand at the end of the counter for a hot dog at Woolworth's.

There were several black doctors in our neighborhood who provided the inspiration for others who came later—Dr. Rudolph Penn, who later built a hospital in the community, Dr. Isabell Butler, the first black woman physician, who opened a hospital in the early 1900s and Dr. Best, a dentist.

The churches provided outlets for social contact with their BYPUs and Christian Endeavors, choir and outings, and many individuals who produced plays, debates, and musical programs and introduced us to Negro history. A few of these people were Hazel Childs, Gladys Brownlee, Eleanor Rowe, T. Malcolm Reeves, and Dr. James Morton.

Questions for Discussion
1. What did Horace and Carrie Franklin have in common in their backgrounds in South Carolina?
2. What activity at Ebenezer Church made it more pleasant for the Franklin family to adjust to the Evanston environment?
3. How was Clarence, Geraldine's brother-in-law helpful to the Franklin family?
4. What was Clarence's important responsibility as purchasing clerk for the Chicago Board of Education?
5. Why were so many black students at Northwestern University forced to the live at the Emerson Street Y or with black families?
6. What might have been a reason the Franklin and Hudson families

decided to build their house at 1846 Ashland Avenue?
7. Why was the Emerson Street Y so important to the Evanston black youth?
8. What were some of the ways blacks were discriminated against in Evanston?

About Geraldine Franklin Cooper

"Gerry" and I first became acquainted with each other when we were class mates in the seventh grade at Haven School. There was one other black student in our room, Margaret Spencer. I think our room was exceptional, because of the warmth of the teacher, Mrs. Grace Keyes, and the friendliness of the students. Gerry made it easy to be accepted, due to her scholarship and willingness to accept responsibilities.

We saw less of each other in our high school activities at Evanston Township High School, but met often at Y activities and other social affairs in the neighborhood. Her observations about the attitude toward blacks at the high school and in Evanston were accurate and characteristic of the city at that time.

Gerry and her husband Andrew, whom everybody called Babe were members of our small social club, which we called a couples club. This club was an informal group of young, recently married couples who enjoyed each other and shared their problems and suggestions for survival. This was before World War II, and most of the men were working two or more jobs in order to survive. Some of the wives were working, too, in addition to rearing children.

One evening while we were being entertained by Jim and Boots Avery in their apartment above the home of Mrs. Flournoy on Emerson Street, the news came over the radio that Germany had invaded Poland. That was in 1939. We were playing a game called Spoons, and Babe* had lost and was required to pay a penalty. The rest of us were happy that he lost because he had bragged about his skill at the game. But as I look back on this evening I realize that it was the beginning of the end of this group, for in 1940 our country began preparations for a possible war with Germany and our employment changed. Some of us went into the military and were stationed all over the world. All of us returned safely, but times were different, and we never recovered the spirit we had before the war.

*Babe passed away in April 1998.

Mrs. Helen Cooper

I am not sure when my father came to Evanston. He was born in Abbeville, South Carolina. What I do know about that, my mother told me. And again, I am fuzzy about who brought him, whether it was the McGrew family or the Cannon family, or the Wideman family. One of the three families spirited him away from his father, who was white. His mother was black and died, apparently when he was an infant. Daddy was born in 1878. He came to Evanston, I judge, when he was about ten or eleven years old. I know nothing about his life beyond that. I had thought I would learn something when I went to a meeting in New York, and a woman asked me, "Where are you from?" I told her, but said, "We know nothing about his family." So, she said, "Well, I bet you I know his family. You ask him if Hiram Cromer was his father." So, I thought, now I am going to find out. So when I came home, he looked at me and all he said was, "No, he was my uncle, and don't ask me another question about that because I am not going to tell you anything. I never got beyond that point with him. So, I know nothing about his relatives on his father's side. And whether the McGriers or the Widemans or the Cannons were related to him, I don't know either, and I have never really discussed it with them.

My mother's family, I think, went up in the underground from somewhere in the South and settled in St. Catherine's, Ontario, Canada. Her mother, Elizabeth Smith, came to the states, I don't know the year, married, and had another family. They settled first in Glencoe, then came to Evanston. Mamma stayed with her grandmother, Sarah Osborne, in Canada. She came here when she was just beginning her teens. I found, in going through some books the other day, her graduation from a public school in Evanston in 1899. I have that diploma. I think she went to high school. I am not sure. She and Daddy met at 1011 University Place. That building is now demolished, but it was just demolished for the Northwestern University Research Center. That is where I was born, and where Billy was born. I guess Peter, too. Ruth was born at 1414 Florence Avenue.

In 1908 they bought a house at 1414 Florence Avenue. Then in 1927 they bought the house at 1819 Ashland Avenue. That was the house that both of them lived in until they passed.

In Reverend Hill's house, down the street here, a family from Cabrini Green moved in. Everybody got terribly upset. I didn't know about the initial meetings, but when I found out about them, I went to them. The wild kind of things that you hear about, my feelings were, and I expressed them, that, "Just because you come from Cabrini Green housing development is no reason why you cannot become a good tenant or property owner." I pointed to the CNN commentator and the Navy man who came from Cabrini Green, as examples. I knew about them. So, it worked out that the family finally moved.

That's the only kind of organization, that I know, this neighborhood has had.

My first dentist was named Dr. Reginald Bess. His offices were where the Evanston Garage is. I think that Dr. Young, also, had offices in this building, in a later year. Then Dr. Howard, whose office was in the 1800 block on Dodge Avenue. Dr. Tarkington came to Evanston while I was away. I knew him and his wife, Isabelle. Those were the dentists I had.

When I came back to Evanston, I began to use Dr. Bruce Reynolds.

The first doctor was Dr. Isabelle Garnett. I knew her because my mother and Billy had their tonsils removed at the same time at the house that she and her husband operated as a sanitarium, Butler's Sanitarium I think they called it, on Asbury Avenue near Foster Street. Then when I was able to make a decision for myself, I used Dr. Hill. After I came back home to Evanston, I still used Dr. Hill, but then I moved into the HMO business. I had my tonsils out at Evanston Hospital in 1912. The reason I had them out was Bill became so ill that Daddy, who was then the steward at the Evanston Club, called in Dr. Danforth. Dr. Danforth immediately called the hospital and told them that he wanted this boy to come into surgery. They said, "We can't accept him, because he is black" Dr. Danforth told them, "You are going to accept him, and you will." So, he went in. He had an appendectomy.

I was so careless that the doctor said, "She has a problem with her tonsils, so let's take them out." That's how I was in the Evanston Hospital in 1912. I remember, even then, how conscious I was of the things that happen to Negroes. They were saying to me, when giving me the anesthetic, "I'll bet you can't count." And I was going to prove to them that I could count. I was conscious at that point of the racial connotations that there were then. I was just six years old then. That was the only time that I was in the Evanston Hospital until I was grown and moved back here. I have been in there a number of times since then.

Dr. Hill was my last physician in Evanston. I had a great deal of respect for her.

For an optometrist, I used Dr. Lawson. Then I was diagnosed as having glaucoma. I was in my late fifties then. He was pretty hurt, because I changed to an ophthalmologist. But I knew enough about medicine and what not to know that as you begin to get up in years, you need to have an ophthalmologist. He felt that he could do everything for me that anyone else could do, but I don't know.

Grocers. The only thing that I remember is there were the Flemings who had a store on Simpson and Darrow. I remember that Ezell and Chlotel Griffin had a store. I also remember Mr. Russell Watkins who was also a grocer. These were people I knew in the community, but most of them were established when I was living away, when I was in New York, or Washington, D.C., so I didn't know a great deal about how they functioned.

Our druggist was, of course, Dr. Morrison. I knew him as an undergraduate student at the University of Iowa.

I assume that somebody remembers William Gill, the real estate man. He had an office across from where the Dempster Street L Station is, right at the corner of Dempster and Sherman Avenue. He gave me my first job when I finished high school, as a typist. And Alberta Carter and I worked in there together. It wasn't for very long, but he published a little newspaper. I wrote columns for it.

Mr. Gill was the kind of person who would dictate to me and say, "Erase that," as if I could go back and erase on the typewriter. But he had a lot of vision for Evanston.

Adam Perry was also a businessman He was the steward of the Evanston Club, but with that he developed his own business, a catering business. He was the reason I was able to go to Northwestern. I worked as his secretary and I could fit my class hours, as long as I got the work done for him. I worked with him and all of his catering, planning, reservations. He had a small business where he sold cigarettes and cigars and things like that in the club when they had their parties. You never hear much about what Mr. Perry did. But I know, for example, that he contributed very heavily to the YMCA. He was president of the YMCA on Emerson Street. He was one of the leaders in the development of the Community Hospital. Back in those days, for somebody to give a thousand dollars, for a black man, that was something. I know he gave both to the Y and to the hospital.

I talked about this at one time at the Evanston Historical Society Board meeting, that there just was no mention of what Mr. Perry had done in material about the Evanston Country Club that should have been mentioned. And I don't see much about it even in recent materials.

I have not seen the thing that Pauline Williams developed and that the bank has shown, you know, for the Evanston Historical Society.

Helen Leaves Evanston to Work in Various Places

I graduated from Northwestern University in 1931. I applied for graduate fellowships to Smith College, to a university in Cleveland, and to the New York School of Social Work and to the National Urban League. The National Urban League and the Cleveland University all offered me fellowships, and New York University gave me a two year fellowship for $1,500 each year, which back in 1931 was an awful lot of money. So I took that. I got sick between my first year and my second year, so I came back home. I got sick in the summer when I came home, and I had to have surgery in October, so I couldn't go back. I worked when I was able to get up, and then went back the next year. The fellowship was still good.

When I finished, I could not do social work in Evanston. I knew everybody. I did not have to do a case history. I could tell you what church they went to, who had died when, where they worked, everything. So, I decided that I would stay in New York.

The depression was just starting then. There were very few social workers in this country who had masters degrees in social work, so there was no problem about getting a job. I liked New York, so I stayed there. And I started out in the what was then called, Home Relief Division of the New York City Department of Welfare. Because of my training, I moved pretty fast.

They offered me a supervisor's job, but because I didn't see myself as a supervisor, I took a supervisor's aide job. When I went to the agency I saw the other kinds of people who were in those jobs and I wanted to kick myself, but within six months I was a supervisor, and as I say, I moved up.

I stayed with the agency. I headed one of the men's division. Then

Marshall Field funded a staffing of the Children's Division in New York, and two other women and I went as the top staff. I headed the Manhattan Division. We had twenty thousand children in foster care. I stayed there, I think, two years.

Then I went to Washington, D.C., as consultant to the Commissioner of Welfare in the District. I stayed there over a year, and then went back and went to New York State as a senior social worker. I went from there back to Washington D.C., with Health Education and Welfare. That is where I stayed until I retired in 1974.

In HEW, I worked in the Washington office. I worked with the staff of the states in region ten, which was Alaska, California, Washington, Oregon, Arizona, Nevada, and Hawaii.

I learned afterward that there was considerable discussion about promoting me and sending me to the California office, because they had never had a black person in a position out in the field, and they did not know whether the state people would accept one. Anyhow, I went, and I never had a single bit of trouble.

I traveled all over. I had a great deal of trouble, because that was in the early fifties, with hotel reservations and that kind of thing. There were some pretty bad situations, but I managed to weather all of them.

When I left California, Dallas wanted me. New York wanted me. Chicago wanted me. Denver wanted me. And I said, "Let me go home." That was 1958 when I came back home. I worked here in Chicago until I retired in 1974 with one promotion here. I went to Assistant Regional Commissioner with the Department of Health Education and Welfare. I got many awards when I was there. The one I am proudest of is the Florida Hold Agency, the Superior Service Award. Then I was nominated and was runner-up for Regional Staff Award for five years. I never got the first prize, but at least I had that.

Even after I had retired, for about two years, I had people calling me from the offices from around the country, asking me what I thought about things. Had I been white and a man, I would have headed one of the HEW offices. I know that it's just one of those things. But it has been an experience that I have enjoyed. I never had any trouble with any of the state people, especially in the west. In the fifties they were not as sophisticated as they are now. Hawaii, for example. We couldn't move for them wanting help. The central states were ignoring them. They thought they knew everything. That is one of the reasons I decided I was going to retire. I could retire, and I decided I would. I told the director of Illinois agency, after having concluded with Washington and that was approved in writing, something he had to do. I said, "Why?" He said, "I went into Washington, and they told me I didn't have to." They never let me know that he had been in there. So I said, "I don't have to put up with this stuff. I've got my years in. I can get my pension. And I can work some place else, if I want to." But I just decided that I had had enough of it.

It was when Nixon and the Republicans came in. It was a big difference in the whole tone and feeling about welfare. I wouldn't be able to work in this climate now because there was no caring about people at all. I know there are many things that are wrong about welfare, but there were as many good things about it, too. There are things that could be done if I, as a supervisor, worked with the staff to help them. But what I found was that people just don't care. One person said to me, "This is the best full-time pay job that you work half-time for" that she had ever dreamed of having. And that was the attitude then.

Social Clubs, Sororities, Etc.

I don't belong to any social clubs now. I have belonged to a bridge club, but I can't go. The bridge club was started back in the thirties. Earnestine Guillebeaux was a member, but everybody else has died off, or like I am, unable to come.

The name of the club was the Sunday Bridge Club. We just played bridge and we bought dirty cards to read to each other on our birthdays, but it's hard to find good dirty cards now.

The club is almost completely new now. There's Leslie Pollard Keeling and Joan Castleberry from Lake Forest. She isn't able to come very much anymore because her husband is sick. Then the new ones are Camilla Harris, Gladys Johnson, and Mame Spencer. I can't think of the rest of them, but these are all new. Guillebeaux, Keeling, Joan, and I are the only old ones from the original group. The other bridge club that I belonged to before that, I guess Rachel Graves and I are the only ones that are left. You know, when you get this old, nobody is left.

Now, the Links, I don't consider a social club. I consider it a service club.

I think one of the biggest services that it has been rendered in the past has been their monetary assistance to organizations in the community. Their scholarships: a thousand to your first scholarship choice; and then three scholarships to that person who is first choice now when she or he enters that freshman year; freshman, sophomore, junior year, if they maintain a B average, five hundred dollars, so that there are three going each year who get five hundred dollars each; so that would be one thousand dollars and 250 dollars. That money comes primarily from the one fund raiser they have during the year, a dinner dance.

For the last two years, when I have not been active, they have been doing a great deal with Family Focus, doing a great deal with volunteer work, being very active in the Family Focus annual fund raising thing, contributing prizes and decorations, selling tickets and selling chances.

I am on the advisory board. Cam Hill is on the advisory board. Lanye Barefield is on the advisory board. Lea McKissisck is on the advisory board.

So, there are four of us who are Links who are very active in that. That's our way of contributing. Other members are active in their communities. We have members from Zion, Waukegan, Evanston, Chicago, Lake Forest, Highland Park. They are active in other ways in their communities. I would say that in the last four years they have made a significant contribution.

Sorority - Alpha Kappa Alpha

You know I am very proud of Alpha Kappa Alpha. I have been a member for sixty-six years. I think that there is nothing, unless it is the church, that I have been more alive in. I have been president of chapters in New York, San Francisco, and in Evanston. I have received the highest award that the sorority gives to a member, which is the Founders Graduated Sorors Service Award. I got the award in Dallas in 1956. They give it every two years. I have served on the National Board for twelve years, first as financial director, then as treasurer, then as parliamentarian, then as chairman of push and L, trying to keep me in. My last work was in 1974. I have just founded a national scholarship. Most people don't know this yet. They were going to announce it in Detroit. The sorority has established a separate foundation, Educational Advancement Foundation. They have almost a million dollars endowment fund, and they have given on the average of fifty scholarships for the last couple of years. There is no restriction as to race. Some of the scholarships are on the basis of merit Others are on the basis of financial need. There are some to undergraduates, there are some to graduates, but I have served until this year when I felt I just couldn't handle it, as one of the graders for the applications. Those of us who initially gave a thousand dollars toward the start of the fund were selected to do the evaluation of applications. And they are interesting. They are really interesting. They are some really great people. This year, for the first time, three of the people who got initial awards have graduated, gone into graduate study, and have established scholarships in their own names.

One of the things that I am proudest of, that I contributed when I went in as financial director, in 1962, I had to sign checks. I began to notice that people were really not knowledgeable about procedure. So, with the help of Mrs. Carrie Preston and Mrs. Hile, I developed a pamphlet, which was published and since revised, that has a chapter on financial procedure. Now, every chapter uses this form for reporting, to the IRS, everything. It is not complicated, I wrote it as simply as I possibly could. I am real proud of that.

When I was the national treasurer, we had a campaign to try to get every chapter to buy a NAACP life membership. I think most of them did.

Alpha Kappa Alpha has been a very important part of my life and I feel I have contributed a great deal toward it. I was appointed in 1986 to a commission. It is known as SOC, Study of the Structure and Operations of Alpha Kappa Alpha. We did a questionnaire thing to all chapters, and then we met from 1986 to 1990 with the regions in their meetings, and the national meetings, and with ourselves, and then made a report of our recommendations. Many were very sound, but Alpha Kappa Alpha was not ready for it at this time. I'm hoping that in the years to come, we will be ready.

My feeling all along was that the sorority members were primarily teachers who don't have the kind of administration experience that you should have to administer a big agency. Their thinking is only in terms of where you go in teaching. Even those who are principals, they don't get the same kind of thing that I got in looking at a state's administration of its welfare program, all of the aspects of it.

Have you seen the AKA building down at Fifty-seventh and Stoney Avenue? It's a three-story building. They bought the land and built it. I was to go to the ground breaking, but we had a meeting with the diocese on the church business. Archie Simmons was the church senior warden. Father and I went up and waited with Jones in his office to discuss it. Archie never showed up, and it made me miss that ground breaking. But that was back in the early 1980s. This year they added another floor, before they could not see the need for a new floor, which was badly needed, and the fee was two hundred dollars per member. The floor was needed, but then you need a base to meet your ongoing expenses. Your insurance, janitorial services, everything that goes into running a building. They couldn't see that. And many of them got out rather than pay that two hundred dollar fee. Some of the people I was surprised at.

How long has the chapter been active in Evanston?
We were chartered in Evanston in 1948 and have been active ever since then.
This is the graduate chapter. There are two undergraduate chapters. One at Northwestern and one at Kendall National College. This chapter was chartered at National because there were girls at Kendall who wanted to be AKAs. We don't get girls from there now. I don't know why. Most of the girls who came in originally were at the Evanston Hospital Kendall nursing program. They phased that out. We lost that big group of girls.

Lodges
My father was a Knights of Pythian when I was a little girl.

Armed Services
Pete, my brother, served in North Africa. He had a plenty devastating experience with discrimination. It startled him a great deal. It was difficult for him to talk about it. I got him to testify when I was on the human relations commission, and we had a series of problems. One of them was on the police department. Pete was then retired. He testified about the police department's discrimination. It was difficult for him to talk about it. Several times I thought he was going to really break down and cry. There was real discrimination. I was the reason that Bud Gidden left. I still have the letter that I wrote to the city manager. I think I wrote it from the Urban League, I am not sure. The incident that really triggered it was when that boy was shot. Gidden never discussed it with us, never brought it up, until we did. So, I went to the city council with it. Anderson was the city manager then. He wrote a letter to the mayor and the city council, and Gidden resigned shortly thereafter.

In the past, I had close relations with city government, being on the human relations commission, then on the commission on aging, or the area commission which is part of the state commission. I served as an officer there. I served as long as I could. I don't think most people know that in 1988 I was inducted in the Chicago Senior Citizens Hall of Fame. It was in the *Evanston Review* and I have a picture of me with Mayor Daley presenting it to me.

Social Environment in Evanston

My feeling is that the social environment has deteriorated. I don't feel that there is a concern in the African-American Community. I am going to say this. I feel that the churches are not doing what they should, what they could do. This may be hearsay, but I think instead of talking every Sunday about loving Jesus and all of that, they ought to be talking about parental responsibility, try to find ways of bringing people into programs in the church, developing programs in the church, because this is where, to me, these youngsters get their training. When the doors of the church close on Sunday, Second Baptist, I think, does more than any other church in the black community in programs. I would be willing to bet that when the doors of the church close on Sunday, they might open for prayer meeting on Wednesday night, but that is about all. There ought to be programs all over the west side.

I don't think there is knowledge of what is being done over the whole community.

Questions for Discussion

1. Describe the way Mr. and Mrs. Cromer met and married in Evanston.
2. What was the attitude of Helen's neighbors when a family from Cabrini Green moved on the block?
3. What unpleasant experience did the Cromer family have at the Evanston Hospital when Bill became ill? How was this problem resolved?
4. What was the name of the realtor Helen worked for? What was her job? Where was the office located?
5. Who was the businessman who was also the steward of the Evanston Club?
6. What universities gave Helen fellowships to complete her studies in social work?
7. Why did Helen feel that she was not appointed to head one of the

HEW offices?
8. What were some of the services that were given to the community by the Links organization?
9. What are some of the awards Helen has received from the Alpha Kappa Alpha sorority?
10. What was a criticism by Helen of the background of many of the elected officers of the sorority?
11. What recommendations does Helen make to improve the social environment in Evanston?

About Helen

Helen takes care of business. I think that statement describes her life and character.

I had the opportunity to work and worship with her at St. Andrews Episcopal Church when she serviced as treasurer and senior warden for many years. She was just as dedicated and efficient there as she had been as a government administrator. But her business-like approach to important matters did not interfere with her having fun, because she knew how to do that too.

Helen has been in the fight helping people and fighting injustices a long time, so nature has taken its toll and placed the burden of troublesome arthritis on her now. She moves slowly, but her mind is as sharp as ever.

Reverend Larry W. Edwards

United Faith Missionary Church

My family is originally from Ecru, Mississippi. About thirty-five or forty years ago they came to Evanston, and like many blacks from the South, looking for job opportunities. We lived in Evanston most of my life until I was married in about 1978. I then moved to Desplains, and we later moved to Buffalo Grove and eventually to Deer Park, where we currently live. And we commute back and forth to Evanston. One of the pleasures that I have in coming to Evanston, on a non-church related matter or when I am not here to see family, is going to the Evanston downtown area, noticing the changes and, especially in the summer, running into people I went to school with. To me, that is exciting.

When I think of the business and professionals in Evanston who served well in the African-American community, I think of people like Dr. Elizabeth Hill who was well known in the black community for many years until she passed. In fact she lived in my neighborhood, so we were very much aware of her. She also reminds me of an old relic that we no longer remember in this community, the Community Hospital, which I think most people have forgotten.

There were others such as Lorenzo Kelly, who grew up in Evanston and worked as a banker at the First National Bank of Evanston. Mr. Kelly, who is now serving as a pastor in South Dakota, spent a lot of time encouraging my brother and me, as well as many other young people in the community. While working at the Washington National Insurance Company in Evanston, I met a gentleman by the name of Don Royster who worked as a claims adjuster and has since gone on to become president of the Atlanta Life Insurance Company. Don, I will always remember. In fact, he is my son's godfather. He provided a good role model and was the motivating factor that caused me to pursue a career in insurance. I am currently working for an insurance company in Glenview.

There are probably a zillion blacks that I consider extremely influential in my growing process here in Evanston. And sometimes I know it is rough to point or look for a role model, since the competition is great today.

Our young people are looking more or less in the direction of sports heroes, people who are making the big dollar salaries. In reality, I think there are a lot of black heroes that we have that are not necessarily throwing hoops in baskets or making touchdowns on the fields, and yet are making touchdowns in the lives of many blacks. Even so, I think the gentlemen whom I have mentioned certainly fit within that category.

I worked as a stock boy in Baskins Clothing Store, which is no longer here in Evanston, while I was going to school. I believe this was in my high school days. This job was mostly an after school job which included work on Saturdays. One of the things I enjoyed about this job was the fact that I was able meet a lot of the people in the Evanston community. One of the things that I do note is that, because of the nature of the Baskins Clothing Store, I would not necessarily meet as many blacks or see as many black faces in there as I would, perhaps, in some of the other stores, but I did enjoy the work experience. I also worked as a stock boy for Kresges. When you compare the two, there I obviously had more opportunity to see our people, because when you look in terms of the stores where we shopped, certainly Kresges would be one where you might see more black people shopping than at Baskins. It, again, provided funds while I was in school. I met some great people while working there. One of the beauties of working as a young person in high school is the fact that you work just to pick up money. You are not working as in a career. You are not working looking at a long term type of thing. And I think that one thing we have done in the country, we have taken the joy out of work because we are so conscious of having to make X number of dollars and having to do X number of things in order for the career to work and be beneficial to us. So when I think back over those days, I have a great appreciation for that.

Eventually, I got a job at the Washington National Insurance Company, where I worked in the policy cash surrender department, and later in the claims department. This was interesting, because it was a department of about six people. It consisted mostly of older people. They were ladies. In fact, they treated me more or less as a grandson. It was quite an interesting experience there. But one of the things I was able to do there, I began to grow up. I learned a lot of things in regards to being committed to a job. There was a level of responsibility that I developed which I thought was extremely good. So, I enjoyed my days there. And, of course, I met the gentleman I mentioned earlier, Don

Royster, who was quite influential in terms of process. As I remember, Mr. Royster was a hard worker. As a young black male, he had goals, and he didn't mind reaching for those goals. I'll never forget. Initially, I used to think, boy, this guy is really going above board, but as I got to know Don, and I saw the direction in which he was going, that gave me the motivation to believe that, if I worked hard, I could also reach such goals. So there's a great appreciation in my life for meeting Don Royster.

I worked at Washington National, I think, in my last two years of high school. I worked there afterward when I went to college. I was to get my bachelors degree. Then I went on and received my masters degree. So, Washington National worked very well for me. They were also very acclimated to work programs which allowed many students to receive credit for working there.

When I was about nine or ten years old, my father and mother separated and my father had died, it was extra special to me to have men such as Don Royster and Lorenzo Kelley as mentors.

I attended Foster School, but I suppose there weren't many young black men in this neighborhood who did not attend Foster School. One of the things I remember and I shall never forget is in Ecru, Mississippi, all of the schools were still segregated, and I realized what a difference there was in education. When I came to Evanston, I was ready to go into second grade, and I will never forget when I came in and I compared my background with the students who were already here, this was extremely frustrating for a seven- or eight-year-old about to enter this program. I met a beautiful black woman whose name I will never forget, Mrs. Morey. Mrs Morey talked with me and spent some time with me and actually helped me make it through the second grade. She was certainly a wonderful teacher.

There was another teacher by the name of Mrs. Flagg who impressed me. There were other teachers there who reminded me of drill sergeants, both white and black. I know they were rough, but when I look at what was accomplished, certainly they contributed a great deal to my motivation in terms of moving into the direction that was good for me.

When I went to junior high school, this was probably my first exposure to an integrated environment. I went to Haven School and saw that in addition to other black faces, there were white faces as well. At that age, one of the blessings of youth is there was no great concern in terms of color. So, we had a real good relationship.

The teachers were tremendous. There were not a great deal of black teachers at Haven, but you felt that there was an interest in the students. As I moved on to high school I went to Evanston Township High School, and that was a growing up experience. I shall never forget. The school was so much bigger. Coming from such a small elementary school, such as Foster, going to a larger school for junior high school, and then being sent to a school as large as Evanston Township High School, that was a tremendous awakening. We had some tremendous teachers there, but the problem with the high school was the personal attention, I think, you didn't receive as much as, I felt, you received in the elementary schools. I think one of the things that really was lacking was counseling, and especially for blacks. When you look at a young black person in the system then, you will see someone who may have gone further in school than his parents, or at best, may have parents who have completed school but have gone no further. And if you go to college, you might be the first one in your family to actually receive a college degree. I say that, to say this. One of the things, I think, that wasn't there or was needed at the time, was someone who was acclimated to the fact that you've got young blacks who are through the system now and who are contemplating going on to college. Parents who may not have gone to college or who may not have gone beyond high school would not, necessarily, be aware of those things or the directions that they need to push their young people so that they can, in essence, be prepared for college. As a result, when I got to that point where I was ready to consider college, it was extremely rough, because I didn't have that type of "push." So I went through high school as though I was going through junior high, looking at it from the stand point that this is OK, I've got to go through these four years, and not in the terms of looking at to think, you've got to go through these four years, but while you're going through, you start forming in your mind where you're going to go if you are going to enter college. And that's one thing that I think, during those days, we probably didn't think a great deal about.

On Evanston politics, I'm not a party member. Where I currently live, my exposure to the alderman concerns matters which concern the church. I find, however, that they have been extremely sensitive to some concerns that I have had, and in helping me get through to City Hall.

One of the things that I have seen that is tremendous is that in Evanston, especially in terms of those who are involved in the political structure, I think they are aware of the fact that black churches exist in Evanston, and that we know where we want to go in this community in terms of helping to keep our young people out of gangs, helping to provide some cohesiveness in our community, so I think there is a greater respect for black churches in Evanston. The new police chief, who happens to be a black man, has spent some valuable time visiting with the Ministers Alliance and sharing with us his agenda and his plans for working with the people of Evanston, which I think is very valuable. We need to have a sense of being a part. Unfortunately, in the past we've been called upon when there is a problem that everyone else can't handle. Then we've been asked to come in. To me, because of my business background, that's management by crisis, and management by crisis pulls everyone together. It gets people aware of the problem, but the biggest problem is becoming aware of the problem when the problem is there. If you prepare to work on a foreseen problem, before it gets in a chaotic state, then you can better deal with the problem. That's management by objective, rather than management by crisis. So, I think that is what is happening now. There are a lot of rough edges we are whittling away at, but I think that we are, at least, moving in a better direction. If we continue going in that way, we will see a better product in terms of relationships here in Evanston.

When we think of what has been done here in Evanston, I am very happy to be a part of a generation which has the first black mayor, a female, which is extremely important. I guess it is hard for me to lay down my clergy background, but this thing with role models is extremely important to me. If I am going to look realistically at statistics, let's face it, if you take a thousand young black males, all of them are good at basketball. Statistically speaking, the bottom line is this. Being realistic, there is going to be a small, minute percentage that will actually be able to get on a professional team. That's being realistic. If that is the case, what is going to happen to that large percentage that doesn't make it?

If they have already failed at being a Michael Jordan, or becoming a part of the Chicago Bulls, what do you have left for them? You have closed the door to what they have thought was "success." You have other, what we call ordinary, black role models, those people who may not be making the big bucks but are doing something meaningful in our community. So I am very in tune to role models, and I think that if we're telling our young people that, in essence, there's more to it than sports, we need to have more role models who are in other things than sports. That includes people in the political structure, clergy, deacons, people who are willing to practice discipleship, and pour their lives into a young person, so that young person, in essence, will have the benefits of some of their experiences. There's an old saying, and although there is some truth to it, I am not one of those who believe that experience is always the best teacher. There are some big "ifs." The cost of tuition can be extremely high. It's better for me to learn from your experience, in some areas, and take it for the value that it is, than for me to actually have to go through the hardships, or whatever, and profit from that. That's not to say that there are things that I am not going to have to experience for myself, but there are things that I should be able to sit down and receive from your wisdom, and not have to go through some of the pains that you went through. I am in favor of having young people mentored by adults. I am very big on that.

I attend the United Faith Missionary Baptist Church. In fact, I am very proud to be the pastor. I would like to mention some of the historical members of this church The late Reverend L.M. Geter, who has been well known in this community, was my former pastor. This church is a result of a split from the Springfield Baptist Church. As a result, the first pastor was Reverend L.M. Geter, and I was fortunate enough to have also attended Springfield during the time that he was pastor there. Reverend Geter was a down to earth person, a great role model. He was well-known in the community and well loved in the community. He was that kind of a person. I used to attend his Bible classes at Springfield, and he taught me to have an appreciation for the Bible. I didn't know how to spell the word, never heard it before, but he used the word one night, verbatim, and looked us in the eyes and said, "That means the word of God should be taken verbatim, which is to say, you're to add nothing to it."

I listened to that and I thought, Wow. I had never heard it before, couldn't even spell it, let alone pronounce it. He was very serious and very committed to the word of God. To me that was extremely important. Also, another thing which I appreciated from him was, that unless you have been a pastor, it's difficult to understand the pains of being a pastor. I often look at the size of our church. We're under a hundred people here. And even when you look at the number on the rolls in every church, there's only a percentage of those people whom you see on a regular basis. No matter what size church you have, you have similar problems to those of other churches. You can have a hundred people and have a hundred personalities. No matter how you labor in the ministry, there are people that you're still going to struggle with in order to get them to grow. So, I have a special appreciation for him, because he spent most of his life working with the church and giving his life for that church.

Another very important person in our church is probably one of our oldest mothers who died, Mother Opel Williams, a sweetheart of a lady. At Springfield, she was one of the encouragers for me. I'll never forget. It was a very small thing, but the National Baptist Convention was going on and the church wasn't able to provide funds to send a delegate from our training group. She and those ladies, bless their hearts, pooled together and said, "We are going to send him." That was so encouraging to me. I felt so good that they thought enough to do that, I would sometimes go to some of the seminars and I would miss lunch because I tried to absorb as much as I could to bring back a good report to them. After we returned from the convention, they would allow us to have some time during Sunday School hour. That was extremely important to me. I developed a great appreciation for expanding my knowledge in doing things of that nature. I say that with an underline because I think sometimes in our churches we don't appreciate how important it is to get our young people to attend things like this. You can take the best doctor in world, and when he hangs his shingle outside his door, it says "Doctor Jones" in practice. You can take the best attorney in the world, and when he hangs his shingle outside his door, "attorney at law" in practice. I say that because one of the things that people in the business world learn, and even in the education world, they realize the need to keep improving and becoming acclimated to what's happening in terms of "fine tuning" their knowledge and learning about new innovations.

I say this because I think in the church we need that same type of desire or spirit. And I think that in order to get our young people to have that type of appreciation, it has to be instilled in them. Churches have to feel that is important and they have to want to send their young people to such conferences or meetings, or children will get to the point where there is no interest at all in the church.

I must have been fifteen or sixteen at that time, and that meant an awful lot to me then.

There is one additional person that I would like to mention from this membership here, one of our deceased members, Deacon J.B. Weaver, who was a tremendous source of encouragement for my ministry here. He worked very faithfully until he was no longer able to do it. But you know what? One of the reasons I mentioned Deacon Weaver is that every pastor needs someone who is an encourager. Deacon Weaver and I used to have a private joke. He would always look at me and say, "Pastor, how is it going?" And I would say, "I'm hanging in there." Or sometimes he would look at me and say, "Hang in there, Pastor." Then I would catch him sometimes before he would ask me and I would say, "How are you doing?" He would say, "Pastor, I'm hanging," and I would look at him and say, " All right, Deacon, hang tough." It's a small thing, but I think sometimes we take our pastors for granted and we don't realize how important it is for us to be able to smile and encourage them. And in the ministry you do a lot of encouraging.

I am very in tune with what is happening in the white churches among the white clergy. They have started the talk, long before we did, about the need for clergy to be able to have that source of encouragement. And they have talked about how important it is. We are starting to talk about it, although when we talk about it, we still talk with an eye of suspicion, thinking, "That person doesn't need that kind of encouragement, if I do this, this is going to go to the pastor's head. When we have members who are encouraging, it can turn a bad day into a great day for a pastor. When you think in terms of the way we are going now, all of the pastors in the world and in the country cannot be tele-evangelists, cannot pastor churches with a thousand members. And yet, when you look at the trenches, the trenches have churches of all sizes, and you've got men the size of the trench, and it's so important, I think, to have people that are encouragers. And so, when I think in terms of our history, I also have to include Deacon J.B. Weaver.

When you look at the church in terms of its value to the community, it can be extremely helpful in making the community a happier and safer place in which to live by merely being involved in the community.

I have learned from experience. I can come and talk to you and tell you how messy my desk is, and I can complain about how the papers are disorganized, etc. That's great, that's wonderful. I have good eyes. I recognized the problem. I saw it, bingo. But you know what is more important? Look at the problem and walk over to this desk and start taking those papers and putting them in some kind of order.

We have been extremely critical, I think, as a church. We've talked about the problems and are made aware of them by the newspapers, but I think one of the things that we have to realize as churches it doesn't matter how much we talk about the problems out there, unless we roll up our sleeves, that work won't get done. I don't believe God has called us to be the thermometer Christians. Thermometers are beautiful. They're very valuable, because they tell you what the temperature is. But God, I believe, does not call us to be thermometers. Everybody knows what the temperature is in the community. Instead, I think God called us to be more like thermostats. The beauty about being a thermostat is if the temperature inside is sixty degrees, and you want it to be seventy degrees, you turn it up to seventy degrees. The thermostat is connected to the furnace, and that furnace won't stop working when that thermostat is on seventy, until all of the temperature around becomes seventy. What I am saying is that in our community, the same thing must happen if we are to be viable. I think that when you look at what we can do, we can provide activities for our young people. We have young people who go to Vacation Bible School here we won't see again until next Vacation Bible School. That can be depressing. But then when we stop and think they may not have heard anything about the Lord, either, since the last Vacation Bible School. Now when you plant a seed, it doesn't come up right away, but if the church can plant enough seeds out there, we can provide some positive impacts in our community. The key word is involvement. I can't pretend that we are an island and be happy as long as everything is going well with my members because we are affected by our community. And so, if we are to make a change, we've got to be involved.

Most of my involvement in the Evanston Community centers around my family and the church. We currently have what we call a family gathering here at United Faith. What I am addressing refers to sources of entertainment. Church is my life, other than my family. One of the things that I believe is that I don't think that God is some ogre sitting up there in the sky with a frown on his face and never enjoying himself. And I believe the same thing about the church. I believe that we should be able to laugh. We should enjoy each other's fellowship. When we come here to worship on Sunday, I believe that we ought to be here because we enjoy being here. What we have decided to do here is to come together as a family gathering, usually in every quarter, and play games, Bible games, and others of that nature where people can laugh and have a good time listening to the people chuckle. You might look at them and say, " Is that the church?" I say "Yes," because what I want to instill in my people is the idea that there is joy in serving the Lord. I am not talking about getting out there, having a fifth in your hand, or doing things that are ungodly, but you can enjoy being a part of the family of God. And you can smile. You can laugh. So, we try to do this so that our people can be able to feel happy. Now we can't take full credit for this. My wife and I had attended a church in Northbrook we had been invited to. They had an activity week where they did a lot of things, crafts and things of that nature. I thought, after we saw that, what if we can do this in such a way where our people can come together and have a good time? That was great. I think that in terms of entertainment in the church, I never want to think that our services are entertainment, unless it is for God. Sometimes we feel that way about our musicals. But it is a service. When I look at entertainment as a part of a church, and since this is where my life kind of migrates, that's one thing that I like to think it is something where our people can come together and enjoy each other. I think that this is something that I would even extend, so that we can do a special thing, even in the community where we can bring people in the community to do basically the same thing.

I've been involved with both the Evanston and the St. Francis Hospitals in an internship program that was affiliated with a pastoral care program at St. Francis. It was very good in what I thought was reflecting the care of patients in that setting. I have nothing but positive things to say of my personal experiences with the hospitals here, because I go in so frequently, everybody there knows me. The hospitals provide free parking for clergy. They used to have clergy days that I thought were very encouraging. I don't know why they discontinued those, but the hospitals have been very supportive. I may have a person who is in critical condition or his nurse or the doctor has to run against a dead wall, or someone who is in ICU, I am their pastor. I need to see this person. And they have been very receptive. My people are depending on me to see them. So, the cooperation I have received from both hospitals, I have appreciated.

Having grown up in Evanston, I consider it a home type of place. I am one of those people who, when you sing "May Old Acquaintance Be Forgot," it hits an emotional spot with me. I look at Evanston as it has changed. When I came out of high school in the 1970s, we were dealing with the long hair and the new word "hippy." I look at how the community has changed. There is such a tremendous difference. We knew there were gangs. We knew there were problems with drugs, but the impact was not as great as it is now. It is so funny, because in Evanston now, we are very acclimated to the fact that there are gang members who live in the community. I think that is of a great concern now. Because of management of objective as opposed to management by crisis, we see that there is no community that can say, "No, we have a one hundred percent safe plan to keep this from happening." But right now, because we are so close to the city of Chicago, we are aware that there are gang members in basically all of our communities. Suburbia isn't a safe haven as people thought before. In fact, what it has done is awakened us. But I think that there is a greater need to be concerned about our young people. You know, one of the worst things you can do if you look at it from the church standpoint, is to wait until the young people become teenagers and then start thinking, Why don't we do something with these young people?

The churches have to work with the city, and the city has to work with the churches in order to form some kind of nucleus where we've got that happening. In so doing, I think this will help reduce the occurrences that we have seen of gang activity. The city, I think, is doing a good job in terms of what they are doing now. The police have been very receptive to opening their doors to people from the churches who would like to come in and meet the officers that operate in their particular neighborhoods. I think that's great. I've known a few police who have come in on Sunday to say hello. Everyone was wondering "Are they going to take away my pastor?"

We need to not see police as "bad guys" if we're going to make this thing work. Our churches need to see police come into the church on a friendly basis. I don't have a problem introducing them to the congregation. I know that they are very busy, but then I think in terms of the investment that's being made when this takes place. There is a need for us to continue this kind of concern for our people.

The Black Ministers Alliance has what I call a dual purpose. It's to provide a cohesiveness among the black clergy in Evanston, which is extremely important. I am not a pastor who has an ego problem. I realize that with a church my size, if I am going to have a desire to do those things that I feel the church should be doing in the community, I have limited resources to do them. But I do believe that if I am able to hook in with another church, pool my resources with another church, or with a central church, we can accomplish more. I believe in being a good steward of the resources that we have. If you had a need, a financial need, I believe in attempting to resolve that need and assist you. And I also believe that as a person who is responsible as a steward over things God has given to us, I need to spend some time doing more than just saying, "Here, take this money." I need to investigate. I need to also be able to check other avenues in terms of things I can do to assist you. Hence, when we pool together as an alliance, I think that's a very valuable thing. Also, I see the Alliance's purpose as being a volatile force in our community, that's there addressing some of the issues that are related to the black community. You hear of the Black Ministers Alliance involved in some of the issues concerning the school district. We need to be involved because if we are to talk the talk, we cannot just preach the gospel here on Sunday and expect that once it's one o'clock and the doors are closed, that it ends there, but it's something that we have to preach to the extent that it takes us into the school system where black youths are. It takes us into issues that affect the community. We have got to be visible. I think that's what happens with the Ministers Alliance. We need to know who our police chief is. We need to know who our mayor is. We need to have a rapport with them as black clergy. When we do this, they know that we are concerned. What I see that has to happen with the churches, it's just like at school, my mother, even after she was separated from my father, during high school open house she was one of the few blacks that would be there, and I noticed that for a fact, because I would often volunteer as a hall guard. But one thing the teachers knew, one thing I knew, Mamma cared. We should let our community know that we care.

Some of the issues that are addressed are basically, as I said before, the things that are happening in the community, the black community per se, and that's not to say that it's not going to hold true or overlap into the things of concern also to the white community. But I think, because most of our constituency happens to be black, those issues are extremely important to us. If there are young people in my congregation who are going through the school system and they're not receiving the education that they should be receiving, that's a concern that I have. So, I see the Alliance as being effectively involved in addressing the issues of that nature.

How effective is the Alliance in realizing its purpose? I think not as effective as we would like to be, but I think we are effective to the extent that people are more aware of the fact that we are there.

Should it be a black oriented type of worship service, or should it be more like in the other group. Then comes this other problem of who should benefit from the receipts. They had this seventy-thirty thing last year. Now, the Evanston Ecumenical Action Council, in theory, represents all the churches of Evanston, and then the African Alliance thinks that they should.

The agenda is to come together and worship God, to offer Him that Thanksgiving. When you come with multi-agendas, I think you will run into problems.

Questions for Discussion
1. Discuss Reverend Edwards' family background.
2. Describe Reverend Edwards' work experiences in Evanston.
3. Who were some of the people who made an impression on the life of Reverend Edwards?
4. What example did he give of how a member of the congregation can ease the burdens of the pastor?
5. What does Reverend Edwards mean by mentoring?
6. What does Reverend Edwards mean by management by objective or management by crisis?
7. What problem does he find with the ecumenical attempt in Evanston?

About Reverend Larry W. Edwards
My associate, Prentis Bryson and I met Reverend Edwards at his church on the corner of Foster Street and Wesley Avenue. This is one of the smaller churches in Evanston, but it is in good repair and attractive. There is evidence of love and care of the church property.

Reverend Edwards was well prepared to respond to any questions we might ask him and did so quite fluently.

Reverend Edwards lives in another city and commutes to the church for services and appointments, but he seems to have the youth, vitality, and enthusiasm to perform duties quite well.

He is optimistic about the future, but he realizes that much work must be done in the community to lessen the disruptive elements which are causing some Evanstonians problems and concerns.

He hopes that the black Ministers Alliance and white Ministers Alliance can agree on a common agenda.

Rachel Graves

My mother was from St. Louis. My father was pastor of the church there. They went to Savannah, Georgia, then from there they went to Mexico, and from there they went to Lincoln, Nebraska. Then they went to Marshall, Texas and then they went to Shreveport, Louisiana.

We got married on my birthday, September 20, 1932. Hop had driven down and had brought my sister and his mother and Luella's mother-in-law with him. It took about two days for the trip back to Evanston, so I guess I really started living in Evanston about the ninth of September 1932.

We roomed with Mrs. Nicholson, right across the street from Ebenezer Church. Then we got an apartment at 1028 Florence. We lived there a year, then we moved across the street from Mrs. Nicholson on Emerson Street to a house which was owned by the family of Sonny Robinson.

Then we went to live in an apartment above Mason's Funeral Parlor. That was when Hop and Mason were together in the funeral business.

Life With an Undertaker in Evanston

Well, I know that I had to go with everything that was happening. I had to buy a ticket to everything. I had to make appearances all the time because people expected you to do that, so, you are in business and you have to please them. When Hop got out of the undertaking business, I told him I was so glad. All my life time I had been a minister's daughter and you had to be and act differently from anybody else and forget that you were a kid like everybody else. Then I married an undertaker and I had to do the same thing. I said, "Oh, good grief, finally I can be myself." Even now when I just retaliate and I don't want to go to something, some tea or luncheon, I say, "I don't have to do anything anymore. I can do what I want to do."

When I came to Evanston, I had finished Fisk University. During the war years, I took a course at Northwestern.

Before Hop became associated with Mr. Mason in the undertaking business on Emerson Street, he was with Metropolitan Funeral Home located, next door west of Ebenezer AME Church.

I joined Second Baptist Church. Reverend Borders was the pastor. I played for the BYPU for a number of years, but I didn't do anything in particular in the church. I paid my dues. My mother used to say that I thought I could pay my way into heaven. I wasn't too active. I played the piano, and every once in a while I play now. You know, I have had this dog (a big one, too) about four years. One day I decided to sit down and play. You know, dogs can be so sensitive. She came and stood beside me and looked so strange. Just once in a blue moon, I open the piano and play.

School

When I first came to Evanston, I applied for a job in the Evanston School System. That was not a nice experience. I went down to the board, and the superintendent showed me a list that he had reserved under glass, and it was so old, where it had been signed by any number of blacks who did not want black persons teaching their children. There are a lot of people who don't know this. I was quite surprised at some of the names that I saw. Well, I don't remember now who got together to finally bring about the change. I believe Patsy Sloan was the first black to teach in Evanston. You couldn't come from Evanston. You had to come from somewhere else, but when you were assigned to a job, then you had to move to Evanston. She was the one who broke the barrier. Then others began to be hired as teachers in Evanston. They taught at Foster School.

Church

I had three children, but Chris is the only survivor. He went through school in Evanston without any problems.

My mother was visiting me and had my brother, Charles, with her. Charles is the baby of our family. So, Hop said to him, "We don't have any children, so how would you like to stay with us and be our little boy?" Later on, he said, "I didn't mean for eternity, when I said that." I had a little "thingamajig" over at the high school with Charles. Somehow, I don't know, I guess it was in the registering, I had to go over there. They said that, since his mother and father were living, I would have to pay tuition for him to go to school there, even though he was living with me. Well, I flipped my top about that. I had a very good white lawyer friend, Mr. Ashcraft. I had sewed for his wife. Anyway, I went to him and said, "Mr. Ashcraft, why do I have to adopt Charles?" He said, "I'll take care of that, Rachel." And I never heard anymore from the high school about it.

Charles lived with us until he married. In fact, when he first married, Hop was working out of town, and he and Julie lived here about two years.

Horace Fred was born in 1940. Christmas Day. He went to Foster School, then to Nichols School, then to ETHS.

The Y was my haven when I first came to Evanston. Of course, I was so close because I was just down the street, or slightly across the street from the Y, until Hop and Mason became partners. I used to go swimming. I played basketball. In fact, any spare moment that I had, I was in the Y. I was worse than a kid, although I was a married women, but at that time I had no children.

The Emerson Street Y was the focal point of an awful lot of good. After everything was all integrated, I could get the feel that the people didn't have the same feeling about going down to the Grove Street Y that had been at the Emerson Street Y. That is one time, that I think, being "cornered off" was to the advantage of us.

I remember some of the people who used to be seen regularly at the Y, such as the secretary, Christine Evans, who later transferred to the Grove Street Y and retired from there, A.P. Perry, chairman of the Board of the Emerson Street, Dr. Cotton, who lived across the street from the Y.

You know, at that time, Northwestern did not offer any housing for their black students. Ted Brown and some others broke that barrier. Most of the male NU students lived at the Y. Turk Garret was one.

I remember Johnny Walker who lived at the Y and also played basketball there. He used to shoot the basketball with one hand. And I thought about him while I was watching "Schack" shooting with one hand. You know Johnny used to shoot free throws with one hand.

Some of the girls who played on our basketball team were Bea Young, the Marshall girls, Linda and Ann, Leslie Pollard.

Politics

I guess the one thing that will always stand out in my mind is when I first came to Evanston, Jourdain had just been elected. At the Varsity Theater they were inviting us upstairs. The thing about having movies on Sunday was up before the City Council!. I remember he hung it up that they would have to stop that policy or he would never vote for Sunday movies. And it worked.

Education

There is so much talk about education in general, both white and black, I don't have an opinion about integrating the school system. I don't know whether, I guess it's better than having them all huddled in one school here and one school there, because once they reach high school, they're all going to be together.

School Recreation

Everything was at Foster that wasn't at the Y.

Churches

I backslid.

Hop was very active at Ebenezer. He used to say he had done everything in the church from pumping the old pipe organ to being the janitor. He said he had done everything, except preach.

Clubs

I did belong to the Twentieth Century Golf Club, but it is gone now. Some of the members were Harry Brown, Bill Matthews, Bill Jones, Michelle Laurent, Ruth Cromer, Willie Higgins, Evelyn Peak. These were members from the beginning of the club and had stayed until they passed or the club was disbanded.

The club was started by Joe Howard, the dentist.

We would have some social affairs, two or three fashion shows, but golf was the main thing. We played in tournaments. Once in my lifetime I was able to score under one hundred, and particularly at Northwestern course. My best score was ninety-eight, but I usually scored 103 or 104.

I never played on the Community Course.

I had a terrific slice. Hop used to say, "With it running along the canal, you don't need to go up there, you go on, out to Northwestern, because you won't have a golf ball with your slice. Every ball is going to be in that canal."

Social Problems in Evanston

I am mostly concerned about my two youngest grandchildren. They don't seem to be interested in school. One just finished high school. That one is the baby. She went into high school as an honor student, and we were worried to death whether or not she would graduate. I used to say, "At least they are not doing something bad, and I should be thankful for that. "There are so many kids around here at that age who are getting into all kinds of trouble.

I just don't understand the youngsters. I don't understand this era.

The Music. Everything sounds alike, just a lot of whooping and hollering, with the wild costumes and things that they wear. I'm just two generations away from it. I just don't understand it. I think there are a lot of parents who don't understand it.

Questions for Discussion
1. Discuss Rachel's background and settlement in Evanston.
2. What were her responsibilities as the wife of an undertaker?
3. What contribution did Rachel make to the Second Baptist Church program?
4. What surprising discovery did she make regarding Evanston blacks' attitude toward black teachers?
5. What problem did Rachel have at Evanston Township High School in regards to registering her brother, Charles? Who came to her aid to settle this problem?
6. Why was the Emerson Y so important to Rachel? How did she feel about the eventual integration with the Grove Street Y?
7. What important contribution did Alderman Jourdain make to the black community?
8. What were some of the activities of the Twentieth Century Golf Club?
9. Discuss Rachel's attitude toward the clothing, music, and conduct of youngsters today.

About Rachel Graves

I have known Rachel for many years. She and her husband, Hop, were quite active in the business and social activities of black Evanstonians. I think Rachel stayed in the background and gave the limelight to Hop. His name was really Horace, but his friends called him Hop affectionately.

I was welcomed to Rachel's house by her and her big dog who watched every move I made.

She doesn't move around like she did many years ago at the Y where she swam and played basketball, but she does like to talk about her "terrific slice" when she played golf on the Community Golf Course a few years ago.

Rachel has enjoyed her life and has many fond memories to recall. Rachel is not alone in her failure to understand the youngsters of this era. She is used to a class which is hard to find today.

Bob and Dorothy Hancock

Dorothy: My parents, George and Sarah Butler, were married in Augusta, Georgia in 1906. My father worked at the Augusta brewery. He left Augusta and came to Evanston, Illinois to work in the construction business as a hod carrier, making more money. My mother did not come to Evanston to join him until a few years later. They lived on Asbury Avenue with a family name Mr. and Mrs. George Phillips before moving to University Place where their daughter, I, was born. Their next move was to 1505 Lake Street in a home that sat in the rear of the owner's home, Mr. and Mrs. Major Hamill. These houses still stand.

Among the neighbors living nearby were Mr. and Mrs. William Cromer, parents of Mrs. Helen Cooper, Pete and Billy Cromer, Mrs. Alice Butler and her family, Mr. and Mrs. Samuel Sanders who lived on Greenwood Street with their family.

All of the families improved their lives and their property where they lived.

Among the African-Americans who served the community, that I remember, were Dr. Rudolph Penn, M.D.; Dr. Young, dentist; Dr. Tarkington, dentist; Dr. Scruggs, podiatrist; Dr. Elizabeth Hill, M.D.; Dr. Morrison, druggist. Mr. and Mrs. Fleming were grocers. Ezel Griffin and Leonard Baines also were grocers. Mr. William Dulcon and Mr. William Gill were realtors. Mr. Russell Watkins was a grocer. Bill Higginbotthom was a grocer.

I went to Dewey School and to Haven School. I had one year at ETHS and three years at Lincoln Institute in Lincoln Ridge, Kentucky. I had one year at Sherwood Music School. Before going to ETHS, I took piano and organ lessons from Mr. Thurman F. Charleston School of Music located at 1009 Ayers Place, now known as Garnett Place. Dorothy Lee and I were the two youngest organists at age twelve.

Miss Vera Bently was a piano teacher who had many pupils also.

During my summers from the Lincoln Institute, I worked as secretary to Mr. William H. Dixon Real Estate located on Emerson Street.

As far as politics is concerned, my interest is personal. However, I voted for and supported the mayor in her campaign. As you can see, politics has really changed in Evanston, beginning with the first black alder person, Edwin B. Jourdain, followed by Eugene Beck. Now that number has increased.

I attend and have belonged to Second Baptist Church since early childhood. I had Mrs. Ellen Branch as my Sunday School teacher. Among the members I remember are Mr. William H. Dixon, who was a trustee, Mr. William Gill, another trustee and real estate owner, Mr. D.W. Richardson, another staunch member, and Mr. Thomas Riley.

I remember the YMCA at 1014 Emerson Street. The clubs used to have teas and banquets there. I remember Mr. Hauser as the director for a long time.

There were many entertainment functions at Foster School. Dances were held at the Masonic Temple, such as the Bachelors and Benedicts (called the "B&B" club). I belong to the "Exclusive 13 Club" and held offices as president, vice-president, and other offices. I now belong to a bridge club, the Phi Mu Taus, which meets once a month with a membership of twelve. My dad belonged to the Odd Fellows Lodge. I remember when the members would have a parade and dressed up in their uniforms and marched down Emerson Street. I was just a youngster then. It would be fun to march along with them on the sidewalk.

My husband served in the military during the Second World War. I was not married to him then.

I remember the black Butler-Garnett Hospital on Asbury Avenue. I had my tonsils taken out there. Black people did not go to Evanston Hospital at that time.

My relationship with the various forms of government has improved. When there is a problem, I can consult with them. I find that you can live most anywhere in the city that your money will let you, with the exception of zoning and permits for some locations.

Bob: I came to Evanston in 1936 from a small town, Martin, Arkansas. My sister was living in Evanston at that time at 2015 Darrow Avenue. I moved in with her and her family. We moved from there to Brown Avenue. The first job I had was at the Evanston Hotel on Main Street. From there I worked at the Greenwood Inn on Greenwood and Chicago Avenues. Then I worked at a garage in Rogers Park.

I was inducted into the Army in 1942. I served overseas for three and one half years.

After the war ended, I came back to Evanston. I roomed with Mrs.

Margaret Farmer on Simpson Street.

When Dorothy and I got married, in 1946, we got an apartment in the old Dr. Roberts Apartments, after which we moved into my in-laws' first floor apartment at 909 Grove Street.

I worked at the First National Bank of Evanston for about five years. Then for a short time I worked at the Evanston Post Office. My last job was with the city of Evanston as a gardener, from which I retired.

I belong to the VFW. We just celebrated our fiftieth anniversary in April 1996. I also belong to the American Legion Post in Evanston with a black roster.

Dorothy: I belong to a couples club, a social couples club which originated in the 1950s. Some of the members who started out with us were Joe and Fanny Brooks, Melvin and Pauline Williams, who came in later, Mary and Bishop Harvey, Vera and Otto Lauden. Some members dropped out, and we acquired new members. We had many events that were pleasurable, such as Count Basie's orchestra, and after his appearance we had him come for cocktails, which was quite an event. We got to see some of the entertainers. Among them were Marshall Roth, Frank Foster, Frank West, Al Gray, Sonny Payne. That was the M & M Club (Madames and Messieurs).

The concert was held at the Evanston Township High School.

Each year we would go to concerts at Ravinia. Also, we went on a boat cruise to Muskegon, Michigan, also to Paw Paw, Michigan where there was a resort which was very, very nice. We had the whole house and use of all of the facilities. We were there over night.

I am a member of Second Baptist Church, and have been since childhood. I was in Sunday School with Mrs. Branch as my Sunday School teacher. Also, I remember Mrs. Eddie Garrett, Mrs. Laura Whitaker an older member, and I just came up through the church. I enjoyed the church work. I participated mainly in musical events. I belonged to the Senior Choir. I just enjoyed music. I wasn't heated up on gospel music. I liked spirituals and anthems. Sometimes we would change with other choirs from Chicago and Evanston. One time our choir, the Senior Choir, competed with choirs from other black churches in Evanston, and our choir won the prize.

From the beginning of my membership at Second Baptist, I remember Reverend I.A. Thomas. Then we had Reverend Balou, then Reverend Borders, then J. Gentry Horace, then Reverend Hawk, then

Reverend Hysel Taylor. I was acquainted with all of these ministers. Now, we have Reverend Taylor and feel that he is a good minister. Some things we like, and some things we don't, as with all of the ministers. We do have a large membership. We have two services and they accommodate a lot of people. We have different types of activities going on that are very good.

Bob: I was christened in the Baptist Church in Arkansas when I was a small kid. I did go to church as a youth a lot, Sunday School and all of that. After I came to Evanston, I did go some, but after the war, I went quite a bit, but then it got to be that some of the things that went on got to me. Some of the people were coming up with politics. I thought that that was something that shouldn't be in the church. That is one of the reasons I don't go to church now.

Dorothy: One thing that I think is that our children go to school and they don't have a dress code, and they are just loose, and I don't think they pay attention to their school work. Instead, they think about what somebody is wearing, or what somebody else is doing. This creates a problem. And the parents don't seem to follow up on their children to see that they are getting the proper education that they should be getting. It could be that the parents are working and don't have the time or the energy to take care of these problems at home. I think that all parents should go to the school's teachers meetings to see what is happening in the school, what grade of education you are getting, and what is offered to them.

As far as social activities are concerned, there use to be a time when we could have a lot of fun, but now days the kids get together and they want to drink or they want to use drugs and it makes it very bad. It interferes and interacts with the activities that the grown-ups have, too.

Dorothy: I think that some of the parents and other older people sanction what these kids are doing too much. Even the ministers hold up for these kids when they are doing wrong. The kids think that education is not for them, just that, "I want to get out as soon as I can to get in sports and make a lot of money." But you know, as I know, that a lot of them are good in sports, but when they get up to the big leagues, they don't make it. Then they have nothing to fall back on. That is what hurts me, to see young kids, especially black kids, who throw away their lives wanting to be something that they don't qualify for and throw away their opportunities for an education.

If the government would, for example, start a program like the old prewar CCC Camps which would put the kids to work, even if it was a draft, they would be controlled better.

Dorothy (on the YMCA): Now the Y has opened up to everybody. You can go there for all kinds of things. They even have therapy and swimming lessons and everything. I am planning to take some of them. I think that has opened up for the blacks, if they would only take the opportunity of going. Some of them would rather hang out in the street with their friends than go somewhere that is going to be educational for them. If we could just impound into their heads that this is the thing that they should do, that once they get an education, they can do anything, they would have the world at their command.

Bob: We have opened up a lot of things for them. For example, we (VFW) went down to the Georgian Hotel. You remember that the Georgian was a "no, no," at one time. We had a breakfast down there. We also had a breakfast at Cooley's Cupboard, and we invited the youngsters to come. Now we still have a breakfast. I see some of them. But you see very few teenagers coming to our affairs. We just had our banquet celebrating our fiftieth year, and no teenagers were there.

If we could open up things for them, and if they would take advantage of these things, it would help them.

Dorothy: Our black parents don't take their children to the restaurants. You go to the restaurants and you see other parents with little babies. They start them out early going to restaurants, learning how to act and conduct themselves, and how to eat. This is what we should do, too. Some of our kids go to a restaurant and don't know which table implements to use. It's really bad.

Dorothy (on politics): Some of the black wards, like the one where Kent is the alderman, are trying to do things that will help the blacks, such as proper integration in the schools. That, I think, is good.

Bob: I was at a senior citizen meeting which the mayor visited. People asked a lot of questions, and the mayor answered them.

Our alderman is black. His name is Drummer. He speaks up. I really don't know much about what is going on.

Dorothy: Almost two years ago our next door neighbor to the north of us moved out, and a family moved in. I have not been able to count, from looking, how many people live over there. They have three bedrooms and one bath. They have people living in the basement. They have folds everywhere. So I was real upset because I didn't think it was fair. You know, it brings down your property values if you see a whole lot of folks living like that. So, I contacted the alderman and told him the circumstances that I was upset about, the ones which would cause our property values to go down with all of those folks living next door. They had real crude ideas of living, I think. Evidently, they didn't know how to live in a neighborhood because the first thing that really set us off was, we have our fence, a cyclone fence, which divides the two properties. They would hang their clothes out on the fence. This is something that is bad. So we spoke to them about it and told them that we didn't want anymore clothes hung on the fence, and that it was our fence. So we got through that deal, but the fact that there were so many people living in one house just really got to me.

The alderman said that they could find out, probably, how many people were living over there, especially if they have children going to school, but he said the only thing was that they couldn't make the people move or clear out the house because when they move somebody, they have to have someplace for them to move to. So this would be the problem. And rather than to cause this dissention we sort of let it drop. But there are still a lot of people living over there. They have a van. In the morning before six o'clock, you should see them marching out getting into the van, going to work. Some walk, going to nearby factories down the street. Then there was an old lady there who kept children, and the folks would come in vans and bring kids. One day in the summer they had all the kids out in the front yard, baby buggies and summer chairs and furniture out in the front yard. This really got to me, but I think I ran my blood pressure up and I sort of cooled down.

Bob: I think some of them have gone now, but it was something we were not used to.

Dorothy: Some of them have gone, but there are still too many living there. They have three small kids, plus young adults, plus older people. There are three Mexican families living in the block. One family lives across the street in an all electric house over there. They have a number of teenagers who come and go, but they don't bother anybody. They stay to themselves.

And then down at the end of the block, at the cul-de-sac, on the east side of the street, there is one family there and they are rather quiet, and I very seldom see them.

The people next door are quiet, but there are just too many of them.

Dorothy: The kids would just run all over the lawn, playing ball from one yard to another. They would be playing soccer, bouncing the ball. Instead of letting the kids play in the back yard, like I would do, they have theirs playing out in the front. All of their cousins and relatives would come over. You should see then. They have a big "to do." They set out long big tables across the yard. That's to be expected, but I tell you, it took some getting used to.

Bob: The lady next door, she said "They better not come over there."

Question: What is the ratio of blacks to whites in this block?

Bob and Dorothy: There are more blacks than whites. But we have had whites to move out and more whites to move in. This lady over here is moving. She is moving in the next couple of weeks. She bought a condo. She sold her house and a white couple is moving in. When we first moved here, some whites moved away, but even back in those days whites would buy in here. In fact, we had a white person who bought a black person's house.

Dorothy: We are living here now, but there is a strong possibility that we won't be able to stay here much longer, because of our age and health. So, our next move would be a place like Primm Towers. I don't know that we would want to buy a condo, because we still would have to keep it up on the inside, and that is what I am trying to get away from. I like this area. I like it very much. It is convenient, in a way. We have a car right now, but there will come a time when we won't be able to drive. I am trying to look to the future, rather than right now.

Questions for Discussion

1. Dorothy's parents came to Evanston from Augusta, Georgia. How do you think this move benefitted their family?
2. Bob came to Evanston Martin, Arkansas. Who gave him assistance in getting settled in Evanston?
3. Why kind of civic and social contributions did Bob and Dorothy make to the city of Evanston?
4. Why do Bob and Dorothy have different attitudes toward church affiliations in Evanston?
5. What are some recommendations Bob and Dorothy made for the improvement of black children in academics and social life?
6. Do Bob and Dorothy think they are well-represented in the city council? Why or why not?
7. The Hancocks live on a quiet, attractive block near Main Street. What is their major complaint about their neighborhood? Why does Dorothy think they will have to move before long?

About Bob and Dorothy

I have known Bob and Dorothy for many years. In fact, Dorothy and I lived in the same house at 1505 Lake Street. Our family lived on the first floor, and her family lived on the second floor. That must have been 1922 or 1923.

The Hancocks and my wife and I have met on many social occasions and usually reflect on those days of long ago.

Both Bob and Dorothy are dealing with ailments which limit their activity in some affairs in which they used to be involved, but their interest is still high and sharp in matters that concern Evanston.

Dr. Avery Hill

In the early 1920s my father moved into Evanston and established residence on the west side of Evanston. I think it was around 1905 Emerson Street where we moved in. Mrs. Smith was the rental agent. She was the mother of Melvin Smith. We moved into that building. I was born there, I understand. Shortly after my father moved there, my Uncle Joe, Joe Hill's father, moved in. They were both members of the Church of God of Evanston, and at that time they were trying to meet with some of the white establishments that were in Evanston, because there was no Church of God for blacks. So my uncle, Joe, being a construction man, a builder, built the first Church of God at Simpson and Ashland Streets, and my father was the pastor of the congregation.

I remember, growing up, that Foster Field was right next to the church. The ball games would be going on while he was trying to have church. He was interested in giving the message, and I was interested in what was going on in the ball park.

We had other family, but most of his other brothers lived in the Chicago region. They all came from Alabama. Some parts of the family were in Georgia, but they were close to the Georgia-Alabama line. They all moved up to Evanston.

I attended Foster School. I didn't think I was going to survive at first because it was kind of a rough and tumble thing for me, being only five or six years old. It seemed that I had to fight my way in and out of the school every day. I had a little friend named Bo Scott who was a little more robust than I was. We became buddies, so he kind of became my protection.

When I was about three years old, we moved from Emerson Street to Jackson Avenue to a house just north of Simpson Street. I remember that address because they had a stairway that came down from upstairs. The stairway went from the ground up to the second floor. We stayed on the second floor. I loved to go outside and sit on the platform where you go in to the second story. I got to squabbling with my sisters, and somehow I got pushed off the platform and down the steps and my head became impaled on a little stick or something that was hanging loose, so I had to be rushed to the hospital. I became an emergency patient at the Evanston Hospital. That was my first experience with any of the institutions of Evanston.

Later we moved to Darrow Avenue. That's when I began to know the people. I was a little older and able to go on my own and look around the community. I remember the Crawfords who lived over there, and some of the Paytons. Those were the families that were near my house. Mr. Jourdain lived across the street. That was the first neighborhood that I can picture in my mind as far as Evanston is concerned.

In that neighborhood, at that time, block clubs were not really necessary, because everybody was everybody else's lookout. In other words, the man across the street was as much my father as my father was, because if I did anything wrong he would correct me, which is something, if we could go back to, it would be a big help.

I guess the first thing I can remember about block club activity was when I lived on Garnett Place. People began to want to fix up the neighborhood and keep it looking nice, decorate at Christmas time and make a safe community and watch out for each other.

I knew all of the doctors who had offices in the Marr Building at Emerson and Dodge Avenue. As a child, I was playing Tarzan, swinging out of trees, and broke my front teeth. That was my first recollection of going up to the Marr Building to see Dr. Tarkington to get my teeth straightened out. They were right in front.

In the Marr building with him were Dr. Washington, Dr. Lawson, the optometrist, Dr. Gatlin, the gynecologist, and Dr. Frye.

There were a doctor or two in the Masonic Temple on Emerson Street.

Dr. Rudolph A. Penn practiced in his home on Emerson Street.

I had a number of small, part-time jobs. I worked for a while there at Cooley's Cupboard when it was going. I had a very important job taking the shells off of shrimp. Anyway, I got into a big discussion there, because at the time, I was living in Chicago and coming out to Cooley's to do my job. Some of the guys would see me getting off the L, and they asked me where I lived. I told them Sixty-first Street. They threatened me by saying that was an Evanston job and they didn't want me working on that job, and the next time I came, they were going to meet me outside afterward. Of course, what they didn't know was that I had a city full of relatives. So when I came out the evening afterward, I had about five or six relatives waiting outside to greet me, so that threat went away.

During the time I was doing those small jobs, I was going to school. After I came out of optometry school, I went into practice for myself. I didn't have too many other kinds of jobs. I worked with Jim Avery for a while in the distribution of newspapers.

In regards to problems I faced in getting my practice started, one of the things I realized immediately was that it was not as easy for me to get out and get funding to open up my practice as it had been for white boys who were in school with me. They immediately got financing, but I had a lot of difficulty. And even though you were borrowing this money to buy equipment, etc., they were very hesitant to go along with it, so I ended up buying equipment that was useful but was not what I wanted to buy, because the funding just was not there. Being a veteran, I went to the Veterans Administration and they sent me to the bank, but that didn't prove to be of any assistance to me. Regardless of that, I got it going. I had originally planned to open in Evanston, and I found in my senior year in school that another optometrist had opened up in the area. That was Dr. Don Lawson. So he beat me in here by about a year. So I didn't open in Evanston. I opened in Chicago.

Later, when Dr. Lawson cut the amount of his time in Evanston, and moved into Chicago, he and I jointly used the space in the Marr building.

I went to the Illinois College of Optometry. It took me about five years to complete my training. Four years of training and a year of clinical work.

While I was in school, I thought that once I got my training and people found out how brilliant I was that they would just start coming in, but I found out that when I got that piece of paper, it was a little more involved than that. You know, getting out and involved in the community and letting people know that you are there is very necessary. Also, there were a lot more restrictions when I opened up than there are now as far as advertising is concerned, because the associations did not want you to advertise. They didn't want to feel that you were being commercial, because they wanted you to be professional.

You needed them, because you needed the certification, even if you had the state license. You needed to be certified by the association.

The association restricted the size of your lettering on your office windows. You couldn't put a great big sign up. They even frowned on signs that would light up. Also, at that time the ruling was that to be professional you should be on the second floor, at least. You shouldn't be on the ground floor. With that background, you had to use other means to attract patients. I did contact the schools to let them know that I was an established optometrist and would appreciate their referring students who required eye correction or examination to me. But I didn't do a lot of it because I found out, when I started doing it, that the school administrators were very careful and said, "You know we can't be steering patients" and this kind of thing. Of course, you had to be diplomatic and say, "Well, I am not asking you to send or steer them, it's just that I would like for you to know that I am in the community and am available if they need my services." I went around and met ministers and let them know I was available. I ended up giving out a few pairs of fresh glasses.

In regards to competition with ophthalmologists, as an optometrist, about seventy-five percent of the eyeglass work comes through the optometrist anyway. The ophthalmologists, most of them are interested in diseases of eye, operations and this kind of thing. Of course, there are some that do it all. Usually, after they become fairly well established, they don't want to be bothered with the eyeglass part of it. One of the fears that we had was that if we referred a patient to the ophthalmologist, he might not come back to us. You would think that if we were friendly enough with the ophthalmologist to send him the patient, he would return the favor. We had to walk very carefully with that. Usually we would find an ophthalmologist that we knew we could depend on and who would return your patient to you. Recently, though, that doesn't seem to be a problem, because the ophthalmologists and optometrists now are working much better together than they did when I started practicing, but I started back in 1948, so that was a long time ago.

Nowadays there are so many different avenues and so many things that are being done in the vision field. Now there is what they call orthocaritology, laser treatment for the correction of nearsightedness. Cataract removal used to mean that automatically you had a patient who needed some very special glasses. Now they put an implant in the eye, so they put the lenses right inside the eye. So there are many cataract patients now who walk around seeing perfectly well without glasses.

There are a lot of myopics who are being corrected with laser. Then there are the myopics who are being corrected with paratology. That diminishes a lot of the eyeglass problems. Of course, there is one thing about vision though. As you get older you need to have added help for reading, so you are going to need glasses for reading, and it depends on how skilled the ophthalmologist was when he removed the cataract or did the operation for the myopia or whether or not he left a lot of residual problems that need to be corrected. If he did, then buying glasses over the counter at Walgreens to read with is no longer an option. They have to come in and see the optometrist. So, we are not worried about the profession going away.

I was born in Evanston, and everyone feels or has the opinion that I went through the Evanston school system. I did go through the grade school, part of it, but when it was time for me to go to the high school, my father had moved to southern Illinois, and one of the reasons for that is I had a first cousin who went to ETHS and was expelled by the principal. My father kind of felt that from his teaching, we had a tendency to want to speak back to people, and especially, speaking back and being black was not very popular at the high school at the time. I remember Daniel got put out and it took the alderman, Mr. Jourdain, to go over there and try to get him back in, and even that wasn't successful. He made it through, but my father felt he could avoid that by sending us out of town.

But I did attend Foster School, and then I went to Dewey School. I think I was there to the fifth or sixth grade. One incident I remember at Foster School. I remember the teacher's name very well, Miss Magnussen, who was my third grade teacher. She had a program going where they were teaching children how to bank, how to save money, so we were to bring money to school once a week and they would deposit it. Well, anyway, I remember one week I asked my dad for some change to put in the bank. He told me he didn't have it, so I told Miss Magnussen I didn't have the money. She grabbed me and shook me, and when she did, I hit her. I didn't wait to be put out of school. After I hit her, I realized what I had done, and I took off. The principal over there was named Miss Rowley. The rumor was that she had a whipping machine in her office, and when they caught you, they put you in the whipping machine.

So I ran, but anyway my dad straightened it out the next day, and I got back in class. But that was the only problem I had with a teacher over there.

My brother was moved from Foster to Haven because his grades were supposed to be such that at the time they thought Haven was a little better school, or something, so they switched him to Haven. Shortly after that, my father moved over on Prairie Avenue right behind Haven School, so we all ended up at Haven. I graduated from Haven. I had one incident there. I don't even remember the name of the teacher. They were having a field trip for our class, so I went over to the school at eight o'clock to go with the class to the Field Museum, only to find that the class had already left. It seems that there was another child at the room waiting also. Nobody was around. It was another black child. What happened was that the teacher had told all the white kids to come at seven and told us to come at eight, so the bus had gone when we got there. Other than that, I think I went through school pretty smoothly with the teachers. I don't remember any other teachers giving me any problems. There was a confrontation between the superintendent of schools because my dad always felt like going to the top about the incident that had happened. Of course, Dr. Skiles, who was the superintendent at that time, promised that it would never happen again. I ended up going to high school down in Georgetown, Illinois.

Politics

One of my biggest heroes in Evanston political scene was Edwin B. Jourdain. He was very intelligent. I always thought very highly of him.

My getting involved in politics in Evanston was the alderman race of John Burton. My brother-in-law, Joe Brooks, came to me with John and said, "I'd like for you to help him in his election." Of course, at that time I didn't know anything about politics. He wanted me to work the area where I was living. I was living, at the time, on Garnet Place. Being that John's base was more Democrat that Republican, I felt I was facing the strongest Republican precinct captain in the whole west side area, who was Leon Robinson. Anyhow, I got out there and worked it. In fact, I took my precinct for John. It brought about a little yelling between me and Mr. Robinson, but at least it worked out. I joined the Democratic party. I think that for the black community, itself, as far as Democratic party and the workings that they have done, I think it's kind of fallen back. I think the leadership in the community has not kept up the kind of organization that we had when I was a young man going in the area. There were Sam White, Eola Richardson, and Grace Boone, when we had a good organization going. Now I don't see any organization. I think it's too bad that they let it fall down, but everyone feels now that all you need is the television. There is nobody out there to pull the vote in. That's kind of sad, because it also affects the school board races and that kind of thing, that there isn't any structure already made up to help pull out the vote in the part of town where the people should be the most interested, especially in the school board races. Black kids need all the support that they can get. The people in the community should try to put good people in who will serve the interest of those people. I remember back when Dr. Gatlin made a statement to me that he was not the representative of the black children of Evanston, he was the representative of all children in Evanston. But then he had to turn that around one day at a board meeting, because he said, "I see that if I don't speak up for the black children, there's nobody who will." So we do need to be able to influence the board a little better than we are. I was on the board for nine years. I lost a lot of sleep. I began to realize a lot of things. You know. I began to realize that the white board members, this is not to bring them down, but I just don't think they realized that if someone isn't there working to try to see to it that all children are being represented, a lot of them are lost along the way, you know, because the average white child is going to get his education. The slow white child and a lot of black children who would do better if there was someone showing them a little more interest, would profit if they had that kind of assistance, and just someone on the board to help push them along.

Teachers, I felt then and I feel now, are not as dedicated as they were, say like when I was coming along. I used to have teachers who would keep me after school, because I knew I was a rascal. The showed me some interest. I think a lot of kids just feel that the teachers are not interested in them. Sometimes it shows in their body language or the way they act toward them. So you need someone who stays on those kinds of issues.

I know one person who is on the District 65 Board, Rose Johnson. She is a very dedicated woman, and she works very hard.

I was on the high school board at the time when Coffin was superintendent of District 65.

I think that Coffin came in to do a job and did his job and got fired for doing it. The power structure felt that he was getting further than he needed to go, but he had the right approach. He felt that both black and white kids had to see that there were black people who could do things and who could achieve things and who were capable of handling positions, and not just broom pushers or window washers. So Coffin began to hire black administrators and more black teachers. When he started doing that, he got some resistance from the white power structure who said, "We brought you in here to integrate the schools and not to integrate the faculty situation." So, I think they went after him. It's too bad we couldn't get more of a ground swell in the black community to get the votes necessary to keep him here. How they did it was by slowly taking school board members who were in favor of Coffin and voting them out of office.

Advantages and Disadvantages of Integration

The biggest advantage is that a teacher is paid to teach, and it doesn't matter whether it's white or black kids. The thing is that white kids are not going to suffer by the fact that black kids are sitting next to them in class. A black kid is going to gain because he is listening to the same thing that the teachers are telling the whites, so he has got to compete with his classmates. So, he gains knowledge. It helps the whole structure. It also helps the kids in the class know that there are black kids who are doing as well as they are doing. White children also need to be taught that black children are capable of learning just as they are.

Teacher's Attitudes Toward Integration

There is no doubt in my mind that some white teachers felt intimidated in having to teach black children. More black kids were brought up for expulsion because the teachers felt that the child was being sassy, when they would accept the remark from a white child, but just the idea that a black child might speak back would create problems.

One of the positions on the board that I had to take, and I was happy that I was there to take, was the expulsion hearings, because ninety to ninety-five percent of the expulsion hearings were black children. You would be there and listen to both sides of the story. A lot of times the story was very simple. The white teacher was just completely shaken up over the fact that she or he and this black child were having this confrontation. So, I became the advocate for the black child quite often. There were some I lost. I don't think any black child that came up for expulsion while I was there, unless it was really blatant, was ever expelled, but there were some who never showed up at the expulsion hearings, and I lost them by default. Sometimes a parent would say, "If the teacher said this, he must have done it." So, I lost a few of those battles. I never missed an expulsion hearing because, whenever one came up, I made it a point, if I had to cancel something else, I would make it out there to see what the expulsion was all about.

Progress Made in Black Appointments in Administration to the Evanston School System

Joe Hill was appointed superintendent of District 65, and Dr. Ruth Labat was superintendent of Evanston High School District 202.

I am not saying that every superintendent we have should be black. I am not saying that at all, but it does give you a feeling that you have got a little more support or blacks understand more the conflicts that go on in education. I think the education system has to be better because these two superintendents were here. Both of them worked very hard to straighten the system out. A lot of the plans that Margaret Labat brought up at the high school, even though she was not able to complete them, other superintendents came in and took her old plans and went forward with them. I think that was a great help. Finally, I feel that both superintendents were let out a little earlier than they should have been. If we could have kept them a little bit longer, things might have been still better.

One of the things I felt bad about was the fact that some of our opposition to Dr. Labat was black as well as white. I think that was because she was a woman. They thought the position should have gone to a black man.

Dan Phillips and I were on the board at the same time when Dr. Labat was taken in as the superintendent.

We did have two other blacks that we were considering at the time. They were Dr. Dorothy Magette and Dr. McKinley Nash. I think both of them would have made very excellent superintendents. I think Dan and I both would have been happy with either one of them. But we found that in trying to get either one of them the position, it was practically impossible to get them in. After meeting Dr. Labat, we were happy with her and we had a couple of the white board members who also felt comfortable with her. So we knew how we were going to be able to get her in?

Church

I was raised up in the Church of God because my father was minister there. In fact, when he died he was the presiding elder out in Los Angeles. After I got married, my wife belonged to Ebenezer and I didn't feel it was important enough to argue about. I felt that I served one God and it didn't matter which building I went to. Since she was already at Ebenezer and loved it, I went along with her to Ebenezer. So that's where I am now.

You know, the churches, through the times, have been the more or less the leaders in the black community. It was the black ministers who were respected by the power structure, at least in a dialog with them. Usually they were also in dialog with the financial institutions. Also, there was a moral position that was held up by the church. I feel that we need the church. We need the ministers to be involved with the community.

In the past the minister was the one who had the time, because most of the rest of us had to work and had much less time to be involved with community affairs.

I think the churches in the black community have done pretty well.

I think the building of Primm Towers was a great help to the community.

I was on the board of Primm Towers. We really had to struggle to get the project started. We spent a lot of hours on it, but now I am happy that we did spend it. There were people like Bill Jones, an ex-policeman, Mr. and Mrs. Russell, Leon Robinson Sr. If it hadn't been for this group of people, we never would have gotten that place built. We had all kinds of problems. They were coming from outside the community, trying to stop this thing from going over. Northwestern had given us the property, but with a stipulation that we start building at a certain time. We had our financing, we thought, all in place. Then we found out that there were people who we thought were helping us who were trying to see that the financing was held back. So, we had all of that to overcome, but we got it built. We had a few problems after that. But since Reverend Wade came to the church, he has helped straighten out practically all of that, so it is running pretty smoothly now.

Who were some of the people who were standing in the way of your progress in building Primm Towers?

At first there was, even in the black community, some talk about there being a hundred and five units, and who was going to come in, and one of the things with HUD was that we couldn't say that it was a building for black people. When they found that there were whites who were trying to come into the building, then the blacks started saying, "What are they doing coming in here?" But the building was integrated from the first. We had white tenants before we had blacks. We were concerned that we were going to be overrun, and some of these tenants were coming from up on the North Shore. They were elderly people whose families felt that they would be in a safe apartment. They were near downtown, and transportation. Many of the old ladies get out and walk down to the shopping center. That gives them their exercise.

Reverend Blake was concerned with people bringing furniture in because he felt that we might end up with a lot of pests that we would have trouble controlling, so when we first started out, we furnished the apartments. Later on, we began to let people bring their furniture in. We had an exterminating room where they brought the furniture before it went into their apartments. A lot of people complained about it. But we said, "You can't go up to the apartment until your furniture has been debugged." We had an exterminating service, but we just didn't want anything to get started. Reverend Blake was particular about that.

I began to realize how important the Ministerial Alliance was through my politicking for the school board. I met with all of these different ministers and I met with the Alliance as a group and I began to realize what kind of work they were doing. I don't think the general public is as aware as maybe you or I what the Alliance is doing for the community. I know they worked to elect black school board members. The fact that we have a vehicle there that you can go to whereas the white board members have the Women's Club and this club and that club for their support. So, it helps you to get into a wider base which would involve most of the black churches. The candidates would come around to the churches. Maybe some of the ministers would not permit them to speak to the congregations, but they would be introduced by the pastor.

YMCA

It was the center when I was a kid living in Evanston. It was the place to go to where there was something to do. Between that and Foster Field, those two places raised me with Mr. Bouyer and Mr. Hauser, Hummons, Louis Moseley.

It was such a shame that they closed that Y. The only time I went to the Y on Grove Street was for some kind of board meeting. But other than that, I just never felt welcome at the Grove Street Y. I never felt that I was even wanted over there. They said we were welcome, but we have to feel it. The feeling never came through.

Closing of the Emerson Street Y has resulted in a great loss to the blacks of Evanston. For a long time it had the only swimming pool we had. I think a lot of blacks who went to ETHS felt that they didn't have a pool at the high school. Some of them said they used to cover it over so we wouldn't see it because they didn't want us over there. So the Y was the only place you could go to swim.

Sports

I said before that when I was a kid, I used to be more interested in the ball games going on at Foster Field on Sundays than the church services I had to attend at the Church of God across the street. I remember such players as Blue Warden, Herman Warren, Homer Fleetwood. That was part of my childhood, going over to Foster to see those Sunday baseball games. I remember Blue Warden so well because there was a fly hit to center field and Warden was out there and lost it in the sun and the ball hit him on top of his head. Everybody laughed, but Blue got up off the ground and was all right.

Most of the sports I enjoyed as a child were out there at Foster. I would go over to Boltwood when they played Foster, but if the Foster team was winning, I learned to leave Boltwood a little early, so I would stay out of the fight. If they won the game, they had to fight their way out of Boltwood Park.

Northwestern had some great teams when I was growing up. Then I remember Claudius Britt and Cornelius Champion playing football at the high school. But I felt that the high school limited their black players to one or two a year. When Joe Brooks became a member of Dad's Club, he found out when he got there that he was the only black, so he was uncomfortable. So many of the Dad's Club members didn't care if the team lost, as long as they played the white players. Play their sons, it isn't important whether we win or lose. So don't be loading up the team with those black players. These things you don't forget. They stick with you.

Entertainment at Foster School

I can remember the neighborhood night they used to have at Foster

School once a week. Pikey Powell would get most of those things together. Nick Butler would whistle and sing. Earl Butler was the comedian. We had great entertainment in those days. There was a lot going on.

We also went to dances at the Masonic Temple.

I kind of enjoyed house parties more because you got to meet all of your old friends, sit down, and get in conversation. It was more of a close knit thing than a dance, but I did like dancing. I didn't get into too many night club situations. About the only one, and that was after I had become grown, was Archie Simmons' club over on Simpson Street. I enjoyed going over there. I was kind of sorry to see him close it up.

I belong to the North Shore Twelve Club. I wasn't one of its original members. It's a group that I really enjoyed. I was sorry to see the club disband. I guess it got to where too many of our members became lame and needed younger replacements. The younger replacements were voted in, but they didn't function. I don't know whether it was because there was an age gap there, or what, but they just didn't function, and I think that was what brought the club to a close. We would have taken in more, but the ones we took in were really not carrying their load. The original "Twelve" worked well together. Everyone did a job. You could depend on them to do the job. As the younger ones came in, that dependence wasn't there.

Some of the original members were Byron Wilson, Evus Charter, Jack Moss, Wilbur "Rudy" Frazier, Forest "Pikey" Powell.

I pledged to the Omega Psi Phi fraternity. Mr. Hummons was the one who read me the riot act. He came to me early one morning and talked to me about the fraternity. It was the graduate chapter. After I got into it, it just seemed to slow down, and I haven't been to a chapter meeting in quite a while. But I did pledge to Omega.

Some of the Omegas where Ashbury Garry, Eddie Stevens, J. Willard Harris, Tom Hummons, Buford Gordon.

I was in the engineer aviation depot assigned to the ninth air force. We were supposed to meet up with the 99th Pursuit Squadron, but we never got together. We were down in Florida and we hoped to go to Granite City for further training, and we got into some racial problems down in Florida. It all started in a theater where they were showing movies. The whites felt the blacks should be in certain areas of the theater. I remember some whites saying something to one of the "brothers," and he referred to the white as an MF, and that's when everything started. We ended up in England. When we left England, we went to Normandy. I think they knew we were coming because it rained and the ground was muddy. I think this was about nine days after D-Day.

What we were principally supposed to do was to try to keep up with the infantry. So we were supposed to be anywhere from three to ten miles behind them. If we were three miles behind and the infantry advanced seven miles, then we had to pick up all of our stuff and move with them with supplies, so that they could come back and get whatever they needed, you know, try to keep close to the front lines. We went through Normandy and then up into Germany. That's where I got injured. I was flown back to England. My injury came from working on a Bailey Bridge. A Bailey Bridge is a bridge that comes in sections. A section would be about eight feet long. They are steel, the holes are already in and all they have to do is lock them together. They had pontoons that would float. The part that I am speaking of is metal, and it goes up, maybe not as high as the ceiling, about seven feet or so. Anyhow, one of those was swinging on a crane. They were restocking. I was a supply clerk. I was really where I didn't have any business. I don't know why I was out there, other than "messing" with the guys that were working. But I had my back to this piece of metal which weighed about a ton and a half. It was swinging on the crane, and I didn't see it coming. Someone yelled to me, but what happened was a German plane came over strafing the area, and the guy in the crane, instead of locking the load, jumped out of his crane to run, and I didn't see the steel coming, and it hit me in back of my head and on my legs, knocking me over. That's what saved me, everybody said. It probably did, because what happened was that after it knocked me over, it went over me. It dragged my clothes a bit, but it went over me and it stopped further down. So it broke my leg. The strange part about it was, when I got to the hospital, they didn't seem to be worried about my leg. They were doing all kinds of scans on my head. It took about eighteen months before I finally got out of there, and by that time I was back in the states.

I went through England, Normandy, and up to Germany. We set up a big depot there in Coleshi. It was close to the Elbe River. That's where they had planned to make a big stand, at the Elbe River, but I never got to the Elbe River because of my injury. They sent me back to England.

The Army was just not my cup of tea. I didn't like it, and I think part of the reason was that all of our officers were white, and all the men were black. I remember a lieutenant sitting me down to talk to me and asking me about the Army and did I like that Army. He said "man to man." And I said, "As long as it is 'man to man,' the answer is Hell no." I said, "As long as we are talking, do you like the Army?" The reason he had called me in was that we were up to the Elbe River, and he said that Harry Truman was raising hell about integration of the services, so they had decided maybe they might integrate. He said, "What would you think about joining an infantry?" I said, "Hell, I've come all this distance and I'm in this black organization and we are behind the lines, now all of a sudden to integrate, you are going to put me up on the front lines? I have no interest whatever." He said, "They want to make it voluntary."

I guess it was Adlai Stevenson who was raising hell about integrating the Navy, but I think it was Truman who was raising hell about the Army. He was vice president at the time.

It was an experience that I very seldom think about. I didn't like my Army service at all, the kind of things like seeing people injured or killed and having to just walk by them. I had one experience where there was a bomb dubbed in front of our outfit. A couple of guys and I in a weapons carrier took a cable and wrapped it around the dud and pulled it away from the area. I had had some training in hooking in crane work, so that's why they talked me into doing it. It wasn't until after we did it that we all stood there and thought about how that thing could have gone off while we were dragging it. We were getting away from our surroundings. That's how stupid we were.

Medical Facilities in Evanston

I went to the Community Hospital. I had pneumonia and Dr. Spencer was my doctor. I had found a couple of years before I got pneumonia that I was diabetic, and the combination of pneumonia and diabetes gave me a hard way to go. I guess I must have been in there six weeks before I was able to get out. Dr. Spencer took a lot of flack from that because he had a twenty-four-hour humidifier in my room and it ruined the walls. The steam and stuff was running down the walls and they had to redecorate the room. Mrs. Williams was the one who raised the most hell because they had to redecorate the room. They said, "Did you really have to do that for Avery Hill?" I was glad he was around to do it because I am still here.

I was sorry to see that facility go. It was in the community. I kind of felt that the people at Community were getting good treatment because I think the doctors who were over there were interested because it was community people, people whom they knew. I've got a thing about strangers working on me.

Also, the Community Hospital was a friendly place. People would come to visit someone else and pass your door and say, "I didn't know you were in here." I really think that the environment has a lot to do with a patient's recovery. We had a patient who came in, and I asked him how he was doing. He had just gotten out of a hospital up on Northside. He said, "I'm glad to be out here because everyone else was speaking Spanish and even the television was speaking Spanish." He said, "I am glad to be out among my own folks." So, I know how he felt, like an alien in a foreign land.

I think the loss of the Community Hospital was a great loss.

Government of the City

I haven't felt any hindrance from the city government. The biggest problem I had with Evanston politics is the other community trying to influence ours as far as our election of alderman. With the Jourdain thing, I know there was a real effort by North Evanston and East Evanston to get Jourdain removed, because he would "set" with them, and I felt that we had somebody there who was in our corner.

I struggled to try to keep that city manager form of government out because I felt that it diluted the power of black community, because of the influence the black aldermen would have on electing who you wanted as mayor of the city. I still think that was their main purpose. Jourdain was able, I think, to influence who the mayor was there a couple of times, and they hated that. They didn't want any block vote. I know that even as a member of the Democratic Party they used to complain about the fact that I would be working in the Fifth Ward Democratic Organization. On these situations where you would elect three people, I was telling them the importance of voting for one guy and forget the other two, which in essence gave that individual three votes. They said, "Avery, that's dirty, you shouldn't do that." But I would have only one person that I was interested in, and as a black you know, if I could get that Fifth Ward Organization to give the person we're interested in three votes, it made a big difference in the outcome of the election. Of course, they knew it, too.

I am not in a ward organization or anything of that nature, but just trying to get people into public office that you feel are in your corner. I don't think the government itself is evil. I think Evanston is a community that tries. That is why I came back. You know I went out to Schaumburg and I moved back to Evanston because it is my kind of community. I have learned to love it. I do think that it is a community that cares. It's just that you have to show them how you feel and what you feel that they ought to do.

Not only the schools are integrating, but the community is integrating. When Gregg left, a lot of these relationships between blacks and whites began to leave with him. I don't know whether they felt that if he was defeated what's the use, or what. There was an official at Garrett Institute whose name was Dick Ford. Dick passed away, but before he passed, the two of us were talking. We were trying to figure out how we could try to get that kind of alliance back together between blacks and whites, so we could bring back the same kind of cohesiveness that Gregg Coffin started. I don't think he started out being a great community organizer, he was just doing his job as a school administrator, but it began to bring the two races together. When they fired him, I think they destroyed something there which was good.

Social Environment

When I spoke about Gregg and that kind of situation, and the pastoral alliance, that is what we have got to really get into. There has got to be more social integration than what is going on now. You can't really trust a stranger, and this is what happens when you don't know people. Then you don't know how to react to them or you don't know how you feel about them. I have even had people angry with me over something that I was not even responsible for because they conceived that I was the problem. They were angry with me. That's what happens between the races as well as with individuals.

We have got to know each other. You can't just stand back and look at a person and draw an opinion like he's white, so he is wrong, or he's black, so he has to be bad. We must begin to try to understand each other.

The Black Ministerial Alliance and the City Wide Ministerial Alliance are the kinds of groups that can bring about some more peace and understanding.

Gangs and Dope

I really didn't get into the heatedness of this police chief thing that we just went through, where the chief was released. What I felt was happening with him was that more or less why he was brought in was he had come out of Chicago where the situation is strong, and he possibly had some ideas and some methods to deal with the gangs. Whether it was his manner of doing things or what, I got in on the tail end of this. I just wonder if they weren't too hasty. You can't give a man a job to do and then tell him he has to do it your way. Your way may not be the best way. He may have a better idea about how the job must be done.

A key element is the police department in working with these gangs, and they have got to work on it, and the community has to work with the police department. You should have community workers out in the street with these gangbangers and know what is on their minds and what it takes to get him out of that mode. You have to have recreation for your youngsters. They must be given some kind of hope. They must be counseled. All of these things play into the program.

Questions for Discussion
1. Describe Avery's early experiences in Evanston.
2. What were the block club contributions to Avery's neighborhood?
3. Discuss Avery's early employment.
4. What were the steps in Avery's preparation for optometry and getting started in this field after graduation?
5. Discuss Avery's experiences as a student in the Evanston school system.
6. How did Avery get started in politics?
7. What advantages to blacks did Avery see in having blacks on the school boards?
8. What are the advantages and disadvantages of school integration, according to Avery?
9. Why does Avery think the church has been the leader in the black community?
10. What does Avery think is the advantage of having the Ministerial Alliance?
11. While in the military service, why was Avery's group shipped overseas in a hurry?
12. How was Avery injured in Germany?

13. What reasons did Avery give for not liking the Army?
14. Why does Avery believe the loss of Community Hospital was a great loss to the Evanston black community?
15. What does Avery recommend for working with gangs?

About Dr. Avery Hill

Avery is a practicing optometrist on the West Side of Chicago. From his comments, you can tell that he has been very active in the professional, political, and education matters in Evanston.

His response to an opportunity to share his ideas and experiences was immediate and enthusiastic. He had a lot to say, and had the training and experience to make his opinions credible. At the time we conducted this interview, Avery was about to have surgery to correct a heart condition. The surgery has been completed, and Avery is in the stage of recovery and then he will go to rehabilitation.

Reverend Dr. Ndung'u Ikenye

Yes, you know we came from Kenya, Africa. I first came here because I wanted to get into Northwestern University, and also to get into Garrett Seminary, and one of the crucial questions at that time for me was, "How are the blacks accepted here in this community." We had heard so many things about, for example, Dr. Martin Luther King and how the blacks were working hard to change the system, and so I inquired about coming to Evanston. I was also considering New York, and going to Columbia University. I was considering going to Portland, Oregon, but the issue that was crucial at the time was how accepted are the blacks in these places. Before dealing with the question of where we were going to live, that was the main question. And so, I ruled out New York because of their overpopulation. When I came to think about Portland, Oregon I had a problem. I felt the minorities might not be accepted there, and so finally, I consented to come to Evanston. I was told that black leadership in the community since the 1950s, and even before that, has existed here. So my choice to come here, the basic question was that, and I did end up getting here. Of course, in 1988, that's when I got here, during the fall of 1988, to get into Garrett Seminary in preparation to get into Northwestern University, which I did, and so I was here for two years. I did my master's degree and did my doctorate also at Garrett.

My family joined me two years later. The African thought is that "you go first, check it out, and if it is possible for us to come and settle there, OK, but you can't bring your family across the sea if you are not sure it is a safe place. So I came here, and I was suited here at the Episcopal church in Evanston, and I felt that it was a safe place to be. I arranged for my family to join me in 1990.

When I first came here, I lived at 916 Noyes Street, and then after my family joined me, we moved to 2108 on Sherman Avenue. We stayed there until we moved to this house, 1930 Darrow Avenue, three years ago, after I was called to be the priest at St. Andrew's Episcopal Church, June of 1993.

My first residence here, on Noyes Street, a one bedroom apartment, was chosen because it was close to Northwestern University. Also, it was close to the L. Transportation was another crucial question. Having to learn how to drive in this country was another thing. It feels that you are driving on the wrong side of the road. I used public transportation for at least three years. I learned all of their schedules, passes, all the trains.

The other aspect was the education of my children, so we finally considered moving to 2108 Sherman Avenue. Then my children would go to Orrington School. If I had come to this side of town to get a house, my children would not have been allowed to go to Orrington School. We had to consider that, and even now, although we are living in this house, the politics of the city has made boundaries of where you can take your children to school. We are still getting permission, year after year, from District 65 for my children to go to school.

The other aspect of my family has to do with my wife's employment. It's one thing that we were not as thoughtful about, in the beginning, how hard it is for black women to get jobs in this city, or how discriminated against they are. My wife started working at Evanston Hospital in food services. In Kenya she was a manager in the YMCA. She had as many as two hundred staff members working for her. She came here and had to go all the way down to begin as a food attendant. It was a big shift. She knew English, so there was no language barrier, but the issue is one with which Evanston has to deal—discrimination. My wife was more qualified than the person who was her monitor at Evanston Hospital, but because she was black and because she was from Africa, that meant that she did not have an equal status and had to take a lower position. She has developed now for the last six years and has proven herself, but she had to leave Evanston Hospital because of the humiliation there. They refused to recognize her expertise there. She was made to feel insignificant, so she moved out of the Evanston Hospital. She went back to college, Kendall College, to culinary school for two years, and now she is working at the Presbyterian Home. She is now an assistant manager there.

Those are some of the things that have affected our family settlement in Evanston.

I call the block around our church the "Holy Square." We have this academy with Bishop Moody and a half a block from there we have Reverend Curry's Church, and then we have the Springfield Church. The four of us clergy have been involved in trying to organize that area. We had a problem: drugs, kids having gang meetings at night, right behind our church. When I came in here, the kids were having their gang meetings at night, so we organized ourselves to fence around and also we asked the police superintendent to send police at night to check our neighborhood. They were to send police at night to check our neighborhood. These were blocks from Dodge Avenue to Dewey and from Foster to Emerson Street. We think we have been quite successful in stopping that kind of activity in this area. Also, many vacant or rundown buildings have been renovated and improved, thereby discouraging undesirable activity on the property.

Also, the mayor was very helpful by encouraging the property owners to keep the alley clean and free from trash and garbage. Now the alley is safe. Before, we had gang signs all over. We asked property owners to paint their houses or outbuildings to cover the gang signs. So now we don't have those gang signs. This clean up required the cooperation of all of us, property owners, police, mayor, and sanitation department.

I never had a face to face confrontation with a gang member, except on one occasion. In front of the church on a Sunday morning, I had to come face to face with one of them. We had backed our cars off the street, and one of the gang members came stealing the hub caps from the cars. I saw him and went and grabbed him and ended up being in a fight. He cut me with a knife on my hand, but that was the only contact that we had.

When the police and I made up our report of this encounter, we were told that their mentality does not have any idea of what is right or wrong, so even calling them and talking to them is impossible. You can't get through to them.

They told us, "Don't worry about it, we'll put this boy away for a few weeks." That was all that happened.

The gangs are now reducing in the neighborhood, but the boys who organized the gangs are still here. But we don't see much activity around here anymore, although they may have moved to other neighborhoods.

We think other block groups could stop gang activity in their neighborhoods like we did. On one occasion we held a meeting with residents and block groups at the Evanston High School. Clergy was there, and with others in the community, started organizing what we called "repossessing our neighborhood." That has continued. Each block is doing that—block by block. They are repossessing their neighborhoods.

But we have a problem because some of the parents are not involved in helping their kids. So you end up having some kids on the streets at night because parents are at work. The kids are on their own.

When I came to Evanston in 1988, I joined St. Mark's Episcopal Church and at that time I was licensed by the Bishop of Chicago to participate and to lead a portion of the service. That became my first appointment in this Diocese. So in 1988 and 1989, and up to October of 1990, I served as an assistant to the priest at St. Marks.

I maintained my residence, even in 1990, when I was appointed again by the Bishop of Chicago to be in charge of the Church of the Epiphany on the west side of Chicago. I maintained halftime employment with the Diocese of Chicago.

The thing that I will not forget is the struggle that any black will have to face in Evanston to mix with the white community. That is quite unique. I don't know whether you would call it unique, but I come from a country where we are in the majority, and here we are in the minority, and so you have to almost really fight your place through the system to be recognized by the system. But it is not easy in Evanston, even when you get to learn the people in Evanston, there is still segregation, even in church. I know when I went to the church at St. Marks, I was told there was a church for black people in Evanston, but since I was living down on Noyes Street, it was more difficult to come to St. Andrew's without a car. So I stayed there as a priest at some level and was not feeling as welcome in the beginning, but after they realized the kind of person I was, then I became part and parcel of the life of the parish.

My sense of it is that for political reasons, it looks like you are welcome, but when you get down to the "nitty-gritty" stuff, you are still not welcome. I have seen that. Even when you go to the stores in Evanston there is a sense of tentativeness. For example, Greenbay Avenue divides us. What I call the more white oriented thought is on the East of Greenbay Road. And on the west side of Greenbay that is where you will find the African-American thought. For me, living on the east side when I was a student at Garrett and Northwestern, there was a sense of disconnection from what was happening within the black community. In fact, I did not meet any members of the black community for around six years. When you are on one side of Greenbay, you don't mix with the people on the other side of Greenbay. Now that I am on the west side, there is a stage transition that you have to go through

Larger politics talk about integration, but when you come down to it, the real experiences, there is still some tentativeness.

My children grew up in a town, so they, growing up in a town forces a person to cross cultural experiences. We have friends who are missionaries who are white, or we had people from other tribes there, but our kids were more used to dealing with other cultures. So their coming here was not as traumatic as we thought it would be. When we got here our first daughter went to Haven School. Our younger daughter went to Orrington, then Kenya went to kindergarten at Kendall College. In all of these places the experience was that we were welcome. The kids do not, as much as we had feared that they would, go through a lot of culture shock, they held themselves together. They assimilated the experience at a slower speed. It was not as traumatic as we thought it would be. The teachers were good, except one who had the attitude that black boys are not good.

I think that as far as my kids are concerned with school activities, and so on, I don't think we have experienced any pressure from the teachers, neither have the kids experienced that. There was only the time when a teacher, meaning to be too helpful, because they thought us to be victims of racism in the educational system, not only in Evanston, but at large, the need to be too helpful, or patronizing. You feel that they were just pushing too hard. I told her, you've got to back up, I am responsible, I know what I'm doing with my kid. You cannot just assume to call up late at night, or early in the morning. You need to back up. We don't need that intrusion.

All of their schools are integrated, but I think integration has not meant a lot in terms of changing the mind set of most of these people. So, we have teachers who still have that attitude, but there is nothing they can do. They have integrated at the school district level, but at their own personal levels we don't know much about that.

The advantage in integrated education is that kids learn to live with other people at an early age. That is the great advantage, knowing that all the world is not only us whites. So, you start giving the kids the tools of dealing with what life is. But the disadvantage of that is the kids have no opportunity to learn about their own culture. That is what I find most difficult. The African-American children do not have ways to learn about their own culture. So, they end up getting the culture of the larger system at the expense of their own culture. Integration without places of education into our people's culture will cause the kids to lose their foundation at the expense of the larger culture.

Question: How do you think that integration affects the personalities or the mind sets of blacks who have been integrated, so called accepted, as opposed to their relationships with blacks who have not been accepted as they have?

The problem we face is who succeeds and who does not succeed. There are kids in all these classes that come from single parent homes and so they are not getting good skills. They are not stimulated academically as they should be at home and end up not being what we call successful. So when they don't succeed academically, they feel like their teacher is pushing them too hard, and they end up with a damaged self image. Then the kid starts a withdrawal. You can see kids having kids. At my daughter's high school there are kids who are very young having kids, or even in seventh grade, junior high school, kids are having kids. You'll find kids using drugs. These are all signs of withdrawing from the larger system which is not acceptable to them.

The teachers play a big role of marginalizing these kids because they are not as well stimulated. The standards which are important here are to help these kids where they are. In other words, a teacher needs to consciously and intentionally go into where the kid is lacking to help the kids to grow academically and socially. That is the problem with integration. When you integrate, the larger system defines what has to be done, and the minority student, who most of the time is not keeping up the standards of the main system falls between the cracks.

I think that if the teachers make conscious and intentional choices to know that this kid is not as stimulated as another kid academically, then one has to lower the standards to reach that particular child. That's what I do in psychology. Go up to where they are. On west side of Chicago I still do counseling with the families once a while and what we have done is that we have first graders and second graders, third graders and fourth graders. Those who can go faster, go faster. Those who can stay with the work of their previous grade, stay with it until they are able to get it, and then they can join the other group. And so they separate them in their tables, but they don't stigmatize them.

The problem of integration, I think, is that you lose the people who are not academically stimulated.

Question: Do you find, also, that in the adult community, when the black family becomes affluent and educated, they leave the masses in the black community? So the black community becomes without educated leaders and role models.

That's what is going in our neighborhoods. Do we have physicians? Do we have people who are well to do? No. When they become affluent they move out of here. I was talking with Mrs. Gardner last week. Her son has a bank in Washington, D.C. He grew up here, but after he begins to succeed, he flies out of here. And so, the neighborhood is improvised by that. I was talking to Archie Simmons. His son is a police chief in another state. So, when people grow in skills and financially, they move away.

I still think there is racial politics in Evanston. It's not used to our advantage, but mostly to our disadvantage. I think the politics of Evanston speaks only to whites or their interests. Whenever blacks are involved, they are used only. They are not equal participants. I feel like they are used. So, politically that is my view. Politicians don't listen to blacks. They use blacks by getting their votes. But I don't think there is anybody, I would say, who listens to us. Our mayor, for example, she is the mayor of Evanston, but she does not have the sole power. We have a black mayor, but what power does she have to change the system? I do sound less optimistic about the way the system works in Evanston.

I have no idea who my alderman is. I haven't seen him or talked to him.

I tell my church one of the things I don't like about politics is the talk, talk, talk. Most of the talk is without action.

We have an African-American Ministerial Alliance, consisting of black ministers in Evanston. When they wanted to introduce another system in Evanston District 65, we opposed it and we stood by that, and they have not affected it yet. For all the black people here, the church is the foundation. We cannot function in politics, we cannot function in our professions without the support of our churches.

The problems we are having right now is the people who are without church affiliation. The people who are selling drugs in the streets are without church affiliation. There are people who are not bringing up their kids well. Most of them are not church affiliated. The church is the center of the life of the black community. People who have succeeded in life have maintained their church affiliations. The church is the mother of change. We go to the church for teachings. Politics has more to do with maintaining the status quo of the larger system, which most of the time does not care about our kids or about us. And so, I think the church has become very important in that sense, as an agent for change.

Our focus must also shift not only to think of spiritual changes, I also want people to grow academically. I like encouraging the kids. We have a program here where at the end of every quarter the kids who made a B average have a good luncheon, and the ones who did not make it are invited, and they learn from that. So we don't exclude them, the emphasis is that we have these examples and you can be mentored by the other children. We think children can be mentors to each other. We also recognize perfect attendance at school.

Our church is now composed of about seventy-five percent Caribbean and twenty-five percent African-American. There was a time when there was a big plurality between the African-Americans and the Caribbeans, but the gulf now is not as wide as it was. I think the issue was the respect for each other, in terms of culture. And this is where the African-Americans and the Caribbeans have to learn and respect each other's cultures. This is the focal point which I have emphasized to them. How do we do that?

We have a typical Episcopal service. What do we do? We have all these flags in the church. That is one way of saying we are celebrating our own cultural differences. We are not homogeneous. Because we are black people, everybody thinks we all are homogeneous. We are heterogenous, even the Caribbeans, because they come from so many different nations, they are not also homogenous. But the tendency I have found is for people to lump all these people together.

The church has to do the work bringing them together.

About the African-American Ministers Alliance, I mentioned to you earlier that I am somewhat disappointed because the African-American Ministers Alliance, which includes all of the black pastors, had not worked together as much as I thought ideal. Of course it continues to the same issue of class. The churches in Evanston serve different classes. Unless we break down the class barriers in the churches, we will not be able to work together successfully. Even among the pastors themselves, they think of themselves in terms of class, and so I have found it amazing that we've been trying to combat class value among us. I don't know how far we will go. Also the age barrier. The younger ones that are in it haven't been coming out to the meetings as much as I thought they would. When you ask them, they say, "When you go to these meetings, they never listen to us." I don't know how we will tackle that problem.

Members of our church go to Foster Center for Senior Citizens, so once in a while they invite me for their annual tea and shows. I attend then. Also, there is the Family Focus.

Medical Facilities Experiences

When a black person goes to the Evanston Hospital or the St. Francis Hospital, they give you as good treatment as they would give to anyone else. That's one thing I have found.

I am concerned that we do not have more nursing homes that are convenient to Evanston residents.

Gangs

If I were the police commissioner or chief I would invite citizens whose neighborhoods were being threatened by gangs to attend a meeting where they could express their fears to the police and design a plan which would involve the participation of the residents to take steps to eradicate the undesirable activity in their area. Perhaps if all neighborhoods would do this, the gangs would be kept on the move.

Questions for Discussion

1. Discuss the matters Father Ikenye had to consider before he came to Evanston from Kenya, Africa.
2. What kinds of racial discrimination did Mrs. Ikenye face in Evanston?
3. Why does Father Ikenye call the block around St. Andrew's the "Holy Square"?
4. On what occasion did Father Ikenye face gang violence?
5. How did the St. Andrew's block discourage gang activity in the alley behind the church?
6. Why did Father Ikenye consider the black-white relationship in Evanston unique?
7. What does Father Ikenye think is the great advantage in integrated education?
8. Why does Father Ikenye think there is racial politics in Evanston?
9. What does Father Ikenye say is happening in black neighborhoods which affects the quality of black leadership there?
10. What is Father Ikenye's opinion of the African-American Ministerial Alliance?

11. How has St. Andrew's been able to accommodate the African-American and Caribbean membership?

About Reverend Dr. Ikenye

Father Ikenye came to St. Andrew's Episcopal Church at a time when the church was losing its status as a parish and was about to become a mission. This was partly due to the fact that many African-American members had become old and disabled and had left the city and could no longer contribute to the church. But Father Ikenye's arrival has been a Godsend to St. Andrew's because he has encouraged the American black members to work with the Caribbean blacks to sponsor programs and activities which have made the church a friendly, lively, and hustling congregation. This is the result of Father Ikenye's positive attitude toward his parishioners. He makes them feel confident in themselves and shows that he cares for them.

St. Andrew's is striving to regain its status as a parish.

The Reverend Terrell Jackson
New Hope CME Church

I came to Evanston in September of 1988 to accept the pastoral charge of New Hope CME Church. I have lived here now for over six and one half years. I came from Kansas City, Kansas. I was born and raised there. Most of my schooling was down there, too.

I now live at 2027 Church Street. That is the only address I have had since I have been in Evanston.

We have tried to organize ourselves into a little community, but it really hasn't worked. All of the neighbors are home owners and know each other. They just sort of speak across the fence. That's about it.

I did about one year at Kendall College. I finished up my undergrad degree here in Evanston. It was a unique experience at Kendall. Strangely enough, Kendall is like a quiet sleeper college. No one realizes it is there. All it is really noted for really is its culinary, but they have other degrees that they offer. It's kind of a family oriented school. The students are all involved with one another. I received a bachelor's degree there.

I am registered as a Democrat. From what I have seen, I think I am well represented There is always some improvement that can be made.

As you know I am pastor of the New Hope CME Church. Our church is family oriented. Something I think our church could do to make our community better is to become more visible in empowering our people to help themselves. Here in the city of Evanston some of the blacks look upon the church for a handout. Most of the people see the church as a place for assistance, but we also try to teach people to help themselves. You know, give a man a fish but also teach him how to fish. One of the things that I hope to do during the coming year is to set up systems whereby training our people to help themselves.

There are a lot of people who want to get off drugs. We have nothing here in Evanston to help people who want to get off drugs as a resource center. I was talking with a young lady who wanted to get off drugs, but there was no place for her to turn. She could go to a program, but what was she going to do with her little girl? So the only thing she could do was to go back to that situation. So I think the church needs away to get together and set up programs where we can set up a house where, if you want to get off drugs, you come here and you will be provided for. You will have housing, you will have food. We will train you so that you can go and get a job and be a productive citizen in this community.

We are now called the Evanston African-American Ministerial Alliance. That is our official name. Better known as the Black Ministers. The purpose we have is to assist people who are economically disadvantaged, those who need rent, light, and gas, also helping people who have problems on their jobs, and to intercede in helping them to find jobs. I think we could do a little better than we are doing.

The latest thing we have done is with the School Board issue. We were leaders in getting the School Board to reverse its decision as far as bussing all of our kids out of this community up into North Evanston, and the North Evanston students to this end of town. We have done an excellent job in getting them to reverse that decision. We are trying to get a more positive opinion of ministers here in Evanston. I don't think some of the Evanston people give the ministers quite the respect as leaders as they should.

Some of our ministers relate to each other, from my own personal opinion, in a brotherhood of a spirit of working together, and then some of the Alliance members have their own personal agendas. I am in the Alliance to help boost the Alliance, not for my own personal agenda, and not for New Hope's agenda. Some of the ministers are sincere about helping and doing, but others have their own agenda.

We have a problem here with the big church and the little church. A lot of our people in Evanston don't come to the little churches, or smaller churches. The only churches we hear about are the large churches that are east of Dodge Avenue. Anything that is west of Dodge, you hear nothing about it. That's something that needs to be changed.

All of us are equal. Maybe you have more resources than I have, or you have more people to pull from, but that is a great problem, the big I's and the little U's. And I think that is one of the problems we have in the Alliance. Most people go to the larger churches or they go to what is considered a "top dog" pastor in the city, and the smaller church pastors are left out. And since they feel they are left out, they kind of pull away from them.

Question: Which do you feel the ministers consider most important, the issues, or themselves, or the image of themselves?

A little of both. "I am going to help the people, and also this will put me in." But not all.

Question: Do you think "self-promotion" is necessarily a handicap in addressing the issue?

Yes, because, I think it depends on who is out front leading the issue, whatever the issue is, because ministers might not want to push the issue, because a particular minister is leading.

Another problem is that some people have forgotten where they came from. They have gotten blessed. The Lord has blessed them and they have reached the place where they are, and have forgotten the rest of the people.

Black Ministers and White Ministers

We have two services a year that we have together, but we are also invited to their meetings and we go to their meetings. We have a few who go. We don't have that many black ministers who are full-time ministers, so most of them have second jobs. But most of the white ministers meetings are during the day, so if you have a job, that makes it impossible for you to attend. I think it is good camaraderie when we can meet and work together, like on the school board issue. In regards to having a ministers alliance instead of a black ministers and white ministers alliance. The black ministers did not want to lose their identity. We had our own, and wanted to keep our own. We did not want to be swallowed up. That was a great discussion.

We have talked about having our alliance together, but several of our ministers have objected, saying, "We have our own worship experiences. They don't worship like we worship. Where they are quiet, we are emotional." Personally, it doesn't bother me, if we don't or do want to set up a fellowship meeting with them, but if we do plan a meeting, it should be at a time when everybody can get there. We have had some business meetings together, usually about twice a year. But the only time we meet it's on an issue.

It is true that the ministers of the largest black churches do not have second jobs, but they say they are too busy to attend white ministers' meetings. They say they have "other obligations."

Question: Do you attend the YMCA? Have you ever been to the Y?

I have only been there to try to help people get rooms there. I have been treated very fairly there. I have no complaints. We helped a young man get in there just two or three days ago. He was trying to get a room there. The cost of the room was about ninety dollars a week for just a bed and a shower, a communal shower.

Also, I was in a mentoring project there, called Project Soar. They also have a good youth program there. There was some black participation. In my opinion the cost to join the Y keeps it low, because some of our parents just do not have the funds.

A lot of our single black mothers are not willing to make the time to invest in the children and to make sure that the child is doing this. As a matter of fact, right here in our own church we have a tutoring program. We have one of the teachers from the high school and the honor students from the high school come here. We have gone to several of the elementary schools where the children in this community go to school, but the parents just won't send the children to the tutoring classes. I think we have programs available for our children, but it's just that the parents won't make the children go. "Johnny makes his own decisions." And that's what we have here in Evanston. Children are raising their parents, instead of the parents raising the children. "If Johnny doesn't want to do something, he doesn't have to."

I have done some substitute teaching here in Evanston, since I have been here. In my opinion the children here have too much freedom. No discipline.

I think there are two reasons for this. First, the mother is doing her own thing. Second, she is too busy working trying to provide for the child.

We are not teaching our children that you have to sacrifice and save. They say, "Gimme, gimme, gimme."

We have no discipline. I had an experience here, right here in the church where there was a child who was "cutting up." Where I was raised, when somebody saw you "cutting up," they went to you and disciplined you, and then told your parent. We had a child who was "cutting up" one Sunday during the service. I went to the child, and I told the child, "You don't act this way in service." The parent found out that I had said this, and the parent came to me and told me that it was not my place nor my responsibility to chastise the child. I think a lot of people don't get involved because they don't want to go through a lot of hassle. Why be bothered? If they don't want me to discipline their child, then I just am not going to be bothered with him.

Strangely enough, as African-Americans, we lost our place in raising children. We are trying to raise them like the books say. We are not raising them like we were raised. We are doing it the book way. The book says, "Put them in the corner and talk to them. Give them 'time out.'" This is no time for "time out." It's our society. If you whip a child now, the child can call the hot line of the child abuse department and say, "My mamma whipped me," and the mamma goes to jail or daddy, or whoever corrected the child. We have lost it, and I really don't know how we are doing to get back to the basics of respect. That is the key word. We have lost it.

In our own community we are scared. We could take back our community if we weren't scared. Take it back from the drug dealers. I think some people are going to have to get together who are not scared and talk. We don't listen to our young people. A lot of young people who are in gangs, that I have talked to, say that "we don't get any discipline at home, and that no one talks to us."

Clubs and Organizations

I am a member of some social service agencies. I have served as chairman of the board for the Family Focus. I have served as a member of the board for BEHIV.

Family Focus is doing an excellent job with our young people. I think it could do a better job if we could just reach other parents. We spend a lot of time talking about disadvantaged youth, but what about that child who is not disadvantaged, whose parents are providing for that child? I don't hear much about that in this city.

Family Focus will provide help for people who are disadvantaged, who have dropped out of school. They are helped to get their GEDs. They provide job placement through a program called Teen Cuisine, and another job placement program, PIC, which is Private Industry Corporation and teaches young people job skills for working in offices and using machines like computers, and typewriters. Young ladies who have become teenage mothers are provided an opportunity to continue their education, and provide baby sitting services for their children.

The basement and the main floor of the building is Family Focus. They rent out the second and third floors with about eighty percent occupancy. There is a fast turn over with people moving in and out. I don't know how rent is in other places, but I personally think that the rent is just a little bit steep. That is my opinion.

I don't have much dealing with the Fleetwood-Jourdain Center. I think we have two social services agencies right there together. They could work together, but they do not. One is run by the city (Fleetwood-Jourdain) and the other (Family Focus) is a private nonprofit organization. They are reaching the same kids in that area, but they are just as separate as they can be.

Family Focus is financially supported by Family Focus, which is downtown. You see, Family Focus has grown. The original Family Focus was started right here in Evanston, and then it grew. So now there are about eleven other agencies that have grown from this one agency here over twenty years ago.

Family Focus Inc. includes Family Focus Evanston, Family Focus Lawndale, Family Focus Aurora, and other locations. The money comes from the corporate offices and is distributed to the various Family Focus Centers.

Our building is owned by Family Focus Inc., but each center must pay for the up keep of the building.

There is a group which is trying to buy back the Foster School unit. The Foster School Reunion Group wants to buy the building from Family Focus Inc. to have a landmark in our community. People in the Foster School Reunion Group are people who have gone to and graduated from Foster School. Their purpose is to buy back the building.

Some of these people are Dorothy Williams, Gwen Davis, etc.

No price has been set.

Family Focus is owned by Bernice Wiseberg, who is one of the big people in the Family Focus Corp.

Question: What did you learn from your experiences in the Marines?

Ten years in the Marine reserves. It had its good days and its bad days. I learned a lot from that. Interrelating with people. I grew up in an all black neighborhood. I went to an all black elementary and junior high school, and high school. When I went to college, it was mostly all black. I never really had any dealing with white people. So, when I went into the Marines, it made me associate with white people and find out that there was nothing wrong with white people, and that white people are just like black people. That is one of the major things I learned in the Marines.

Question: Discuss your relationship with the various arms of the government.

With the mayor, she's doing a good job. The aldermen, at least of this ward need to be more visible and do things in this community to help better the community and improve it, such as sidewalk repairs, painting, etc. I don't see that. They should have some community meeting once a quarter, twice a year. The only time you hear from the aldermen, or any of these public officials, really, is at election time.

The police department, police chief is very open. His door is open. On several occasions that I have had to go there to talk to Chief Cooper his staff was helpful in getting things that I needed done. He is a good, positive person.

Question: Describe the social environment in regards to conditions which threaten the peaceful, progressive lives of African-Americans and other citizens in Evanston.

We need to teach the African-Americans to help themselves and not to look for others to give them something. Honest day's work for an honest day's pay. We have too may social agencies that are helping people who really don't need the help. This makes it hard for people who do need the help. We need to weed out those who don't need the help and make it easier for those who do need help to get it. We need to have a time limit. Six months to a year, and that's it. It's caught up in a bureaucracy. If you have someone who comes to you today whose wife has just put him out and they don't have any money. Where can he go to get some immediate assistance?

I would like to say that Evanston is a quite diverse community and city. It's unusual and not quite like they told me it was going to be when I was coming here, unless here has changed. When I was told that I was coming here, some ministers who had already been to Evanston going to school told me that Evanston was a nice, quiet town where people could leave their doors open, friendly, neighborly, but when I got here, I didn't find that.

New Hope Church

This church has been in the Evanston community for eighty-three years. It has a lot of historical background as far as a Christian Methodist Episcopal Church denomination. We have had several ministers come through here who have gotten their training here and have gone on to reach the highest office that our church offers, which is a bishop. We have had at least four who have reached that, and one in particular who was not only a pastor, but if my memory is correct, he served also as a senior bishop of our denomination. That was Smith. So, this church has been an inspiration to this community, but has not been recognized because of its size.

Ebenezer is an AME Church, and we are New Hope Christian Methodist Episcopal Church.

The AME and AME Zion church was started in the North. The CME church was started in the South. The United Methodist came with the Evangelical and the Brethren churches.

Maybe Reverend Jackson can explain the differences between the various Methodist groups in one thousand words. He will let us know.

Prentis Bryson Comments

This was not one of the new churches in Evanston. This goes back to 1912 and our church was originally located in the same community as Ebenezer and Second Baptist. We were on Greenbay Road, right near Foster Street. There is a gas station there now, where Asbury and Greenbay intersect. There was a dance hall there, we worshiped there on Sunday mornings after they had had recreation on Saturday night. That facility was used not only for church, but for a dance hall. The dance hall became more popular than the worship. It was owned by a Jewish fellow who needed the income derived from the facility.

Questions for Discussion

1. Discuss Reverend Jackson's coming to Evanston.
2. Discuss community organization in Reverend Jackson's block (2027 Church).
3. What is one of his important objectives at New Hope CME Church?
4. What is the purpose of the Evanston African-American Ministerial Alliance? What is their latest achievement?
5. What is Rev. Jackson's concept of "big" churches and "little" churches?

6. What were some of the reasons members of the black alliance did not want to meet with the members of the white ministers group?
7. What were some of the black ministers' remarks about the church tutoring program?
8. What did Reverend Jackson say about child raising of some African-Americans?
9. Discuss some of the Family Focus programs.
10. What are Reverend Jackson's recommendations for an improvement in the African-American life in Evanston?

About Reverend Terrell Jackson

Reverend Jackson came to Evanston in September of 1988 to accept the pastoral charge of New Hope CME Church. He said that Evanston is quite a diverse community and much different than he had expected.

He said that he had been told that Evanston was a nice, quiet town where people could leave their doors unlocked and where the people were friendly and neighborly, but when he got here, he didn't find it so. He did say, however, that he realized that Evanston could have changed over the years. He has high hopes for the future of New Hope CME and its programs in Evanston. The reasons are that the church has been in Evanston for eighty-three years, and because he has confidence that the people they serve can improve their life-styles and become more considerate of each other.

Mrs. Anest R. Marshall

I came to Evanston in 1950. The reason I'm in Evanston, I had no people or nothing in Evanston, but I was living in a place you call St. Mary's, Georgia. That's where I was born. After I finished high school, I started working with children and I started taking care of babies. This family was of a prominent president of this big mill that had come into St. Mary's. This lady, she would always watch me, she liked me, and she had a little baby and she said, "Anest Robinson, I like you, I like your movement. I want you to take care of my baby." The baby was two weeks old, just had come from the hospital. She fired her nurse and she wanted me to take care of that baby. So, I started taking care of that baby and did such a splendid job until that baby got so attached to me, until the baby thought I was his mother. I raised that baby until it was about two years old. Then this president of the big mill in St. Mary's had a promotion to come to Chicago. She asked me if I would come to Chicago with her. At this time I had two children. My husband and I had just built a house. She said, "I cannot go, unless you go." She said, "I wouldn't take this boy away from you because he loves you so much."

So my husband and I thought it over and we talked about it. He worked in the laboratory at the plant. He had a big job there, but Mr. McKinley, that was the man's name, asked my husband and me to just come to Chicago to bring the baby and get them settled with somebody else to take care of the baby. So we decided that we would do that.

So, my husband and her husband motored up to Chicago. She, the baby, and I came up on the train. We were supposed to be here one month, and then go back home. We stayed here for over a month. They really didn't want us to leave. Well, we didn't leave, and my husband started working at the Chicago Motor Club in Chicago. We moved from Chicago to Evanston. We liked Evanston so much that we never went back to St. Mary's.

When the boy got around three or four years old, his father got another transfer to a place called Sarasota, Florida. Well, at that time, I had sent for my two children and they were up here. So the family went back, but I stayed up here.

Since we have been here, we have made many friends. I joined

Ebenezer Church in 1950. I was surrounded by such lovely people, because I am the type of person that can meet anybody and get along with them. I never had difficulty getting along with anybody.

So we stayed here, and I started working in a nursery school, the Mary Johnson Nursery School. After I worked there for, I don't know how long, I decided that I wanted to open my own business, and I went down to the Chicago Loop College and took classes in training and child development and got my certificate.

I opened my own nursery school with seven children. I kept on and I never had to run an ad. Just from one person to another, I became a big school. I started having twenty-five children, and my supervisor would come up and say, "Mrs. Robinson, you are doing such a great job. I think you should have more children than you have." So, I converted my basement into a school. Then she told me that I could expand. I did expand by bringing fifteen kids upstairs. I now have forty children. So, that's how I started in Evanston. I think I have had nearly everybody's child in Evanston. Some are grown, and I have had their children, maybe some grandchildren. I have never had to advertise. One person just tells another person.

I have had a supervisor over me. Then the place had to be really presented properly. I had to meet requirements. That is how we got our license. I have been in business now for thirty-two years. I haven't had any trouble with anybody.

As I said, I joined Ebenezer and I was a faithful member and am still a faithful member. I worked on the steward board. I worked in different clubs. I just happen to be one of the good members of Ebenezer.

Our church was destroyed. We organized a club we called the Two Thousand Dollar Club. We raised over a hundred thousand dollars with that club of just one or two people. We would meet month to month and we would pay so much as we could afford to pay. From time to time, we put all of that money together, and we figured out that we had raised over one hundred thousand dollars for the restoration of the church building.

I joined Ebenezer under Reverend Robinson. During the time the church burned, it was Reverend Powell. Other pastors were Reverend Higginbotthom, Reverend Blake, Reverend Wade.

I have always been a church goer. I have focused on trying to do the things that I was taught to do. My parents came from Florida. My mother married my father, who was a Georgian. After she married him, they moved back to Georgia. I was born in Georgia, but raised in Florida.

We were taught the right way. My parents were very strict. They instilled in me the things about how we were supposed to live. And that's what I instill in my daughter, and she in her children. She has raised four children, and none of them has given her a minute's trouble. She has two in Florida, one in Texas, my grandson who married recently and went to college at Prairie View and now has a good job in Texas. Both of my granddaughters finished Florida A & M and are living now in Ft. Lauderdale, Florida. One of them is married and has two children, one of them is getting married Thanksgiving weekend, so we will have a big wedding in the family then. And we have one grandson in Evanston. He is staying with his mother. My daughter lives in Evanston. She married Woodrow Cannon.

We have found Evanston to be a lovely place to live in. We lived, when we came here, in Mr. Gill's place on Hartrey Avenue. We moved there from Alberta Logan's house on Wesley Avenue. We got along real well until we bought our own home here at 2323 Lake Street.

My first husband died in 1962, at the time my son was just finishing high school, so I had a son to put through college and didn't have a husband. By the grace of God, I got him through college and he is now living in Ft. Wayne, Indiana and he has a lovely family. He has a girl and a boy. His son has earned a five-year scholarship at the University of Indiana. He could have gone to many places. Northwestern wanted him, but after his daddy took him around to all the colleges, he liked the University of Indiana. It's where he is playing football now. His name is Jabar Robinson, if you ever hear of him.

I have a granddaughter. This is her last year in high school. She is one of my son's children. She is trying to see which college she would like to go to.

My son and his wife are living in Ft. Wayne, Indiana. They are doing well. The wife is the director of a Y in Ft. Wayne. My son is an engineer. He works for the city. So all of them are doing great and I am very proud of all of them.

Neighbors

I have always gotten along well with my neighbors. I haven't lived around anybody that I couldn't get along with, because we understood each other, and by me being the person I am, I try to make friends with them instead of enemies. Nobody in Evanston can say anything wrong about me because I haven't done anything but try to do the right thing.

When I worked in the Y over on Emerson Street, I was working for Mary Johnson Nursery School. I worked there for ten years. Everybody thought it was my school. They would come up there sometimes and say, "I want to speak to Mrs. Robinson." Mrs. Payne would say, "Not Mrs. Robinson, she doesn't own this school. I own it." But the children loved me.

Up until now, I have been getting along with everybody in the community and haven't had any trouble with them.

Block Club

In 1970 I married Fred Marshall, and we lived on Hartrey. We had a block club on Hartrey Avenue. I worked with that a lot. We had bake sales and everything like that to raise money to do improvements that we wanted to do around the block.

The way the block club started was this. They decided to have a meeting, and I always take part in things my husband is involved in, so we had this meeting and organized the block club.

My husband was elected president. He did a good job until he became disabled. Then Annie Barnes became president. I don't know whether it is still going on now or not. I don't think it is because I don't hear anything about it.

Some of the Club's Activities

If we saw anything going on wrong, we would report it, and then we would tell each one of them to keep their property up. Hartrey was kept up pretty nice. I think it is mostly what we did.

My husband joined a group which worked as policemen's helpers. They had red jackets and if there was an accident in the neighborhood, they would report it and assist until the police came.

Block clubs are very helpful because the things they would report that were going on in the neighborhood, the police would respond to. That is why they asked everybody to have block clubs and do these things. They are essential.

Another thing the neighbors, like Mrs. Barnes, if they saw anything that was pertaining to illegal activities, especially since they were close to the high school where so many cars were parked, they would call the police. The police would then disperse any gangs who might be around

But over there on Hartrey it was pretty nice. You didn't have too many gangs hanging around them.

Nursery School - "Good Things"

The good things I like about the nursery school, when I first started, my nursery school in 1964, I had a lot of lovely young children to come and they have done so well in life. I had one of Billy Logan's boys. I had Billy Dawson's son. They all went to college. I saw such good work from those boys and I am proud of them. Then I had the Wicks boy who went to college. He came back here the other day and spoke to our little children at their graduation. He told them that he attended the nursery school as a little boy, and now he has graduated from the University of Illinois, and he has a big job. He was one of my little boys, and now he is about twenty years old or more.

He comes to talk to the little children to tell them how they must be, not to get into any gangs, not to be in dope or anything. So I liked a lot of things about a lot of my boys. But a lot of them, I don't know what they did after they left me. But ones I keep up with have been very nice young men. The thing about it, if they are in gangs, they all still have respect for me. I can go into the worst crowd you have ever seen and say, Hello, young men. How are you doing? I bet you are some of my boys I had." They say, "Oh, yeah, Mrs. Marshall, we know you. We used to go to your nursery school." Now, they could be in the gangs, but they never disrespect me.

The boys who have actually gone into gangs kind of stay away from me because when I graduate some of them at five years old, I don't see some of them anymore. I have lost contact with them. But some of them still pass by my yard and say, "Mrs. Marshall, we love you, Mrs. Marshall." Because I used to have gardens all outside the fence, you know, with cabbage and other stuff. They would pass by and say, "Mrs. Marshall, you sure have a pretty garden out here, but you know we love you and are not going to let nobody bother you. We won't let nobody touch your garden." And they would never touch a thing I'd have up beside the fence.

But I haven't had the chance to talk to any of the boys who are really in gangs because when I talk to them, you wouldn't know they were in it or not. They were so respectful.

Question: What are some of the problems in the nursery school business?

The only thing, I have had a few people that would be lying to me about pay—"We don't have the money" or "we will bring it by tomorrow or the next day." Some of them would never show up the next day. Well, with me, if I didn't have anything, I wouldn't fuss with them about it. So many people have gone without paying me. I just leave it in the hands of the Lord. I say, "Probably they need it more than I did." That's the only thing that discouraged me, that people that I respect would promise to pay me but never pay. So, I would figure they were too poor to pay and didn't have it. But other than that, I haven't had any big troubles since I have been in this business. The only thing is that some of them were supposed to pay me and didn't pay me, but then it didn't cause me to not eat or nothing like that, so after they left, I just said, "They won't be coming back anymore."

But it was my home, and I guess they respected my home. It wasn't like I was running a school where I wasn't at home all the time, but I was at home all the time, right here. And I haven't had too many problems. The only problem was some of the parents not paying.

Question: Has there been a change in the parents who leave their children here today, compared with the parents a few years ago?

Oh, yes. There are some big changes now. Let me tell you. The most of them now are youngsters. Young parents. When I had some of the older parents here, I didn't have a minute's trouble. They would have different things like showers for the school, they would buy food, but these young folks, if they pay you that's it. They don't have things for you like the other older parents used to. Young folks don't think of things like that anymore.

Now, the young folks don't believe in making their children mind like the older ones did years ago. The children are much different now. They are louder. They don't want to listen. They figure you can't tell them too much until you get hard and say, "You have got to listen. You can't learn if you don't listen. When you get hard on them, then they do all right. But it is a big difference now because the children now are much louder and they are not well behaved like they used to be. We teach the children how to say "thank you." At one time, you never had to tell a child to say "thank you." When you gave them something, they said "thank you." Now when you give a child something, he is not going to say "thank you" unless you tell them to say it. So, I have been telling them manners.

It's a big difference now. I guess they are more alert, or something. I guess they look at television a lot and see so many more things that there used to be. You could tell a child, "If you do so and so, I will tell your mother," and he would listen, but now if you tell them, they will say, "Mamma ain't going to do nothing." She won't spank them, but when you could have spanked those kids they were much better children because they had something to fear. But children have nothing to fear now.

Question: What were your experiences at the Y?

When I used to work at the Y, we had the upper level floor. There would be activities on the lower floors. I can say that the children were not unruly, like they are now. If they were, Mr. Buley, one of the executives there, could handle the boys, and he never had a whole lot of this that we have now. I guess the dope wasn't in like it is now. But that dope has ruined a lot of things because some of them don't know what they are saying to you. That's why you are scared to open your mouth to someone, you don't know the response you will get.

But at the Y you had men living there, like A.V. Cavinet, he was one of the men who lived there. We never had a problem with people doing anything or hurting the children.

Question: Did blacks lose something valuable to the community when the Emerson Street Y was closed and the Grove Street Y began to integrate their activities?

I am sure that they lost something, but it could be better because it is integrated and they can respect one another.

I would go to the Grove Street Y. I was teaching one of the classes down there. But I never did go for dipping in the teams or anything.

You know, I never had any problems because when I was with the other race, I was just myself and I tried to be intelligent like I was raised. So when my daughter came here and started to high school, they told me that the black people did not attend the meetings, and if you have a child in high school, be sure and go to PTA meetings and do things like that. So, when I put her in ETHS, everything they had, I was there. But sometimes I would be the only black there. They weren't

Conversations with Blacks in Evanston, Illinois • 137

going then to the PTA meetings or nothing, only a few. But I was a stranger here. And I noticed when you go to these schools and show an interest in your children, they will help you. And that's what they have done. Because one of the teachers of my daughter said she never talked very much. She was kind of bashful. So, this teacher said, if I could just get her to talk more, but you and I are going to make her talk. So, when I would go to meetings and different things around the school, I'd visit and Cynthia would be in class, sometimes a change of class, he'd say, "hi Cynthia" before all of these people, and make her respond back to him. By he and I working with her, you can't beat her talking now. That was the teacher and I. She was encouraged. That was by me visiting the school. I went to PTA meetings, and a lot of times I would visit. We did this and she did not know it. We were just trying to get her to open up. It worked. But I notice, if you visit these things and show that you are interested, you will have help. Somebody will help you. So, the teacher and I got her out of that bashfulness, and she was one of the nicest students around.

My son went to Foster School. Mrs. Morton was his teacher. Mrs. Robinson was his teacher. When he finished Foster, he started going to Haven. Then he went to high school. Then he went to Central State College where he finished. He is now an engineer.

Cynthia was teaching over at the high school. She left there and was in Glencoe, and I asked her if she wanted to take the nursery school over. She told me she would have to think about it. So she thought about it and she came and is now the director and everything at the school. I am so glad I had her because it is a good business. It's hers now. I am getting tired, but I still help.

She is taking care of the school. She is doing a beautiful job. I only have two children. It's theirs anyway, because it is my private school.

Politics

You know I never was a really good and tall politician. I am a Democrat. I have always been a Democrat, all my life. I don't know why, but I just feel more comfortable with them than the Republicans. I am not caught up in politics and all of that. I respect my alderman, Dennis Drummond, now. It used to be Betty Burns.

I don't know what to say about politics.

I've known the mayor ever since I came to Evanston. Lorraine, I think she is a beautiful person. When I was going into nursery school, we always met different places and we are very good friends.

Lorraine had my child in her school, and she saw me all the time. I think she has made a good mayor. I don't know if she is running again, but if she does, I will vote for her.

Question: Changes in Evanston which may result in the deterioration of the quality of life here?

Old folks are dying off. The young folks do not want too much responsibility. That's why they are selling the old folks' homes now, and the whites are coming in. You take Garnett Place, Garnett Place used to be all white at one time, but they started selling to blacks. Now it's going back to the same thing it was at first because whites are buying back into Garnett Place, because the older people are dying out and the young people are selling. So that's what is worrying me. The white folks are coming right back in the city and buying these homes that the black folks are selling, and these black people are going somewhere else in these apartments and high rises and are not going to be bothered with these old homes.

Question: What about the blacks who can't move?

They get in trouble. That's true. Some of them have moved from here and I don't think they are doing all that good by not staying. They could have stayed and kind of kept things going, but they don't want that. There's one thing about our black folks, they are getting lazy. They don't want to do things that they should do. You take these drop outs. There are so many of them dropping out of school, they are too lazy to study. They want somebody to give them something. There are a lot of our black children like that. They just want somebody to be giving to them all the time.

Question: Why do you think that is?

Now, I don't know. I don't know whether it is the times or what? I think the parents have something to do with a lot of this thing about raising children. It's all in the parents. Some of these children, now, the way they talk to their parents, if I talked to my parents when I was growing, I wouldn't have had a mouth or nothing, because I would have been backhanded. But that's one thing that has disrupted the whole thing. You can't do nothing to your own child. You can't chastise them. All they know now is to call the police. The police aren't helping, so who are you going to call now.

One day I heard a parent say, "I can't do a thing with this child." I said, "What do you mean?" He was cutting up in the store. He was a little boy. He wanted something, and she didn't give it to him. He was all on the floor. I walked in there and she said, "Mrs. Marshall, what can I do for him?" I said, "You have started too late. You should have started while he was younger, chastising him and telling him what is right and what is wrong." I said, "When they get around eight, nine, or ten years old, you can't do nothing with them. You should have started with them when they were younger. Now you can't touch them, because if you do, someone will call the police."

I noticed that there was somebody downtown who was trying to get the child to go and get in the car, and the child wouldn't get in the car. A passerby called the police and said the man was abusing the child. Now the man was just trying to make the child mind.

These children have got sense now. I had a little girl come in here and she said, "Mrs. Marshall, he just doesn't want to do what I tell him to do." I said, "Well, you must make him mind you." She said, "Well, if I pull him or jerk him he will holler like I am killing him. So he has sense enough to holler to make people believe that I am hurting him. So I don't know what to do." She was a young mother.

I said, "Well, honey, charity begins at home. You make him mind you by talking to him, you don't have to scream all the time. Just talk to him and say, 'Mind Mother, now. You've got to listen. If you don't listen, you'll get hurt.'" I said, "Find something to get him to listen to you." She said, "All right, I'll try, but I can't do a thing with him. He starts screaming and hollering and people think I am killing him."

It's terrible.

I feel sorry for the young folks now. They can't enjoy themselves like we used to enjoy ourselves. They can't have parties without somebody crashing the party. I just feel so sorry for the young girls. I had a talk with some young boys. I said, "Why are you all leaving the black girls and going with the white girls?" One boy said, "Well, I tell you, Mrs. Marshall, they are much nicer to us than our own color. All our colored girls know is to cuss us out and use all kinds of bad language. The white girls are very nice. We will go out together, they will help pay the expenses sometime. That's why we go out with them, because they are much nicer than our own color."

Question: Are the boys accepted by the white girls' families?

Some of them are and some of them are not.

It just worries me about the black people now, especially to see the girls like that. How are they to get good husbands? That's the way things are now that most of the black women are very independent. They get their education, and if their husbands don't want to do right, they will go just to themselves. I know a lot of mothers who are the only parent. They have their own apartments. They go to work, bring the child here, and they have good jobs. They can't depend on the young men. Why, I don't know. But I feel real sorry for a lot of the young women.

Question: Has the church been effective in enabling the black kids to conduct themselves properly in society and to make progress?

I think the church could do a little more than what they are doing. We have a pastor now who is really dedicated to the young people. He tries to get the young people into church, but it looks like it's not the ones that we need. We need these wild ones that are in the street. It looks like we are not able to draw that kind into the church. We even have big meetings, but ones who are supposed to hear about these things are not there. They do not attend. The ones who need to know will not come to church. We have been having Bible classes to try to get people to come to church, but they join and then don't come back.

I don't know how we are going to reach them. We have been trying everything, by talking to them I have talked to a bunch of youngsters. I say, "When am I going to take all of you to church?" "We'll go with you sometime," they say. I say, "When will that sometime be?" "Oh, soon. We'll let you know." They never let me know. Now what can you do, when you ask them to go and they give you that excuse? It's a question. What can you do?

Question: What about the Family Focus program?

One time we went over to the Family Focus building and talked to a bunch of the girls and took them refreshments. We sat down and talked with them, but I do not know about them because I am so busy myself with my school that I don't have time to visit them more. But they say that it is a good program because I know a lot of people who work with the youngsters and their babies.

A lot of sororities volunteer and do things there. I know, my daughter, she is an Alpha Kappa Alpha, and they have been going a lot with a bunch of youngsters.

I think that helps, but I don't know whether it's helping enough because, as I say, there is one crowd there but you can't get some of those who really need the help to come in there.

Question: What is the future outlook for a certain group of youngsters?

The future doesn't look too good for the blacks who are getting into this dope stuff. There are so many of them. A lady from Milwaukee told me that there was an eleven-year-old boy who had another boy on the roof of some house, watching for the policemen. They were paying him a hundred dollars a week as a lookout for a crack house. I was astonished when this lady told me this. She said it is so terrible that they are ruining these little children.

Question: Do you think it is possible to keep dope out of the neighborhoods?

I don't know, because over there, farther down on Lake Street, they tell me there are different houses where it's so annoying at night, when this little bunch gets together. You call a policeman, the policeman comes, they scatter, and when the policemen go back, they still come again. So, I don't know what to do in that situation.

Sometimes it makes me believe the officers could do more than what they are doing. One thing, they are too lenient with these boys who go round with this dope. They will put them in jail one day and let them out the next month or so. They can do it again. So, I think they are a little bit too lenient on the boys. I think if they had stronger restrictions on the boys, it would break up some of this stuff, but I don't know how they can do it now.

Question: What about boarding up dope houses?

I think that is a good idea because if they open it up, they will probably start doing the same thing they have been doing. They should get different people in there who are not in the dope selling business. If they open it up and the same people are there, they are going to have problems. I don't see how they could get rid of it because they are going to keep on doing the same thing.

One lady who lives in the 2100 block of Darrow Avenue where there is a cul-de-sac, complained that her area was "dope heaven" and she was sick of it, but she feels helpless.

The policemen seem to be afraid of them.

You know, we don't have any airplanes or stuff to bring this dope in to the neighborhoods. Now that is where you are going to have to get to the bottom of this. The ones who are bringing it in here have to be stopped. The big man is sitting back, but it is the little man who is catching the devil.

Questions for Discussion
1. Describe Anest's background before she came to Evanston.
2. What do you think was the most important reason that Anest came to Evanston?
3. What kind of preparation did Anest have before she opened her own nursery school?
4. Why did Anest have to expand her nursery school? What changes in her house did she have to make?
5. What was the purpose of the Two Thousand Dollar Club at Ebenezer Church as described by Anest?
6. Anest has a grandson who is on the University of Indiana football team. What is his name?
7. What did Anest say about the advantages of their block club on Hartrey Avenue?
8. What were some of the good things Anest has experienced in her nursery school?
9. What were some of the problems Anest had in her nursery school?
10. How does Anest describe many of the modern parents today?
11. Why does Anest feel that integrating the Evanston YMCA could be helpful to blacks and whites?
12. How did attending the school meetings and affairs benefit Anest's children?
13. What are some of the changes taking place is Evanston which may

result in the deterioration of the quality of life here?
14. What advice did Anest have to parents who have trouble with their children's behavior?
15. How effective has the church been in helping the black kids to conduct themselves properly?

About Anest Marshall

Anest is rather short in stature, but appears to be a bundle of energy. It is easy to see how she has been so successful in her nursery school business. Her smile puts all who meet her at ease. That is especially important in her dealing with children and their parents.

We found the physical environment of the nursery school spotless and attractive. Children had access to a well disciplined playground area which provided apparatus which was entertaining and safe. No wonder they loved it here. Also, Anest had a thriving garden which supplied the school with nourishing vegetables.

Now that Anest's daughter, Cynthia, has taken over the school as director, Anest has more time to do other things to improve life in her community and other places in Evanston.

Louis Moseley

I was born in Chicago, and I came, in 1937, to Evanston, Illinois from Chicago, Illinois. I lived in the 5400 block on Prairie Avenue in Chicago. But prior to coming to live in Evanston, I had visited Evanston as a youngster. For about six summers, I spent all summer with my aunt, Mrs. Black, who lived on Ayers Place, now known as Garnett Place. She moved to the 1900 block on Dewey Avenue.

I enrolled in Foster School and graduated from Foster School in 1939. I entered Evanston Township High School in 1939 and graduated in 1943. Then, I entered Northwestern University in September 1943 and stayed there until June 1944. In September, I enlisted in the Air Force and I was accepted for pilot training at Tuskegee. I reported there in November of 1944.

I did very well at Foster School. I had been in a Catholic school, Corpus Christi, in Chicago, and was a pretty good student at that time. I skipped from sixth grade to eighth grade. My sister was a year ahead of me, so we both graduated at the same time. I got a perfect report card throughout my entire sixth grade, so they skipped me from seventh to eighth, and then I had a perfect report card all through eighth grade until I graduated.

At high school I ran track for a short time. That was my freshman year. I was a dash man, but I had pulled a muscle so bad that I couldn't run dashes anymore, so I switched to cross country, and that was just to stay in shape. I had wanted to go out for tennis at Foster Field because I was a pretty good tennis player at that time. I was playing tennis at Foster Field and some of the other field houses. They had good tennis programs then. Dr. Fred Clark and I won the city championship for juniors while I was a sophomore in high school.

When I went out to play tennis at high school, they wouldn't accept me. They wouldn't accept me because of my race.

In fact, I was told, at the time, that I could play some other sports, but because the tennis team traveled to other schools like Oak Park in Suburban League, they wouldn't permit me to play on the courts. The tennis coach told me this. I was very disappointed about that, so as a result of that bad experience, I just didn't pursue any activity at high school.

I did very well in my studies; however, I made the honor roll, was accepted at Northwestern and did very well in my freshman year there.

I scored very high on my aptitude test for officer's training school when I went into the Air Force. The minimum score was 110 and I got 141. So, that helped me in my military career.

I went into basic preflight training at Tuskegee in November 1944. And I was at Tuskegee for about five months. I was in the 301st Squadron of a fighter group, and most of the men in my group were being phased into different parts of the Air Force, because the war was taking a turn in our favor in Europe. That's what we were told. Most of us were sent from Tuskegee to Sulfridge Air Force Base. That's where the 332nd Fighter Group later on trained, and they began to phase out the classes at Tuskegee.

While I was at Sulfridge, I did some advance training. Then they cut that class out. Then they sent me to the South Pacific. And I was the only black in a B-29 unit, which was very unusual at that time. I lived with my plane captain who was plane commander. He was white. I lived with him and the copilot on the B-29. I was assigned to their crew. I got a lot of additional flight training under him and another white lieutenant named Lieutenant Phillips. They knew I wanted to fly. This was something they did on their own. It had nothing to do with the Air Force's policy. We lived off-base together. They liked me.

At the time, I was head of the military police near the Clark Air Force Base. I had ninety-three military policemen under my jurisdiction I supervised and also taught classes, four hours Monday through Thursday in unarmed defense.

Prior to going into the service, at the time I was thirteen, I became interested in the martial arts, Ju Jitsu, and I started training in Ju Jitsu, so by the time I entered the service I was one step under black belt. I was a first degree brown belt. So, with my I.Q. they promoted me to staff sergeant.

The military police unit was mixed black and white, because the whites served one part of an area, and the blacks served the other, but I was the officer in charge the of whole unit.

They needed somebody to train the occupation troops as military policemen, so with my credentials in martial arts, I was selected to go to Japan and I went to Ju Jitsu school in Japan for about twenty-two weeks. There I got my black belt. When I got back, I was put in as the head instructor for the military police command. I stayed there until I was rotated back to this country.

At Clark Air Force Base in the Philippines, I used to fly by myself in the advance trainer under the jurisdiction of Captain Rochelle, who was my commanding officer. We flew the AT-6. Captain Rochelle was also my instructor. He would let me take the controls in flight, but not in landing or taking off. This was kind of a continuation of my training I had at Tuskegee. I was fortunate that I ran into a very unique situation at that time. Toward the end, we didn't do too much flying because I moved into another area, still in Clark Air Force Base, but my duties became more and more restricted to the military police. I enjoyed this work very much. I had a supporting staff of about six noncommissioned officers who worked with me. I was a staff sergeant at this time.

When we left Clark Air Force Base, I returned to the U.S. to be discharged from the service. I was discharged at Sulfridge Air Force Base. I then went into the reserves and entered the National Guard and graduated highest in the class from the Officers Training School in Fort Sill Oklahoma. I then became a survey officer for the 184th Field Artillery Battalion in Chicago for about a year and a half. I later resigned my commission as a second lieutenant.

I went back to school and opened up a martial arts school and I was no longer able to fulfill my obligation as a second lieutenant, where their needs were going to be more than I could contribute, because I was primarily getting very much involved in the martial arts and other things. So, I wrote to Springfield and resigned. As a veteran, that was what I had a right to do.

I was employed many years at the Emerson Street YMCA, and was also employed for twelve years with Allstate Insurance Company, but that was in recent years, from 1981 till 1993. In years back, I worked at the Y as the physical director and the youth director, and somewhat as night director when the executive director didn't come back for specific programs. I was physical, youth, and programs director for many years.

I worked under Mr. Hummons, who was the executive secretary, Mr. Boyd, and then I worked the entire time that Mr. Buley was at the Emerson Street Y. And during the interim, before, I was in charge of the Y for about a year, and I worked under Jack Price, who was my supervisor at that time. When they were searching for an executive director, after Mr. Boyd, before they hired Mr. Buley, I was hired by Jack Price to be in charge of the Y. Then I worked seven days a week. I was doing everything. If they had parties, I was in control. The youth program, the physical programs, swimming programs. I qualified as a physical director because of my martial arts. I had the first martial arts school outside of Chicago at the Emerson Street Y around 1954. The next school was in Milwaukee.

From the time I came to the Y in 1937, I received a fellowship every year which sponsored me. And I took my beginning swimming test and went all the way up to senior life guard. Then later on, I took the aquatic leaders examiners class. That is the same test that the lifeguards give other lifeguards. So, I was certified to do that. With those credentials, my aquatic leader examiner certificate registered by the Red Cross, and continually updated my lifeguard certificate plus my martial arts, I was a physical director there for many years. They had never had any until they used me as the physical director.

I had classes in the martial arts on Tuesdays, Thursdays, and Saturdays. We had beginners and advanced classes.

We also participated in tournaments. Advanced students and beginners traveled all around to represent the Y.

We had class designation as beginners, intermediates, and advanced. We organized the YMCA Club, called the YMCA Martial Arts Club. They elected their own president and hired me as their instructor. The members of the club had a constitution, and they could expel anyone they felt was degrading the club, or doing something that was against the principles of the club. I had the final say so on expulsion.

I attended only part of the meeting, just to check up on them. Then I would leave so they could conduct their own meeting. They actually hired me on a monthly contract.

This club put on exhibitions at the Fleetwood-Jourdain Center, in Waukegan and quite a few other different places.

Another fellow and I were the two hired instructors.

I was responsible to the executive secretary of the YMCA. I gave a monthly report, and the board would visit our classes periodically to see how we were doing.

There was no cost to the Y, because the dues which we collected from each member were enough to pay my salary and get the materials required. The only thing the Y did for us was, on several occasions, they bought mats for us. We were self-supporting.

Also, we were kind of publicizing the Y. In our activities, we participated in all of the major tournaments in Milwaukee, Ohio, Indiana, Michigan, and Iowa, so we represented the Emerson Street Y.

The only requirement made was that every member had to be a member of the Y. We had about forty-five members. We maintained that number for about five or six years. Most of them were from freshmen in high school to adulthood, in their thirties or forties.

They seemed to be attracted to this program because we tried to make it a fun activity. They got their belt rights. At the time, my immediate teacher was a cousin of a Judo Black Belt Federation of America member. He was the overseer of our school in Evanston. He gave us the charter. We were under his jurisdiction, and that made things very interesting. Also, we went swimming, and had social activities where the club would invite their girlfriends or wives and have a little affair downstairs in the Orbit room. We were well organized.

I was fortunate enough to have some other noteworthy instructors in the area who would come out and take over the school every so often. And we would give them a stipend of something like twenty-five dollars for coming out. And they really enjoyed that, and these people would bring their philosophy to the group. Some of them were national champions.

One was a very good friend of mine that I used to work with, and he used to come out, and the men seemed to enjoy that.

We had strict rules that anyone who misused or brought about bad feeling to our club was subject to review by the membership, and if the membership felt that they had violated any of our principles of sportsmanship or conduct, they were automatically put out of the club. I had the authority to override it if I thought it was too harsh or maybe the person should be put on probation. I never had an occasion to, because in all of the years I was there we had to expel one person. And that was because that person was demonstrating the use of Ju Jitsu and Judo outside, and after he had been drinking. Reports had come back to me from the chief of police of Evanston and several other places. So, that was automatic.

The club did what it was supposed to do, and as far as character is concerned, those I would see outside the Emerson Y, carried themselves very well, I don't know of anybody who got into any kind of trouble. They demonstrated good character. All of them.

We also went swimming. Since I was a lifeguard, and the executive director gave me authority after class, we could loosen up in the swimming pool. They enjoyed that, too.

I taught swimming with Mr. Barnfield for maybe six or seven years in the tot swimming program. We used to have that every Saturday. He was an excellent swimmer.

I taught at least six or seven years. We had the only tot swimming program in this area at one time at the Emerson Street Y. Mr. Boyd brought that with him. I was generally in charge of all the adult and high school level swimming classes after school hours. I usually served as lifeguard. That's when I was on the payroll. I was the head lifeguard. I had several people who would come up for senior lifeguard tests, and they would assist me, and I would give them credit for the number of hours that they put in. And when they took their tests, I would site how many hours they had put in instructional hours, how many assistant hours, teaching, etc. I did the same thing in my martial arts school. Every person who came up for an advanced belt had to go through a training program and put in so many hours as an assistant instructor and learn the discipline, etc.

Anyone who enters the martial arts, open island style, the Japanese style, basically starts with what we call the OB, and the OB represents—what it really represents is two things—the rank that you hold and also tells someone that you have a certain level of experience. So every student starts with a white belt. The majority of the schools have a testing phase where the instructor can give a person a belt when he thinks that the person has accomplished certain things. But I don't like that system. I prefer the system of having the student approach me to request belt testing, and then have that student go through the belt testing, and then we grade him. It seems that the person feels that he has earned something a lot more than if it were given to him. After you have reached one level, we have certain forms, certain you things you must do at the next level. You can't perform anything which is at a level above you. You can perform something from the next level you are trying to attain. In other words, a person who is in the yellow belt won't demonstrate the quality or the capability to do something that a green belt or brown belt would be able to do, because he just doesn't have it. That would be unfair to him, and would be prostituting the belt rank if you did that. So, immediately when a person takes his test, we say, "You are now going to join a general class with everybody in it." If you have a large gym I would say, "OK, now the green belt class will go over to this section, the brown belt class will go over to another section, and the blue belt section will go to a different section, and the yellow belt section over there." That's when the advance teachers begin to document their training and their ability, because they are advancing to where they can teach. They don't test them at this point, but they train them. As the chief instructor, I walk around and make sure that they are being trained properly in each category. I will have my assistant instructors at their grade levels meeting the other students and training them. I oversee the whole thing.

The other instructors are not paid because they are members of the Amateur Athletic Union. I get paid because I am the only one who is a professional. I am no AAU. Everybody else in the school is also a member of the AAU.

Most of the tournaments we have are affiliated with the AAU. The instructors are generally considered professional, because we get paid.

We have white belt, yellow belt, blue belt, green belt, purple belt, third, second, and first degree brown belt, so we have all those different levels. You don't get to black belt until you have been through all of those other levels. It all depends upon the ability of the student, and how much time the person has to participate in the art.

Anything below the black belt is called ungraded. From black belt up is called graded There are two separate categories.

A fully certified teacher is only at the black belt level. I can have somebody act in my absence only, but that person cannot run the school. That person cannot be hired by the city of Evanston or anything to open a school and teach too, because he is not certified. There are ten degrees of the black belt. Those with degrees one through five wear a solid black belt. Degrees six, seven, and eight wear a red, white, and checkered belt. A solid red belt would be a ninth and tenth degree.

The head of my organization is in Japan. There is only one tenth degree. That is the head of the organization. He can delegate someone to succeed him when he retires. His successor will be a ninth degree, the only one.

The eighth, seventh, and sixth are usually regional directors, etc.

At this time I wear a white checkered belt. I am a seventh degree.

I am the Midwest Regional Director for the Unites States Karate Association. There are four of us in the county, the Southern Region, Eastern Region, Western Region, and Midwest Region.

There is one eighth degree in Florida. The head of our organization in this country is a ninth degree in Phoenix, Arizona. That's where the headquarters of the Unites States Karate Association is.

I am considered a Master. From the seventh degree on up, you are considered a Master. The ninth and tenth degree are the Grand Masters.

We have a Board of Masters, consisting of those of the seventh degree on up. I am automatically on that board because of my rank. This board selects the Grand Master. If he dies, one from the board of Grand Masters is selected to be Great Grand Master. Our Grand Master is eighty-two years old. He is in Japan. He is still practicing.

In Japan and in China there is martial arts called Tichee. It is real slow, and anybody can do it. This is especially for older people. Before

Louis Moseley

I retired I was teaching that kind of martial arts at Great Lakes to senior citizens. We also have a Tichee class here in Evanston for seniors.

This is basically exercise because there is a different purpose involved with the older people than for younger people. Ninety-nine percent of students who stick with the martial arts will go all the way up through years of hard rigorous training which will be four to five years to get a black belt. With discipline, etc., that's the only way to the belt. They will have to demonstrate the quality of their lives, discipline, etc. And they will have to demonstrate their ability to teach and all of that. So there is a different purpose with the younger students than with the older ones. When a person is taking Tichee, he learns the serenity part of life where you learn to be calm. It's beautiful for people who might be slightly nervous or something, because you learn to calm yourself. For people who may have some physical problems, there is no exertion. It just tones the muscles. You do inner breathing, which is called the inner spirit of the body. That way, you have to use some mental gymnastics for that. You have to learn to control your inner breathing and all of that in tune with what you are doing to get that calm state, you know. The Japanese say, "The mind flows freely, as the water." You have to learn to do that. That is called the "inner spirit." It has nothing to do with the "outer spirit." In order to be effective in the martial arts, somewhere, you will have to learn that. You must understand that.

Emerson Street YMCA

At the time when I was at the YMCA, we also had the High Y Club. Mr. Thomas Garnett was sponsor of that club. We also had the Tri Hi Y, which was the girls section. We had very active group when Mr. Boyd was there, and also when Mr. Boulee was there; I don't know when the Orbit Room was finished, or built, but we wanted to have a control over how we used the room. We decided that the best way to control it was to have, in an organized fashion, types of clubs, which would sponsor different kinds of activities, have their own parties, and when people came into a club, we would tell them what we expected from them, as far as their conduct, their discipline, and other do's and don'ts when they came to the Y.

The orbit room was down in the basement of the Y, right of from the gym, where the pool room used to be. The whole room was made like the inside of a space ship. So they called it the Orbit Room. We had hot dogs. We used to get donations from Jewel food store and places like that who would give us cases of beer. In fact, sometimes we would just go up and talk to the management and tell them that we were having a party and if there was anything they would like to donate, we would appreciate it. They usually would donate buns, hot dogs, drinks. We would take it up to the Y.

For two years a program called CETA, which was a government program, chose the Emerson Street Y. I was the director of this program. The Y was chosen because it was close to the kind of community for which the program was designed, and because it had facilities such as the swimming pool, gym, cafeteria, day care center. We had all of these facilities which were convenient for their program.

I had a staff, I had two people under me. We also had N.U. students who also came under the CETA program. They came over and got hours credit for working there in the summer in helping us manage this program. So, we tabled our program from June to about the first of October and ran the government program. We did this for about three years.

The government paid all the expenses for this program. We had to have a strict accounting for everything we spent money for, because the government audited records.

We would have to show them all the receipts that we had for money we spent.

One of the people we had from N.U. was from the business school and that person was assigned to audit the things that we did. Also, we gave a formal report every week to this person, and he sent this report to Washington, D.C.

So, this was a very good program, and I think it really benefited the kids.

We also had chaperones. We had a ruling set up that groups were notified in advance that their affairs would be chaperoned.

We set the programs up so that the kids sort of ran the programs themselves, although we monitored the programs. But if they couldn't get a chaperone, we could not have their function. What we tried to do was to train them to assume certain responsibilities.

One night I was there, and no chaperone showed up. The Y was packed with kids and they wanted to have a party. The group had been advised that the details of their affair, including the selection of a chaperone, had to be given to me at least a week before the party, but they had failed to do this, and no chaperone had been obtained.

Therefore, the party was denied. As a result, there were a lot of long faces, but that never happened again. I did teach them that it was their responsibility, their show, and if they miss one link in the chain then the whole thing falls apart.

That was in 1967.

I got married in 1953. I was working at the Y in 1952. I had my martial arts school there in 1954. I was there from about 1951 until the Y closed. I was the head counselor and youth director. Mr. Garnett was the counselor for the High Y boys. He did a wonderful job there. All of the boys liked him. He also was a photographer and took many pictures of the boys and girls in their activities. He was particularly helpful to me that one year when Jack Price hired me when I was the interim director there.

When Mr. Buley was there, we used to go, every year, to Muncie, Indiana. They would have an open house for us. We played a basketball game, and they would have a banquet hall there full of food for us. It was a wonderful trip.

We would rent a bus. Tom Garnett was with us every time and took pictures. This was the entire youth group from the Y.

The Tri Hi Y was the girls. One of their counselors was Winnie Collins, who went to Tempe, Arizona and graduated from college there. She was my assistant for a long time.

Having the boys and girls in supervised groups helped to control the conduct at the Y. If anything got out of had the Y was automatically closed when I was in charge. I would tell them, "You can have fun here but the minute something gets out of hand, "That's it. It's closed. And they knew that. Even the people out on the street would come in, and I knew who they were. I said, you are welcome here as long as you conduct yourself. So we had very few problems.

The boys under a certain age had to stay on the boy's side of the Y, and when they reached a designated age, they were permitted to enter the men's side. We had men living in the Y. Most of the men did not have their own TVs, so we had a central TV which was kept in a locker. The residents usually came down and sat in the lobby for as long as they wanted, even after the doors closed at 10:00 PM, when we put the young people out. That was their home. Nobody else went into the dormitory. That was locked.

They had a pool table and ping pong on the boy's side. When they went swimming, they went from the boy's side.

Lobby side was for visitors and adults who lived there.

There once was a pool table for adults down stairs on the same floor as the gym, until the Orbit room replaced it. Then we took the pool table out. The Orbit room became our youth center. Our youth director worked on the desk in the boy's lobby. He was a part-time employee, usually a college student. So, what he would do, if you signed up for a pool game, and you lost, you would leave the building, and not wander about the Y.

After ten o'clock, the adults could play ping pong, shoot pool, but before ten, this side of the Y was reserved for the youths.

Northwestern students were welcome to come to the Y and use the facilities when ever they wanted to, if they did not disturb the organized programs. In fact, my wife and I belonged to a young adult husband and wife group. We used to play badminton and swim. Johnny Raynor, the undertaker, Ted Boyd, and myself, Frank Reid, Norman Barber and his wife, and one of our fraternity brothers who just died, Bennet Gray.

We set aside one day a week for married adults. We had hot dogs, a grill for hamburgers, and the pop was always donated by someone from the Hilo store. They thought our program was so unique that they donated about forty-eight cans of pop to us. I would go up there once a week and get it. We would put it in the cooler and reserve it for our married group.

That was a very good group because it kind of brought the young adults into fold. We would eat and swim and so forth. As a result of this, all of these people bought Y memberships. They now had a reason to join.

My feeling is that the biggest thing that we could ever have lost in Evanston was when they closed this Y, because from ten to twelve hours a week, I taught martial arts at the Emerson Y, plus we had your adult and adult swim classes. These were women who did not want to be mixed with young kids.

They transferred me and gave me one hour at the Grove Street Y to teach martial arts when they closed this Y. That was the end of my martial arts class, for there was nothing we could do in one hour. When I left the Emerson Street Y, there was not one person in any of the programs that I managed there that followed me to Grove Street. Nobody did, and I used to ask kids and they would say they didn't want to come up there. They said, "I don't listen to their music," and each person felt that he was not wanted. You see, it is very difficult to change a person's feelings because you open the doors and say come on in, when you have sneered at them through a looking glass and made them feel unwelcome.

My personal feelings is that integration is fine, if you are going to give the same opportunities and have everybody intermingle and never think about the color of a man's skin. It's wonderful. You have a certain amount of pride in what you have. In all the years I went to the Y, I never thought about ever going anyplace else because I was happy with what I was doing.

Questions for Discussion
1. Describe Louis' coming to Evanston and entering elementary school and high school.
2. Why did Louis say he couldn't play on the Evanston High School tennis team?
3. When Louis completed his flight training, what responsibility did he assume at Clark Air Force Base?
4. What were Louis' responsibilities when he was employed by the Emerson Street Y?
5. Louis went to Ju Jitsu school in Japan and got his black belt. What position in the army did he get after he received his black belt?
6. When Louis became an employee of the Emerson Street Y, what were some of his responsibilities?
7. Describe Louis' martial arts program at the Y.
8. What are the levels of achievement in Judo before you get to black belt? What level is Louis now?
9. Louis was director of a program called CETA at the Y. What were some of their activities?
10. When the Emerson Street Y closed, Louis was asked to teach Judo one hour per week at the Grove Street Y. How did the kids from the Emerson Street Y respond to this move?

About Louis Moseley
Louis is a fraternity brother of mine. Our chapter is called Zeta Xi Lambda, and our national fraternity is Alpha Phi Alpha. In addition to this relationship, Louis has been a friend of my wife, Betty, since they were youngsters and lived in Chicago.

You must have enjoyed Louis' interview in which he shared his many interesting experiences. I hope the readers will appreciate the contributions Louis has made to the physical development, not only of himself but of others who have had the good fortune to benefit from his instruction.

Louis did not limit his interest and energy to physical challenges. He is a devoted churchman at St. Andrew's Episcopal Church.

A few weeks ago, Louis' wife, Joan, passed away unexpectedly. Louis was devastated, but he has recovered and is ready for more challenges.

Reverend John Norwood
Mt. Zion Missionary Baptist Church

My family and I came here in 1968 from Atlanta, Georgia, having lived in South Carolina, Alabama at Tuskegee Institute, then Evanston. When I came here in 1968, housing, open occupancy, really, we couldn't deal with that problem. They hadn't settled the question. The thing that fascinated me was the way they got around it. You would see a small house, worth then about thirty or forty thousand dollars, but when a black showed up, it went up to about one hundred thousand. A lot of the white realtors wouldn't take you to houses in white communities. There was a Mrs. Nixon who was a rebel realtor, I guess. Every white house that she could think of that was in the price range, she would carry us to see it, and would laugh and scoff at people who were reluctant to show it to us. But we finally bought from a German family on Fowler Avenue, which was fairly mixed at the time I came. There were three brothers, I think three houses, right in a row in the 1400 block on Fowler. The older brother was the last one to sell, and I bought that house directly from them. They wouldn't deal with a black realtor. Rather than let a black realtor handle it, they sold it themselves. But I had a black realtor, anyway, and forced them to pay the six percent commission to Fred Hunter. We became friends after that. Civil rights is my thing.

Black people moved in on Fowler, and all of them had a batch of children, like myself. All of those children have grown up now and gone, mine and all of them. We are getting a lot of Hispanics now with a lot of children.

We have had about two Hispanics who have become members of Mt. Zion, but they have sort of faded out. They would come in, stay a while, and kind of fade out. I have had several people from the Jewish religion become members. They were mostly men who were accompanied by black women.

We have had quite a few white people join this church. As a matter of fact, I have two white families coming now who are very consistent. It's the daughter who joined, not the parents. The daughter is just a teenager. She is friendly with a little black girl in the neighborhood.

They are always together. She said, "Can I join the church? I am white." I said, "Are you, really?" But she was just like all the other kids, hugging and kissing each other. Chances are that they had that kind of relationship with their neighbors. Some kinds you can tell are superficial, but others are genuine. They are the only child in each family, and they are really sisters. The black girl's mother is active in the church, but the white girl's mother is not. The congregation has changed tremendously. We don't have more than twenty of the older members who are still alive. All the members that we have now are relatively new, and joined since I have been here, which will be nineteen years in September. We have a completely new congregation, save for about twenty or twenty-five people. All the rest are completely new.

We had a telethon last night to all of our members. We are trying to build an education building, a 2.8 million dollar building on the back of the church. We are using the plans that were drawn by the founders of the church. The original plans called for a three story educational building. When the architectural plans were drawn for this building, they drew the plans for the education building. We have made only three changes in those plans, except putting in an elevator, which is required by law, and we are planning an atrium in the front, using more natural sunlight throughout the building.

In 1904 they had a vision that was far greater than one could imagine. We had copies of the actual plans. When you look at the dimensions, size, material, and all that kind of stuff, you can see how advanced they were mentally in their foresight in drawing the design for the new building and for the church. The thing that has always interested me is that we have only been able to maintain the building since I came here. The building had deteriorated. The pews were splintered and we had to take them out. The church had graveyard windows. I couldn't take them. There is not a drain plug anywhere in the church. So when water came in, you had to dip it out and mop it out. But beyond that, the building is solid and will last another one hundred years because of the condition of the building. We had to do a lot of maintenance and patching and stuff to get the church back to where, I think, now it is possibly one of the prettiest churches in town.

But the people who made all of this possible were the older members. The desire, the psychic, the taking religion as a viable part of their experience in sharing their relationship with God, that is vanishing now. The new breed has no ties, they feel that giving and religion are two separate things. They don't tie them together as one. So, I don't know where we are going in the next one hundred years, in terms of that kind of commitment. People like myself are old-timers. They don't hesitate to tell you that. On our telethon thing we had 140 thousand dollars pledged for cash. A doctor said to me, "Oh, that's great!" But to me, that's nothing. Out of eight hundred people, we only need two hundred people to give us 2,500 dollars. That's a half million dollars, and to me that should have been simple, easy. No one can tell me if we take an act of faith, or the second step of faith, and say twenty-five hundred dollars for the first phase, it's really nothing, nothing to give when we have had this church for one hundred years. You come in, and it's air-conditioned. The toilet facilities, the food we give to people, we are always helping people, and for a person to tell me, "I have to think about it." The schools are failing, no place for kids to go. We don't have a black place that is in a good community where you can go sit down to a meal. Our churches have to rent a hotel. We don't have services for senior citizens made available by the church, as it used to be in this church which was an institutional church. It provided those services. The building which we have deigned will have one office to be given to a gerontologist free. They must treat patients in this building at the lowest cost. We will take all risks. We bear all the burden. And all they have to do is treat people at a minimum cost and give them the kind of service that, hopefully, they won't have to go to some of these other offices and be patted on the head, etc.

Another thing is that we don't have a place for kids to go. The Jews teach their children before they are confirmed to their religion. Our kids are failing, and we don't have any place. We don't have any door that is open at little or no cost to parents to educate our children and pull them up, so that they can perform with anybody else in school. The little five hours spent in school is not enough. It is not going to do it. The kids are just not going to make it. And you've got to subsidize their education and pull them in. Our building will have legal classroom sizes. My intention is to start a school from the preschool through the fifth grade, and a have a tutoring program from the fifth grade to the twelfth grade.

The school will be staffed with professional teachers. That's needed, and for somebody not to see that need really makes me angry. I just don't think stupidity should reign that much. You go and buy a new car or a new refrigerator or whatever you need on a monthly basis, and when it comes to God, your life, you've got your future, who has everything that you have in His hands, and you are going to cheat yourself of an opportunity, to really rob yourself of an opportunity to trust God to help you build something that's going to be an asset to your community, it defies my understanding my reason, and my religion. I get mad. I get angry. It becomes difficult for me to understand. I started off, I pledged ten thousand dollars to be paid in ten months. Where in the world is my ten thousand going to come from? I don't know where it's coming from, but I know that every extra dime I get I pay on my pledge. I don't ask my members to give what I don't give. And I haven't had one single member to say "Well, Reverend, if you can pledge ten thousand and sacrifice, I am going to pledge ten thousand." Not a single one. Where is faith? Trust in God?

If the older members had been alive, there's no doubt about it, twelve years ago, I would have had those members to even will their homes. They would have willed their homes to build their church. That's commitment. That's faith. Since I have been here, I have seen the church and community go together.

When I first came to Evanston, they didn't have a black person on the school board. People asked me, "Why are you running for the school board?" I said, "I am a citizen. I'm of legal age. I have a right to." The whites really tried to beat me out of running. They said I didn't go before this committee or that committee. But I don't have to be legitimized by a committee. I am a citizen, and I am in good standing. So I ran, and I won. I served two terms. I came back and wasn't satisfied. We had never had a black run for mayor. I said, "Why not run for mayor?" Deep down in my heart, though, I knew I was not going to win. But the point wasn't winning. The point was I hoped that I would have ignited in some young person a desire to say, "Oh, he did it. He survived." Nothing happened. It didn't work the first time. The second time I ran it was the same thing. My own members didn't support me. They said, "We don't want to lose you as a pastor." That's stupid.

How stupid can you get? The person you have been running to for favors—"get me out of jail," "my son is in trouble," my daughter needs to go to the hospital," "this person has to be buried," "can you marry us?" They come into a place which you have developed, they see that you have changed and made it available to them and they don't want to "lose you."

The third time I ran, we finally got a black mayor. People were wrapped up around this sexist thing and what have you, and of course they finally got a black mayor. I think that they probably would not have had a black mayor if I had not kept running. But to get rid of the thorn in the flesh, white folks always empower a woman over a man. That hasn't changed. That was some South Carolina stuff. They always will do that. They will give a woman anything, but won't give a man a thing. I found that to be very present in Evanston, and just the reverse down South. I have a cousin who became the first senator since Reconstruction, state senator of Greenville, South Carolina. He ran in a white district and won overwhelmingly over four white candidates. I have a another school mate who is supreme justice of South Carolina. I have another school mate who is the secretary of the bar association of South Carolina. I see the legal system there hires black men, while the other systems shut them off.

Evanston, I think, is unique in the sense that people are so complacent. The fighters who make the shakers are gone. We don't have persons even striving to get in the limelight or not just in the limelight, but get in position to make decisions and make changes. I haven't seen it.

Integration

There was a black woman on that school board, a Mrs. Eason. One of the struggles I have always had about integration, I never thought that it was workable, because of the housing and stuff. I never thought it was workable because I don't think the white people, though well intended, knew black children well enough to really be interested in them to the point of caring. And when Evanston went all out, it maintained its position as a head light school district, head of the nation in terms of policy changes in racial relationships. That was Coffin's concept. He wanted to be out there and ahead of the law.

My best understanding of it is, when I go down South, I watch the clouds as if it is going to rain. I try to run ahead of the storm and keep ahead of the shower. Coffin stayed ahead of the shower. As a result, he got a reputation in the district. But we have too many ethnic groups for it to really work. We have the Jewish community, whose influence was very strong, also we had the whites, then we had the blacks, so when the push became a shove, everything the blacks owned became of no value. Black schools, etc. lost all of their value. Of course, to me there was another manifestation of a seal of superiority of anything the white folks touch. So, as a matter of fact, our children are going backwards.

The remediation funds from the federal government, to me, was a disaster. You know, they give your money to teachers to teach speech therapy and all this kind of stuff. The people in the schools made proposals and got all this money and they didn't do any therapy. So the district in Evanston became loaded with specialists doing nothing. We should be one of strongest school districts in the nation because of the federal funds that were made available because of the integration.

Ida Lawler, proposal writer for District 65, was an excellent writer, and she got all kinds of funds, billions of dollars. They had this hearing specialist, this visual specialist, this reading specialist, writing specialist. But our kids started going backwards. And only a few profited from that, and those few were from the Jewish community, and the white community. And blacks were selected, one or two, and at the most three to participate in the project.

When it was over, and they lost their funds, then they started talking about the gap, and I think it's a direct result of the lack of teaching with inspiration of children, lack of knowing who the kids are.

I served as a principal in South Carolina for three years, back in the fifties. My contention was that you couldn't teach students you didn't know, and I required all of my teachers to visit the homes of their students. You can't do that now, because the unions won't let you. But that was the requirement. When we sat on the board with the superintendent, the two questions I always asked were, "How many black homes have you visited to have dinner?" "How many black churches have you worshipped in?" And, if you hadn't done any of that, to me, you weren't qualified. I don't care how many degrees you have. But if you have been invited to a black home to have dinner, somebody has accepted you as a real friend and has seen you as a person, rather than as a white man.

I have never voted for anybody for superintendent who has not spent an hour in a black home for a meal with the family, or has not spent an hour in the church worshipping, at the invitation of, or on their own. So, integration has been a curse to Evanston, and a curse across the nation.

Maddox, in Georgia, did more for education in the South, I think, than any other person. And he was a "nigger" hater. But his premise was "Give him a trade. If he is not going to college, give him a trade." So he built trade schools all over the state. Make them available. Don't make kids have to leave home to learn a trade. There are trade schools all over Georgia, all over South Carolina. Every little town of any size, five thousand, six thousand or more, you can go to a trade school, state owned and operated. So a child is measured to see where he is academically and where he is skill wise. They test them to see what strengths they have. And if they have good use of their hands, or with metal, take up trade school, take up metal.

We tried to get a trade school here, but that was embarrassing. They couldn't do that. So what we have got now is people maybe three generations later, out on the street and can't do anything. Their eyes are not coordinated, their hands are not coordinated, they can do nothing. One time some group went so far as to get some union to say "Yes, we will let some of them come in." But the high school fought it. They didn't want it. So, integration for us in Evanston, I think, has been a red curse.

We don't know literature any more. We don't know geography anymore.

Lack of Activities for Youth

There are no places for kids to participate in activities such as skating, pool, or do anything but basketball, perpetuating the "Michael Jordan Syndrome"—plenty of basketball. That's all. And if a girl doesn't play basketball, she is out. There are no tennis courts.

We tried to save the Emerson Street Y building, but Hari Krishnas bought it.

Prentis

What had happened, the Grove Street Y was really carrying the Emerson Street Y and we were a liability to them, because we weren't able to do our share in the black community. So they wanted to sell it to us, at first. They offered it to us for thirty thousand dollars. We didn't have enough blacks with the backbone to get it.

Foster Center

There was a white woman, Alice Kramer, who didn't want Foster School opened, and got in with Martha Fromberg, who was the president of the board. Martha got John Buck, and they came back and switched the decision we had made. They closed it. After we closed it, I got Bishop Moody who was interested in starting a school at that time. I was interested, but serving on the board, I couldn't. He had gone much further with his proposal. I had just started getting all of the papers together to file, papers that he already had prepared. They said, "We will sell you this building for 100,000 dollars." We finally got them down because of the repairs that had to be made and maintenance required. Bishop Moody decided that the cost was too great, so he withdrew his interest.

Then the Family Focus Community organization came up. Bert and myself said, "Let's get Foster School." Everybody in that meeting began to say, "That is a white elephant. Why do you want a white elephant?" Bert backed down, but I said, "I am not going to back down. That building has potential. It is there, and eventually we can own it." The white people who were paying the rent on Church Street were going to give us some money to get Foster School. So we kept on talking about it. I finally went and talked to the Wisebergs. I asked him what he would do if his name was written on something in the black community and would be there as long as the city of Evanston. He said, "What are you talking about?" I said, "Foster School."

So, one night we were at the school board meeting, they agreed to sell the building for 100,000 dollars with ten thousand dollars required for earnest money. Mr. Wiseburg called me to him and gave me a check for 100,000 dollars and said, "Here, take this check up there and see what they say." I looked at it, and there was 100,000 dollars on the check. It cut all of the argument completely out.

Then some of us were saying in the black community, "Why don't we buy it from them." I don't think we got ten thousand dollars pledged. It would have been a good chance for the black community to have a center with a central building that could house everything they had to offer. The spirit is not there. There is no interest there. Just think about how little money you are talking about. If just two hundred people give 2,500 dollars, they could buy and repair the building and have one of the finest centers anywhere in the country.

I just don't think the blacks in Evanston are putting their resources where they ought to be, for the good of the community.

Save for black churches, I don't know if there is that much more community property owned by blacks.

This church owns two houses. We did own four, and we divested of two. These two were given to us by whites. They were houses that they were renting to blacks and the blacks died. They said, "Reverend, would you accept this house in the memory of the Kellys?" I said, "Of course." They said, "I will renovate it, it will only take about fifteen or twenty-five thousand dollars to renovate it, and I'll deed it to the church, title free." This was just a token of expression of love for the Kellys. Then our members said, "Why don't you sell it?" The house needs some work done on it. They wanted to get some engineers in on it. I said, "No, all we have to do is to jack the house up and pour a stronger foundation." It was on sand, and you know sand had gotten wet for a long time and had gotten soft.

I jacked the house up myself, and poured some cat feet foundation under that. The house is still sitting there. Nobody came to me and said, "Reverend, you saved us a house." Nobody. Not a single [person] out of eight hundred people. Then they said, "How come you aren't charging that woman more rent?" "That must be his girlfriend." So, the kind of mentality that is in Evanston, for most people, it's "I." It's what "I" can get. There is not a sharing, or a real community spirit.

At my last campaign, I spent ten thousand of my own personal money. I knew I wasn't going to win, but I just didn't want to have a ridiculous campaign. You would think all of the professional people in Evanston know what it costs, and that some of them would say, "Hey, Pastor, we are going to give you a hundred dollars." But, nothing. Nothing. So, there isn't a mind set that gives to the community, to want to leave something to posterity. I don't see that spirit.

Social Environment

Social life is limited because there is nothing available or accessible. After you leave the church, it's like it was before, they have a theater up on Central Street. They have a theater on Chicago Avenue, special plays and some live theater. Besides that, there are no other avenues for socialization. They have beaches, but I haven't been to the beach since my children left home thirteen years ago. The lake front is not that accessible to you. So families are no longer encouraged to go down there. There is no zoo or anything like that here. From my vantage point, unless you have something like a little education or the desire to really expose yourself and your children, there is nothing to do. As a result, I think one reason that we are becoming a hotbed with gangs and drugs is because the alternatives are not present. We have the ice rink on Main Street for ice skaters in the summer that is a structured fee, etc. Most black kids are not interested in ice skating in the summer.

African-American Ministers Alliance

African-American Ministers Alliance is a direct reflection of what the Evanston community is. It's not doing anything. It doesn't hardly meet. It's really sad. This is the only place that I have ever known where they have never had any real ministerial alliance that had any influence, that had had any real feeling among the brothers and sisters of the alliance.

They are still fighting on the women's issue. There are still some who feel that women should not be preaching. They are resentful of them coming to the meetings and having anything to say. All have little or no vision when it comes to giving, except one or two. We started a food program here several years ago and after we had gotten the forms and had established the bylaws, tax exemptions, etc., I turned it all over to the Ministerial Alliance. But it got stuck. Now it's gone.

We started the Alliance going from church to church. We met here several times. One of the ministers decided that he wanted to have it at his church. Then he started charging for it, that negative attitude. It got to the place where I just don't go. When you go in for a devotion and sit down and share some theological understanding, the whole thing is on dealing with what your are going to do with this or that, when you really are going to do nothing. We tried making a benevolent pool, that every fifth Sunday of the year, or every fourth Sunday of the month, all of the churches would take a free will offering and send it to the Alliance treasury, and we would send everybody who comes to the church for assistance to the Alliance. I think his church and my church were the only two churches that ever made a contribution to that fund. Nobody else did, so we stopped. It's a direct reflection of where the leadership is in this community. It's almost nil and void and sad.

Questions for Discussion

1. Describe Reverend Norwood's move to Evanston in 1968.
2. To what extent has Mt. Zion become integrated?
3. How has the congregation changed in the last twenty years?
4. In what ways has the church deteriorated, according to Reverend Norwood?
5. Why is Reverend Norwood discouraged by the poor response he has received in his campaign for funds to improve and expand the church?
6. What are some of the services he hopes the church will provide with

the addition of a new building?
7. Describe Reverend Norwood's venture into school and city politics.
8. What are some of the reasons Reverend Norwood believes true integration in the Evanston schools is not workable?
9. Why does Reverend Norwood believe that "Governor Maddox in Georgia did more for education in the South than any other person?"
10. Why does Reverend Norwood believe that remediation funding from the federal government was a disaster?
11. What efforts were made by Evanston blacks to buy Foster School? Why weren't they successful?
12. Describe the way Mt. Zion Baptist Church became owners of rental property.
13. What is Norwood's criticism of the black social environment in Evanston?
14. How effective is the influence of the African-American Ministers Alliance in Evanston?

About Reverend John Norwood

Prentis Bryson, an associate of mine, accompanied me to interview Reverend Norwood. It was a morning meeting, and Reverend Norwood was in coveralls and getting ready to do some physical chores around the church. That was characteristic of Reverend Norwood because he was always ready to take the lead in doing something that he thought had to be done. He hoped the congregation would follow his example.

Reverend Norwood was installed pastor of Mt. Zion Missionary Baptist Church on April 5, 1978. He had served as a school principal, pastorates in South Carolina and Georgia, district superintendent in Alabama, interim president of Gammon Theological Seminary, and retired as assistant secretary of the General Council on Finance and Administration of the United Methodist Church.

This was my first meeting with Reverend Norwood, and I was impressed with his ambition, determination, and frankness.

Dan Phillips

I got to Evanston because my wife and her family lived in this area. My home is Pennsylvania. That's where I was born and raised and went to school, and I met my wife in Pennsylvania, but we got married here in 1940. We moved back to Pennsylvania to live. We lived there for two years and since my wife was an only child and her mother was living here by herself and wasn't in the best of health, and my wife was coming back and forth to see her, when we came here on vacation one summer, in 1942, I said that if I found a decent job, maybe I will quit my job in Pennsylvania and move here. So I did. I read an ad in the *Tribune* that was advertising for a person. I applied for it and I got hired. We packed up all of our stuff and moved here and have been here ever since.

We lived briefly with my wife's mother in the twenty hundred block of Dodge Avenue. Then we all moved to a large place on Emerson Street. Then we bought a house at 1830 Laurel Avenue, where we still live.

The neighbors have had a few excursions at organizing a block club. They weren't too tightly organized, and usually their programs were mostly a backyard picnic or barbecue, or something like that once a year. Maybe if there were some city-wide issues, a half a dozen of us would get together and talk about it.

Business and Professional People

I was a good friend of Dr. Frye for a long time. He and Dr. Gatlin and I used to play a lot of volleyball and basketball together at the YMCA and at the Grove Street Y.

Dr. Bryant was our family doctor. My experience goes to the fact that for medical care in Evanston, African-Americans could not go to the Evanston Hospital at that time. My first child was born in 1946, and Dr. Bryant was our doctor. We lived on the same block. Something was wrong with his car, so I picked him up, and he and my wife drove down to the Provident Hospital. That was the nearest place he could get service. So my oldest child was born at the Provident Hospital.

That was one experience which was probably a hardship in relation to medical treatment in Evanston. At that time the Community Hospital was not up to par. It was an outlet for the black doctors and it was inferior in equipment, so Dr. Bryant chose to go down to Provident as the best choice.

Over the years I have done business with the black business people in Evanston. I was on the board of ECDC, the Economic Development Corporation. It was federally financed and aimed at neighborhoods and areas that needed economic and financial support to develop. The office, with about three to seven employees, was located at the corner of Dodge Avenue and Church Street. The building was owned by the city, and the city contributed a portion toward this operation. The main purpose of ECDC was helping the minority business men to improve their condition and business. It operated for about twelve or fifteen years. The funds dried up, as most federal funds are these days.

They did a variety of things. Among them was to help business people in the area to get loans at very low interest rates to improve the facades of their businesses. They also helped with job training type programs for minorities.

This activity took place back in the late seventies and eighties. In fact it has only been closed down since about 1985.

Question: Does it appear that in the black community now there is as much business activity as there used to be?

I don't think so, because restrictions have loosened up, you don't have to stay in your neighborhood to buy or sell. People are more comfortable going down town to Davis Street and shopping for the best service at the best place. Now most of the small businesses in the African-American neighborhoods are owned by Asians, Arabians, or other foreigners.

Employment
I am in real estate now, as a retirement job. I was plant manager of Federal Tool and Plastics for the Evanston plant. This plant was located at 1618 Hartrey Avenue at Hartrey and Seward, just North of Oakton Street. We were adjacent to the Rustoleum plant. Our plant employed about one hundred to one hundred fifty people. We were doing electroplating on plastics.

I took a job when I first came here. I answered an ad in Chicago for a job with a company on the West side. I worked for them about five years. I was the chief chemist in charge of their laboratories. They were a metal stamping house and did electroplating. Back during the war, everything we did had to be related to government projects. This was a pretty big outfit with over five hundred employees. In our electroplating department we must have had about one hundred employees. I had charge of the laboratory control of the electroplating process. Most of our work was with parts for radio and radar. Our customers were Zenith, Motorola, Philco, and other companies like that. We made the parts, stamped them out in steel and electroplated them with whatever plating was called for. We did zinc plating, cadmium plating, copper plating, chrome plating, nickel plating, gold plating, silver plating, etc.

I left there and I went with a couple of guys from the company and we started our own company. I was president of the corporation. We named it Lincoln Plating Company because I graduated from Lincoln University in Pennsylvania. That's my alma mater, Lincoln University. So we started the company as the Lincoln Plating Company and we stuck together for eight or nine years. Our first operation, we bought out another small plating company on the North side of Chicago. It was on Lincoln Avenue, just North of Belmont Avenue. We were there for several years, then we moved near downtown on Kenzie Street, just across the street at the back of the Merchandise Mart. We had a pretty good operation going there.

About that time, the Korean War was going on, and when those kinds of emergencies start, the particular chemicals or metals that are necessary become scarce and, unless you are working on a government job, then you can't get the materials you need, so we really had to stop the operation, because we couldn't buy the chemicals that we needed.

So we closed that place, and I went to work for another plating and stamping outfit on the West side of Chicago, U.S. Plating and Mfg. Co. I managed their plant for several years. It was a much larger operation. We had put in a lot more automatic equipment for the production line. We had three shifts, twenty-four hours a day.

About that time, I was active in the National Organization of American Electroplates Society. Things were developing in research which I wanted to get involved in. The owner of the U.S. Plating Company didn't want to spend the money to become involved, so I knew another company out in Franklin Park, MSL Plastics, and they were interested in having someone run their plating operation and also incorporate plating on plastics. Plating on plastics is contrary to what electroplating is expected to be, because electroplating is a process of running electrical current through a part, and by electrolysis, to plate another metal on top of something else. It was quite an involvement learning how to do this. Plastic is a natural insulator, and we had to convert it to become a conductor. I got involved and did some research on that. So I left U.S. Plating Company, because I wanted to learn this process and move in that direction. So, for the rest of my career I was in some type of plating on plastics.

The MSL Plastics Company out in Franklin Park wasn't in a very good position because it was a company that was composed of two different plastic companies which had come together. The factions in each company were fighting each other, and production was poor because of that. I came from the outside and didn't belong to either of those companies, so I wasn't involved, but I wasn't getting anything done either. I found out about another job here in Evanston, The Federal Tool and Plastics. Their main office was in Lincolnwood, but they had this operation in Evanston on Hartrey Avenue. Through the American Electroplating Society and the Society for Electroplating Plastics, I met the guy who was the vice president of Federal Tool and Plastics and he invited me to come over and work with him. So I did and stayed there my last twenty years.

I learned a lot of innovative things in plating there. The company was bought out by Ethyl Corporation. They branched out and were buying up plastics, molding companies and that sort of thing. So they bought Federal Tool and Plastics and they were in the process of moving it to their headquarters in Baton Rouge, Louisiana, and since I had reached the age for early retirement, I opted to take that. That is when I resigned.

At that time I was also a member of the Rotary Club in Evanston. I was at lunch one day with Walter Keem, who was the president of Cyrus and I said, "After the first of the year, I am retiring and I am exploring about what I am going to do." I had been doing some consulting then in electroplating, and I could have continued and expanded in electroplating consulting, but it called for a lot of traveling. One day I was in Detroit. The next day I was Louisville. The next day I would be someplace else. At sixty years old, that's not as glamorous as it would be if I were much younger. So, Walter said, "Why don't you come on into real estate?" I said, "I don't know. I will think about it." He said, "Come over to my office and I will tell you all you need to know in one half hour." So I did. I went over to his office. At that time he was managing the Wilmette office. We had two offices then, this one here and the one at Wilmette. So, we sat and talked for a while, and by the first of the next week, I was enrolled in the courses I needed to get my state license to sell real estate. Since 1980, I have been here. I have enjoyed it. It's a lot of fun, because in all of the years prior to this I was under the pressure of profit and loss statements and corporate managers, presidents and vice-presidents looking over your shoulders at your sheets and your production and your corporate percentage all that kind of stuff. I was on call, even though my office hours might have been eight to five, but I was managing a twenty-four hour operation five, six, or seven days a week sometimes. I wasn't there all the time, but I had supervisors, superintendents, and foremen running the operation on different shifts. It was still my responsibility. I would go out in the evening with my family and get home about midnight and instead of going to bed, I would run down to the plant to see what was going on. Those were the kinds of things you had to do.

But when I got into real estate, it was a completely different picture. I am responsible for one man. That one was me. I set my own schedule, my own time. Of course, that is good and bad too. On the bad side, you have clients who are really telling you what they want and when they want it. They are the boss, but you do have control over adjusting the appointment. I can say, "I can set an appointment with you for two o'clock this afternoon," but you might want to come at noon. I would say, "I am sorry, I have something else to do now." It might be a basketball game. It might be a tennis match. It might be that I just want to lie down and rest. It is up to me. So I have enjoyed it.

Question: Have the markets been open, as far as prospective black purchasers of property on the North Shore or any place in particular where they are not as open as they are in, other places?

Well, there is, and there always has been, to a degree either covertly, or openly, different types of prejudices. You really have to be alert to watch for it. In this business I am on the board of directors of the North Shore Board of Realtors. That is all the Realtors between Chicago and Wisconsin. I got elected to the board of directors, because for five years I was chairman of The Equal Opportunities Committee of the North Shore Board. I blew the whistle a few times on other realtors and had some hearings to straighten out some matters, but in most cases, especially on the North Shore, the owners and operators are wise enough and savvy enough that they don't let themselves get caught in anything that is overt. How much of it goes on in conversations at cocktail parties between individuals, you never really know.

I have tried to really stress the fact that you should be loyal to yourself, be loyal to your family, be loyal to your personal finances, and be able to account for what you have done. It's not easy. My dad was steel worker. I didn't have much, but my dad was very close on how he handled his money. We learned that from him. I have seen some very good examples of that. The other day, a young couple came in here to see me, whom I had just sold some property to. A black couple. They are now living in Minneapolis, Minnesota, and doing very well. They came here from New Jersey. He is now working with a finance company in Minneapolis and he is making a very good salary. He is a good example. Of course, he was in financing. He was in banking. He came here to work for Continental Bank.

I see a lot of that. But I still see a lot of our people who would rather flash their money, show their money than save it.

Going back to the Civil Rights days, the late sixties and early seventies, when here in Evanston our so called black leaders were pounding their chests and wearing their afros and dashikis and getting on top of the desks in the city council building and all this kind of thing, I met with them. Most of them were younger than I was. Men like Ronald Lee, Bru Alexander. They would say, why don't you say this and that. I said, "Look, number one, I can make more progress negotiating with a man or a couple of men across the table with a cup of coffee between us than I can by running up and down the street shouting and making a lot of noise. Number two, you get a job over here in this plant, but what are you doing? What is your job?" They were seldom production line type jobs. They were service jobs. They were jobs that were not necessary. They gave you a desk. They gave you a telephone. They gave you some paper to shuffle.

But two things are going to happen. One, they are going to find out that all this noise you have been making doesn't get you anything. It's a lot of fake. Number two, they will find out that you don't know anything. Number three, they are going to find out that they don't need you. You are not the one who is making a profit for that company, and all a corporation needs is people who are going to supply something that's going to make money for the company. They will find out in a hurry that the little job you are doing over there in personnel is not important. That little job you are doing over here in publications is not important. They don't need you. They need the guys who are engineers, or a guy who is going to design a product or improve a product, or get the production out so that they can ship it and sell it and get the money. Just as soon as things begin to level off and find out that they don't need to be afraid of you anymore, because you are nothing but noise, anyhow, they are going to start firing.

That is exactly what happened; they had overstocked their company with personnel that they didn't need.

We have to compete.

I came from a small town, Sharon, Pennsylvania. In my high school, in my graduating class there were three hundred. Three of us were black, all boys, and we were in three different fields. The whole school had only about twelve blacks. Just like any other association between the two races, they looked down their noses at the blacks to start with. At that time, I decided that to beat me, you had to beat the heck out of me. I am not going to let you side step me. I am not going to let you go around me. You have got to come through me, or over me.

Before I graduated, I was captain of the track team. I was co-captain of the football team. I was treasurer of our senior class. These were things I did because I just kept busy. I kept active, and I developed skills. And those same skills I have been using ever since then.

I haven't been in any group or association that I haven't been a leader. I figure that if I am in something, or involved, I am going to give it all I've got. I'm competing all the time.

I'll be eighty years old my next birthday. I play tennis with guys who are forty or forty-five. I get tired, and I don't apologize for it. I puff and blow, but I am giving it all I've got.

I was the first black or white when we organized the park and recreation work. That was started through a referendum, city wide. Gene Beck recommended me. There were five people appointed by the mayor, and I was one of them. At one of the first meetings, Joe Rose who was the city commissioner at the time, said, "Dan, what is it your people want?" I said, "Before we go any further, let us get something straight, I was appointed by the mayor to serve the city of Evanston as a member of this committee. He didn't say anything about anybody's people, or anybody's ward. He said, "The city of Evanston, and I intend to serve the city of Evanston. And I am going to make a decision on everything that happens in the city of Evanston, from Howard St. to Wilmette. So let's get that straight. My people are the same as your people. All of the people want the best. There was a lot of apologizing and turning red in the face and all of that. Then I said, "Now that we are friends, let's get this thing going."

I stayed on the recreation board for eighteen years. I was president for ten years.

Then I was on the school board.

When my oldest daughter got ready to go to Foster School, I was concerned about my little five-year-old girl. I went to Oscar Schute who was superintendent. He and I sat there from nine o'clock until almost noon, talking about what I didn't like and things I wasn't going to stand for, and if it wasn't made right I was going to take my kid out of school, and put her in a private school, or a Catholic School. So we sat there and exchanged ideas. He said, "Write these things down, and I agree with you about this" and so on.

I said, "the principal is a crime. The lack of respect she has for the black people out there is a shame." Before we left, by noon that morning, he said, "I tell you what, if you promise me to get involved with parents in the schools, I'll promise you to take care of these things that I do agree with you on and are delinquent, and start right away." We shook hands. Oscar Schute and I are friends today. I had lunch with him last week. That's what got me started in the schools.

He got rid of the principal at the end of the year. That was her last year.

Another of my complaints was about Foster School getting all of the old books from the other schools. They stopped that. They got new books shipped in to Foster. I didn't like the idea that the junior high kids, seventh and eighth graders, were retained at Foster, while at other schools, the seventh and eighth graders went to Haven or Nichols. So he stopped that immediately, by the next year.

So, I became a member of the PTA, and I went to the city-wide PTA meetings. They said to someone, "Who is the ultimate authority in the school system?" They said, "The school board." I said, "How do you get on the school board?" They said, "There is a caucus, you have to get in the caucus." I said, "OK, I'm going to be Foster's delegate to the caucus." So, I became a member of the caucus. Then I found out that the ones who made the decisions were on the executive committee consisting of eight people. So I politicked to get elected to the executive committee. From then on, I was one who was making the decisions. I said, "Where are the blacks?" That was in 1963. I stayed on the High School Board for twenty-five years. I served about eight or ten years as president of the board. In the main hall of the high school, right by the superintendent's office, there is an oil painting of me, a life size painting.

So, you see, those are things you can do. You have to persevere. Some times you have to take a lot of crap, but as long as you are wading through crap and know where you goal is, you never give up. Back in 1989 the mayor proclaimed and the school supported a Dan Day. All Sunday, they had an afternoon program, a dinner in the high school, and presented this painting, which I didn't know they were making.

When I went on the board, they had only one black teacher. That was Charley Thomas. So, one of the first questions I raised was how do we search for teachers. Dr. Hall was assistant superintendent in charge of personnel and he made a tour of all the major universities every spring picking out top graduates. So, I suggested, and he accepted, including in his tour visiting Howard University, Fisk University, and I got him to include three or four black colleges in his tour. Out of that we began to hire one or two more blacks here and there, and we soon had a pretty good representative number of blacks coming in from good schools, good representatives. It increased to where we had a black woman as superintendent.

Dr. Magett became a principal. The school was divided up into four schools, and we had four different principals. We had, at one time, two black principals at the same time, Tom Cross and Mac Nash. Then Magett took over for Tom Cross when he left town. So we had several principals. We have had several other principals then. Right now, up until today, Denise Martin, an Evanston kid, is an associate principal in charge of the Freshman School, which is one of the top jobs that blacks have at that school today.

Margaret Labat became superintendent of District 202 a few years back. She didn't last too long. She was not quite prepared for the type of school that Evanston had. There are people who did make it easier for her, but she didn't make it easy for herself, because she didn't have her arms out, she had her fists punching. That was her attitude and that doesn't get you very far. Back to what I was saying before, you can get a lot further by sitting down, one on one with a cup of coffee or a sandwich between you and talking sense, than you can by being confrontational.

Of course, times and attitudes changed nationwide. At one period there we were, back in the late sixties and early seventies, in what I referred to as the revolutionary war. There were three different revolutions going on. There was the youth revolution. There was the teacher's revolution, they were demanding to be heard. And then there was the black revolution. All of this was going on at the same time. This was the time when I was elected president of School Board 202. The elected me president because I was the only black on the board. I said, "In the first place, you guys are afraid of the competition with the citizens and you think I can act as moderator between whites and blacks." One of the members said, 'Well, you are the bridge between us. You can stand on both sides of the issues and talk to both sides. You are the bridge between the whites and the blacks and the blacks and the whites."

That was the time when I called a meeting of the board and some times people in the audience would come marching in carrying signs and demanding this and demanding that. It was not an easy time.

But we got through it without anything serious happening. We never had a strike. That was the first time the teachers union began to negotiate with the board. I headed that up. The first negotiation between the teachers and the board was when I was president. We had some tough times, but we were able to keep everything under control.

Dr. Coffin's Effort to Integrate the Evanston Schools

I think integration could have been done better and smoother, if somebody else had been involved, besides Coffin. Coffin came in and was going to be the "white savior." A lot of his stuff was phoney. A good example. When he came in, he gave Joe Hill a job with the title of assistant to the superintendent, and Joe and many of his supporters were very inflated. So I called Joe aside one time and said, "Joe, do you know what that title is?" He said, "Yes, assistant superintendent." I said, "Assistant superintendent is just glorified way of calling you an office boy. That's all it is. You are a go-for." His eyes popped. I then said, "What authority do you have? Who can you hire? Who can you fire?" That's the same thing I was talking about when Bru Alexander and those guys were raising all of that fuss. Some will throw a title at you, give you a white shirt and a desk. That's not a job. It's camouflage. And if the white folks have done anything, they pulled that over our heads and we ate it up, lock, stock and barrel. And that's what we did with Coffin. They embraced Coffin like he was Jesus, and Coffin didn't mean any of them any good. It was a shame.

Oscar Schute had started a plan of integration, which finally developed, but being a conservative and older guy, he was trying to do it the way he thought was right. Of course, when the revolution started, that was too slow. Of course, when Oscar Schute saw that what he was doing was not going to be acceptable, he resigned. That's when they hired Coffin.

I was at some social affairs with Coffin. Coffin had more disheiks than I had. He was trying to emulate and imitate and act like he was one of the boys.

Back to the Kids

I don't think that integration hurt the kids. Our black kids have not grown academically the way we had hoped they would, but it goes back predominately to their parents. It's not the schools. It's the parents. The schools are not breaking their backs to make you learn. They shouldn't have to. If you are coming from a home where you have some discipline and your parents demand that you be respectful to yourself and to other people, you will make more progress in school than if those demands are not made upon you at home.

I have been on cases where we almost begged the kids to go into some of the higher or honor classes, and they didn't want to. When they don't want to, it's because they are lacking parental support or they are afraid of their peers. They are afraid of the other black kids who think that they are trying to "be somebody." "Who do you think you are?"

Our Problems Still Lie with Us

How many kids had I talked with when I was on the school board? I was always involved with athletics. I was always a big supporter of the athletic teams because I was an athlete in my life, but my father said, "If you don't keep your grades up, you can't play football." It didn't have to be in the rule books. That was my rule at home. Father's rule was, "If you don't do you chores at home, you don't play football or track or any other sports." But the kids don't get that anymore. No one demands them to do the right thing.

I was the oldest child in my family. There were six of us. I was the one responsible. I was in high school at the time. I guess I was playing out in the streets and my family had gone to church. I came in and I had forgotten that I was supposed to scrub the kitchen, so that night after I had gone to bed, my father pulled the covers off me and made me get up and do my chores. I didn't forget anymore.

Question: What are some of the serious problems that threaten the community?

Part of the problem is we are not concentrating enough on one central point or central location.

It used to be the churches, and it still is the churches, but the churches are not really as magnetic as they once were. It used to be that no family did anything socially that was not dictated by the church.

As a result of school integration, the unfortunate part was that integrating weakens the blood lines. Of course, that's what Hitler said. Mixing with other environments, mixing with diversities, takes away the strength of the African-American life. Our social life was much more ethnically strong and satisfying, or probably satisfying, when the big event was a dinner at the Emerson Street YMCA. When the women dressed up in their best clothes and best dresses to go to the Annual Dinner at the YMCA. Nowadays there are very few times when we have a big affair that is all black.

I belong to the Rotary Club. We had a big formal party up at the Botanical Gardens. All of the black members were there with their wives, but we were only ten percent of the crowd.

The same was true at something at the school. When they have a big affair, its naturally integrated. There is strength in diversity, but we lose the strong African-American type culture that we are used to.

Question: Do you think that the blacks who are integrated into these wider societies have the tendency to lose their identity with the black community?

Yes, I think so. I think so at least in the eyes of the black community, but not necessarily in their eyesight.

I go back to the Rotary Club as an example, where there are black members.

Ted Downing is president of the Bank One. Sonny Robinson is the richest black man on the North Shore. They are involved in anything that might come up that's all black or all African-American, but they are also just as involved, or more so, involved in diverse situations. I don't think that makes them any less concerned about their black neighbors or black friends.

Question: Can you say that their integrated activities take so much of their time and energy that they don't have as much energy to spend on the black community?

That could be true because the energy, time, and money are limited and you must spend it or use it where you think it does the most good for you and the group. You can't do it for the group, if you are not enjoying it yourself.

The social affairs that are all black are usually focused, either around the fraternity or sorority, or clubs like Bachelors and Benedicts, Links, Chessmen, FAAM (Federation of African American Men) which deals mostly with kids. They do a good job. There is a case of reverse identity. You would be surprised how many whites are being attracted into FAAM. One of the things that FAAM does is that it runs a basketball program all year long, for girls and boys from fifth grade up through high school. The guys like Gene Bell, Bill Logan serve as coaches and as leaders. Right now, I would say that The FAAM league activities are about one third white. Their parents come to support and contribute time and money to FAAM. They have been busy now for the last twenty years.

Question: How can we counter act the tendency for young men to form gangs and engage in delinquent kinds of activities?

Well, it's a tough battle. To tell you the truth, FAAM is doing something, also the Chessmen are doing something. The YMCA is doing something. They are having what they call The Outward Bound Program. Those are all groups that are working. I am president of a group called YOU, Youth Organization Umbrella. What we do is work with kids at risk. If there is a problem, we try to solve that problem right away. If a kid gets in a gang, he is looking for somebody to solve his problem. He is looking for support.

Right here, Walter Keith, the guy who is president of our company, is in a mentoring program connected with the School District 65. His wife is a teacher, and she got him involved because she has some black kids her class who need mentoring. No male images were in their families.

Walter takes this little black kid, whose whole family siblings are involved in gangs or in trouble, his sister had a baby and all are living together with an elderly mother who can't control any of them. Walter goes over there and takes this kid every Saturday. He spends a whole day with him. Now he is playing softball with him. He plays soccer with him. He takes him, as if he was his father, to all of his practices. He takes him out to eat. Since I get passes to the high school football and basketball games, I took both of them to New Trier to a football game, and we all sat together.

If you take these kids and give them role model images, this is what a man is supposed to act like, to look like, to be like, to talk like, the only way you can do it is to do it with them. You can't write it out and say, go home and read this. That won't work.

Like you and I were saying, we got started because we had a role model at home. We had strong arm at home. They don't have that at home. They probably have a one-parent family, or maybe a one-grandparent family for many of these kids, because the mother who had them wasn't old enough to have them in the first place. And she doesn't know what to do with them except throw them some food. That's where the problems are. If we could work with groups like FAAM, Chessmen, and the YMCA. We could help a lot.

Question: What about the churches? Can they help?

The churches are not doing as much as they should. Too many ministers are caught up in "I." They all want to be king. They want to be emperors. They want to turn that church into fiefdom. This is not what Christianity is all about. A lot of people don't like the idea, but I worked hard in the AME Church. I held every office in the Bethel AME Church, and the appreciation you get, the cooperation you get? Maybe one or two here or there. They take me for granted.

I have been a member of the church at the corner of Hinman and Church for the last four or five years now. I am doing everything there. I am accepted there and I don't have the hassle, and I don't have finger pointing or anything else. I do what I feel urged to do. Just last month I was elected to the trustee board. They knew what I had done before at the AME church.

Questions for Discussion
1. Describe Dan's coming to Evanston.
2. What experience indicated that some blacks in Evanston did not consider the Community Hospital on par with some of the other hospitals in the area?
3. Dan was active with the Economic Development Corporation in Evanston. What services did this group give to black Evanstonians?
4. What qualifications did Dan have to obtain his first job in Chicago?
5. When Dan left that job, he and some partners opened a business of their own. What was the name of that business and why did they give it that name?
6. Why did Dan's company have to stop their operations?
7. Where did Dan work after the Lincoln Plating Company of Chicago closed?
8. How did Dan become involved with Cyrus Realtors?
9. What is Dan's personal philosophy? From whom did he learn that?
10. What was Dan's criticism of blacks who make a lot of noise demanding rights and opportunities?
11. What did Dan say about competing?
12. What was Dan's complaint against Foster School? What was the outcome of this complaint?
13. What was Dan's complaint of Dr. Magett, ETHS principal at that time?
14. What did Dan say about Dr. Coffin's efforts to integrate the schools?
15. What was Dan's opinion about the effect integration of the schools had on blacks?
16. How can we counteract the tendency for young men to form gangs and engage in delinquent kids of activities?

About Dan Phillips

I remember when Dan first came to Evanston. We met at the Emerson Street YMCA. He was a part of a group of men who were in business or professions. We played volleyball at the Y and softball at Foster Field. Our softball team was called Fleety's Fumblers. The name Fleety came from our sponsor, Homer Fleetwood, who was the director of Foster Field at that time. "Fumblers" more or less described how we played.

Dan also was involved with the Y's Men's Club, a group of men dedicated to the improvement and advancement of youth.

Dan, of course, has retired from his electroplating business but is active as a broker with the Cyrus Realtors, 2929 Central Street, Evanston, Illinois, 60201.

We appreciate the time he gave us for the interview and his words of wisdom and encouragement.

Albert Price

We came to Evanston in the early twenties. I know that, but the exact year I can't remember. My mother was from Brooklyn, Georgia, where I was born. My father was from Augusta, Georgia. They lived at 1915 Asbury Avenue until the Second World War. Then we went to 1910, then to 1928 Jackson Avenue, from there we moved to 1460 Pitner where we live now.

In between that time, in moving, friends were very nice to us, let us live with them until our house was ready.

I don't know why my parents came to Evanston. They never discussed it. They never brought it up.

We didn't have any block clubs on Asbury Avenue and down on Jackson, but all of the parents, at that time, were second parents. If you were bad or disorderly, or did anything wrong, those people took care of you and then told your parents, and they would take care of you after you got home. If there was any disturbance in the neighborhood, everybody knew about it and they would cooperate together to try to correct the situation. They were all a community together as a group in each of the neighborhoods.

Business People
Watkins, up there on Emerson Street had a grocery store next door to the Masonic Temple. Mr. Flemings had a store near Mt. Zion Church on the corner of Clark and East Railroad. Later, he moved his store to Simpson Street and Darrow Avenue.

In those days the black people had their own businesses and that was another thing that knitted the community together.

The Masonic Temple was built right before the depression. You had doctors, lawyers, dentists, barbershops, tailor shops, restaurants, and all of those places were clean. They were well managed. Everybody had clean uniforms and stuff on, first class, until The Depression hit.

Things changed after The Depression. You know, they lost the building, you know, the Masonic Temple. All those people were gone.

Jack's Employment

I just worked to make money. I had that independent streak, like my mother. I carried newspapers. I didn't carry them in the morning, but I used to help Rollin Davis and Babe Cooper and all of them up on Asbury sometimes in the morning to get their papers out, because they had to go to school. I was an afternoon man, *Evanston Index*. And I made good, because at Christmas time I had won a bike and things like that, a watch and all that, for being a good carrier. I never used the bike. I walked my route. My route started at Davis Street down there where the Lyon and Healy building used to be, and go over East to Orrington, then on Orrington to Colfax, of course all of the side streets going North. I always threw the newspapers up on the porch, so they wouldn't get wet. So, at Christmas time, I would get fifty to one hundred dollars from many houses. I would come home with over five or six hundred dollars. That was a lot of money during the depression time. Of course, I had a little scheme there. The maid would see me coming to the door and hand me a check with a certain amount of money, and I would say, "This can't be for me," if it was lower than fifty dollars. So later on, when I delivered their paper, they would come home and ask me if I had received my Christmas present, I would say, "No." They would say, "You didn't get it?" I said "No, you usually give me fifty to one hundred dollars." They would run into the house and make another check for a larger amount.

I remember a man who live in the 2300 block of Orrington Avenue. He ran a big insurance company in the loop. In the winter time he would see me out here delivering papers and he would have the maid come in and tell her to fix some hot cocoa or tea and some cakes and cookies and things like that for me, and then have his chauffeur get the car out of the garage and drive me home. At the Women's Club it was the same way, there at Chicago Avenue and Church Street. The secretary in there, she would have a little box and she would have all kinds of sandwiches and cookies and cakes and stuff in there, but she would make me first sit down and have some hot tea before I went further North and that sort of thing. So I just loved that route.

Another job I had was at the Robin Hood's Barn Restaurant on Chicago Avenue, between Church and Davis Streets. I was working some place else, but I took this job to make some extra money. I was washing dishes and pans and pots, but I never liked to do that, even at home. I only had my mind on being independent and making money.

My mother had set me up in a Christmas Club at a dollar a month, and that never got out of my system. Always save some money. That's what started me on this money kick, I guess.

Then at Mt. Zion Baptist Church, you know I grew up in there. I think it was William Pyant who came around one Sunday. He was asking the churches, clubs, lodges, fraternities, and all that to sponsor somebody for membership in the YMCA. The deacon board at Mt. Zion decided that I would get the membership.

Going over to the Y on this membership, I knew all of the kids over there, and Mr. Pyant noticed and said that I had leadership ability, especially in handling the boys in the lobby. So he decided that the Y would pay me a little something for doing this job. Then Mr. Hauser put me in charge of the boys department, supervised by Mr. Bouyer and also Owen Washington. Now I was on a salary, so, I was in charge of letting them in to go swimming or go the gym, the locker rooms, clubs, and the lobby.

Then after the students came over from Northwestern, they worked under me. Some time when they wanted to get off, I would take over their duties. These students were paid under a government program.

After the kids came over from Northwestern, we started a powwow. I don't know how I thought of that, but other kids went away to college from Evanston. So when they came home at Thanksgiving, and especially Christmas, they had a longer weekend, and I asked them to bring in some brochures from their schools, colleges, or universities that they went to. And they would present the material to the seniors at the high school here, explaining to them about finance, etc. That was the first night.

The second night they would review it, and then they would have a social for them. Get together one on one. Then we would have a little music and dance, and refreshments, etc. We went to the Older Boy's State Conference, and from that I got the idea that we could have a Local Older Boy's Conference. I think you know how successful that was. Then Inez Washington wanted one for the girls, so I helped organize the girls. The other thing was the Black History. We had one day at that time, but I extended it for a week, and then it was extended to a whole month.

We organized the clubs by age group. They had their different times for going on the gym or swimming or other activities, but they always had to go to club meetings first. Then, by the time the group that was before them got through in the gym or swimming, the club period would be over.

We had every preacher in town taking turns giving devotions to those clubs, so I knew all of the churches and their preachers. I made a schedule so that they knew when they were supposed to meet with the clubs.

The clubs elected their own officers. They had their door keepers. They learned to develop leadership and character, how to debate, and that sort of thing.

The older boys went to the Hi-Y. They went to some of those conference and found out a lot of things and brought back ideas which they used at the Emerson Street Y.

We also had the Y's Mens Club, composed of young men. That became a big thing. These men were out of high school and either working or going to some kind of school. We had guys like Dan Phillips, who was one of the prominent leaders.

The Older Boys Conference got so big that we had to have the whole gymnasium down there, and that's how it really started with organizing at the Y. I was on the Older Boys Committee. Being a young fellow, I knew all the kids, so naturally I knew their fathers. It was easy to get them there to bring their kids to the Fathers and Sons Banquet. We have a lot of pictures of these meetings.

Question: Jack, how were you able to get the cooperation of the parents in sending their children to the Y?

I went around to see the parents regularly. If kids were bad or were not at the Y when they should have been, I let them know. I also went around checking memberships and to let them know that payments were due, especially if they were paying on a time payment plan. So while I was going around collecting the payments, I could talk to the parents about the kids.

The parents were very supportive. Of course, in those days, all of the parents were, especially the women. They were very "on the ball" and wanted to know everything. If the kids were even late getting home, they would call and let us know that the kids were not home yet.

Question: How did the Y program fill in for the boys who did not have fathers?

We tried to get them connected with their best friend's father, so they would always come together and be together. The father would take him under his arms and that sort of thing. And then we would give them special counseling in the office there. We always try not to show favoritism among the boys. Sometimes we would call them into the office and talk to them, tell them what they are doing good or bad, pat them on the back, and that sort of thing. Or if they were cutting up in the lobby or pushing around the smaller kids, have a nice friendly talk with them. We tried to be calm with them because they were just playing and trying to win games. They are all friends anyway, so we tried not to be harsh with them.

Older Men in the Lobby

Most of the men you would see in the lobby lived there, such as the Walker brothers and the Helms. Also some of the older men dropped in from their homes, shops, or offices. Dr. Cotton came over, and Dr. Scruggs, but he mostly played pool.

Most of these older men were supporters of the Y and came by to see how things were going. They were working like everything on membership drives and making big contributions themselves, so they were very interested in seeing how things were going. They would become involved there with them, and that would be a break for me, for they would be there for hours at a time. Some of them would be late for their appointments at their offices, but it gave me a chance to do something else that I thought was important.

The way men got on the board of management was by not only making a good monetary contribution to the Y, but also by spending some time with the boys.

Fathers and Sons Banquet

The Fathers and Sons Banquet was a big affair. We had some of the biggest preachers on the South Side of Chicago to come out to speak at the banquet, for the Hi-Y. They would even lead devotion services. They said it was a relief for them to come out to Evanston. Everybody liked to come out to Evanston. Everybody was so down to earth, they could relax more. It wasn't stiff like it was in Chicago. At the same time, I was active with the Wabash Y in Chicago. I was also active in the NAACP in Chicago, the Urban League, and the Negro Business League.

When we were discussing integrating the YMCA, Helen Cooper

and the North Shore Branch of the Urban League saw that we were about to come to a conclusion on the integration of the Y and they became involved. But I knew the president of the Urban League in Chicago, so I went down and talked to him. Since we were right on the verge of integrating, I didn't want to go back.

We had been working on it for about two years, or more. I think they were just trying to rush it along. We were too far along for them to come in at this time. We didn't need any help at this point. We needed help in the beginning.

Mr. Bouyer

Mr. Bouyer was patient with you and would reckon with you—very patient, very considerate—but if you were doing wrong, he would come to grip with you. Now, Mr. Pyant was the same way, as far as come to grip with you. Now, Mr. Pyant was the same way, as far as club work, but Mr. Pyant was always rushing here and there. I went with him to the NAACP meeting in Cleveland. Then I went with him to Pennsylvania on Y business.

All of those things were just a part of me. I wasn't trying to make a history or be a big shot or all of that sort of thing. If there was anything I could do to help or push the organization or an individual, it was just part of me. That's all, and that's why I can't remember the names and dates, even the integration, but I really worked on that.

So, after the fellows worked on the Fathers and Sons Banquet, I started pushing them to get on the Committee of Management of the Y, and also the Y's Men's Club, like Phillips, Bryson, Ted Harding, Merrit St. Clair, and Bill Jones. I picked those who wanted to be on the committee and would be an asset to the board. They went from the Boy's Work Committee to the Committee of Management, and from there to the Grove Street Y. Phillips finally made secretary of the Grove Street Board.

Black Attendance at the Grove Street Y

Everybody was pushing for integration at that time. When I went into the service they were talking about it, and when I came out of service in 1945, that was on everybody's mind. Everywhere you would go, they were saying we should have only one YMCA. A P. Perry wanted to give it up as chairman of the Board of Management. So Mrs. Duggard, Mr. Gill and others came to see me about it. I said "No, I want to talk to

Mr. Perry, first. I don't want him to think that I am trying to undermine him." So Mrs. Duggard made an appointment with Mr. Perry, and I met with him at the country club. He said "Yes, he wanted to give up the chairmanship of the Emerson Street Y board. He said, "I think you are going to have a tough fight with this integration. I have been here all these years, and I am not ready for that, but you will be just the man for the job." So, that's how I got into it. We made a pledge, and I told him I would take it under one consideration, that cooperation from every member of the Board of Directors must be given to me. Also, we must put our ears to the community first, before we make a move to make sure that this is what the people want. I added that "blacks are beginning to want integration in everything everywhere so we have got to do this, do it fast and do it right." They said, "You're right. You're right." So, we agreed on this arrangement.

We started getting ready. Everybody was for integration and we finally were integrated with the Grove Street Y.

But when we got integrated, blacks did not have a headquarters like the Y for social, religious, educational, or just civic meetings. Then many blacks were sorry they went into it. But it was too late.

We really lost something when we lost the Y, just like the Masonic Temple, when we lost that. We had one of the finest restaurants in there. The barbershops were spic and span clean. Their uniforms were clean. The beauty parlors were attractive. Mr. Aikers ran a first class tailor shop. Upstairs there were offices for professional people like Doctor Bess, the dentist, and others. The washrooms were always clean and not smelly.

Sports

At Northwestern, I knew the ticket manager. Somebody told him to see me at the Y. I don't know who. He wanted the students at Northwestern to feel welcome at the Y. These students were mostly the black football players. So we would have some of the young women over to socialize with them on the weekends. Some of them made dates and established relationships. Then we were asked to entertain the students after the games. I got Chuck Glass on that, but I had to help him.

There were too many kids involved for one person. We made contact with the chief of police, some of the big stores, the mayor, and all of those, and they would get buns and hot dogs hamburgers, drinks, etc.

The ticket manager at Northwestern also knew me from the *Chicago Defender* because I knew Abbot. So, he would give me a ticket in the press box at the games. Up there, you know, you get your lunch, drinks, you're inside, the elevator takes you up, good seats, almost in front every time, same seat in same row. You could eat with the press and drink with the press.

I never did bother Chuck Glass about tickets because I was the one who set him up over there.

The only sport I had in high school was recess softball. I liked to play short stop. They used to say, "Price cleans up on that short stop." Other than that, when they practiced in the afternoon, I was working carrying papers, or I was working at the Y. The band and the orchestra, I played clarinet at Foster School, even, but I had to go to Haven for music. Then a guy encouraged me and got me in the music hall at Emerson and Sherman Avenues. So I went there for lessons once a week. From the band I went to the orchestra. I only played with the band during football season. I was taking music appreciation along with my band music, because it was during class time.

Politics

I started out with Professor W.W. Fisher. He was a great orator and he was from down in Kansas. I think he was an auditor in some college or university down there. He said he had to leave there in a hurry, but he was such a great orator and such a big man in the Methodist church, they sent him around to different big churches in the United States. He knew all of the bishops and elders, all of those people. Somebody introduced him to Charles Dawes, the vice president of the U.S., so from then on he was a big shot in the Republican Party speaking bureau. He spoke at churches, lodges, etc. He was working for the candidates of Dawes in the Republican Party.

On Asbury there, you know, he lived next door to the undertaker. He had political meetings, and they would bring literature and stuff there, so he used to always send me to the store down on Greenbay Road. He called me one day and asked me to help him sort some literature, so I would help him separate the literature and stuff. Then he had me up there when he had the meetings to pass out the literature about the different candidates and, at the same time, he asked me to get the guys to come and deliver it around the Fifth Ward. So, I would get Rol Davis and the rest of them. It was good money then, you know.

He paid well for that age and time.

Then Dwight Green was running for governor, and he won. W.W. came over to Foster Field, didn't even call up. He said, "Get your guys together now, we're going to get those good jobs, get some good jobs, state jobs, highway jobs, they pay good money. I mean they pay good money. You know they don't want Negroes to have these jobs, we've got good backing." They did turn out to be good jobs, because [Jim] Avery had one of them. They didn't want any office jobs because they weren't paying anything. They wanted those jobs out there on the county highway. In fact, they got me out there on one. You know, the cosmetics place there at Greenbay and Golf Road and Waukegan Road. We made good money spreading gravel on that property.

After the war, we went back to the state, Avery, Warren, and all of them, back to work for the state. One of the guys was with the county, and Avery and he got along pretty well together. He was one of the supervisors on the state, so Avery really got the best job. Warren got one of the heavy duty jobs.

After they lost the state election, of course, there wasn't nothing there but a few jobs with the county downtown, but they weren't paying too much. I was working down there, too, after Hauser (at the Y) and I fell out. When I came out of the service I went to the Veterans Administration. You see, I was helping officers with there papers before I came home from overseas. That was the only way I could get away from over there. I had made up my mind that I was going to stay in Hawaii. I had two or three chances to come home before, and they wouldn't let me come. They tried to persuade me with warrant officer, second lieutenant, and first lieutenant, but I couldn't come to the states and do it. They wanted me overseas because they needed me over there. I wouldn't compromise, or I never would get back to the states.

One of the generals came to headquarters and said, "Sergeant Price, what are you doing here? Everybody's gone except you." I said, "Yes." So, he said, "Tomorrow morning you pick up the mail, and your orders will be in there." And sure enough they were there. I used to see that he got fed. He was a big old guy from Texas. He didn't want no white cooks. He came all the way over to the office to get someone to take him over to the mess hall to get his breakfast. Those cooks knew how to cook for him, and in the meantime, going and coming, he would see white officers riding around in jeeps when they were supposed to be saving gas. He would make them walk, get out and walk. Here I would be riding with him in the jeep with his chauffeur. You see, I used to take care of him. He said, "Tomorrow we will book you on a plane, and you will be on it." And sure enough I was.

Gangs and Dope
They got another kid at high school last week. He was carrying a gun down there on Greenwood and Dempster and Fowler; there's nothing but dope addicts there.

Remedy for Gang Activity
I haven't talked to many people other than Reverend Norwood, pastor of my church. He talks to the people and discusses what we should do. We should get to the parents, rather than the general church, the parents of all of these kids. Talk to them and organize them, all of the churches, to see what can be done to handle this bad activity of the gangs. This is how you are going to straighten this out.

Prognosis?
The future looks bad. I don't have any faith in it. I think things are going to get worse.

Questions for Discussion
1. Describe Jack's arrival in Evanston.
2. What did Jack say about neighborhood control of their affairs?
3. What benefit to the community came from black owned businesses?
4. Explain how Jack used psychology on his paper route patrons.
5. How did Jack get his first membership to the Emerson Street Y?
6. Whose idea was it to start an Older Boys Conference at Emerson Street Y?
7. What were some of the ways older men supported the Y?
8. Why was the Fathers and Sons Banquet an outstanding event for the boys and dads?
9. Why was the Emerson Street Y closed?
10. How did the Emerson Street Y cooperate with the Sports Department of Northwestern University?
11. How did W.W. Fisher become a popular politician in Evanston?
12. What benefits did some Republican supporters receive for their campaigning?
13. Jack talked to Reverend Norwood, his pastor, about kids in gangs.

Reverend Norwood suggested organizing the parents in their respective churches to see what can be done to handle the gang problem.

About Albert "Jack" Price[*]

If you should ask any black in Evanston over sixty years of age, "Who is Jack Price?" you would be told that he was a YMCA man, a politician, a churchman, a war veteran, and a man who likes a good drink and a good cigar.

Jack knows class when he sees it, and when class is not there, Jack does not bother with it.

When Jack was on the Emerson Street Y staff, he used to visit my house at 1715 Emerson Street and talk to me about the Y program. I was sixteen years old at that time. Jack asked me to take on the responsibility of program chairman for our spring Older Boys YMCA Conference. With my parent's permission, I agreed to accept the challenge. From that point on, Jack left the job up to me. I wrote many of the local and Chicago leaders in law, medicine, politics, and education and asked them to speak or lead discussions with the young men who would be attending the conference. Not one person refused to accept the invitation, even though they were told that we could not pay them. The conference was a tremendous success, and we have photographs to show how well and orderly it was attended. I don't think anyone will deny that the success of the Emerson Street Y Older Boys Conference was due to the salesmanship of Albert "Jack" Price.

---

[*] Albert Price passed away on February 21, 1997.

Allen Price

My mother came here in 1900, and she came from Staunton, Virginia. Her maiden name was Bell. My father came from Tennessee. Now whereabouts in Tennessee, I am not quite sure. Somewhere around Memphis. It was a small town near a big city. They were married and had eleven children, seven boys and four girls.

Talk about moving, when I was young, we grew up on Lyons Street and my father died when I was two years old, so my mother raised the family and kept the family together until World War II. I can remember moving and living in the 2000 block on Darrow Avenue. Within four houses there were forty-four kids, thirteen Perrins, eleven Prices, ten Turners, and ten Robinsons. And across the street there were the Mims, Tates, Davises, Palitos, and there was another Italian family across there and they were kin to Joe Bichecci. I can't think of their name right now. But there must have been something like seventy kids in that one block. Oh, Henry Brown lived right there on Simpson Street, so we had the Brown family right in there, too. There was quite an aggregation of kids down in that neighborhood.

When you think of the family itself, when you have that many sisters and brothers it's hard to remember anything, because everything I got was handed down. You didn't think too much about it because everybody was in the same shape. We didn't have locks on our doors. We could go and come. We attended Mt. Zion church. Afterward, we went to the Springfield Church on Dodge Avenue. After they had the big fight over at Mt. Zion Church in October of 1929.

Other than that we were just family. All of my brothers played football and things like that. Living down on Darrow Avenue, they called it dead end. When we ran out of fellows to play football, or softball, we used Gladys Tate, Lila Perrin, her sister, Gertrude, Idelle Turner, and Effie Harper. They would fill in for us. My sister was as good a half back as any boy. She could really run with a football. I don't think the girls realized that they were girls up until they were about seventeen.

We had no uniforms. We just played. That was just growing up at that time.

The family structure, that was funny. My uncle, Roy, he was more or less like a father to me. You know, Roy Bell. He was my mother's brother. I used to reflect that when I was young, walking from Darrow Avenue, 2100 block down to the 1700 block to get a hair cut and a bald head. On my way back, everybody I passed gave me a lick on my bald head. There was nothing exciting in my family. We were just poor. All of us worked and tried to make the best of it. In those days, they didn't have what you called block clubs. Families just cared for each other. Like if Mrs. Perrin saw you doing something, she would crack you and tell your mother when she got home, then you got another crack. It was the same with Mrs. Turner and Mrs. Robinson. They used to look out after each other's families, and as I said, there were no locked doors on our homes. When the Perrins ate, I ate. When we ate, the Perrins ate.

Mr. Jim Morton lived next door to us. Every year, on New Years Day, he would slaughter hogs and everybody in the block got meat. When he shucked his corn, everybody got corn. Mr. Perrin plowed and had his garden, so everybody had vegetables, same way with Mr. Robinson. We had a small garden, too, everybody shared. Joe Bichecci, he was the fruit man. He was around the corner and he was always bringing stuff by because he knew we had a large family. So it was a neighborhood that wasn't a block club, but they looked after each other. But you don't find that today. You don't find that closeness. You may find some, but not much.

Mr. Ellered Scott had a store on Simpson Street. Ellered thought he was a boxer. Mr. Small had a bakery right next to him. He used to give me a quarter to clean the pans. Some of the professionals in the community were Dr. Joseph Roberts, Dr. A Rudolph Penn, Dr. Washington, Dr. Bryant, Dr. Young the dentist, Dr. Schruggs the chiropodist, Dr. Tarkinton dentist and great golfer, and my good friend, Dr. Jake Frye. He was the best doctor that I knew. Then there was Dr. Elizabeth Hill, who I thought the world of until she told my mother that I could not play football any more. And then I left her and went to Jake Frye who was an avid football fan, and baseball fan, so I knew he would never tell my mother that. So I was safe to play football.

Oh yes. There was a real estate man, Dixon, on Emerson. Also Mr. "Slick" Gill, the real estate man. Than there were Porter and Owen, undertakers. Also, Mr. C.L. Mason, and Horace Graves, undertakers at The Metropolitan Funeral Home on Emerson Street next to Ebenezer Church. And there was Professor W.W. Fisher. He would give me a quarter and I would go down to the lake and tell him if the tide was in or out. That was a quarter I earned. I really appreciated that quarter.

I don't know what Professor Fisher was professor of, philosophy or what he was, but I know he was a politician. He was an orator. He had a good gift of gab. I used to go up there and listen to him speak and touch the palm of his hand.

Oh, yes, there was Dr. Fairfax. He moved to Maywood, Illinois.

My mother worked as a domestic worker for a family named Campbell. My brother, Charles, worked for Burkett's Drug Store down on Sherman and Church Street. He was a delivery man there for some time. My brother, Clarence, worked for the Evanston Scrap and Iron Company over at Foster and Greenbay Road, my other brother James worked at the Perfecto Cleaners. He was considered a washer. He washed the clothes. My brother Harry, he was a construction worker. He worked for Weiboldts. He helped to build Weiboldts Store, and quite a few other buildings around town. My brother, Leon, he worked for the city. First, he was a custodian at Fleetwood-Jourdain Community Center, which was the old Foster Field at that time. Then he was promoted to supervisor of maintenance for all of the parks and recreation facilities. When he retired, that is what he was doing. My brother, Joe, was a handyman. He could take a hammer and saw and do wonders with it. I am a shoe repair man. My sister, Virginia, she worked for E.V. Searles. She retired from there. My sister Gertrude, she went to California, but I don't know what she is doing. My sister, Beatrice, she moved to Chicago. My oldest sister died at an early age.

Three of us are living now. My sister, Virginia McClain who lives here on Church, my brother Harry, the one they call Pity, lives in Cedar Rapids, Iowa. He is in a nursing home there. [Pity passed recently.]

Education

Well, I went to the red brick Foster. Mrs. Rowley was the principal. I remember my first kindergarten teacher, I think I was in love with her. Her name was Miss Wilson. Some of the other teachers I remember were Miss May, Miss Budeball who was the gym teacher, Miss Klienbell, Dan McTaggert, the Sloan Sisters, Miss Moon the librarian, and Mr. Huff the janitor. He was always getting me in trouble.

When I started that school, it was mixed because on Dewey Avenue it was all white. Right around on Dewey, there, they started moving out. The only whites I remember who stayed there a long time were Art and Harry McZure, Peter Farreri, Bichacci stayed there, and Gus

Pallito. I think those were about the last whites that I remember that stayed at Foster, unless they graduated. At that time they went from kindergarten to eighth grade. They didn't have a football team. They had a music program there. They had instruments and Dan McTaggert would try to teach you to play some instrument, but that didn't last too long. The greatest thing that I remember at that school was when Mr. Charles Bouyer came. He came from the South Side of Chicago to Evanston. That was the greatest thing that ever happened to the black male in this community. He left an impression that will linger with young people my age "till they go to their graves." He was strict with that stick, and he would use it. He was something. Mr. Bouyer was something, and there was another janitor there, but I can't remember his name. He was the finest of all the janitors there. He was a little short fellow. He wore glasses. He retired from there. He used to let us in school to play after school when it was cold. I remember the ice rink over at Foster Field. I remember Bill Logan, Jimmy Morton, we called him "Hooks" because he was bowlegged. There was also a fellow named Bobo who could skate, too. English Bobo. The Holliday Boys could skate, too. All of those fellows grew up and went to Foster, most of them are deceased.

Some of the fellows in the neighborhood got into trouble and had to serve time in St. Charles or other juvenile institutions, but most of them came back reversed and did wonders. But, you know, at that time Mr. Worthington was the juvenile officer, and he had no regard for young blacks, and neither did Henry White. LaVelle was a much more compassionate officer than Henry White. Tony Schultz, you could talk to, but some of those policemen, you couldn't talk to. So, Foster School was a good school, but I tell you one thing, I remember every Tuesday you had to bring money and bank. That was bank day. If you didn't have any money, Miss Rowley would send you home. We had problems, but they were good problems.

Politics

Politics has really changed in Evanston over the years. I remember when I first started dabbling in politics was when Ed Jourdain was running for alderman in the Fifth Ward. I will never forget the campaign song. In fact, I think the young folks did more work for Jourdain than the old folks. I remember Eola Richardson used to give us a dime to pass out hand bills. You know, she was a staunch Democrat, and she was a big time politician. Then there was Sam White, who I thought the world of. Professor Fisher was a big Republican. Then came Gene Beck. Gene Beck gave me a job on the State of Illinois Highway. I have never forgotten that. I voted for Gene Beck every time he ran, but I just couldn't pull myself to go in there to vote for some of those Republicans that he was backing. So, I used to tell them that. I used to tell Bill Ericson who was their sponsor, the same thing.

There were a lot of people who thought they were politicians, but they were not politicians that were in this community. I used to tell my good friend, Jack Price, I said, "Jack, you are a good man, but don't be staunch and don't be blind. You know there are two sides to everything." I always split my vote. I never voted straight. I used to tell Jack that there are other things. When I was a precinct captain, we beat Roy Neal and Leon Robinson. That was my greatest thrill, to beat them two brothers-in-law. And then, you know, I worked in a lot of aldermanic elections. I worked for Mame Spencer, Edna Summers, Roosevelt Alexander, but that was my biggest disappointment. He disappointed a lot of people. One of the young men I admire right now is a Republican, Dennis Drummand. You can call Dennis up. You can talk to him and he understands both sides of the aisle.

There is always one thing that I remember, Joe Bichecci and Sam White. They fought against the city manager type government. For African-Americans, that is not the best type of city government because they are not accountable. You can't put them in office, and you can't kick them out of office. And to be accountable, you have to have somebody you can put in and take out. We used to have eighteen aldermen here, and at that time all we needed was ten votes and he could keep his job, but now, we have nine aldermen and all he needs is five and he can keep his job. But if you have to answer to your constituents, then they can put you in or kick you out like they do with the aldermen, and I think it is better under those terms. But they say, sometime, that in a community like this it is better, but I don't think it is for poor people.

Mayor

Wonderful, I worked hard for her, and I did something I wasn't supposed to do. At the VFW breakfast, we are not supposed to get politically involved, but that morning I got up on the roster and I said, "I am supporting, and I am working for Lorraine Morton. This is a chance of a lifetime for us. If we don't take advantage of this, we are going backwards." And she won by a narrow vote, but she won. And she has been a pleasant, pleasant, pleasant mayor.

Church

I am a member of Mt. Zion, but like a lot people my age, I don't attend church that much. But I do help them financially if they come by, and stuff like that. I admire Reverend Norwood, because Reverend Norwood does something that a lot of the ministers don't do. He services the community. There are a lot of funerals for people who do not have church homes. He has them in his church. I know a lot of people who have talked about how he has accepted strangers in his church for this service. I give him great credit for that because some ministers say if you are not a member of my church, don't even bring the body in. I think that is wrong. I think that if some of your family has been going there for years, or maybe not, they should be able to have the services there. But I don't worry about that when I go. I go to church three or four times a year, but I don't like to go on Mother's Day because it depresses me. They seem to make it depressing. The Bible says, "Cry when the baby is born and rejoice when he leaves." We do just the opposite. I visit the churches. I haven't made up my mind where I will go before I die. I may not go to any before I die. I will be frank with you.

YMCA

Well, I don't go to this Y now because it is still in the back of my mind that they don't want me down there, especially at my age. So I found other homes at Fleetwood and other places. But the Emerson Street YMCA, that was home. Every Friday night, in the winter, you had the basketball games. You had the swimming pool. You had Queroque games, you had ping pong. I remember Owen Washington when he was there. I remember Jack Price when he was there. I couldn't get along with him, but he was all right. Jack used to kick me out every other day, but that was all right. And Mr. Pyant was a fine man. And Mr. Hauser, and then after Mr. Hauser there was Mr. Hummons, and Ted Boyd, and the Mr. Charles Bouyer. I have to go back to Mr. Bouyer. He was the man. He had the 135s, the Flashers, and the Wildcats basketball teams. On Friday nights you couldn't get a place in that Y to watch those games. I remember he always brought in outstanding teams from the South Side of Chicago. That was the first time I saw some of the Harlem Globe Trotters like Rosey Brown, Sweet Water Clifton, Agis and Cleve Bray, Iron Man McGinnis. All of those guys came and played at the Y. And I remember the one shot they use now, Johnny Walker was using that for years. Back when I was a little fellow, Johnny Walker was using that shot.

Then we had the bean eating contest and pie eating contest on Saturday. Oh man. Then we had swimming. They would tell you to go and take a shower before you go into the pool.

Del Alexander, Del the quarterback, had a good mind. And there was Chuck Glass, another good mind. He did a lot of recruiting for Northwestern. They called him "Doc." There were a lot of fellows around here who could have played in the National Professional Football League. I know one, J.B. Harmon. All of the Harmons were great players, Cord, Ellis, and J.B. Cord was a good quarterback. He went to Phillips, you know. Then there was Dyche Smith, Bill Jones, Sad Sam Jones, they all went down South to college. There was Freddie Brooks, an excellent basketball player. All of these guys came off Foster Center.

Also Pettigrew, Wilbur Carter, and Junior Temple—now art editor for Johnson Publishing Company. Oh man, we had so much talent around here. And this was before the war. After the war we had the Rams, and we joined the Central State Professional Football League. Bill Johnson was our coach.

Dick Lee was manager of the Evanston Boosters baseball team. I remember when Dick Lee played Mason Park. Cliff Adams was his ace pitcher. But there used to be a family that lived right around the corner from you, on Darrow Avenue, upstairs where Hattie Rogers used to be in the back. You know that big house in the front. There used to be a fellow up there. He was a left handed pitcher. His aunt lived up there. And Dick Lee would go down to Chicago and get him and have him warming up in Foster Field and had Cliff Adams warming up at Mason Park. Just before it was time to play, John Dixon came in his Model T and brought this left handed pitcher over. And all you could hear from the Mason Park hitters was swish, swish, swish. We beat them two to nothing. Dick Lee said, "I'm going to teach you all a lesson." You know at that time Mason Park had a couple of guys that were supposed to be pretty good ball players and property of the Chicago Cubs, especially their first baseman. But that used to be a pretty good rivalry between Mason Park and Evanston Boosters.

After the war we had a football rivalry with Boltwood. Every Thanksgiving we used to go down there and play. That was a big game. Even if a guy was hurt, he would play in that game. I remember, Lad [James Freeman] had both shoulders busted up and we padded him up with sanitary napkins with his pads on and he played. And a fellow named Henry Bond, he was dragging one leg, and played. Scoot Moore was dragging, but he played in that game.

Entertainment
Well, you know, we used to have the Y dances. You go to the Y and you dance at proms and things like that. But after you got a little older, you went to the Masonic Temple. That was the big thing right before the war. Then after the war Tom Butler had a place called the Subway, downstairs. That was pretty nice. But there was a place called Shorty Pitts. They were selling booze back there, if you drank. They had gambling back there if you gambled. If you shot dice, if you played Georgia Skin, he had everything. And the barbershop. The barber wouldn't start cutting hair until about six or seven o'clock at night, and he cut all night. This was called Cannon's Barber Shop. Old man Sims had the restaurant right next door. That stayed open all night. That was the place to go and party. And then there was Hattie Rogers over there on Darrow Avenue, and there was Slim Barber's place out on Grey Avenue. And there was Louis Collins' behind Watkins' Grocery Store over there on Simpson Street. And right there on Wesley and Foster, Neal's, that was a skin house. The fellows had a lot of places to have fun and entertainment. For those who wanted to participate in those things, there were plenty of places to go to. And then there was "policy." Everybody wrote policy. Toussaint Massey wrote policy. Mich Purdue wrote policy. Now and then they would get busted, but wouldn't amount to anything. Country Jennings had his wheel there. And Jack Perrin had a wheel after he came off the police department. It was just another kind of entertainment.

There were a whole lot of house parties. We use to go out to Edora Taylor's house on Grey Avenue. At twelve o'clock, Mr. Taylor would take that stick and hit on the floor three times. That means you've got to go. And then we had Joe Cater who played the piano. Willie Langston played the piano at those house parties. We used to call them kerosene parties. They furnished the lamps, and we brought the kerosene. It was a good time, very little trouble. We always had a good time.

Policy Wheel

Benvenuti had a wheel down town. John Dixon was a big man in policy. Drawings were twice a day. You could play as little as a nickel. Toussant Massey would get on the bus at Simpson Street and Dodge Avenue. And by time he got to Davis Street, he had written his "book." I don't know how much was in his "book," but I know it was pretty good. You know, a lot of fellows never had a job. All they every did was write policy, like Bubba Thompson. And everybody knew it. The police knew it. Police LaVelle would call and say, "We're coming to bust you." And they would clean house so the police would find nothing.

LaVelle was a good policeman, nothing like Hank White, the old man.

Social Club or Lodge

None.

My brother, Harry, was a Mason. He belonged to Mt. Moriah.

After I came out of the service, I made up my mind that I was not going to join anything else segregated. The Masons was segregated, and I have nothing against that, and sometimes I wish I was a Mason, but my brother joined and I just didn't see joining. Reverend Bradford tried to get me to join the Knights of Pithians. You know my father was a Knight of Pithian in the Uniform Ranks. You know, when I tell people that my father had the largest funeral that's ever been in the city of Evanston, they don't believe me. Then I tell them that they had people stretched out from Mt. Zion Church all the way down Clark to Ridge Avenue, from Ridge to Church Street, Church Street all the way down to Darrow Avenue, then Darrow Avenue to Lyons Street. That's when they broke ranks. There were so many bands out there that they couldn't get them all in the church. They used to call my father "Chicken Bill." My father was a sparring partner for Jack Johnson, the prize fighter. My mother was a Corinthian. Mr. Jerry Reed, Dad Reed, was a Knight of Pithian, also, Mr. Ballenger, Mr. Searles, and Mr. Irving who used to live over here on Wesley and Emerson. He was one. Oh, they had a big uniform rank. They had a big uniform rank. The Knights of Pithians were big. They used to parade on Sunday. In those uniforms with swords at their sides, white gloves, they were really proud. They would throw those feet out there and really be walking. They had a band from Chicago. You know the funny thing about it, we were at an affair one time, and one of the fellows who used to play the bass drum in the old

Nights of Pithian band, he kept looking at me, and Rudy Frazier said, "That man's looking at you." I said, "That man don't know me." Then the man said, "Boy, aren't you one of Chicken Bill's boys? I can tell by that head." Rudy and Squirrel Head Wilson just laughed and still laugh every time they see me. Rol Davis still calls me Chicken Bill.

Problems in Our Social Environment

Well, babies having babies. That's one. Parental guidance is almost nil now. Parents are just not there. One other thing is the system. The man has used us, has brainwashed us that we are part of the system. We feel that we can't make it without food stamps, can't make it without the welfare checks. Which is wrong. That's how they keep jobs, and we don't progress. We don't become self-reliant. We don't have the initiative to do anything, so that's one of the things. The other thing, I find, is when they start telling you that we don't need affirmative action, that we need to go back and give the states the money, instead of the federal government, to run their programs, so you know what that's going to do. I tell young people today that they had better fight to keep affirmative action, because if they don't, everything that we won in the sixties is going to be lost. And I don't think that I went to World War II to fight for that. A lot of the veterans are upset about that. As you know, we were the forgotten soldiers in World War II, and we are going to be the forgotten people again if we don't get political action. Some people say, "I don't want to become involved politically," but I think everybody should be politically active, for the simple reason that there is your means of living. They make all of the decisions in Washington. If you don't write your congressman or senator or your state representatives, you are lost. The president is only one man, but if you write enough letters to your congressmen and to your state representatives, they will listen because they understand votes. They know that votes put them in, and votes can take them out. Once they get to Washington and begin to live pretty good, or to Springfield and begin to live pretty good, they want to stay there. So, they will listen. That's why I feel that when they say that ministers should not get politically involved, I say they should get involved because they have the largest congregations of any African-Americans at eleven o'clock on Sundays. If they can't do something then, we are lost. I see us losing a little bit everyday.

Every time there is an Afro-American in a key spot, they are going after him. They got rid of Dr. Elder, the Surgeon General, going after

Ron Brown now, pretty soon they are going after Jesse Brown because he is the head of the Veterans Affairs.

I want to say this, and I am a vet. Our president may not have fought for and served his country, but I can tell you one thing, for the minorities, he has done an awful lot for putting them in key spots. He stuck his neck out, and if we don't back him, then we are in trouble. I don't care what party you are in, I look at the man for what he is. Take Dr. Foster, for example. I know they don't want Dr. Foster because they want somebody else in there. It's the same thing that's happening in Chicago with the school board. They're putting in a white man now, because they are starting all over from scratch again. Any time a program hits rock bottom, they put us in charge. When they think they are going to get money and something new, they want to take over and say, "Well, we will handle this." Now when the school was in bad shape, they always interviewed black folks. Now, the Republicans are saying, "It's our turn now. We are going to do some things differently." So, you can see that is what is happening across the board. In California, by executive order, affirmative action has got to go. When they are saying that, they don't know about the quota system when I was in the service and rode in the back of the bus while in uniform.

Young blacks don't understand what their grandparents and great-grandparents fought to get for them. They are just sitting around letting it pass by because the man has inundated us with drugs. Quick money, drugs, drugs. Quick money, drugs, drugs, drugs. They say, "Take it to Harlem, take it to the South Side, poison their minds with drugs, give them those pistols, let them kill each other." And we don't have enough sense to understand that. It's pitiful.

Gangs, white powder, and money. That's the problem with the black communities today.

How can we stop that trend?

Change the laws. Legalizing drugs could solve some of the problems. But I think that one of the things we have to do is to take a good look at who is bringing in the drugs, where it is coming from. We can stop it. We can stop anything else. So we can stop this too, if we want to. So, stop it. It doesn't matter how high we have to go to do it, but stop it. Are some neighborhoods keeping drugs out?

In Brooklyn, New York there are some blocks where a drug pusher will not dare to go. There are some blocks in Washington D.C. where you can't pay a pusher to go. They break their legs. Break their hands. Who does that? The elders in the community. But you see, the first thing they say is that they are afraid of somebody coming back and threatening them or doing something to them if they turn them in. But I was telling some fellows here, if you take one of those young boys and give him a good whipping with a baseball bat, you will alleviate some of the problem. You have to start working with kids early. Our problem is we don't have enough black males working with our kids. I have been out here for forty some odd years, and I know that you can't get enough men to do this. Some men say, "I'm not going to work with those hard heads. Sure they are hard heads, but eventually they come back when they are twenty-one and say, "Thanks." I found that out for thirty years working with these kids. He will stand beside me and I will put my arm around him and tell him, "You are my man," and he's an adult. Arthur Albright, and Skip Johnson, all those kids I had on the drill team, they come back and stand around on the fourth of July, and they will be up on Central Street.

Drill Team

When I came out of the service where I was taught discipline, I knew that if we were going to get ahead, we must have some kind of discipline. I started out with Richard Johnson, Leonard Matthews, Bob Brown, Raymond Bell, and Charlie Thomas. Charley Thomas is a superintendent. Bell is in Dallas, Texas working for a university. Sonny Matthews just retired from the school system. Buddy worked at Fort Sheridan for years, and he retired. I had Ed Jourdain. I had Stanton Payne, who is now a principal at Westinghouse. I had Phil Johnson's son and daughter, Iva and Skip. They are in business in Chicago. I had a lot of wonderful kids. I will always remember when they came back and gave me my night in 1976. They came back from all over the country. Who would have thought that these kids thought that much of me? The only birthday party that I ever had in my life, my kids out of the drum corps gave me. They did all the cooking and everything. They had it at the Center and had a packed house. So I have been blessed. I've had my eulogy, because Reverend Ulysses Robinson came out from retirement and came that night, and he spoke. I told him, "I don't have to worry about my eulogy, because I have just heard mine. It has been great working with the drill team and drum corps.

Questions for Discussions
1. What were some of the advantages of living as a child in Bo's neighborhood, the 2000 block on Darrow Avenue?
2. Allen said that there was no block club in his neighborhood, but there was something else there which seemed to control the behavior of the residents. What was that?
3. Allen had close contact with the business and professional blacks in the neighborhood. What does that tell you about their contributions to the blacks in Evanston?
4. Describe Allen's Foster School environment. How do you think he felt about his experiences there?
5. What were some of Allen's political views?
6. Describe Allen's experiences at the Emerson Street Y. Why did he now want to go the Grove Street Y when the Emerson Street Y was closed?
7. Discuss Allen's description of the black entertainment and sports figures in Evanston.
8. What were some of Bo's recommendations for improving the social environment of Evanston?

About Allen "Bo" Price

I first met "Bo" when we played games such as football, basketball, and softball at Foster Field and the Emerson Street Y. He is a few years younger than I, but he was there. My father and his father were in the same lodge, Knights of Pythian. Dad used to call Mr. Price "Chicken Bill," Mr. Price's nickname, and laugh about the experiences they had.

Bo is probably one of the best known black men in Evanston, maybe on the North Shore. This is due to his tremendous achievement with the drill team and drum and bugle corps, which he organized.

Edna Summers

My paternal and maternal grandparents came to Evanston in the early 1900s. Samuel White I and Alice brought their eight children. Grampa White drove a horse and wagon for the city of Evanston.

Hannah McCoy brought her daughter, Evelyn. I never knew my grandfather who my grandmother always referred to as "Old Man Peter McCoy."

Hannah was a born slave. Her mother was the seamstress in the "Big House." Hannah's job was to take "Missy" to school every day. She waited outside, under a tree, until it was time to take "Missy" home. Hannah was nine years old when "freedom" came.

Reading was always very important to her. We were taught to read very early because we had to read the Bible to her. I never really knew if my grandmother could read or not, but she certainly corrected us if we mispronounced a word or skipped over some words.

My father, Samuel White II, married my mother, Evelyn McCoy. They rented an apartment and had five children. My father then worked for the city of Evanston. He drove a truck.

When my mother was pregnant with her sixth child, the landlord asked them to move. We then moved to an area that was primarily prairie, with no paved streets and only a few houses. The family moved in a car, but the furniture was brought in a horse and wagon.

My father bought a house which had wild strawberries, fresh mint, and beautiful wild flowers. One family near us owned horses and a farm. A short walk from our house there was a cow which we thought to be wild. We ran because it was said that a cow would attack you if you wore red. We did not know any better.

There was an Italian family who owned goats, and a Polish family who ate margarine without color. Our area was very open.

We played softball, kickball, and rode on the backs of boys' bicycles. The boys had bikes because they had paper routes.

Summertime brought the circus to town, as well as carnivals, which were set up just down the block in the field that is now the high school football field.

Every year we went to Dyche Stadium for the fireworks display.

My father's job was to put up the barricades and to take them down later, so we could always get in free.

During The Depression, we had other family members living in our house. My mother would set up the bedroom like dorms. Sisters, brothers, and cousins slept three or four in a bed. The family set up the basement as a large kitchen with a huge round table. All of the aunts and my mother cooked huge pots of food. I did not know until many years later that those members of the family could not afford their apartments and they had moved in until they could "get on their feet again."

My mother often called our house "the house by the side of the road" because it was always filled with friends, relatives, neighbors, and sometimes hoboes stopped by, and she would give them a bit of food. My mother was always at home when we came home.

The thing I remember most about growing up is that we "always" sat down for dinner. My father said the blessing and served the plates. There was always company and a pleasant conversation. I always felt secure.

In retrospect, I had a glorious childhood and I did not realize we were poor. I did not know that the reason Christmas Eve was so exciting was because my father got the Christmas tree for free, because we got what was left over.

We used whatever we had on hand to trim the tree. One year we used Christmas cards from the year before to trim the tree. Many years later, a Christmas tree decorated with cards was described in the paper. We just laughed. During Christmas, everyone came by. We had food and then were sent to bed.

During my early years, everyone we knew was a Republican. Abraham Lincoln freed the slaves. After Franklin Roosevelt was elected president, my father became a reformed Democrat, but my mother remained a Republican until, finally, my father persuaded her to become a Democrat. My mother died first, so under my father, I became a Democrat. Every year I try to attend the Lincoln Day Republican Dinner as a tribute to my mother.

I was raised to be a wife and mother. My husband served in World War II and was in the army of occupation in Germany. Later he was a truck driver. He drove an eighteen wheeler "over the road." We have four children and nine grandchildren.

My activities were limited to the church and PTA.

Our parents were always in politics. They worked for aldermen and mayors. We were exposed to state officials. We were in New York when Adlai Stevenson was chosen for president at the convention. We met Alan Dixon at lunch in Niles when he first ran for office. We were at dinner in Northbrook when Mayor Richard Daley introduced John Kennedy. We went to the airport to greet Lyndon Johnson. We have pictures with Hubert Humphrey.

I was a very late bloomer. I was forty-nine years of age when I entered the "World of Politics." To my father, it was a natural progression that I run for public office. Altogether, I served fifteen years.

I was, indeed, a pioneer.
1. Early member of National League of Cities (Black Caucus).
2. Early member of Black Elected Officials of Illinois.
   There are now over six hundred members.

I have had lunch at the White House with President Carter. I have been in several editions of *Who's Who in Black America*, *Black Elected Officials in America*, life member of NAACP, and a life member of the Illinois PTA.

Danger Signs in Evanston

What has happened to our bright young people is that they are taking their talents and moving away.

Has desecration destroyed our children? Do we need a strong black base before we expect our children to carry the burden?

Something is going wrong! There have always been poor people, but with a lot of pride. More and more black children are going to college these days, but are they coming back to Evanston? People bought homes and sent their children to college, but what is going to happen to these people and their homes, if the children do not come back to Evanston?

Are we all of good will destroying our children?

Questions for Discussion

1. Discuss the progress of the White family from the time they came to Evanston to the end of Edna's political career.
2. Discuss the way the White family helped others survive financial difficulties and The Depression.
3. Edna said she "always felt secure." What particular event in her family life made her feel this way?
4. What did Edna say about her family's political differences that

indicated her respect for them?
5. What did Edna mean by "something is going wrong in Evanston"?

About Edna Summers

Edna said that she served fifteen years in public office. I remember best when she was alderman of the Fifth Ward. Her concern about the people of her ward was great, and she became quite popular with them. She never tried to gain publicity by being a "muckraker" in the political sense, but she was persistent in caring for the welfare of the constituents of her ward and the city of Evanston.

Mrs. Martha Walker

My father came to Evanston from Davenport, Iowa, where he was born. His mother and her sister shot their master somewhere in the South and got as far as the Mississippi River, and they came up the river and my grandmother settled in Davenport. Her sister went on up to Minneapolis on the river. So, I did have, at one time, an aunt in Minneapolis. The only relatives that I have are those two, my grandmother and my aunt. I have no other relatives that I know of.

In Davenport, my father grew up. Incidentally, he was born in Davenport. He grew up on the river. My grandmother had a friend, a Reverend Woods who had some knowledge of Evanston. I am not sure what the background was, but he was black. He knew about Northwestern University and when my father became a young man, Reverend Woods decided that he would make good material to go to Northwestern. Northwestern was a Methodist school, and I think it still is. So, he brought my father to Evanston and he did go to Northwestern University for a period of time. I don't know how long. He lived in the dormitory, the old tower that was on the lake. In Clyde Foster's book, in which he wrote about early Evanston, he tells the story of how Daddy said that he and his roommate had a potbelly stove and they had to go to the basement to get the coal, and by the time they got to the basement and back upstairs, the fire would be out.

Then he became a regular Evanston native. At first, as far as I can remember, and as far as he has told me, he had a barbershop. Evanston was peculiar in that it was settled primarily by blacks who came to work for the very wealthy people who inhabited Evanston and had come to Evanston because of Northwestern. They built Northwestern University, primarily, to take care of their wealthy children. That's how Northwestern started. So when they began to come out to Evanston from Chicago and other areas, they needed people to clean those great big mansions and that sort of thing, so, people came here to work, because it was advantageous. Those were good jobs. But you did not find professionals, black professionals here, because there was no need for them. At the time that I can remember, the doctors that attended to blacks here usually were the doctors who attended to their employers, until we began to get settled.

Now that was my father. My mother came from West Virginia, near Charleston and the Harper's Ferry area. Her mother was a slave for the governor of Virginia. She was black, but she had some Indian blood in her. She was a house lady. House ladies were notoriously taken by their masters to be their own whatever they wished, and my mother was the product of one of those types of relationships. However, it was advantageous to her because, evidently, as she grew up she must have shown some promise, or something. Anyhow, her father sent her to Carlisle to be educated. That was an Indian school, so that is where she went to school. She had a brother that I only knew when I was very, very small, who was a product of her mother, a slave. Uncle John still lived in West Virginia, I guess, when I was three years old was the last time that my mother went back, and she took me. While we were there it seemed as though the people, her other family, wanted to keep me. So we hurried up and left. Now, that's the story that mother tells. I don't know what the circumstances were or anything, but she did not want them to have me, so she hurried up and left. So, anyway, we came back to Evanston and mother came to Evanston at the instigation of Aunt Charity Davenport who was the housekeeper for Charles Dawes, the vice president at that time. She knew my grandmother. Aunt Charity and my grandmother were friends. She knew my mother, and she knew that she had been educated. So, she sent for mother to come and be the governess for the French family. So mother did. She stayed with Aunt Charity. Aunt Charity's house is still there. The house is on Fowler Avenue, and was last owned by Mr. Howard Mack. I remember that there was a large mulberry tree in that yard, and Aunt Charity and the Cromers and Mrs. Finland and Mrs. Cannon used to have these beautiful lawn parties out there in the yard. And when we were little, those of us who were around then, had a ball out there because that was just like being in the country. In fact, across the street, the Bowman Dairy people had a farm along the canal there. It was called the Emerson Farm. That's probably where Emerson Street got its name.

That was one of the good times we had. They had a club, and I think that the outcome of that club was the Dunbar Club. These were all the ladies of that club. And they were ladies. I think that if we had a few ladies like that today, maybe we would have a different type of relationship with children. I don't know. Maybe not, but to me they had class. Those are some of the things I can remember about the good times we used to have out in that yard. Anyhow, that's how my mother came here.

Then Daddy got interested, I don't know how, in the printing business. The only thing that I can recall about that is that there was a Mums Print Shop. And I think that's where he got the press and probably where he learned his skills. I don't know. But, anyway, he had the printing office there in the area where Chandlers is. Also, where the fountain used to be, they called Twiggs' Lot. The kids played baseball there. He became acquainted with Clyde Foster's family and people like that. He later became keeper of the seal at city hall. I can remember, as a very little girl, going to the city hall with him and sitting at his desk while he worked. He got the job as a political appointment. I think Clyde Foster and several of those men were instrumental in that. Their friendship lasted throughout the years.

Clyde Foster owned Quinlan and Tyson, but he had his hand in everything. He wrote a book which I had an autographed copy of. I loaned Ebenezer Church the book, and I have not seen it since. I think the book might be available in the Evanston Historical Society.

I have no other relatives other than those that I have spoken of.

The only relative I ever had, that I know of, and I am sure it was the only relative, was my aunt that went on to Minneapolis. She had a son, Dave, and Cousin Dave came back to Chicago to live and he was married to a very wonderful, smart woman. I was so little that I am not sure about what went on, but Cousin Dave was instrumental in the Assembly Club in Chicago. When I was a little girl he, to me, was very old. He might have been no more than fifty years old, but to a little girl that was pretty old.

Anyway, they went back to Minneapolis, and I never heard anything more about Cousin Dave.

When Daddy came to Evanston he lived at Northwestern University and was living there when he met Mother. She was living at the French's because she was the governess and she lived on the place. The first place that I ever heard them mention about living was on Oak Avenue where Weiboldts' Parking Lot ended, right around the corner from the Zion Church. They lived there, and I think that's where my sister (Kathryn) was born. Both Kathryn and Willard were born there, I am sure. Then they moved further down on Elmwood. That is where the other children were born. This house was later moved to the east side of Dodge Avenue, between Foster and Simpson.

My parents moved to Emerson Street from Elmwood, and it was here that my father set up his print shop on the first floor. The family lived on the second floor.

My parents had me late in life. Mother was almost fifty. She was in her late forties. Agnes was the baby and she was seventeen when I was born. Daddy decided that he was going to build a house for me, and the little house on the back of our lot was my house. He actually built the house himself with the help of a friend. He rented the house later.

Virginia White's family lived there when she was born. Her mother was Lou Gonzales' aunt. That was also Carlos "Brother" White's mother. They then lived across the alley, in the little house which was attached to the hospital.

Then Harry Jackson lived in my little house. I remember when Harry lived there. His mother used to bake bread. She would make the best homebread. His father had an old car. It must have been a Ford or something, and we would sit in the alley there in this car, and she would bake this bread and cut in the middle of it and fill it with butter, and we would just sit out there and have that bread and butter.

They lived there for quite a while. When I got married, I got married at Sister's (Kathryn) house on Ashland Avenue because they had built the house, but Doctor McDonald was not ready to give up his practice in Boushnell, Illinois, so when they built the house, Daddy was afraid that there would be some vandalism because there was nobody in the house, so he elected to move, with Mother and I, over to Sister's house to stay there until Sister and her family would move in. Ken and I were married in Sister's house. Our first home was doctor's offices because they had a little entrance to his offices separate from the other part of the house. It consisted of two rooms.

When we left there, Daddy had rented my house on Emerson Street. We finally got the people out, and that is when we moved in and where we raised all of our kids, except Chris.

Daddy and Mr. Jackson were members of the Masonic Lodge, and my mother and Mrs. Jackson helped to found the women's group, called the Eastern Stars.

When I was little and lived in the house, the man who had the first undertaker parlor, where Mason's was, lived on the third floor of our house. There was an apartment on the third floor of the big house in front.

Then my aunt, Retta Stewart, and her husband lived up on the third floor at one time, and they had an ice cream parlor down on the first floor. And somewhere there is a picture of me sitting on the long steps, you know, that were in front of 1315 Emerson Street, with ice cream all over my mouth. Yes, they had an ice cream parlor there, on the one half, not on the printing side. On the other half, mother had a beauty shop.

Mother went to Burnham Business School downtown in the loop and learned the beauty culture business. She learned not only how to do hair, she learned about the ingredients that went into making pomades and hair dressing stuff. She made little round hair pins, and Daddy printed labels for them.

Women used to comb their hair, and they had something to take the combings out of the comb and they saved them. Then they would have something called a "switch," an extra little piece of hair that, when they had buns up on the top, would wrap around them.

When they would bring them to mother, she had a flat piece that had a lot of wire points, and she would run the hair through until it was smooth, and then she had a loom that had four black strands of thread, and you weave the hair in and out, and in and out, twist it back, and when you got it all filled, then you have your base because the thread was there, and you push it together, you sew it, and you now have your "switch." You can buy them now. They belonged to the women because that was their hair. This was common practice among all women, not just black women. Everybody was doing it.

Mason moved in his building when I was a little girl. He learned of things in the black community because he was connected with the insurance department and things like that, so when they would have something happen in the black community, a shooting or some criminal activity that involved death, they had the hearings at Mason's Funeral Parlor. Mr. Mason got most of the bodies. He got almost all of them, until Mr. Porter of Porter and Owen came along and opened on Asbury Avenue. That was near Cannon's Barber Shop, and Frank Smith's Drug Store, Winters had the market.

Mason controlled the funeral business of Evanston, as far as the blacks were concerned. He started out in the original building that was there when this man who lived at our house had it. Mr. Mason's wife came from a family which had money, some place near Chicago. I think she had the money. They built the building around the original building. The front was always the original building, and then they built up for them to have living quarters. That's where their son, Clarence, was born. They built it up out in the back, and Rachel lived in the living quarters in the rear, she and Hop Graves.

Hop Graves was with Mason, but I don't know if he was a partner.

Mason stayed at this location until his death. They found him dead in his country house in Michigan where Babe's county place was, Paradise Lake.

Mr. and Mrs. Mason went to Mexico on vacation a couple of times. At this time they were retiring. Clarence was a chemist and worked for the Parker Pen Company. If you go to Tuskegee now, there is a building named in memory of him for the work he did along with Dr. Carver.

Anyway, when Mr. and Mrs. Mason went to Mexico, they thought about retiring there, but the altitude affected her and she died.

Then Mr. Mason was found dead at his summer home in Michigan. Freddie Hutcherson used to go up there all the time.

Mason used to sit out in the front on his bench on the steps. I can see him now sitting in his chair, reared back. And he knew everything that went on.

And there was Mrs. Anderson's grocery store. A candy store where the record shop was at one time. Mr. Volt had the tailor shop, where the barbershop is now. All of those buildings at one time were a school. It was not a part of the regular school system, but a special school where the students lived. They say that our house was formerly used as a dormitory for the school.

Uncle Sam Cannon also sat there on the steps and he would be ordering people around. He also brought people here from the South. He brought the Parks family here. I remember very well when they came. Mr. Parks was very, very fair. There was nothing about him that looked black. And his wife was not far behind. They came, I believe, from Georgia. How they knew Uncle Sam, I don't know, but he brought the family here and saw that they got settled in the house on Wesley. Evelyn and I were little, and Mamie was really little. Albert was older than Evelyn.

As soon as they got here, Uncle Sam had me over taking care of them. Evidently he had done that for several families. He looked like a southern colonel, like you see in the movies.

He ruled the roost. There used to be people who ruled the roost. You used to know you didn't do anything in their presence, or anywhere near where they were, because it was going to get home before you got home. That is what controlled the young people. That is what we need

Conversations with Blacks in Evanston, Illinois • 219

to have today. My kids still can remember, when they do something, and they get home and I will know what they have done, as far back as that.

Back then, you weren't alone in the black community. Almost everybody knew everybody else. If you were ill, or if there was a death in the family, or a birth in the family, there were people who were going to be there as soon as those things happened. You didn't have to worry about something to eat, or a place to stay. Somebody would say, "Well, you can come and stay with us." In fact, my earliest recollections of the Y and the churches and all those things were that, whenever they brought anybody in from the outside to do any job in Evanston in the black community, they stayed at our house. Like the Y secretary, Marie Ross, and kids who came to Northwestern, the black kids, they were sent to 1315 Emerson Street to get acclimated to what to do, etc. Then they usually ended up on Garnett Place at someone's house. The Culture Club was over there. The Dunbar Club met at the Y every Thursday at two o'clock. We weren't allowed, at home, to make any plans for Thursday. That was mother's day off. She went to the Dunbar Club.

I can remember that group of women, and I think back on what a wonderful group of women they were, because they were strong. They kept their families together, and they took care of their families, and they took care of their husbands, no matter that their husbands were philandering and doing otherwise, but they kept the families together.

Do you remember Dr. Young? Dr. Young played football at the University of Illinois. He maintained his practice up on the second floor across from the Davis L on Benson. He was a dentist. He was the only black dentist that we had. His son is a member of St. Andrew's now. Do you remember Eleanor and Jean? They came to live with him because his wife was their aunt, and I guess their mother must have died. We were good friends.

At that time, Dr. Young and his wife and two or three other couples, all of whom were very fair, formed a little community in the area where Haven School is now. There were three houses up on Prairie, and Henry Butler was in Mrs. Priscilla Taylor's family. The two nieces did not associate with black kids. Add Mrs Breckenridge to the group she was a member of St. Andrew's.

Dr. Tarkington came along. His wife was Isabelle, they were later divorced. Her nieces were Helen and Jeane Young, Dr. Young's nieces. After Dr. Young's wife died, she took them. They were teenagers.

I forgot Dr. Bess. He was here about the same time as Dr. Young. Didn't Dr. Bess belong to the Knights of Pythians? Yes. He was a West Indian, I believe. That was about the same time that Dr. Penn was around.

You know Dr. Garnett and Dr. Butler, Art Butler's father. They were before Dr. Penn. I remember them. Dr. Butler founded the hospital. Dr. Butler was about the most handsome man I ever saw. He used to stop me. I had a thing as a little girl because Dr. Butler used to come through the alley every morning. Dr. Scruggs lived next door to the hospital. Mr. Cannon used to come down the alley. They always had something for me. I remember Dr. Butler who founded the hospital. They were there before Dr. Penn, I am sure. Dr. Garnett birthed me. Their sanitarium was there in the front and they also had the little house that sits back in the yard, all that was part of the hospital.

Dr. Penn came, since I can remember, he and his wife. She was an Indian from the get go. She was very large and looked just like an Indian. Fred Roulette was her nephew.

Dr. Penn built the brick house which later became the Community Hospital.

Questions for Discussion
1. Describe the journey of Martha's father from Davenport, Iowa to Evanston.
2. According to Martha, what was the reason for black settlement in Evanston?
3. Describe Martha's mother's background.
4. What did Martha say about the Dunbar Club?
5. Describe Martha's life and neighbors when she live on Emerson Street.
6. How did Martha describe "Black Togetherness" when she was growing up?
7. Who built the Community Hospital building?

About Martha Walker
Martha grew up in a family which had a great head start on her. Mr. Twiggs had been well established as a businessman and civic leader, and his first three children had reached adulthood when Martha was born.

She must have been considered a great event in the Twiggs family because they treated her like a princess. No doubt the tender loving care from her family made her the bubbling, enthusiastic person she is today. Martha and her husband, Kenneth, were considered a popular couple in the black community of Evanston. Ken passed a few years ago, but Martha is still very much alive.

Evelyn Williams

Well, I was born in South Carolina. My grandfather and my grandmother lived next door. My grandmother passed away. I don't remember when, and my grandfather and my aunt came to Evanston with his brother, Willis Acker. Then, when my mother died when I was ten and a half years old, I came to Evanston to live with my aunt. I don't know why they moved to Evanston. I don't know that part at all. But I was on my own when I was sixteen.

I don't think there were many changes in our residence from our house at 703 Greenleaf, but we moved to a house on Prairie Avenue where we lived with my uncle and aunt, Mr. and Mrs. Joseph Murphy. He used to have a riding academy on Dempster Street where he taught women how to ride. I don't know about him because he died not too long after I came to Evanston.

My longest residence in Evanston was when my husband, Henry, and I moved to our house on Pitner Avenue in 1959. I lived there for twenty-five years. Henry died three years before I moved. We didn't buy our unit, we just rented. I moved to a building at Ridge and Noyes where I stayed for four years, and then I came to this building and have been here ten years. Most residents here are either senior citizens or handicapped.

I like it very much here because the rent is not so terribly high, and it's quiet. But one thing I don't like is having to go downstairs to answer the door. That's really the only thing I don't like about it. Another good feature about this building is a convenient parking lot where my friends can park when they come to see me. I don't socialize much with the residents here though, because I'm more of a loner.

G.W.W.: Can you comment on African-Americans who have served the community in business or professions?

E.W.: Mr. Bryant used to have a grocery store on Emerson Street, and we used to trade there quite a bit. Doctor Bryant was our doctor until he passed away, and with Dr. Morrison at his drug store.

I had Dr. Davis for a dentist, and Dr. Lawson for an optometrist. I went to a podiatrist, Dr. Alvin Keith, a couple of times, but we didn't set horses too well.

I remember Mr. Watkins, the grocer, and his wife, Marie. Also, another grocer named Higginbotthom.

G.W.W.: Describe the types of jobs you have held in Evanston.

E.W.: When I first came to Evanston in 1923, it was domestic work that the people were doing. They stayed on the job and worked together as couples. That's what my aunt did and that's what I did until I retired two and a half years ago, when my arthritis made me stop working.

G.W.W.: Many people who worked in service had excellent relationships with their employers.

E.W.: I know a couple that I used to work for where our relationship was like that. I hear from them on my birthday and at Christmas time. We stay in touch with each other. I left them under good circumstances. I got along with the people I worked for very well, and the ones I did not get along with, I did not stay there.

I know you know of Jim Finks who used to be with the Chicago Bears. I worked for them for eleven years. We got along fine. I still hear from her. She lives in New Orleans, but we still keep in touch.

I had another employer named Mrs. Murphy. Her husband died about ten years ago. He was a certified accountant. She still lives in Winetka and has remarried. But we still keep in touch.

G.W.W.: Describe your education in Evanston.

E.W.: I went to Central School on Main Street. That's the only school I went to. I went to work, but I enjoyed school and never had any trouble while going to school. I liked all of my teachers.

G.W.W.: What is your interest in politics?

E.W.: I just don't go in for politics. It's all a dirty deal to me, but I do vote. They promise you a pie in the sky, but you don't get results from any of them. I just vote because I know I should.

G.W.W.: Who were some of the popular politicians that you remember?

E.W.: I remember Jourdain when he was alderman, but, like I said, I just wasn't a politician.

G.W.W.: How about Gene Beck?

E.W.: Just to speak to him.

G.W.W.: Edna Summers?

E.W.: I knew Edna, but just to speak to her.

G.W.W.: Bru Alexander?

E.W.: I only knew of Bru Alexander.

G.W.W.: What about your church activity?

E.W.: I go to church because I enjoy going to God's house. I think we all should, and I enjoy the Eucharist because it helps me to get along from day to day.
　　I remember some of the historical people at St. Andrew's like Mrs. Helen Cromer, Mrs. Byrd, Mrs. Peak, Mr. and Mrs. Sweatt, and Mr. Ralph Jackson.

G.W.W.: You know both Mr. and Mrs. Sweatt have passed?

E.W.: Yes.

G.W.W.: Do you remember Father Birney Smith?

E.W.: Father Smith was the priest I was confirmed under. I thought he was a nice, religious man. He just made me angry once, but I got over that. I liked him. At confirmation class he said something that made me angry. I started to walk out of St. Andrew's, and if I had, I wouldn't be a member there today. But I said no, I'm not going to let him run me away.

G.W.W.: Father Smith left, and several other priests came to St. Andrew's and left. Now Father Ikenye is your priest.

E.W.: I like him. He comes to us every Sunday with communion, except the first Sunday. Mr. Allison and I go downstairs to receive the communion. I like him.

There was only one priest I didn't care for very much and that one was Father Spaulding. He was too demanding. That's why I got out of the choir.

G.W.W.: Did you enjoy your experiences in the choir?

E.W.: Oh, I loved it. I sing by ear, but I really enjoyed it. I also used to work with the altar guild, but I had to give that up because of my arthritis. You know, going up steps was kind of hard, but on Saturday before Palm Sunday I usually go over and fix the palms.

G.W.W.: How do you get to church now?

E.W.: I take a taxi, and Ruby Taylor brings me home.

G.W.W.: Your mass is at ten o'clock?

E.W.: Yes.

G.W.W.: Did you ever go to the YMCA?

E.W.: Yes. I used to be a member, but I didn't go very much. I went on a convention to Saugatuck, Michigan with the YMCA. I enjoyed it, but I had to work, so I just wasn't too involved.

G.W.W.: What about the YMCA on Emerson Street?

E.W.: Well, I think I went there once to a basketball game, but I knew all about the Y. Mr. Baker, you know, had a restaurant there, and I worked as a waitress there for a while. Mr. Baker now lives in Glencoe.

G.W.W.: Were you a Cubs or Sox fan?

E.W.: Well, I guess I'm a Cubs fan.

G.W.W.: Are you a Bears fan?

E.W.: Well, yes, but when Mr. Finks went to New Orleans, I used to be a New Orleans Saints fan, as well as a Bears fan.

G.W.W.: Do you watch hockey?

E.W.: I watch them play, but I really don't know what I am watching. But I still like to see them do it.

G.W.W.: What kind of entertainment have you enjoyed in Evanston?

E.W.: Henry and I used to go to a lot of dances at the Masonic Temple. We had good times. And house parties? We used to call them house rent parties. There was a lady who lived on University Place, right in front of Maple Avenue, who used to have them every Saturday night. I used to love to dance, but I wasn't drinking or anything like that.

G.W.W.: Do you gamble?

E.W.: I'm not against gambling, but that never was my bag.

G.W.W.: You have heard about policy wheels, haven't you?

E.W.: Yes, but I never played it. Henry used to play, but I never did. I don't even care for slot machines, but I have been to Las Vegas once.

G.W.W.: Did you have any luck?

E.W.: I didn't leave any of my money there, but it was just kind of fascinating to see. But it was so noisy. It seems like I could hear those sounds after I left.

G.W.W.: The machines?

E.W.: Yes. I went on one of the casino boats in Aurora, but I still didn't gamble. They served us a delicious lunch, all free.

G.W.W.: Where did you catch the bus?

E.W.: At Foster-Fleetwood Center. We had to be over there at seven AM. That was early for me, but I wanted to see what it was all about.

G.W.W.: Where did you catch the boat?

E.W.: In Aurora.

G.W.W.: Did you win any money?

E.W.: No. Because I didn't bet any. You know, Henry used to be gambler, and I said that one gambler in the family was enough. But he gave it up before he passed on. But I will play Keno now.

G.W.W.: Do you belong to any social clubs?

E.W.: Yes, I belong to the Exclusive 13 Club. We really don't do much, except among ourselves, but we do give baskets of food or certificates or something during the Christmas holidays for the needy persons.

G.W.W.: Who are the Exclusive 13 Club?

E.W.: Well, let's see, Beverly Mason was one of the younger members. Some of the older members are Fannie Brooks, Vera Louden, Dorothy Hancock, and Ann Abare.

G.W.W.: Why did you join the club?

E.W.: I had a friend who was a member, and she asked me to become a member, so I joined and I'm still sticking. We are meeting this Saturday. We do it in the afternoon, instead of the evening, before 4 PM.

G.W.W.: Are most of the members younger than you?

E.W.: Yes.

G.W.W.: Do you belong to any sorority or lodge?

E.W.: No

Questions for Discussion
1. Describe Evelyn's coming to Evanston.
2. Who was Joseph Murphy? What was his business?
3. What are some of the features of Evelyn's present residence that she likes? What does she dislike about her building?
4. Describe the kind of work Evelyn has done in Evanston.
S. What is Evelyn's attitude toward politics?
6. Discuss some of Evelyn's joys while attending church in Evanston.
7. Discuss Evelyn's social activities.

About Evelyn Williams

Evelyn and her husband were faithful members of St. Andrew's Episcopal Church. Evelyn was a popular member of the choir, and Henry provided delicious barbecue for affairs given by the St. Andrew's Mens Club. Evelyn also participated in the Birthday Club, a program which provided monthly breakfasts for members of the congregation. Her month was September, the same month as mine.

Evelyn no longer sings in the choir, but she attends church whenever she feels able to do so.

She usually has a few of us "old timers" over to her apartment during the Christmas holidays for food, drinks, and talk.

She is a very thankful to be in such a nice building with friendly residents and convenient parking. She said the only thing she dislikes is having to go downstairs to get her mail.

Dr. Donald Lawson

I was born in Canada. My family moved, in 1938, to Detroit because opportunities in Canada were not too good for black people. My father was an electrician and also a designer of electrical fixtures. He worked in Detroit. He crossed the river in a boat. That was long before they had the bridge or the tunnel. He crossed to Detroit to work every day. In 1938, with his children, some of them getting older and reaching a point where they had to think in terms of their futures, he felt the opportunities were not there in Windsor, Canada. As a consequence, he decided to move to Detroit.

So, we lived in Detroit and enjoyed Detroit. However, it was becoming time for me to think of my education and my family, the Lawson family in optometry. We were the first black optometrists in the United States. My father had a brother, William, Dr. William Lawson, who practiced optometry in Detroit. My brother followed him. Then my uncle's son followed my brother. Then it was my time. So I came to Chicago to study optometry.

When I completed my education in 1946, actually a short time before I completed it, as a matter of fact, in my senior year in school, I met Frank Smith who had been a long time resident of Evanston. As a matter of fact, he had a liquor store in Chicago. I used to go there, because I lived on Fiftieth Place, just a couple of blocks from Frank Smith. We became very fast friends. Frank used to tell me, as I was completing my education in optometry, that I ought to come to Evanston to practice. My family was in Detroit. I had an uncle, a cousin, and a brother practicing optometry there, and all of my friends were in Detroit. Frank brought me to Evanston in his car on several occasions and he tried to tell me about the stability of Evanston, with no unemployment, good living, and this type of thing. As a consequence, he introduced me to Mr. Clarence Marr. Mr. Marr was a gentleman who had a grocery store on the corner of Dodge and Emerson Street. He had a severe problem with his hearing.

After giving it a good deal of thought about the fact that Evanston was very stable, I began to think seriously of it. And one of the things that precipitated this was the fact that Detroit was, at the time, a "boom and bust" city. I can recall my uncle, in Detroit, having practiced many years he said there were times when the Ford Motor Company, General Motors, and Chrysler went down and business stopped. It was like turning a spigot and the water off. Things were bad. Then they would return, but you would have good times and bad times.

As a consequence, having met Mr. Marr and talked to him, he said to me that he had a dream and that dream was to have a building where he could make a contribution to Evanston by having a place for black professionals to practice.

So, in 1947, on the thirtieth of June, I opened my practice in the Marr building at Dodge and Emerson. It was the same day that Dr. Alwyn Gatlin, who was in obstetrics and gynecology opened, and Dr. Jacob Frye. We all opened on the same day. We were joined by Dr. Charles Monroe Tarkington, dentist, who had been practicing there for a few years, and Dr. John Washington from the University of Illinois in internal medicine. Dr. Washington had just come out of the Army. He had been in practice for a couple of years. Dr. Frye and Dr. Gatlin, both had just come out of the Army. So, there were five of us on the second floor of the Marr building.

As I reflect, for many months, and even perhaps a year or two, when anyone walked up those steps, we all seemed to congregate in Dr. Tarkington's waiting room because it was on the corner, and Dr. Tarkington had one of the first televisions. TV had just come out. We used to sit in the waiting room, and every time anyone would come up the steps, all the heads would turn to see where that patient was going. We were anxious to see who that patient was going to because we were all vying for patients.

I had one good fortune in that Reverend Jones, who was the pastor of Ebenezer AME Church, was from Canada, and he knew my father very well. Reverend Jones, when he heard that I was coming to Evanston, came by and insisted that I come out to church. I did, and he had me come up, and he talked about me and my family and I got a "crass" start. Through the years, Evanston treated me very well. I did very well in Evanston in my practice. As a matter of fact, we used to compare notes, and I was doing, from a financial standpoint, far better than Dr. Gatlin or Dr. Frye.

In 1953, I built my home on the corner of Davis and McDaniel Streets. I had three children, three daughters. I was quite happy with a leisurely type of practice because we didn't open our offices until eleven o'clock in the morning, and we there from eleven to one, and then we took a two hour break, and then from three to five, and then we worked every night, however, from seven to nine. But all of people in the building did that.

Well, time was moving on, and my children were getting older. Charley, the oldest of my three daughters, was ready to go away to school. I was sending her to Howard University. Dr. Gatlin made a move. You know, he came to Evanston, incidently, as result of Dr. Bryant, J. Edmund Bryant. He came under him. Dr. Gatlin contended that he did not feel that we were making the type of progress in the health care field as fast as we ought to in Evanston. He moved to Chicago, Sixty-third and Green. He kept his office in Evanston, but he went to Chicago. And, after eighteen months, he said that he was making as much money in Chicago as he had been making in Evanston. That was about 1960. So, in thirteen years, he practiced in Evanston exclusively. And in less than eighteen months, he was making as much, or more money, in Chicago than he was in Evanston.

You know, Dr. Tarkington and I actually put in more hours than the physicians, because they came in a little later in the day. They had their hospital responsibilities and things like that. So, Dr. Tarkington and I became fast friends, and we used to go to the race track a lot. Arlington Park was close and we used to go to Arlington Park. In the summertime, we used to go every day. We would just go for a couple of hours. We could go out there and play a few races and come back. Well, I met, at the race track, Reverend Clarence Cobb. Reverend Cobb at that time was probably the most powerful black minister in Chicago. We became fast friends. After a short time, he said to me, "You know, you don't belong in Evanston. You should go to Chicago. Come to Chicago. If you do, I will put my church behind you." And I gave it some thought. I thought of what Dr. Gatlin had said, and I realized that now that my oldest girl was going to Howard University, my next girl, Donna would be ready for college. And let me say, I made five thousand dollars the first year that I was in practice in Evanston, and that was a lot of money in those days. When I say a lot of money, let me put it in context.

My office rent in Evanston with Mr. Marr was fifteen dollars a month. My residence at 1815 Darrow Avenue, across the street from Dr. Hill, the Hut House, a two flat building, my rent there was twenty-two dollars and fifty cents a month, with heat supplied. So, my rent for my office and residence was thirty-seven dollars and fifty cents a month.

As I said, I made five thousand dollars in my first year of practice. Far more than Dr. Gatlin or Dr. Frye. We used to compare notes.

However, you know, in a small town, you tend to peak. You earn rather quickly, but after a certain point, you reach a peak, because at that time, if my recollection is correct, there were about six thousand black people in Evanston.

Now, one of the good things you can say about Evanston is that there was very little unemployment, but most of those people worked as domestics. They were chauffeurs and domestics, good people, but they had limited earnings. And many of those people who sought professional care were directed to the practitioners of those they worked for. "Mrs. Jones," who worked for "Mrs. McCormick," would be directed to "Mrs. McCormick's" doctor. So, what it did was reduce the number of people that you had to make a living from. And certainly from the beginning, you drew from black people and six thousand people are not a lot. And, at one time, there were nine black physicians in Evanston. Nine. And all of them were making a living. They all did not have flourishing practices, but they were making a living.

So, as a result of having met Reverend Cobb and his telling me what he would do, and having listened to Dr. Gatlin say how he was doing in Chicago, I decided to open an office in Chicago. I said, "I will go into Chicago during the morning hours every day and keep my Evanston office." I did this. At that particular time, my Chicago office was at 6326 Cottage Grove Avenue, on the second floor. I was in practice with two dentists.

I found that things were better, indeed, in Chicago. After one year, I moved into the Maryland Building on Sixty-third Street. Now the Maryland Building, at that time, was the largest black professional building in the United States. There were about forty black professional people. All disciplines. It made no difference what particular thing you were interested in, what branch of medicine, there were those doctors in the Maryland Building.

And I took off. My practice really began to flourish, with the help of Reverend Cobb, as I said. And a short time later, Elijah Mohammad was introduced to me. And I became his eye doctor. I took care of him, his wife, and his sister, Anna, until he died. During those times, I also took care of the many, many of his followers, and at the school they were directed to come to me every year.

I stayed in the Maryland Building for sixteen years. My roots, however, were in Evanston, and the physician who was caring for me was in Evanston. And I developed a physical problem, a problem in my neck where I had to have surgery. I was in the Evanston Hospital. One Sunday morning I happened to turn on the television and I heard a minister by the name of Robert Schuler. Robert Schuler made a statement, a very strong statement to the fact that if there was something you wanted to do, you should do it. Get at it. Don't worry about the end or how you are going to do it and all the other things, do it. And I came out of Evanston Hospital and went back to my office in the Maryland Building where I was doing very well. I found that I had difficulty finding a place to park. I found that when I went to enter the building, after having been out for over two months, there were people standing around with wine bottles in paper bags. And I went into the lobby, and it seemed sort of depressing, and the elevator seemed ill kept. You know, when we see these things every day, sometimes we don't recognize how things actually are. And having been away for a couple of months, and seeing this, I said, "Is this what my patients have to come to every day?" So, I mentioned it to my wife, the fact that I wasn't happy and I felt that I needed to move. She thought I was crazy. Because she knew that I was doing very well. Why would I want to leave the Maryland Building?

But I had made up my mind. Reverend Schuler had implanted something in me. So I made a call to a real estate broker. I said "I think I want to move." She said, "You do? Where do you want to go?"

I said, "I have no idea. However, I want to go into an area where the transportation is good and where parking is good. I don't want an old ragged building." Basically, these were my requirements.

She said, "I don't have anything, doctor, but I tell you, I'll get on it."

Twenty minutes later she called me and stated that something came across her desk, the Adams Woodsell Feldhoff Funeral Home, on the corner of Eighty-Seventh and Dorchester.

Well, I am an impetuous person. I said to her, "It sounds great. When can I see it?" She said, "Let me call Mrs. Feldhoff."

The result was that, after the second day, Mrs. Feldhoff permitted me to come. She wanted her daughter there with her, because she was getting up in age. Her husband had died, and she wanted someone there with her when I went to look at the building.

I was very impressed with the building because it was not an old building. It was about eighteen years old. The architecture of the building was fantastic. And I immediately began to negotiate. Again, my wife was not convinced. She felt that I was doing so well at the Maryland Building, why should I even entertain the thought of moving?

I said, "Well, baby, this is a decision that I am going to make." And I bought that building, and certainly, it was one of the best moves that I ever made.

My Recollections from Evanston

Perhaps I should say that at that time, when I bought the building, I had discontinued my Evanston practice completely. That was about 1977. It was about twenty years ago. I found Evanston to be an excellent place to raise a family. And I thoroughly enjoyed living in Evanston, the friends I developed there. I enjoyed the schools that my children went to. All of the schools were very, very fine, as compared with Chicago.

I became involved, I don't know how it came about, but I became first involved in the Urban League. We developed a tutorial program. I was the chairman of that program for over ten years.

We developed a tutorial program in Evanston which was the largest tutorial program in the United States. It got to the place where it was so large that we were able to even bus children to areas for tutoring. We reached out to Northwestern University and the National College of Education for students to assist, and we got them to work on a one on one basis. And we had an outstanding tutorial program.

One of the great disappointments that I had was when we went to W. Clement Stone, who was a noted philanthropist, and he refused to give us any financial help. However, we had outstanding people working with us. Erwin Salk from Salk, Ward, and Salk. Jack Korshak, who was a former alderman. We had Bill Erickson and his wife, Margery. Bill was the president of the American National Bank. We had some excellent people. And certainly, Dr. Grace Jaffe who was one of the stalwarts in the tutorial program.

For some reason, that program became recognized. Near the end of that time, there were severe problems in the school systems in Evanston. I was elected to the board of District 202, the executive board of District 202. And I served on that board for a number of years.

During that time, there was a good deal of trouble. Dr. Gregory Coffin was brought into the district from Boston to get things straightened out. Dr. Coffin was a liberal person. His being liberal was not digested too well by some people in Evanston. They thought he was moving too quickly. They wanted him out. And there were certain forces in Evanston, at that time, white liberals, who developed an organization, and they asked me to head that. And I became chairman of citizens for Coffin.

There was all kinds of publicity and notoriety. As a matter of fact, during the years of the Gregory Coffin situation, it was on the first eight pages of the newspapers of every Chicago newspaper for many, many, many months.

It was that hot an issue. I said that I never, ever wanted to see another television camera in my lifetime. Every channel was at my house or in my office for interviews every day and many, many times a week. You would just get tired of it. You lose your life.

However, we met at the Unitarian church. That was our headquarters. We had large mass meetings. And we had the board members. They were hot times, I'll tell you, in Evanston.

At that time, also, I was asked to run for mayor of Evanston. Of course I said, "No way. If I could ever get out of this, I will have made my contribution."

The Evanston Chamber of Commerce awarded me their most outstanding citizen in Evanston, and I developed many good friends in Evanston.

Ultimately, however, we were not successful. Dr. Coffin remained for a certain period of time, but he had to move. They couldn't take Gregory Coffin. And it is interesting, as I look back on Evanston, those whites who were liberal are now very conservative. The whole complexion of Evanston changed.

As I talk to people who know people, they tell me how these people have changed. It almost blows my mind to know they could have been so conscientious and liberal in those days and now to be just the opposite.

Let me say this one thing. I have always, in my practice, had love affairs with my patients. When I say that, I want that to be understood. And in many cases, my patients have loved me. I have developed close ties with many good people. I thoroughly enjoyed Evanston.

However, you know, as I go back to Evanston now, which does not happen too often, I don't see the changes that I would expect to see. It surprises me that in 1947 or 1948 there were nine black physicians and today there are not over two or three practicing there. You would expect there to be as many or more, but it has completely reversed.

As I go back to Evanston, I don't see the change, the progress that one would expect to see so many years later. It appears that things are almost the way they were before. But I understand, now, that many black people have moved to Skokie and other areas. But, to me, there seems to be a stagnation in Evanston.

I am very close to Leon and Alice Robinson. They certainly have done exceptionally well, not only in Evanston, but all over the United States.

They have a very, very successful operation. That stems back to the parents, Josephine and Leon, whom I knew and was close to for many, many years. They pioneered. Most people are not aware of the magnitude of the Robinson empire. I call it an empire because they own more real estate in Evanston, probably, than any other person, black or white. And their operation with the Robinson Bus Company is not only an Evanston Operation, but also Chicago, Detroit, Philadelphia, it's in many other cities. It's a very, very big and successful operation.

I talked to the son-in-law of Frank Smith, who is still living and is approximately one hundred and five years old. He still lives on the corner of Fowler and Davis Streets. I intend to get over to see him very soon.

Deterioration in Evanston

I think one of the things that is contributing to the deterioration of Evanston is the fact that blacks now have the opportunities to go elsewhere for services, something that they could not do in the earlier years. They have opportunities to live in other areas, so many have moved out of Evanston. Of course, the Asians have moved in and taken over black businesses, but that is prevalent in Chicago. It is prevalent all over. Probably, the best part of the country is the South. And many, many black people are moving back to the South. They are going back to their roots. It's a sad thing. You know, it has been my observation that black people, basically, don't like themselves. They have low opinions of themselves. We are the only race of people who don't help each other. We tend to pull each other down. Asians, Chinese, Italians, Irish, or any other ethnic group tends to stick together. They tend to support each other. Black people don't do it. We don't do it. I don't know what the answer is. I wish I did. We have so many billions of dollars that we spend in the United States. If we put our money together, there is just no limit.

I have discussed, as a matter of fact in a club meeting yesterday, I was saying what a pity it is that the black athletes now, who are making millions of dollars, could not, somewhere along the line, get together a group of men and contribute to a pot.

Now, these are people who have not had big amounts of education. It varies, however, but they control probably more money than any other segment of the black community. And if that could be corralled in some manner, and we could get them to work and contribute, a great deal could be done.

But one of the major things for many years has been that the black people don't get out and vote. They don't exercise their power. They could very well do many, many more things.

At another club meeting that I attended on Friday, I was told about Harold Washington when he died, something that most people are now aware of. When Harold Washington died, two billion dollars worth of business, finances that had been channeled by him to black businesses, black law offices, black operations, was lost. It's gone. It's just evaporated. It's all now going back to the white community.

It's a very difficult thing. And we are being replaced by Hispanics. Their numbers are and they are getting a much bigger piece of the pie.

In Chicago, Daley has entrenched himself to the extent that he will be mayor as long as he wants to be. And he is doing nothing for black people, in the main. He has two or three, but the masses of black people are just out. And it is a sad commentary. Chicago once was a progressive city for black people. It has been replaced, as there are many other cities now that are far ahead of Chicago, as far as black business is concerned.

The operations like Soft Sheen and Johnson's Products and all of these other places are being sold to whites. And the black basis is just leaving us. Soft Sheen is still owned by Soft Sheen, but they are seeking a buyer. What they want to do is, they would like to maintain some ownership, but they don't want to maintain the operation. They want to be free from the operation itself.

I keep referring to club meetings. We were discussing the role of the black church. This role is the same in Evanston, Chicago, Detroit, in any of the other big cities. There is no question in my mind that the black ministers, the black church has more influence on black people than any other source. And it is sad that they are not working together and doing more for each other. Now, I cannot speak at this point for Evanston, but I can say this for Chicago. Some of the top, the most powerful black ministers, are in the pocket of Richard Daley. One of the ministers, Clay Evans, said to his church, "Give us this day our Daley bread." Which, in my judgment, is a disgrace for a minister. But, he is only concerned about himself. Too many black ministers are apparently interested in themselves than they have the power to join forces and really have a power base for black business and black success in the community. They are failing to do that.

Question: Do you see any change in that in the future?

You know, I would hope that I could say, yes, I do, but I don't. I really don't. And I really don't know what it is going to take. You know, the most unfortunate thing to happen in my lifetime, as it relates to politics, was Harold Washington's death. I think had he lived, even another term, that the whole complexion of Chicago, and even Evanston, would be changed, because not only was Harold Washington doing things for black people, he was doing things for white groups, and they liked him because he was a fair man. He was fair. They were getting things done that none of this predecessors did. There would have been opportunities for black entrepreneurs to have flourished, if Harold Washington had lived a while longer.

But there just seems to be now a conservative movement in Evanston, Chicago, and all over. They tend to get rid of blacks, and one who has power. You go back to Malcolm X, to Martin Luther King, and your liberals like the Kennedys, they're rid of them. Now, they are not able to handle Farrakhan, and frankly, I think that says a lot about Louis Farrakhan. I don't agree with everything he does or says, but he is telling black people what they need to hear. They need to get together and pool their resources and do for themselves. We have the power to do that.

Questions for Discussion

1. How did Donald Lawson happen to enter the profession of optometry?
2. Name two Evanston residents who were influential in getting Don to come to Evanston.
3. What was the result of Clarence Marr's ambition to provide a place for black professional to practice?
4. Who were the other doctors who had offices in the Marr Building?
5. How did Dr. Lawson's income compare to the incomes of the other professionals in the building?
6. What minister encouraged Dr. Lawson to move his practice to Chicago?
7. What were some of the factors that limited the amount of business that would go to black professionals in Evanston?
8. Dr. Lawson said that when he moved his office to the Maryland Building in Chicago, his business "took off." What did he mean by that?
9. Why did Dr. Lawson decide to move from the Maryland Building?
10. What was the Urban League program in Evanston that Don became the head of? Name some of the features of this program.

11. Dr. Gregory Coffin was a controversial figure in Evanston. What was Don's opinion of him?

12. In what ways does Dr. Lawson think black life in Evanston has deteriorated?

About Dr. Donald Lawson

If one word could describe Don, it would be "competitive." We used to have a group of business and professional men in Evanston who would meet at the Emerson Street YMCA and play volleyball during the fall and winter months, and in the spring and summer months we would play softball at Foster Field.

Well, Don was the most energetic man on the floor or field. I used to wonder where he got so much enthusiasm and aggression. He seemed to really enjoy competing with the rest of us.

Obviously his desire to be the best in his field has led to his success in his profession. I don't know of anyone who can say that Don has given them an incorrect prescription for an eye condition. His success has been well earned.

Evanston lost a valuable citizen when Don moved to Chicago, but their loss is a gain for the Beverly community on the South Side. When I called upon him for our interview, he looked right at home in his opulent surroundings.

We ended our session by taking a short trip to his office at Eighty-seventh and Dorchester. It was a pleasure to enter an attractive, busy, efficient optical office. I am sure that Don congratulates himself many times for moving from the Maryland Building to this place.

Many thanks to Reverend Robert Schuler.

Mr. Spencer Jourdain

My father, Edwin B., was from New Bedford, Massachusetts. He came to Evanston after his graduation from college. He went to Harvard College. He arrived here about five years after his graduation. I am not exactly sure of the date, but I think it was late 1926. His reason for coming was basically to increase his economic opportunities. The businesses were moving out of New England, and there were very little economic opportunities, especially for people who were colored, but in general. So he came to Chicago where there was an increase in economic opportunities.

My mother came from the rural area of eastern Georgia, near the South Carolina border, and they came in 1919 or 1920. They came as part of the great migration. Economic opportunity was the reason.

My family lived on Asbury Avenue between Greenbay and Emerson Streets. Then they moved to Emerson Street, on the same block as Ebenezer Church. Then my mother married my father and then they moved over to Darrow Avenue.

I left Evanston in 1957 to go to college, so I haven't really lived in Evanston since then, but I remember that the whole block looked out for the youth and each other in that area.

I am now a consultant in education and business aspects of education, and pure education itself.

But my dad, as you know, was an alderman in Evanston, and after being an alderman he was assistant superintendent of schools of the state of Illinois. He held a number of different offices for the state. He was also head of the NAACP from 1942 to 1944. After that he was an educator at Roosevelt University. He then retired.

Some of his earlier jobs were with the *Chicago Defender* newspaper. He was the first manager of the Regal Theater. He tried to start his own newspaper, the *North Shore Whip*. That did not make it. There wasn't a big enough market.

I went to Haven School from kindergarten through the eighth grade. It was one of the best experiences of my life. The teachers, by and large, were terrific. I think I got a very good education. I enjoyed it very much.

In Evanston Township High School it was the same. The teachers in high school were even more outstanding. In grammar school I remember a teacher, especially Mrs. O'Brien, who was my eighth grade teacher. She had a very good influence on me. And in high school there were tremendous teachers like Miss Caravetes and Dr. Mattson, and others who were very good.

I went to Harvard College. And when I got there, the education which I got at Evanston Township High School was equivalent to the education of the prep schools like Andover and Exeter, etc. There was no difference. In fact, I think I had a much more well rounded education at ETHS. But academically, it was the same.

Politics in Evanston

The high points of my political experiences in Evanston were when my dad was involved.

He came to Evanston and served as an usher in the Ebenezer Church and got to be known in the community while he was working as reporter in Chicago and as manager of the Regal Theater.

He was drafted to run for alderman of the Fifth Ward because of the tremendous political spirit which was growing among the black residents. They were no longer satisfied with the inferior representation they were getting from white representatives. They wanted to elect one of their own, and because of my dad's educational background and his service in the church community, they asked him to run. He had also done things like organizing "black awareness" at the Emerson Street YMCA and he was teaching black history on Sunday afternoons, so they knew he was a leader in the black cultural movement.

So he was asked to run, and he did run for alderman of the Fifth Ward of Evanston. He ran in 1931 and was elected, but the election was contested. He had to run again in 1932, and he was elected by a landslide. From then on, he represented the community until 1946, when he lost.

The reason he was my hero and the hero of many people in Evanston was that he represented the pride of the community, the insistence on learning, emphasis on education, emphasis on self respect, and he did a lot of things to better the community, like bringing people such as W.E.B. Dubois and Oscar DePriest and Bill Dawson, and many others to the community to speak to the people and try to give good values to the kids and teach them to have pride in their own heritage, as well as the heritage of America. I think that during that time, black people in the community and also whites and women benefitted from his service, because he was always a great proponent for women's rights. He supported Daisy Sandridge for alderman just as much as she supported him. She was the first female alderman in Evanston. He was the first black. So he was as much concerned about women's rights as he was about blacks rights.

I think that during that time there were all these causes advanced, and there were many advances in the black community, like the theaters were desegregated under his leadership. Many of the restaurants were desegregated under his leadership. The lights were put in on Foster Field under his leadership. Black baseball prospered. The community had a spirit under his leadership that it has not had since his administration. There is no question about that. Many of the older people talk about that.

Desegregation of the Evanston Theaters

I only hear what was told to me, but I think that when my father entered into negotiations with Balaban and Katz Organization which owned the theaters, Varsity and Valencia, basically he requested that there be a change in the seating policy. After one brief episode where he had the theater closed, they agreed that it was better to end this type of segregation in the theaters.

But informally, it went on for a long time. Blacks would sort of sit in the balcony because for so many years they had been doing that. But officially segregation in the theaters was ended.

YMCA

During the summer we would go to the Y twice a day. They had swimming in the morning and in the afternoon. We would go over there, and Mr. Green was the swimming instructor for a while, and then my older brother was one of the lifeguards there. And Louis Moseley and Ollie Jones, one of the twins, Ollie and Oliver, was an instructor and lifeguard. That is where I learned how to swim, and that was a major occupation of our time as kids in the summer. It gave us a place to go and something to do in the morning and afternoon. I really enjoyed that.

We lived one block from Foster Field. We played softball, a little basketball, and on tennis courts is where I became a pretty good tennis player.

My grandfather was one of those people who were caretakers of Foster Field. Fleety was the head of the park, and Doc Cohen and my grandfather, "Poppa Joe" Hardwick were the caretakers. So I was over there a lot.

Of course we loved watching the Rams and the Flashers.

In high school I was big fan of the ETHS teams. We had great teams when I was in high school. I was in the class of 1957. The class of 1958 had a great team. In basketball, we went down state—guys like Art McZier, Tom Mims, and Harold Howell was a great center. McZier was a forward. We had tremendous team spirit, and I remember it was really enjoyable going to the football and basketball games.

Northwestern

We used to go Northwestern during the 1948 season and watch them practice. That was the year they had a great team. We had a lot of awe for the college football players, like Ron Burton who became an All American, and Fred Williamson, and the Kimbroughs, Sam Johnson, and Wilmer Fowler. We used to go and watch those games. Oh yes, Irv Cross was a stand-out.

Evanston Entertainment

We had a lot of fun growing up. Of course, since I left at the end of high school, the entertainment I knew was entertainment as a kid or an adolescent. Basically it was in people's homes where we had house parties, but usually it was around sports and at Foster Field.

Harvard College

Kids of alumnae always get certain perks, but I had a very good academic record in high school and did very well on the SATs. I think I scored second highest in the state in English. I also won a scholarship. They still say that was the peak academic performance time of Harvard and that they are still trying to get back to the standards of the fifties and early sixties. It was a top period for academics there. It was very, very tough, competitive. You just studied all the time, but it was a tremendous training experience. I had incredibly great professors like Arthur Schlesinger and other famous people.

Campus life was integrated, but basically revolved around, for me, studying. But there were a lot of things to do. There were intramural sports. I didn't play any college sports, but intramural sports we played.

I think I was sort of a "grind," but I did wind up graduating with honors, so that was worth it.

I studied seven days week, twelve hours a day, eighteen hours a day. I had to do this to compete with a lot of brilliant people there. I did want to be an honor student, so it just took all of my time.

Occupation Experiences Since College

I have been a consultant my entire career. I have found that it gave me the flexibility that I wanted in terms of developing my own career, and I was very much involved in the economic development, the black economic development movement of the 1960s and 1970s, and I was part of the movement to get things like Minority Small Business Investment Companies, I was on the advisory group to SBA, along with people like Mayor Hatcher of Gary, Indiana, counseling to businesses that were being started at that time. That went for about ten years, and then I did documentary film production, consultation, and basically, it was pretty neat because the package, in terms of the decade, the sixties, was economic development. The seventies was documentary film. And the eighties was communications consulting and then getting into educational communications consulting. Education has been the center of my consulting, basically, education in terms of history, social studies, and studies that lead toward development of business skills.

History and economics were the two key course categories that gave me the background for my consulting training. After college, I also took individual studies in accounting, finance, marketing, production.

I am an individual consultant. Since last year, I have been spending most of my time writing, writing about history, writing about educational development, and I would say now that my time is equally devoted toward writing and consulting activities.

I feel very satisfied that is where things seem to be going now. Corporate employment is less the total of total employment in the United States, because of corporate downsizing, and the outsourcing of work to small groups of consultants is the trend. So I have just sort of been in that same mode all along. It hasn't been any kind of transition for me, because that is always the way I have been doing business.

I think this project is a very good one. I am glad that this project is being done because Evanston has had a very unique history as a city, and I am glad to see that we as a community and as black people in the community are recording our history and our experiences. And I think, particularly, the history of folks who are maturing now is important, and we need to start to set some inspirational examples for the kids who are coming on now, and leave ways of wisdom for them in how we made it.

Questions for Discussion
1. Why did Spencer's father come to Chicago? Where did he come from?
2. Where did Spencer's mother come from?
3. What is Spencer's occupation now?
4. What were some of the positions held by Spencer's father?
5. Describe Spencer's educational experiences.
6. Describe Spencer's impressions of his father's political and civic activities in Evanston.
7. Why did Spencer say that his father was his hero?
8. Describe Spencer's sports activities.
9. What was Spencer's campus life like at Harvard College?
10. What have been Spencer's occupational experiences since he left college?

About Spencer Jourdain
Spencer has been a busy young man. He travels a lot, performing services as a consultant in the field of education. He is well qualified, having been an honor student at both Evanston Township High School and Harvard College.

It is apparent that his father has been a great influence on his life. Spencer seems to be ready for success.

Bill Logan

I was born and raised in Evanston. My family came from two different locations. My dad's family came from Greenwood, South Carolina. My mother's family came from Des Moines, Iowa.

The reasons they left are not very clear. My dad's family had property down in South Carolina, but still they chose to move here. His father had passed away earlier in his life, so it was just the mother and about nine kids who came up to this particular area.

My mom's family, the Powells, lived on Church Street in the 1800 block where there was a barbershop, which my great great grandfather had. I think my dad's family, a lot of them were domestics for a long period of time. My father did some domestic work, but he was also involved in construction for years. He worked in areas where he was the only black, out in the western suburban areas. Eventually, he ended up with the post office and retired from the post office.

My mom, she did clerical work. She also did domestic work and clerical work. She retired from a printing firm here in Evanston many years ago.

I went to the old Foster School. I remember some good experiences there with some of the teachers, like Mr. Bouyer. He had an influence on my life. From there I went to Haven School for junior high school. In those days it was seventh and eighth grades.

I had some pretty good experiences there. I really don't remember a lot of teachers who were prejudiced there at Haven School. A lot of kids that we associated with, of course, were ignorant about blacks. They would ask, for example, if the lines in the middle of your hands were made by chocolate candy, or if your mom fed the baby was it chocolate milk. But the experiences at Haven for me and other blacks were not so bad.

Probably the one that slapped me in the face the most was my experience at Evanston Township High School where I ran into so many prejudiced teachers.

They were very blatant and open with their prejudices. That had an impact on me about the reality of the world I was facing in Evanston. But with my dad and mom being very strong, I was able to overcome a lot of the stuff they were putting up with.

There were some very strong examples. I will never forget, there was an English teacher here. I will never forget her as long as I live. She was very open that she didn't care for blacks. In fact, she wanted to flunk me and she flunked my two sisters who, unfortunately, ended up with her. But she was the type of teacher who, if you raised your hand in class, she would not acknowledge you. She wouldn't answer any questions about homework, and when you came to the school the next day, she would be at the front door and if you didn't have your homework ready, and you tried to explain it to her, she wouldn't even let you in the class. She would just kick you out. So, she was just about the toughest one I faced there.

But there were some good teachers there, too. She was about to flunk me my freshman year. I was an athlete. She was going to give me a failing grade, so I went to my homeroom director, a man by the name of Carl Erie. I told him what the story was and he said, "Come on with me." So we went to the teacher and he told the teacher, "I want you to do me a favor. If you are going to flunk Bill, why don't you give him a passing grade, and I will see that he goes to summer school." She reluctantly gave in to that and gave me a passing grade. When we walked out of the office and down the hall he said, "We got what we wanted. Forget the summer school. You don't need it."

I had social workers and counselors who said I wasn't college material. For example, I didn't need to take college preparatory courses, because I wasn't going to college. But I think I overcame all of those kind of "good" things. Being a three sport athlete, I was the only black on the baseball team, and all of the racial comments and things from places like New Trier and Highland Park and Cicero and getting hit with pitched balls were tough. But I over came that.

In football, I was the first black to win the Myerson Award for excellence in football for four years. I was told that I was the first black captain of a football team. But I know there was a tremendous number of great black athletes who went on before me, but because of the prejudice that they faced, they never got that kind of recognition.

In basketball, I had a prejudiced basketball coach. First of all, he didn't like blacks, and second, he didn't like football players. But I went out, and he put me on the junior varsity. I was the only black on the junior varsity. I was the leading scorer. He was dressing all of the white boys on the team for the varsity game. I asked him one day why I didn't dress. So, he told me to dress for the next game. So, I dressed for the next game, and it was a blow out. Evanston was winning by a big points. Everybody went into the game and when thirty-one seconds were left in the game, he told me to go into the game. I refused to go in. I quit. That was the only time I ever quit anything in my life.

But on the other hand, I had a good experience with Carl Plath. When I was a sophomore he started four blacks on the basketball team. I remember when we were playing here on the gym, we had a lot of white parents who were screaming epithets at us and everything. My mom came home from a couple of games and she was crying because they were calling us "niggers" and all of that, and asking why were we playing and all that kind of stuff. But he stuck with us. Later, he was my varsity coach in my senior year. So, those were the kind of experiences I had, some good ones and some bad ones.

I was the senior class vice president. They tell me I was the first one, but we also had George King, who was the class president. I was also told that I was the first black president of a homeroom. So the experiences here were good and bad, but I think I overcame them with the backing of my parents. I remember being in a class, the only black in the class. Some kids were talking in class. The teacher told everybody to stop talking, or she was going to kick them out of class. But I had never said a word. So, she turned around to the board again, and the kids started talking. She pointed her finger at me and told me to get out. And I wasn't even talking. But there wasn't anything I could say to change her mind.

Community Spirit

There was a lot of community support in Evanston then. We were more like a family. I remember people like the Flemings and Smalls, I worked for the Smalls. I remember "Doc" Morrison and his stores on Lyons and Darrow, and on Church Street. I worked for him for a while. I think all of these people had an influence on my life.

Dr. Hill brought me into this world. They claimed that it was between me and Bettyjeane White who she first brought into this world at the old Community Hospital. All of those people leave a little piece of themselves in your life. I remember the man who had the hardware store on Emerson and Dodge Avenue, Mr. Clarence Marr and Marie Marr. They also had a big house on Dodge, right behind the store.

Sometimes I give talks about the whole community and family

situation that I see is lacking today. I remember when a kid by the name of John Ingram and I got into a fight at Foster School. The fight was broken up, and we had to stay after school. On the way home, I lived in the 1900 block on Foster Street, I got stopped about two or three times by adults who said that they had heard about the fight and that I shouldn't be doing this, and they jumped on my case. And then I got home and my mom was waiting with a switch, already. But it was that whole community feeling. The people were concerned. But now it is not like that at all. Kids are afraid to cross certain streets, you know, they are afraid to come to certain areas, because of the gang problem and all of those kinds of things. That had a positive influence on us, but I don't see that influence now.

I went on from Evanston High School. I received a football scholarship to Western Illinois University. I went down there and played ball for two years before I had to go into the military. It was primarily a white town. There were only eleven blacks in the whole school. Ten of us were athletes. There was only one black female in the whole school. When we walked down the street downtown on Saturday, they would tell us we had to walk out in the street and let the white people get by and all that kind of stuff.

I had to go into the war, the Korean War. I was with the U.S. Air Force. I spent four years there, and I spent two years in Japan and Korea. I played ball there. Then I came back to the United States and was discharged. I was stationed at O'Hare Field.

At that time the Air Force had not been integrated too long, so there were some difficult times. We had some instructors in basic training who made it very clear that they didn't like blacks. But we were able to overcome those. I remember being called names on the ship when we were going to Japan. I never will forget. One Indian guy called me a "nigger." He didn't want to sleep on the same bunk area where I slept. He said he didn't want to sleep with "no niggers."

Then overseas, of course, we ran into prejudice from Japanese who wouldn't hesitate to tell you that they thought we had tails.

We had bosses in the military who didn't like blacks and made it very evident, but I had the rank of staff sergeant.

I remember coming back from overseas and being stationed at O'Hare Field. I was a staff sergeant at that time, and the lieutenant, when he wasn't there, left me in charge of the shift that I was on. I was in communications. I will never forget, the captain came in one day, and asked for the lieutenant, and I told him the lieutenant wasn't there and that I was in charge and asked if I could help him. He looked at me and he said, "We don't put niggers in charge of anything like this," just out in the open like that. What could I say? He stormed on out of the door. I guess he chewed the lieutenant out the next day for putting me in charge.

I think I hit more individual prejudice in the military than I did from the Air Force itself, particularly individuals from the South, you know, who didn't want to have anything to do with blacks. But over all, the experience wasn't too bad. It was a good learning experience.

I was discharged from O'Hare Field and came back to Evanston. I didn't know what I wanted to do after I got discharged. I was floating around. I worked at the Nash Brothers for a while. When they went on strike, I was walking the picket line in January. I went home and told my dad, I said, "I can't take this." So, he showed me an article in the *Evanston Review* about a position which had opened up in the police department called the "Policeman-Fireman." You were hired as a policeman, but you would be trained as a fireman, also.

So, I went down and put in my application and I was hired.

At that time, there were only six or seven blacks on the department. Mr. White was gone, but Babe Cooper, Bill Jones, Pete Cromer, and Zelty Edwards were on at that time. So, there were only a handful of blacks on the police department.

At that time we couldn't patrol in the white neighborhoods. We were assigned to the black areas. Only in the emergency situations could we go into a white area.

We had that old promotion system and assignment where there never had been any blacks promoted. A lot of black guys had been to college and had good backgrounds, but they couldn't get promoted. Some of the assignments, blacks couldn't get into. If they did get in, there would be limitations as to how many could be assigned there. For example, Zelty Edwards was the first black to be in the traffic bureau. He rode a two wheel motorcycle, which was an elite bureau at that time. When I applied for it, they wouldn't let me go up. So, eventually they transferred him out, and then they moved me up. So they only kept one of us there out of twelve.

On the detective bureau they had two on each shift. There were two shifts. We worked on the west side.

So, we ran into a lot of prejudice there, shift commanders and sergeants who were prejudiced. But the promotion system was the thing.

Nobody could get promoted. I almost gave up on that because I was thinking, hey, they aren't going to promote any blacks, so maybe I'll find me another field.

But a couple of things happened. I had an opportunity to be Dr. Martin Luther King's bodyguard when he came to Evanston to speak back in the sixties. As a result of that, we had some conversations, and I remember the last time I spoke to him, we were standing in front of the Orrington Hotel. He was waiting for the car to come and take him to the airport. I was talking to him about no blacks ever being promoted in Evanston, and that I was concerned about that. He said that I needed to keep the faith and never stop dreaming my dream and hold on, and that things would get better.

Then I thought about that time that I quit the basketball team, because of prejudice, so I just made up my mind that I wasn't going to quit. They were going to have to do something to show me why I wasn't eligible or qualified to be a sergeant on this police department.

So I went back with kind of a new attitude and took advantage of working every bureau. I went to all the schools that were offered. I took a course at the University of Michigan, Michigan State, Wisconsin, Illinois, Northwestern. I took police courses.

I took the exam for the first time and I came out about twelfth on the list.

I will never forget it. It was about two weeks before the list was supposed to expire. There was a vacancy, and the chief was a red neck from Oklahoma City. He called me in and said he was going to interview me. I was twelfth on the list, and there was a white guy who was eleventh on the list, ahead of me. He said he was going to interview both of us and ask us one question to make up his mind who he was going to promote. So he asked this question, "What is the biggest problem facing the Evanston police department?"

Now, I knew this guy graduated from the Northwestern University Traffic Institute. I was in the Juvenile Bureau at that time. I told him, "Traffic accidents and fatalities. That is the biggest problem."

So, he called the white guy in and he asked him the same question.

This guy thought, Logan has been in here, and he has been in Juvenile Delinquency, and I know what he told him, Juvenile Delinquency. So he said, "Juvenile Delinquency."

So he jumped this white guy and made me a sergeant. I became the first black sergeant. But there was a little bit more to it than that. I will also have to say that the NAACP was pushing very strongly, also at that time, to have more blacks promoted in the police department. They played a strong role pushing for that.

From then on, I was a full sergeant. The reason, of course, they had given before, why they had not made any blacks sergeants, was that whites would not obey or work under a black sergeant.

We didn't have that problem. It worked out OK. So, two years later, I was promoted to lieutenant, and two years later I was promoted to captain, the first black in each one of those positions. I think, about ten years later, I was promoted to first deputy chief. In 1984 I was appointed the first black chief of police.

I remember the first time I applied for the position of chief. The city manager at that time had advertised in the paper that he wanted somebody who was well versed in community relations. I was the only one. I started the Community Relations Bureau. I was the only one involved in community relations. To make a long story short, he ended up making a white guy chief, which was probably a Godsend for me, for I probably wasn't ready at that time. Then they said that the reason I didn't get it was because I didn't have enough administrative schooling behind me. So, I ended up going to the FBI Academy to prepare myself. That is one of the premier schools in the country. And I took supervision and management courses at Northwestern University. So, all the pieces were in place.

I had experiences at the FBI Academy when J. Edgar Hoover was head of the academy. He had a known history for not caring for blacks. Out of the one hundred police administrators around the country, there were only two blacks in the class, me and a guy who is a close personal friend now and is assistant director of security for the National Football League, named Chuck Jackson. He is married to Mary Alice Crocket. She was an Evanstonian. They live in New York.

So, we were the only two blacks there. We ran into some tough situations there. We had whites who wouldn't sit with us at the lunch tables where we ate. We had whites who would chastise other whites who would sit with us. I will never forget, we had some heated arguments with some of the police officers who were from the city where Martin Luther King got killed. They took it as a big joke. Of course, we responded to that and almost got into some fights. Now this is in the FBI Academy.

They were talking to us one day, and I raised my hand and asked a question about who had ordered the wire tapping on the telephone of Dr. Martin Luther King.

The FBI guy almost choked on his cup of coffee. He said the president of the United States ordered it.

So, that was quite an experience there at the FBI Academy. It was the first time I had faced that strong racism from other police officers, particularly from the South. It was really something. My buddy and I were saying, "My God. How can blacks stand a chance in the cities where these officers are in charge?

I was captain at the time. They had not promoted anybody else. The black police officers came together and met and decided that we were going to file suit with the EEOC for lack of promotion of blacks and unequal treatment in discipline, not assigning blacks in certain areas, and all those kind of things.

We had a huge law firm in Chicago that came to our defense and defended us personally, so we filed suit. It ended up going to court. The other black officers realized the position I was in, being a captain, and said they would understand if I did not participate with them, but I told them that there was no question about it. I was going to participate. So, I participated, which was good because people like state senators were calling me. Our senators from D.C. were calling me, since I was like the coordinator of everything. We had a chief from Oklahoma City who would never meet with us. Finally, when he was forced to meet with us by the city manager, he wanted to record our conversation. Then, he lost his job over a case where there was a black youth who was shot in Woolworth's store and across the street there was a jewelry store on Davis Street. The alarm went off there about three o'clock in the morning. Police officers responded, but didn't see anybody. Some officer said he saw some kids up on the L tracks. The police officers took off to the L tracks and started firing. They hit this one kid from Chicago. They shot him in the hip and he was paralyzed for the rest of his life.

There was a big public hearing on that. Ben Williams was head of Human Relations Commission at the time. The Chief of Police at that time, Giddens, tried to justify the shooting. He said a felony had been committed, and that's why the kid was shot. I got up and testified against my chief and told them that it wasn't justified, that nobody saw anybody committing a criminal act other than these kids running and the kids should never have been shot. To make a long story short, he got fired.

Then the next chief came in, Bill McCue, and it was at that time we ended up with our suit.

The city manager invited me out for lunch. Coming back from

lunch, he said that he hoped that in the future I would not participate in those kinds of things. He said if I wanted to be supportive, fine, but not to be out there in the open against the officer. I told him, "I will do the same thing in the future that I did now. In my heart and soul, I am going to do what is right, and if you don't like it, that's too bad."

I was one of four captains at that time, and the chief wouldn't speak to me for about six months. He would look at me just like I wasn't there.

I can remember going to places responding to calls and they would open the door and see that you are black and they didn't want to talk to a black officer. I will never forget the time when I was chief, I went to a meeting here in Evanston. I forget the name of the group, but they had called me to come and make some remarks. Here I am with my uniform on with four stars and had my assistant, a white guy, we walked in together and they walked up to him and said, "Hi, Chief," and shook his hand, just like I wasn't even there.

We overcame a lot and accomplished a lot on the force, but we ran into a lot of prejudice.

Eventually we won our suit, and black officers were promoted. They were given assignments in all of the bureaus in the police department. Because of our suit, women even became full fledged police officers. At that time, they weren't considered police officers, even though they were police, there were only certain things that they could do. Mrs. Washington, for example, there were only certain things she could do and she could never get promoted when she was a police officer, and they got less pay. We equalized that with our suit. All of that was equalized as a result of black officers coming together and getting those kinds of things accomplished.

So, we accomplished some things. Now we have blacks in all of the ranks. They work everywhere in the city. We had another black chief that you know about.

At the time when I was chief, we also had a black fire chief, Sam Hicks. He was a very close personal friend of mine. We retired within three or four months of each other. He was the first black fire chief in Evanston.

I had spent about thirty years on the department, and hadn't thought about retiring, and Dan Phillips came to me one day and said, "Bill, they are going to have a position open at the high school, head of security, why don't you think about coming over. You've got your pension coming, come on and draw another salary."

I said, "Naw, I am not even thinking about leaving."

Well, I went home and talked to my family, and I talked to other people in the community, particularly other people in the black community that I knew and who knew me, and got their opinions on things. They said, "You would be crazy not to leave the department."

So, I retired. I left there on a Friday and started as security chief at ETHS on Monday.

Fellowship For African American Men (FAAM)

I was one of the founders of FAAM. This is our twenty-eighth year. We started a basketball program because School District 65, for financial reasons, stopped all of their after school activities. We said, "Well, we were concerned about our black kids, our black males not having something to do." So, we formed it. Eugene Bell and myself, and Andy Rodez, Henry White, we all put this together.

We started out with four basketball teams. It was a black program. We went on for about eight or nine years or ten years. We were growing every year. Then we started integrating the program. Today we have all races involved in the program. We have twenty teams now, including four girls teams and sixteen boys teams.

We have never backed down or changed from our mission, and that is to provide positive role models and mentors and to help our black kids make it through life.

We even get money from the city. We are a nonprofit organization.

Two or three years ago there was a nice article in the *Tribune*, a full back page, on our basketball program. They called the program "Books and Balls" because we emphasized education as well as athletics.

We follow our kids through school. We stay with them. By my being here at the high school, one of the staff persons, and Eugene Bell, we stay on top of our kids who come to our program into the high school.

This year, for the first time, we even gave one of our former graduates a scholarship to college. So, it has been a really tremendous program. I think we have had a real good impact on our black youth, and we have received a lot of support from the families of the kids. We don't turn anybody away from this program. We have a fee, but if they can't afford it, we find some way to work it out.

The other program which has had a nice influence on the community is the Chessmen Club. That club was founded by a friend of mine who is now deceased, a police officer, Andy Rodez.

We were riding together in the squad car one day, and we dreamed up this concept of the Chessmen Club to be a civic organization in the community, so we formed it. That was back in 1957. It has been in existence ever since.

For all of those years, we have given college scholarships to black students who graduated from Evanston Township High School and we have branched out into the suburbs, since we have members who live in Glencoe, for example. This past year, we gave out over ten thousand dollars in scholarships.

We also have a program where we try to follow a kid through college and give him support every year, rather than just a one time thing, and support that kid for four years.

We also try to support other organizations which are trying to do things, such as FAAM.

Also, every year, we give out numerous Christmas baskets to the needy. We deliver those first hand. We go to senior citizen homes. We get information from other people about those who need food, and we will help them.

Social Environment

I have been involved in gangs for a good many years. When I was chief of police, I started the first gang unit. We had a zero tolerance policy. We worked closely with the Nichols neighbors who were having big problems there. We put a lot of people in jail. We had a lot of killings back in the mid-eighties, gang killings in Evanston. And we had a previous administration, including the city hall and the police department, who didn't want to admit that we had a problem.

I remember a meeting with some of the gang members at the police department, which I got some criticism for, but I wanted to hear from them first hand and let them know where I was coming from. The biggest thing that they said, at that time, was they belonged to gangs, because drugs weren't prevailing then, was jobs. They couldn't find jobs. So we talked about that. We did get a few people some jobs. Others went on and ended up in some jail, but I told them we wouldn't tolerate illegal activity here. But I think we had a pretty good hand on it in 1983 and 1984. We put a lot of people in jail. The gangs had decreased from over five hundred down to two hundred people. I am not saying because I left, but when I left, the feeling seemed to be that everything was under control, so nobody did anything. Even the chief, at that time, said the same thing.

I also said that enforcement was good, but there are other things that need to be involved, such as working with the gangs and kids and their families. You have to do other things. You can't just depend on the Police Department to put people in jail. There is more to it than that.

Now the problem has started to creep up again, one of the big concerns is the drug traffic. Also, there are so many younger kids in Evanston now who belong to gangs, more than we had before. I am talking about the Junior High Schools and even fifth grade. We have some who belong to gangs.

There are a lot of reasons why kids join gangs. Peer pressure, wanting to belong to something, it provides camaraderie that some of them don't get at home. We look at our single family structure now and cases here in the school where we have problems with our black kids, the issues of violence, and who comes in for the meeting or who comes in for the hearing is the single black mom, or black grandma. No dads. You see very, very few dads. So, I think the family structure has an impact on that.

I still think that a lot of it is tied into the money situation. Because, now, with the drugs, the kids can make these easy bucks. They laugh off a job at McDonald's $4.50 an hour, when they can make a hundred and fifty dollars in a couple of hours on the street. So, the gangs are controlling those kinds of things now in this community. A lot of friction is over territory.

But this is a threat to the schools here and everywhere, the violence of the gangs and intimidation that goes on.

What we have found here is that, with the police department and some of the people that work here and people in the community who are nameless, a lot of people, but I know a lot of them are working to keep the school a neutral zone. And we pretty much have that at Evanston High School, even though we have gang members that come to this school. But they pretty much keep it as a neutral area. Now, some things happen after school that may go down, but it is pretty much controlled in the school.

We had one big incident last year. No, there were two. There was another incident at a basketball game, but they weren't students. They were adults who came in the building during a basketball game and caused some problems. We had to have them arrested.

But they pretty well keep it under control here. The problems that the gang members are having are pretty much among the young kids who seem to just go all off on their own. But the people up top want to try to keep this under control here.

But we do have it. And it can impact upon the school setting, the school grounds where the students are concerned about their safety. We had a shooting here year before last. As a result of that, the school and community came together with a task force, fifty or sixty people in there. They met for a year and a half and came up with all kinds of programs to help solve some of the problems of violence and civility and all of those kinds of things in the community. A portion of that is to keep kids out of gangs. Gang resistance.

The police department has a session in their program where they talk about gang resistance, so there are some efforts there to work with the police department, work with youth groups, work with parents.

In my opinion, right now, it still has not come together as much as it should come together. For the city to deal with the problem, I think that if it were more of a white problem, we would probably have more support to deal with the issue than it being isolated to blacks. So, therefore, you find a reluctance, I think, on the part of the community to come together and deal with the issue of the community.

When we were talking about the gang problem, the real estate people were screaming, "You are going to hurt our practices!" We have some of the same stuff now. People don't want that publicity out about the problem that we have.

It is a problem. We have to deal with it. Until the community deals with it as a whole, it is not going to go away.

Block Clubs

A couple of months ago we had a major incident on Jackson Avenue. As a result of that, we had a public hearing on safety and I chaired the panel at city hall. We had a lot of people in the community speaking about the problems of the community. I remember Howard Santo from Chicago was on the committee. He made a statement to the group, as a whole, that the people are the power. We need to do what we need to do and not turn to the government and ask, "Can we do this?" We do it because we are the power.

The second thing that happened as a result of that is that Reverend Hycel Taylor has formed a group called the United Block Clubs of Evanston. We are working to mobilize the whole community in this whole block club concept, getting the block clubs together to deal with our problems and use the power that they have.

As a result of that, we are having a conference here on September twenty-eighth, here at the high school, to bring all of the block clubs together and help others to form. We are trying to pull this whole block club issue together, all over the community.

We are going to have Warren Friedman from the Alliance on Community Safety to be one of our speakers. Our superintendent here is going to speak on the task force report which also talks about community.

So, there is a move under way now to mobilize everybody in the community to form block clubs, those that don't have them, and work with those who do have them to bring them together to deal with these issues like crime, safety, government, everything in the community. We are hoping it gets off well on the twenty-eighth of September.

It's got to be the community. You can't just depend upon the police to deal with all of those problems by themselves. It just is not going to work.

There is definitely a lack of leadership in Evanston these days. We don't bring pressure on city hall for some of the things that have to be done. Right now we don't have any black department heads in the city government. We have a mayor, but department heads that are on the day to day operation of things are not there. The mayor's position is nice, but it really doesn't have any power in this community. It is symbolic. There was a push for me to run for mayor, and I wouldn't do it. To me, it just doesn't have the power. The city manager has the power. It's nice to have the mayor. She does some good things, and she is beautiful speaker, but the position, itself, has nothing to do with her. She just doesn't have the power that the mayor in Chicago has.

Our aldermen, I would like to see more blacks get involved in the aldermanic races. Of course, they cut the city council in half, from eighteen to nine, which has made another impact. But the people said they wanted that done, and there it is. But I think it took away some of the possibilities for more power for blacks in the city council. Now we have only two black aldermen out of the eight members of the city council.

I think we are kind of splintered in the community. For some reason or other, we are reluctant to support each other in the black community. We look at what Hysel Taylor has done with coalition of block clubs. We look at people who will not come to the meetings, or may come once and then you may not see them any more. So, for some reason or other, I don't know what it is going to take to make us realize that we have got to come together as a community and work and stop all this problem with personal stuff.

But that's been our problem throughout our history.

Questions For Discussion
1. How did Bill's family background prepare him to overcome the prejudice and discrimination he was to face in Evanston and elsewhere?
2. How was Bill's reaction to the discrimination he received under Rocky Hampton different from when he was denied a promotion to become a sergeant on the Evanston Police Department?
3. What expression did Bill use when he named community people who had made an impact on his life? It begins with "all" and ends with "life"
4. How did Bill's association with Dr. Martin Luther King affect his determination to become successful?
5. When Bill was competing with another policeman for the position of sergeant, what strategy did he use to get the appointment? What other influence was helpful in getting this position?
6. How did Bill prepare himself for police chief after he had been passed over by the city manager?
7. What motivated the founders of FAAM to establish this group? Describe the activities of FAAM
8. Describe the founding and activities of the Chessman Club.
9. Why did some of the gang members say they joined gangs?
10. How are they keeping Evanston Township High School a "neutral zone" for gangs?
11. Why does Bill think the city is not dealing more effectively with the gang problem?
12. Mr. Howard Santo from the Chicago Police Department spoke to a panel at city hall. What was the statement he made about the responsibilities of the community?
13. What changes would Bill like to see in the city government?

About Bill Logan
I met with Bill in the offices of the security chief of the Evanston Township High School. The offices were spacious and very impressive, attended by two charming young black girls.

Because I had returned to ETHS only a few times since I graduated from there in 1936, the changes seemed to be remarkable. I remember when there were two police guards at the school, but to have a suite of offices for security meant that maintaining order there had become a major concern.

Bill's experience certainly has prepared him for his responsibilities as security chief. He has the advantage of having been born and reared in Evanston, and his family is well known by other residents. His military experience and duties as police sergeant and chief of the Evanston Police Department have given him the judgment and empathy he must have to be effective in this position.

I was especially impressed with his interest in the people of the community, especially the youth. We trust that he will be successful in helping to mobilize the people of the area to control their neighborhoods.

Bill Saulsbury

When I went into the Army, I was working for Clayton Mark. I was a turret lathe operator. Before then, I was cooking. I didn't want to go to the Army, and I thought if I got into war work, I could stay out of the Army. After a couple of years, I did get two or three deferments.

The manager there was Fred Hossenflug.

At that time Grabriel Heater was still saying, "There is good news tonight," and I wanted to get my hands around his neck.

My brother came out of the Army before I did. He worked at the Philip Lochman Company. At that time, he was the only black working there. He said, "I am not going to continue working here because I am going into business." He went into business on Central Street with a fellow he formerly had worked with. His name was Nick, a Greek fellow. He said, "I think you would like this job very much. I think you can do pretty good with it."

When I took the job, I was making about fifty percent of what I was making at Clayton Mark. So, I said, "I will try it."

I had told Fred that I would be back to work at Clayton Mark, but I said, "I am not going to work for anybody for six weeks, after two years in the Army." He said, "Just call me when you want to come back, and I will put you back on the job."

When I came back, I went to Philip Lochman. Well, I started there in April 1, 1945. I said, "Well, I will just see how it is." I liked the job. Mr. Lochman was very considerate. He said, "Well, the black community is one tenth of the population of the United States. So, for every ten white employees, I will hire one black."

So, I worked for him. I first started in the shipping department, but I helped in the manufacturing of the different products.

After I had been there a little less than a year, he gave me about three hundred dollars in a bonus one week before Christmas. Everybody else was getting $750. He said, "You haven't been here a full year. When you have been here a full year, you will get the same." The following year, and every year after that, I got $750, and he gave it to me one week before Christmas and said, "Buy your wife a present."

The work was interesting, and it wasn't hard, physical labor. There

Conversations with Blacks in Evanston, Illinois • 263

was no heavy lifting or things like that.

I had thirty-eight products that I made. These products were for graphic arts and for lithographers and engravers.

I used to make developers. Then I used to make cold top enamel.

After fifteen years, he retired and went to Arizona. So, I asked if I could have the job as head of production. He said, "Well, Bill, I don't see any reason why you shouldn't do it. You know about making the products as well as anyone else here, other than Jewel Marquart." Marquart was a Frenchman.

So, one week passed. Two weeks passed. I was feeling kind of funny, because I was the only black, and I was not going to get it. Then he came to me and said, "Bill, you've got it." He said, "You are in charge."

I had thirty-eight products at our peak. I had two helpers. It went very well. I had one product that I was making thirty-five hundred gallons of a month. It was Cold Top Enamel, Friendopher Cold Top Enamel.

Right after the war, we were terribly busy with this because Friendopher was in Munich, Germany, and he had a big plant there. But during the war, it closed up. My employer was of German descent, and we were doing all the work that the plant in Germany was doing. We sent products to Cape Town, South Africa. We sent products to Rio de Jeniero, South America. We sent products to Herpinrose in England. We sent to a plant in Zolikan, near Zurich, Switzerland. We were sending all over. We were busy, and there were times when we were over a thousand gallons behind. We had a backlog.

After the death of Mr. Lochman, his son-in-law and his daughter took over. I liked them very well, too. But, at this time, we got to the place that business had grown so that we had an airplane.

One company in New York owed us money, and we took over that company. Chuck was the pilot of the airplane, delivering some of these things to the company. At that time we had seven salesmen, but finally, I started cutting down on my time there. I was getting too old.

My present employer, his mother, was working there with her husband. Then she retired. She asked me. She said, "Bill, Phil does not know these chemicals like you do." You see, when I started working there, he was twelve years old. He was going to college in Wisconsin. Finally, he took over. He and his brother went into another business. We have two businesses going on down there now, not only Philip Lochman's Photochemical Laboratory, we have REF. REF is the silkscreening company. REF is Randolph, Emil, and Frank. Frank was the husband of Lynn, who was the daughter of Mr. Lochman. Emil was the superintendent. Randolph was the son of the daughter.

There was a lot of tax which they had to pay on chemicals, so the younger generation started getting away from the chemicals and going more into the silk screening.

We now have eliminated all of our explosives.

I make about five or six different products now. Yesterday, when I was there, I made forty-four gallons of gum Arabic. I made forty-five gallons of pre-ex solution, and I canned some asphalt solution.

I work five hours a day, one day a week. Up until last year, I was going two days a week. Beginning this year, I cut it to one day a week. I'll keep on until I cut it to none.

Phil's mother asked me to stay with Phil. She said, "He doesn't know these chemicals." And that is the reason I have stayed there.

Phil's mother is the biggest stockholder in the company. Her father, Mr. Lochman, had only one daughter, Lynn. After Mr. Lochman died, Lynn and her husband, Frank Hatsell, took over. They retired, and their son, Theo, took over. He is not a chemical man, but he is a smart man. He is a college business major. He knows that I know the chemicals.

Lynn comes by now and then, and she will hug me. But I said two days a week is getting to be too much for me, so I cut it down to one, where I am now.

American Legion Activities

I have been a member of the Thomas Garnett Post of the American Legion since its founding, and have been post commander eight times, including the present year.

I have enjoyed working with my comrades over the years. Some of the original members were:

Harrison Black	George Brown	Henry M. Collins
John Daniels	John Fleming	Thad Freeman
Jack Hill	Eugene Hut	John Landry
Logan Lewis	Henry Payton	Bruce Reynolds
Leonard J. Robinson	George Sampson	William Terry
Haywood Thomas	Leonard Ward	Sam Butler
Edgar Elkins	Miles Gill	Eugene Kelley
Alfred Parham	Homer Roberts	Abel S. Shields
Odis Walker		

All of the above members were World War I veterans.

Neighborhood Changes

It is the generation change. This is what happened after World War II.

When I came to Evanston, and Mary and I married, we would go to the Valencia Theater, and I would leave my front door unlocked. Now I am scared even with my doors locked. I am not kidding. You could walk the streets without fear. I don't like to drive the streets at night now. Can you imagine Evanston being like that? I get the *Evanston Review* every week. The first thing I read now is the "Police Blotter." This old man was held up at three o'clock in the afternoon on a lot on Chicago Avenue. Even on the L platform you are not safe. Where are you safe? You're not safe in your home. If anybody would tell me that I would have to live in Evanston and would have to have a gun beside my bed, I wouldn't have believed them.

Now, the streets have changed. When I first came here, Emerson Street was the roughest. Then Church Street took over. Now Simpson Street has the record. Everything happens on Simpson—arrests, dope, shootings. What is the answer?

When I first came here, it seemed like everybody here was from South Carolina—the Holmes, the Robinsons, the Butlers, and I could name many more families who were from South Carolina. They all knew each other and felt safe.

After World War II, many people who had served in nearby forts and naval posts liked it here and decided to bring their families here.

When I went into the Army, I thought I knew everybody in Evanston. If I didn't know them by name, I knew them by face. I am now talking about the blacks. But when I came out of the Army, I would walk to the corner, I have my uniform on, everybody would be passing by and when I saw some face I knew, I ran up to him and started talking and almost wanted to hug him.

That's how things have changed. That's how neighborhoods have changed.

I tell you, it happened too suddenly for a lot of people who had been deprived of their civil rights and privileges to come to a place where they could enjoy such rights and privileges. Many people didn't know how to use this new freedom. So they have come up here and are ruining it for everybody. That is a step backwards.

But once you have something good, but is going bad, you always hope that it will return to what it used to be.

That is the situation that I think Evanston is in today. I do not know the answer. I only hope and pray that it will get back to somewhat like it was and the things that we have gained are not outnumbered by the things that we have lost. I have a recording of a song sung by Brook Benton in which the words are "I got what I wanted, but I lost what I had." So, I hope we haven't lost what we had here in Evanston.

We had a meeting at the city hall two or three months ago. We all got together and did a little organizing. It was unfortunate that I was in the hospital and could not attend. They are trying to organize for protection. We talked with Tom Gunther. He is a white police officer who is working with our ward, the second ward, just this precinct.

Since the meeting, I was talking with some who want to do what we did two or three years ago. We had lights put in our alleys from here to Church Street. About four families paid for one light. It runs about twenty-five dollars a year. There is a captain to collect the money. This money will be collected as long as the lights are here.

Since the last meeting, the members in the block going up to Grove want the same thing.

One of the other things we discussed was the congestion in our block. We have a lot of congestion from people coming to the soccer games at ETHS, and also the football games.

I had a very unfortunate incident at one time. Then, my driveway was not as wide as it is now, just a regular size driveway. And when I came in, there was a car stuck halfway across my driveway.

I was much younger then. And I pushed that car out into the middle of the street. Then I sat down on my stoop there. Pretty soon a squad car came. Evidently, somebody had reported the car.

The next thing, they took the license number of the car. Then I heard them announce on the speaker, "Such and such a license number, come and move your car." Then I saw two young fellows come and get in the car. They didn't say anything to me. I wanted them to say something to me. But they didn't accommodate me. They drove off.

Now, every Saturday when there is a game, the neighborhood is crowded with parked cars. Fortunately, I have a driveway, and can pull up into it, but some of my neighbors have two or three cars and have to park one or more on the street.

That was the discussion that went on at this meeting.

The officer was saying that we could get a permit for about ten dollars a year. Each car would have a sticker. Cars that do not have a sticker could not legally park there. That has its bad points, too. You have friends who are visiting you and could not park there, unless they have a ticket.

Not being at the meeting where I could ask questions about this, I have to rely on what takes place at the next meeting.

The meetings are to get together and see what we can do, with the help of officer Tom Gunther, to promote crime prevention, and how we can recognize and help our patrol officers. In fact, the latest patrol officer I didn't know myself. Before then, one had come by and introduced himself to me and gave me his card.

I am going to tell you the honest to goodness truth. Living alone is hard. My immediate neighbors are the Ransoms, Pettigrew, DeWitt, and my next door neighbor, Sharon, who is married to a Mexican fellow. The Ransoms have a key to my house. Pettigrew has a key to my house. So does DeWitt Talbert.

Being eighty-four years old and alone, if they don't see me for a day or two, they will call, come over and check to see if I am all right. If I am fishing or somewhere else, they will watch the house, if they are not with me. We all look out for each other. We have been looking out for each other for many years, but now we are involving the whole community.

I can also recall when Charlie Fisher sat on his front porch from morning until night, after he retired, and he knew everything that was going on. He would just sit there and see who was coming. If you were not at home, he would tell them. It was kind of a comfort to have someone like that around. He didn't do anything else. When he retired, he retired. But he made a good look out. And he had a strong voice.

Right now, as I said, we are in the stage of development. I have hopes that community efforts will turn out very well.

Questions for Discussion
1. What advantage did Bill have by working for Clayton Mark, in regards to his military draft?
2. Why was Bill's decision to take a fifty percent cut in pay at Clayton Mark, in order to work for Philip Lochman, a good one?
3. What did Philip Lochman say about hiring black employees?
4. What were Bill's responsibilities as head of production at The Lochman Company?

5. When the Lochman Company reduced its chemical manufacturing program, what operation did they take on?
6. Bill is getting tired, now, but he still works at Lochman's. Why does he do this?
7. Bill's American Legion Post was established in 1935. What did these members have in common?
8. How many times was Bill elected commander of his post? Who was second in the number of times commander?
9. What are some of the changes in the Bill's neighborhood that he complains about?
10. What does Bill mean by "I got what I wanted, but I lost what I had," in regards to the neighborhood changes?
11. A few years ago Bill and his neighbors did something to brighten the neighborhood. What was that ? How much did it cost per year?
12. How have neighbors helped Bill to feel more secure as he has grown older and is living alone ?

About Bill Saulsbury

Bill is a person you can depend on to carry out any responsibility he has assumed, and he assumed many of them.

First of all, he takes care of his home. In a block of attractive homes, his property is maintained as well as, or better than, the property of his neighbors.

His garden includes vegetables, flowers, and plants of many kinds. His lawn is always well trimmed and includes a bird bath which attracts birds and a squirrel which Bill has given a name. Many neighbors and friends enjoy coming over to Bill's to eat, drink, and chat.

For the last two years, Bill has begun to feel the stress that has been imposed upon him by advanced age—he is eighty-four—and responsibilities, but he still has that happy spirit which makes it hard to believe that he is in any pain or discomfort.

It is no wonder that his American Legion Post has elected him to be their commander for the eighth time.

Epilogue

In summary, let us see if the families of the interviewees were successful in obtaining the freedom and progress they hoped for in Evanston. How can this success be measured?

Perhaps we can use the social class structure which is described in *The Status Seekers*, a book by Vance Packard, published by D. Mackay Co., New York. He said, "The majority of Americans rate acquaintances and are themselves being rated in return. They believe that some people rate somewhere above them, that some others rate somewhere below them, and that still others seem to rate close enough to their own level to permit them to explore the possibility of getting to know them socially without fear of being snubbed or appearing to down grade themselves." (p. 6)

Packard describes a system of horizontal social structure to illustrate what he means by levels.

Upper Class:
    a. Board members of local industries, banks, etc.
    b. Send their sons and daughters to good colleges.
    c. Have heavy investments in land, industry, banks, etc., much of it inherited.
    d. Fashionable doctors, lawyers, architects, Episcopal ministers.
    e. In smaller communities, "old Family background" is especially important.
    f. Old real-upper-class people accept new rich only when they become so powerful that they must be consulted, only if they have enough money.

Upper Middle Class (p. 40)
    a. Mostly confident
    b. Energetic
    c. Ambitious
    d. Went away to college
    e. Decision makers, serving as managers, technologists or persuaders
    f. Professional men or successful local business men

Lower Middle-Class
   a. Respectable, proper, cultured, socially above the working masses
   b. More conforming, more morally proper, and more active in churches than any other group.
   c. The "noncommissioned officers" of our society
   d. In offices they are the clerks, excepting the routine machine attendants and secretaries.
   e. On Main Street they are clerks in the quality stores or the small shopkeepers, or the smaller contractors
   f. In industry they are the foremen, technical aides, and skilled craftsmen. They also are the smaller farmers.
   g. They include lower ranks of the genuinely white-collar world and the higher ranks of the blue collar world, the aristocrats of labor.
   h. They feel they haven't arrived, but actually most will never get very far, and eventually realize it.

The Working Class (p. 42)
   a. Heads of families of this class frequently have not finished high school.
   b. They work steadily, in good times, at jobs that require little training.
   c. They constitute the backbone of industrial unions, and numerically are the largest class.
   d. Most are skilled operatives, like truck drivers, semi-skilled factory operatives. Some wear white shirts and man machines in offices or work as delivery men. Others are truck drivers, miners, filling station attendants, supermarket clerks, and attendants.
   e. They are "the good solid people who live right but never get anyplace."

The Real Lower Class (p. 43)
   a. People everyone looks down on
   b. Live in decrepit slum areas
   c. Usually leave school as soon as legally allowed, if not before
   d. They work erratically at unskilled or semi-skilled tasks and try to find their pleasures where they can.
   e. People in this class are so used to living on the edge of hunger and disaster that they have never learned "ambition" or drive for higher skills or education.

f. They require a minimum of physical security.

g. They don't fear losing a job because they expect it anyway.

h. They know that when everything is lost, friends and relatives will take them in without any loss of respectability. There is little to lose.

i. Unmarried male spends his nights in sexual explorations. He lives in a world where "visceral, genital, and emotional gratification is far more available than it is to most of us."

j. The people know that most of us look down on them. There are two natural reactions to this contempt, either kick back, which youths do and then are arrested for juvenile delinquency, or retreat in apathy, which is what the older lowers do.

k. What these people need more than charity or prosperity is *RECOGNITION.

A review of the responses of the interviewees should enable you to place them in one of the social classes described. The readers must determine this for themselves. I believe most of them will fit in the working class to the upper class.

Evanston seems to have been a wise choice for the people or their parents, because most of them have achieved the status of at least lower middle class. A few have achieved upper class.

However, as a result of social stratification among blacks in general, and also in Evanston, there appears to be the lack of communication between the blacks of higher status and blacks of lower status.

In Packard's *Status Seekers*, page 54, he said, "Some Negroes seek to separate themselves as far as possible from the general run of lower class Negroes through achievement and life-style. The higher status Negroes pattern their behavior after what they perceive to be the white model. They speak softly and precisely to show that they are not noisy, low class Negroes. They shun emotional religions, they have small families, they encourage their children to study Latin as a mark of culture, and they prefer to shop at higher class white stores."

One of Chicago's department stores was considering building a branch in an upper-middle class Negro neighborhood. The management was advised by local informants, in effect, 'Don't come. You'll become a Negro store. The people would rather go in town to your white store.'"

*(See Appendix I, *The Jack Roller Book Review*.)

Perhaps this attitude of the upward mobile class of blacks in Evanston explains why black business and professional services have diminished in the black community to the extent that many blacks feel like Ruby Alexander when she said, "We don't have anything now."

A major problem facing the black residents of Evanston is the growing number of delinquent youths and their delinquent parents. In describing the "real lower class" group, the author said, "What these people need more than charity or prosperity is recognition." (See Appendix I: "Juvenile Delinquency: A Group Tradition")

How will the people of Evanston give this type of recognition to the youth?

The appendix of this book contains material which describes some of the outstanding youth programs that are being sponsored by various organizations, but recognition of youths who are in the lower class and at risk is not indicated to any great extent. This is unfortunate, and it illustrates how serious the loss of the Emerson Street YMCA has been to the blacks in Evanston. The Y used to be a place where fatherless boys and girls could enjoy education, recreation, and discipline. Evanston must give more recognition to those in the lower class.

Appendices

Appendix A - Churches
Ebenezer AME Church
New Hope CME Church
St. Andrew's Episcopal Church
Mt. Zion Missionary Baptist Church
Second Baptist Church

Appendix B - Emerson Street YMCA
Photographs
Founders of YMCA
First Section of Y
YMCA Expansion 1929
Local Older Boys Conference 1934

Appendix C - Evanston Community Hospital
"The Sick Can't Wait" - A history of the Community Hospital of Evanston from an article taken from the Fleetwood Jourdain Art Guild publication "The Shaping of Black Evanston," January 15, 1996

Appendix D - Sororities
Alpha Kappa Alpha
(Material taken from UNITY publication June 25, 1995, Community Scholarship Recognition Reception)
Delta Sigma Theta
(Material taken from UNITY publication June 25, 1995 Community Scholarship Recognition Reception)

Appendix E - Social and Civic Clubs
North Shore Illinois Links by Beulah Avery and Carmella Hill
The Dunbar Club (Material submitted by Martha Walker)
UNITY History by Yvonne Davis, UNITY publication June 25, 1995
Twentieth Century Golf Club of Evanston by Willie Higgins

Appendix F
"How To Apply For Scholarships in the African-American Community" and 1995 Scholarship Award Recipients (June 25, 1995 Community Scholarship Recognition Reception)

Appendix G - Tech. Sgt. William Benjamin Snell Post No. 7186 of The Veterans of Foreign Wars
Snell Post Commanders
Drill Team
Ladies Auxiliary VFW
Ladies Auxiliary Past Commanders

Appendix H - Alpha Phi Alpha Fraternity
Founding of the Fraternity, National and Local
Dr. Martin Luther King Jr. Award
    a. Application
    b. Enrollment verification form
    c. ETHS form to college of entry
    d. Letters of appreciation from previous award winners
Report from the 57th Anniversary Convention of The Alpha Phi Alpha Fraternity, Inc.

Appendix I
Book review of Clifford R. Shaw's *The Jack Roller*, University of Chicago Press. The study and treatment of the delinquent child.

Juvenile Delinquency: A Group Tradition

Appendix A

EBENEZER A. M. E. CHURCH
1882 - 1965

Book I

THE REV. GEORGE H. HANN

About 1880, less than a quarter of a century after the town of Evanston was incorporated and when its population was only a trifle more than 4,000, a group of colored citizens gathered at the home of Richard Day, on Davis Street, between Sherman Avenue and Benson Street, to worship God.

From those devout prayer meetings evolved a Missionary Sunday School. Because some had ties to the Methodist church and others to the Baptist denomination, the Methodist members conducted services on one Sunday and the Baptists on the following Sunday.

But these people sought even further religious expression. They wanted a house of worship and they wanted a place to carry on the good work they had started. So, the Illinois Annual Conference (later to become the Chicago Annual Conference) of the African Methodist Episcopal Church sent the Rev. George H. Hann to the field to hold services for those of the Methodist faith. A Mr. Joplin opened his home to Rev. Hann for the first prayer meeting.

Formal organization of Ebenezer A. M. E. Church, which took place October 30, 1882, with the Rev. Hann as its first pastor, was made possible largely through money and influence contributed by Madam Taylor. Numbered in that first small, dedicated congregation were Mrs. Henry Butler, Mrs. Ellison, Mrs. Owens, and James Hill, Sr.

Other men and women among the first Ebenezer members were Edward Long, Henry Burrell, Mrs. Stephens, Mr. and Mrs. Osborne, Mariah Humphrey and Mollie Thomas. Sarah Ackis was the first to transfer her membership to Ebenezer; she brought her letter from Holly Springs, Miss.

Mollie Thomas

Madam Taylor

Sarah Ackis

278 • *Williams*

Mr. and Mrs. Lewis Dixon, Joseph Hadley, Sr., Mr. and Mrs. James Thompson, and Nick D. White were early Ebenezer members who joined under the Rev. Hann's pastorate.

At mid-point of the century, on May 31, 1850, nine men — three Methodist ministers and six laymen — met in Chicago to pledge themselves to "found a university near Chicago that should be the fountain of scholarship for the area that has been known as the Northwest Territory." Dr. John Evans, physician, religious leader and educator was one of the laymen.

In August, 1853, a university site was acquired — 379 acres of land along Lake Michigan from the present Dempster Street to Lincoln Street. After the purchase, a portion of the land was platted and lots for the prospective village were sold.

Northwestern University was founded in 1851 and the village that accommodated it was named Evanston in honor of Dr. Evans, who had become the first president of the board of trustees of the University. However, it was not until December, 1863, that its citizens voted to incorporate the village of Evanston as a town.

The university increased its land holdings to a peak of 680 acres during the period 1860-70. Time and again parcels of this land was used to help new churches and to create city parks

Like so many other Evanston churches, the first Ebenezer A. M. E. Church building stood on land leased from Northwestern University. The Rev. Hann built the church, a structure large enough to accommodate 150 persons, on Benson Avenue, between Clark Street and University Place.

W. H. Twiggs was a pioneer business man and Evanston's first Negro printer, with his print shop located on Sherman Avenue, between Church and Davis streets. His printing press is included in the Evanston Historical Society exhibit. In later years, Mr. Twiggs engaged in the real estate business.

Nick D. White was an influential citizen of Evanston with an interesting family, all of whom were connected with Ebenezer. Brother White donated a large bible to the church in memory of his son, Harry. Both Mr. White and Mr. Twiggs served Ebenezer as trustees for fifty years.

In the spring of 1882, Mrs. Dorsey Dixon came to Evanston to join her husband, Lewis, who had migrated earlier from Abbeville, S. C. A deeply religious young woman, she attended the Missionary Sunday School. When Ebenezer A. M. E. Church was formed, she became a charter member, remaining faithful in service for seventy-four years, until her death in 1957, at the age of 90. A beloved woman, Mother Dixon helped to organize the Faithful Few Club; she served as a Stewardess for fourteen year; a l oness for thirty-eight year; and a class leader for twenty-eight   rs.

William H. Twiggs

N. D. White

Mrs. Lewis (Mother Dorsey) Dixon

The W. H. Twiggs Family

Conversations with Blacks in Evanston, Illinois • 279

SOME EARLY MEMBERS

L. J. Ashmore
Florence and W. E. Bell
William and Rebecca Beck
Ida Blunt
Emma Butler
Mary Berry
Jane Byrd
Carrie Breckenridge
Martha Bush
Prudence Burrell
Preston and Anna Beck
Solomon and Mary Bowie
Catherine Blackwell
Grant and Lula Blakeman
Vera Bentley
Hattie Ball
Len Ballinger
Lucinda Bobo
Frankie Bobo
Sallie Crockett
Horace and Janie Callahan
Walker and Janie Callahan
George and Georgia Combash
H. O. and Amelia Cannon
Samuel Cannon
Joseph and Sarah Collier
Sarah Crump
Dr. Thomas and Lillian Cotton
Martha and J. A. Collier
Lewis and Dorsey Dixon
Liza Dixon
Urijah Davis
Minnie Dickerson
Thomas and Allene Davis
P. R. and Lola Y. Downs
Mary and Baker DePugh
John and Sadie Duggard
Violet Elmore
Robert Elmore
A. H. Edmonds
Josephine Ellis
Monroe and Marie Floyd
Fred, W. W. and Jamie Fisher
Mary Fleetwood
Horace and Carrie Franklin
Tillie Finley
Ed. and Julia Foster
Geo. and Gertrude Foley
Isaac and Mamie Pollard
John and Cora Griffin
Roxanna Green
Mr. and Mrs. W. F. Garnett
Isaac and Marie Gresham
Richard and Georgia Gash
Lorenza Griffin
Donna Griffin
Mamie Griffin
Mr. and Mrs. Pless Howland
Grace and Willis Howland
Lucy Hester
Emma —
Major — Emma Hammett
Elizabeth and Hugh Heimes

Nancy Hayes
Robert and Julia Hadley
Lawrence and Melissa Hadley
Joseph Hadley
Elton J. and Cassie Harding
Mrs. E. D. Hart
Mattie Horn
Elijah and May Irwin
Florence Jones
Thomas and Virgie Jones
Lula James
May Jones
Jennie Johnson
Catherine Johnson
Arthur and Ella King
Havana Kanter
Elizabeth and William Kincad
Edna Ketchum
Jas. W. and Millie Lindsey
Julia Lights
Hulda Lights
Mary Lyons
Frances Lee
Vera Bentley
Ora Mack
W. T. and Lucille Mason
Ella Miller
Howard and Marie Miller
George and Beulah McCravey
Lucinda McBride
Butler and Emma McBride
Solomon McBride
Prudence McBride
Jennie Miller
J. R. and Goldie Moore
Rena Myers
Irene McAllister
James McAllister
Sam McGrier
Frances Morris
Thedeus and Lethia Morris
Louie Owens (Rev.)
Amelia and Louis Owens
George and Angeline Pressier, Sr.
Mr. and Mrs. Jas. Prather
Carrie Pope
Sadie Phillips
Georgiana Pope
William and Mamie Pollard
Emma Persadey
George Roberts
Elijah Riley
Emma Richardson
Thomas and Eola Richardson
Lucy Robinson
Julia Robinson
William J. Russell
Dennis and Sydney Sims
Mary Smith
Birdie Smith
Lillie Smith
William and Loretta Stewart
Alice Sanders

Louise Snowden
E. J. and Jessie Slaughter
Marshall Sherrod
Mary Sherrod
James and Mary Singleton
Mamie Smith
Ellen Smith
George Smith
Dr. C. B. and Alice Scruggs
Hattie Smith
Pansy Smith
John and Anna Smith
S. J. Starks
Chelsea Taylor
Mariah Thompson
Wilma Tillotson
Joseph and Beatrice Thurman
James and Alice Thompson
William Tate
Andrew Tate
Sena Tobias
Wm. and Mary Terry
Taggart Brothers
Betty Turman
Sallie Wideman
Augusta Walker
Harvey and Minnie Walden
Jesse and Sisie Wideman
Bert and Susie Wilson
Lizzie Watts
Mr. and Mrs. Forest White
Florence White
Carlos White
Amelia Woodson
Sam and Alice White
Caroline Washington
George and Effie Williams
Bessie Williams
Julia Wilson
Moses and Cora Watson
Hester Weems
Rev. and Mrs. Washington
Henry Wideman
Carl F. Wilson
Mahalia Wright
John and Minnie Young

TRUSTEES

George Pressley
J. W. Webb
J. S. Martin
J. R. Moore
W. F. Garnett
Joseph Prather
W. H. Twiggs
N. D. White
E. J. Harding
George Combash
Bert Wilson
Andrew Tate
Hosea Hammett
J. R. Moore

A. P. Perry
William Jackson
Joseph Thurman
W. T. Mason
William Stewart
Walter Willis
W. W. Fisher
Sam Nichols
S. J. Fountain
George Barr
C. H. Walker
H. Walden
J. L. Porter
M. A. Floyd

SOME OF THE EARLY SUNDAY SCHOOL TEACHERS

Emma Daniels
Mary DePugh
Martha Twiggs
Belle Graves
Mamie Pollard
Nettie Banks
Gertrude O'Neal-Jones
Effie Osborne
Julia Hadley
Susan Bailey
Ida Benton
Lulene Perrin-Taylor
Florence White
Lena Tibbs Neely
Ophelia Neely Otey

STEWARDESSES WHO SERVED

Mary Bibbs
Susie Brown
Lucinda Bobo
Sarah Collier
Laura English
Georgia Combash
Nancy Hayes
Cecelia Webb Hill
Emma Howard
Lula Hughes
Mary Ann Jackson
Lula James
Janie King
Mary Lyons
Beulah McCravey
Cecelia Morton
Rachel Miller
Carrie Murray
Gladys McCraven
Carrie Pope
Emma Richardson
Alice Scruggs
Mary Singleton
Lula Sherrod
Alice Sanders
Sadie Straughters
Mollie Thomas
Birdee Wideman
Susie Wilson
Susie Wideman
Minnie Young
Sally Bowman

CHRISTIAN ENDEAVOR LEADERS

Julia Hadley .... Rev. Marvey Walden
Lydia Davis .... Wayman McPhear
Walter Willis .... Margaret Palmer

OUR EARLY CLUB PRESIDENTS

Faithful Few .... Effie Williams
Church Aid Club .... Belle Graves
Men's Club .... Sam L. Cannon
Mother's Club .... Lola Y. Downs
Sewing Circle .... Mae Jones
Pastor's Aid .... Mrs. W. W. Fisher
Kentucky Club .... Fannie Griffin
 .... Pauline Holt
F. N. C. Club Native Ogleton-McCaskey
 .... Mrs. R. S. Wilson Organizer
South Carolina .... Novella Markness
Willing Workers .... Nora D. Brown
Organ Club .... Lula Blakeman
 .... Addie Lawton
 .... Rev. R. C. Henderson
 .... Organizer

SOME OF THE EARLY CLASS LEADERS

Susan Bailey
Elnora Bell
Lucinda Bobo
Nora D. Brown
Georgia Combash
J. W. Collier
Dorsey Dixon
Laura English
Lawrence Hadley
Cecelia Webb Hill
Pless Howland
Carrie Franklin
Thomas Jones
Mack McDuffie
Marie Miller
Jessie Wideman
Sallie Wideman
Moses Watson
Evelyn White
Georgia Williams
Ione Harris
Effie Williams
J. W. Washington
Nelson Gaines
H. J. Roberts
D. D. Martin
Lucian Gunn
Bert Wilson
Roger Bell
Anna Mayo
James Singleton
William Matcher
Willis Howland
T. W. Banks

THROUGH THE YEARS

ORGANISTS
Ethel Hadley
Josephine Webb
Mr. Morris
Ora Mack
Fannie Griffin
Walter Gossette
Thurman F. Charleston
Hillbert Stewart
C. C. Iles
Florence White Powell
Deram Richardson
LaJune James Fisher
Hazel Bailey Walker
Bessie Lee White
Beatrice Snibbaling
Faith McBride

EQUIPMENT:
Electric duplicating machine
Office storage cabinets
Paper cutter
A Protomatic card duplicator
New choir seats
New metal chairs for basement
New tables
Drapes for the Walnut Room

WORSHIP AID GIFTS:
Bibles-250 for pews given by Mrs. Louise G. Smith and Mrs. Katherine Barrett in memory of their mother, Laura Virginia English.
Communion Tables-memorial to Fannie Brooks (Mrs.)
Missal stand-a memorial to Fannie Brooks (Mrs.)
Portable lecturn-given by the Willing Workers Club
Communion bread plates-given by Mrs. Marguerite Penn
New amplified sound facility-a memorial to: Mary Mitchell, Roger Ball, and Susan B. Stickney
Communion service-given by Mrs. Edna Walden in memory of her mother, Mrs. Sallie Craddock
Robert J. Ball Room-memorial gift of Mr. and Mrs. Kenneth Ball
Memorial gifts for the R. J. Ball parish house from friends
Memorial Library in memory of Mrs. Margaret St. Clair
Time Box given by Mattie McDowell

CANDY-ICE CREAM-VARIETY
Dora Auston
Mar'i's
Pressleys

PROFESSIONALS
M. D.'s
Garnett
Butler
Dr. A. D. Garnett
A. E. Penn
Kingslow
Dr. E. Hill
Fairfax
Beck
J. C. Washington

D.D.'s
Garnett
Roy M. Young
Reginald Best
Tarkington
F. D. Moore

THOSE WHO ENTERED THE MINISTRY FROM EBENEZER
Cecil Fisher
Harvey Walden
Benjamin Moore
Fred Jordan
Louis Owens
Walter Willis
Ernest Dyett
Eugene Seales
Carlyle F. Stewart
Benjamin Brooks
Lewis Dixon
Andrew Cooper, Jr.
Joseph Patterson
O. T. Carpenter
Bessie Johnson
Elizabeth Kincaid
Oryx B. Robinson
Josephine Johnson Payne
Bessie Tate
Lizzie Lovell

NEW ORGANIZATIONS AND REACTIVATED ONES
M & M Courtesy Club
M J H Male Chorus
Junior Missionary
Calendar Club
Class Leaders Guild

SOLOISTS
Lola Y. Downs
Robert Hadley
Mayme Wilson
Dora Dunn
Euphemia Osborne
Helen Owens
Herbert Lyons
Emily Smith
Elijah Irwin
J. Allen Spencer
Gertrude O'Neal Jones
Richard Lee
William Pollard, Sr.
Howard Mack
Cora Cooper Moore
Ruth Powell
Ethel Daugherty
Mildred Black
Alice Stewart
George Rowe, Sr.
Charles Morris
Albert Carruthers
Wilma Hudson
Louise Snowden
Horace Graves
Charles Fisher
Beatrice Gaines
Lois White Dudd
Dorothy Lipscomb
Minnie Kennedy
John Revis
Wilson Holmes
Gertrude Fuller
Claudine Lytle King
Allie Adams Jones
Alfronso Bowie
Agnes Searles
Sallie Rogers

DOUBT and FAITH
Doubt sees the obstacles
Faith sees the way!
Doubt sees the darkest night,
Faith sees the Day
Doubt dreads to take a step
Faith soars on high
Doubt questions 'Who Believes'?
Faith answers — "'I'!!

CHIROPODIST
Thos. C. Cotton
C. E. Scruggs
Tilman Weatherall
Scott
Jennie

OTHERS WHO SERVED
Rev. J. W. Washington
Rev. C. W. Turner
Rev. Brice
Rev. Gibson
Rev. Ben Moore
Rev. J. T. Smith
Rev. Branford
Rev. Horace T. Hudson

EBENEZER A.M.E.

It may come as a surprise to many that among Evanston's oldest churches is Ebenezer A.M.E. This, as its name indicates, serves a Negro congregation.

For a period longer than the life span of most Evanstonians, Ebenezer has been an integral part of Evanston. Although it has necessarily faced financial difficulties since its congregation is not affluent, it has played its share in building up the ideals of home and community and spiritual life which Evanstonians like to think are typical of their city.

These seven decades, too, have seen progress in the reduction of racial prejudice and discrimination — not enough progress, to be sure, but the important thing is that there is continuing progress.

The people of Ebenezer have good reason to be proud of the record of their church, and Evanston also can be, and is, proud of this 70-year-old institution.

DON'T YOU QUIT
When things go wrong, as they sometimes will,
And the road you're treading seems uphill
When the funds are low and the debts are high
And you want to smile but you have to sigh
When care is pressing you down a bit
Rest if you must — but don't you quit.
— Edgar A. Guest

RECREATION
Chas. Breckenridge
John Revis
L. Watson

CARE OF CHURCH PROPERTY:
Replacing of broken art glass windows and symbols
New window frames where needed
Double copper protective screens for windows
New concrete floor over the entire basement
Concrete driveways and stairs at the parsonage
Parish house paneling
Basement tiled at a cost of $4,200.00
Acoustical tiling
Tiling of hall floors
Concrete steps west side of church (rear)
Painting sanctuary and foyer
Painting exterior of building
Tuckpointing where needed on church
New choir seats
New roof on church
Butler's pantry remodeled

ICE, COAL, WOOD
Sol Moore
Dad Griffin
Chas. Taylor
King
Adams Bros.

MUSIC STUDIOS
V. E. Bentley
T. F. Charleston
Herbert Lyons and Homer D. Jones
LaJune James Fisher
Sophronia Hudson
Daram D. Richardson
Tanya Frocks—
Leona Downs Morton, Prop.
E. S. Gaines Haberdashery
Evanston Sanitarium

TRUCKING
J. W. Lindsay

TAILORS-CLEANERS
Akers
Clarence Cunningham
John McAllister
Thurman F. Charleston

PLUMBERS
Mack Williams
Elliot Green
Langford

New Hope Christian Methodist Episcopal Church

The following article was printed in a religious publication entitled *The Christian Index*, dated August 8, 1912 under the byline of Prentis A. Bryson, 1719 Lyons St. Evanston, Illinois.

Dear Christian Index:

Kindly allow me space for a few words regarding the organization of our church here in Evanston.

Some time in April, five CMEs who have been residents of Evanston for some little time, one of whom has been connected with the AME church for ten years by virtue of the CME not being here, decided that they had waited long enough for a church. The result was that we had several meetings among ourselves and got in touch with Reverend T.L. Scott, pastor of St. Paul CME Church of Chicago, and Reverend W. A. Jackson, presiding elder of the Illinois District, who gave us an encouragement and set a date for our organization.

On Sunday, April 26, at 4 P.M., our church was organized and five souls were made happy. Reverend T.L. Scott, the organizer, came out and preached all of his spare time and set this town on fire with his wonderful sermons.

Another great aid to us was Reverend W.H. Parker, pastor of the Englewood CME Church, who came out and preached for us every time he could get away from his church. We have learned to have a great love for these two valuable CME preachers.

Reverend T.L. Scott has been especially kind to us. When Bishop Lane was making his visit on the Illinois District, Reverend T.L. Scott was the direct cause of Bishop Lane including us on his schedule.

The Bishop's visit in this town was indeed a memorable one. He preached to a packed house. The words of his sermon are still ringing in our ears.

Our first quarterly conference was held here on June 28-30 by Reverend W.A. Johnson, D.D., P.E., of the Illinois District. It was certainly a success. Reverend Scott and Reverend Parker, both pastors of our churches of Chicago, came out and brought their congregations. $16.25 was raised on that day.

Our membership has grown from five to ten. Reverend John G. Williams has been appointed our pastor, and we are praying and hoping for him here one great success.

Personally, we feel we have in Reverend Williams a clean cut Christian man and one who is conscientious of his work.

Prentis A. Bryson
1719 Lyons Street
Evanston, Illinois

St. Andrew's Episcopal Church

The parish of St. Andrew's, Evanston, was founded as a mission in November 1919. The primary goal was to care for the spiritual and Christian needs of the residents of Evanston and the surrounding areas.

Three matriarchs, Mrs. Esther L. Bryant, Mrs. Mary F. Jackson, and Dr. Louise Scott, under the leadership of the Holy Spirit, made a petition for a mission status to the Rt. Reverend Charles Palmerston, Bishop of Chicago. The signatures to the petition were Eugene Sr., Harriett, Eugene Jr., Davidson and Richard Hutt, Mary V. Jackson, Louise Scott, Ester L., Katherine and Charlotte Bryant, Lula M. Jackson, Joseph O. and Jessie G: Jackson, Frances Lash, Beulah Lee, Nettie Penn, Albert Pickett, William E. Stewart, Flora Poston, Irene Best, and Walter Bell.

The Reverend Henry B. Browne was appointed the first Priest-in-Charge on September 8, 1920. Father Browne came to Evanston from Denver, Colorado, where he had been Vicar of the Church of the Redeemer. The first services were conducted at St. Mark's Episcopal Church, Evanston, Illinois.

Beginning Sunday, September 26, 1920, services were conducted at the YMCA on Emerson Street. The Rt. Reverend Sheldon Munsion Griswold, the Suffragan Bishop, officiated at that special occasion. The parish church services were later moved to 1930 Darrow Avenue, now the rectory.

The present brick church building was consecrated on Advent Sunday, November 27, 1935. In 1945, the St. Andrew's Church was granted the status of a parish. Changes in membership and environment led the parish to a mission status in 1985.

The church has been served by the Reverends Henry B. Browne, William J. Weaver, Edwin L. Braithwaite, George E. Stams, Birney W. Smith, who was the first rector, Harold L. Young, Grosvenor M. Needham, E. John Gwynn, Norbert Cooper, John A. Spaulding, and Ed Howell followed by interim pastorates and Ndung'u J.B. Ikenye, the current permanent vicar. Dr. Ikenye hails from Kenya, Africa.

Mt. Zion Missionary Baptist Church

Highlights of History

This church was organized in the spring of 1894 when the Second Baptist Church granted letters to nine women and six men, namely, Andrew Scott, D.J. Marion, Frank Scott, Sandy Trent, Robert Fields, Joseph Young ,and sisters Mary Fields, Laura Scott, Susan Scott, M.L. Trent, Maria Robinson, Julia Minor, Rebecca Marion, and Lou Ann Truesdale.

Meetings were held from house to house for a couple of months until a mission was formed and the Union Hall (New Chandler's) was rented to hold services. The Reverend Harry Knight of Chicago was asked to meet with the members and decided to call a council for church organization on August 15, 1894.

The Council of Ministers for organization included the Reverends J.S. Cruchon as moderator, J.J. Anderson, G.M. Davis, H.W. Knight, and R.H. Walker as clerk. Thus, Mt. Zion Baptist Church was born.

Ministers who first served the church as pastors were the Reverends Moses Porter, G.M. Davis, L.E. Hamilton, and James Swanson, under whose leadership the first parcel of property was acquired at 1113 Clark Street in 1902. In 1904, the Reverend E.H. Fletcher was called to pastor and served for twelve years. He left the church debt free and with a balance of $1600 in the bank.

The Reverend W.R. Ashburn was elected after Reverend Fletcher, and additional land was purchased and the first unit of the present building was erected.

In the fall of 1918, the Reverend E.P. Jones, president of the National Baptist Convention, was called as pastor. During his administration, a mortgage was made on the church, and, in 1922, the main auditorium of the present structure was completed. It was during his pastorate that the pipe organ was installed. Dr. Jones passed away after serving six years, in November 1924.

The Reverends C.A. Long, J.H. Abernathy, Orlando Mitchell, J.C. Olden, and F.W. Penick followed as pastors during the Depression years. The church went through many hardships, tears, and sorrow during these short terms of leadership. Many members scattered. Despair and confusion were prevalent throughout the membership, but through prayers and faith the church survived.

In May of 1940, with the help of the Holy Spirit and guidance of Dr. Henry Allen Boyd, the Reverend G.W. Wilson was encouraged to come and preach at Mt. Zion. He was immediately called as pastor. He proved to be a great organizer, leader, and financier. During the first four years, the church was remodeled. All loans were paid off. Membership increased. The baptismal pool was moved to the rostrum, and the downstairs was remodeled. In 1944, the long overdue mortgage was burned during the celebration of the Golden Anniversary. The present parsonage was purchased and paid for.

Under Pastor Wilson's leadership, the following deacons were ordained: Robert Adams, Nathan Rogers, Wadie Daniels, Robert Macklin, and Charles Hicks. The Reverend William Marion was also ordained and licensed as a minister.

Pastor Wilson passed away in September 1952 after serving twelve years and four months. He also left the church debt free and with a sizeable bank account.

The church remained without a pastor for eight months. In June of 1953, the Reverend A. Alton Hill, a native of Texas, was invited to preach and was elected as pastor. He, too, was a great teacher, spiritual leader, and astute financier. His first aim was to organize the church into a Christian body where everyone, young or old, rich or poor, would feel that they belonged to this Christian family.

Pastor Hill soon realized that much had to be reconstructed around the church because of new building codes. The parsonage was completely remodeled. Choir seats and carpeting to match were purchased. New windows and roofing were installed. The kitchen was equipped. Office equipment was purchased. The balcony was reconstructed. The floors were tiled all over. Two adjacent lots were also purchased for a future expansion program. These renovations increased the value of the church's holdings to over $200,000.

The church began a Crusade of Community Awareness. The membership was responsible for meeting many needs in home and foreign missions. Mt. Zion was the first church in the community to hold a life membership in the NAACP. Pastor Hill was always active in the State and National Conventions. He also took an active part when the World Council of Churches met in Evanston.

The following deacons served or were ordained under the Reverend

Hill: Ulysses Mackey, O.D. Walker, Theodore Turner, Jerry Eubanks, Robert Adams, Robert Guillebeaux, Nathan Rogers, Richard Henry, Luther Avery, Linsay Langston, Morgan Forehand, Calvin Parker, John Haugabrook, Raymon Huff, Otis Keller, James Banks, Leslie Gayles, George Fike, and Herman Davis.

Some of the trustees that served were Frank Bacon, James Kidd, J.H. Fleming, J.H. Eubanks, Leslie Gregory, James Davis, Roscoe Harris, Julius Brown, Elizabeth K. Henderson, Albert Dent, Ruby Manson, Minnie and Thomas Wilson.

Pastor Hill became ill and in August of 1976, the Lord said, "Well done thy faithful servant, enter into the house of many mansions that I have prepared for you."

After almost 24 years of continuous leadership, the chairman of the deacon board, Morgan Forehand, had the task of trying to hold the church together. Many visiting ministers were invited to speak.

In September of 1976, the Reverend John F. Norwood was invited to deliver God's message to our congregation. He served the pulpit for seventeen months without compensation. On November 20, 1977, by formal vote, he was chosen as pastor-elect and was installed on April 5, 1978 by Dr. L.W. Mingo, president of the National State Convention.

Original Second Baptist Church

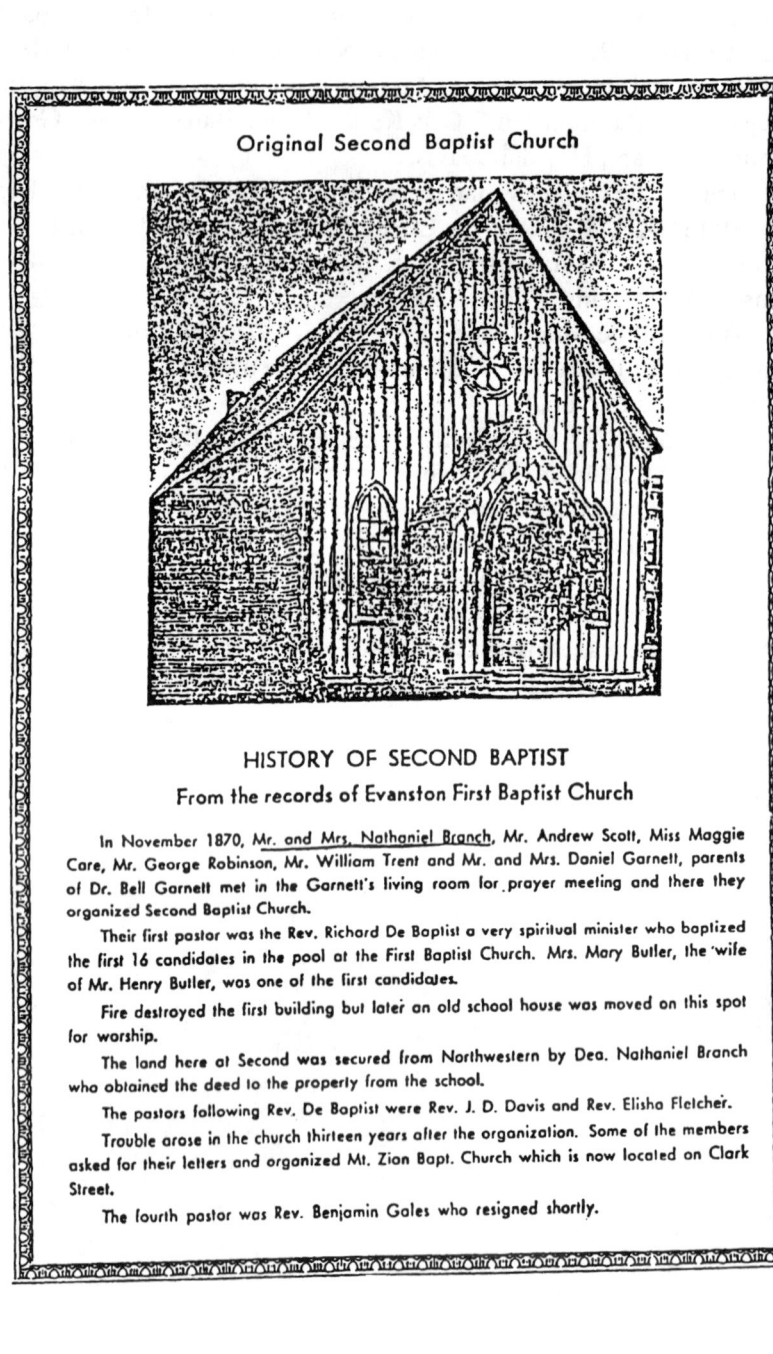

HISTORY OF SECOND BAPTIST
From the records of Evanston First Baptist Church

In November 1870, Mr. and Mrs. Nathaniel Branch, Mr. Andrew Scott, Miss Maggie Care, Mr. George Robinson, Mr. William Trent and Mr. and Mrs. Daniel Garnett, parents of Dr. Bell Garnett met in the Garnett's living room for prayer meeting and there they organized Second Baptist Church.

Their first pastor was the Rev. Richard De Baptist a very spiritual minister who baptized the first 16 candidates in the pool at the First Baptist Church. Mrs. Mary Butler, the wife of Mr. Henry Butler, was one of the first candidates.

Fire destroyed the first building but later an old school house was moved on this spot for worship.

The land here at Second was secured from Northwestern by Dea. Nathaniel Branch who obtained the deed to the property from the school.

The pastors following Rev. De Baptist were Rev. J. D. Davis and Rev. Elisha Fletcher.

Trouble arose in the church thirteen years after the organization. Some of the members asked for their letters and organized Mt. Zion Bapt. Church which is now located on Clark Street.

The fourth pastor was Rev. Benjamin Gales who resigned shortly.

Appendix B

Left to right: Mr. Jerry Reed; Mr. D.W. Richardson; Mr. R.C. Williams; Mr. A.P. Perry; Mr. W.H. Twiggs; Mr. Wm. H. Gill; Dr. Charles R. Scruggs; Mr. James Allen (not shown). The men above were responsible for starting the Emerson Y.M.C.A. These men were responsible for forming the basic structure that has held the Emerson Branch together since 1914.

The first section of the Emerson Y.M.C.A.
Building erected in 1914.

Ground was broken for the building December 29, 1913; on February 8, 1914 the cornerstone was laid. At this time the city of Evanston contributed money to the Y.M.C.A. of which $10,000 was allocated to the Branch project. During this year the first building costing $23,000 was officially opened. The structure now located on the site was completed in December 1929 at a cost of $107,000.

The expansion of the Emerson Street Y.M.C.A.

The expansion of the Emerson Street YMCA was completed in 1929. The building was located at 1014 Emerson Street.

The facilities included a swimming pool, gymnasium, youth center, adult lobby, youth game room area with table tennis, pocket billiards, television, and other small games, nineteen residence rooms, four club meeting rooms, auditorium, special exercise room with bar bells, exercycle, punching bag, and other devices for fitness programs.

There is ample space in the rear of the building for parking space or other outdoor recreational use.

Emerson Street YMCA
Fifth Annual Local
Older Boys' Conference
1934 (photo on page 294)

Row   Name (Left to Right)
1. George Williams, Bill Jones, Pikey Powell, Tracy Gray, Mr. Prather Hauser, John Barber, Albert "Jack" Price, Charles Smith, Owen Washington, Clyde Arnold

2. Charles Whiteside, Alvin Brooks, Joe Warren, James Avery, Bill Byrd, Jack Bracken, James "Lad" Freeman

3. Carl Wilson, Herbert Foster, Robert Stringer, Melvin Smith, Elbert Lee, Mayo Partee, Harry Kingslow, Bobby Brown

4. John Burton, Purnell Davis, Robert Sutton, Sonny Brown, George Young

5. Sammy Mathews, Claudius Britt, Douglas Reynolds, Hecky Powell, Jerry Banks, Bebward Reynolds, Rollin Davis, Herbert Barton, Aaron Halley, Owen Boudry, Mickey McGrier, Roy Griffin, James Harvey, Eddie Moses

Conversations with Blacks in Evanston, Illinois

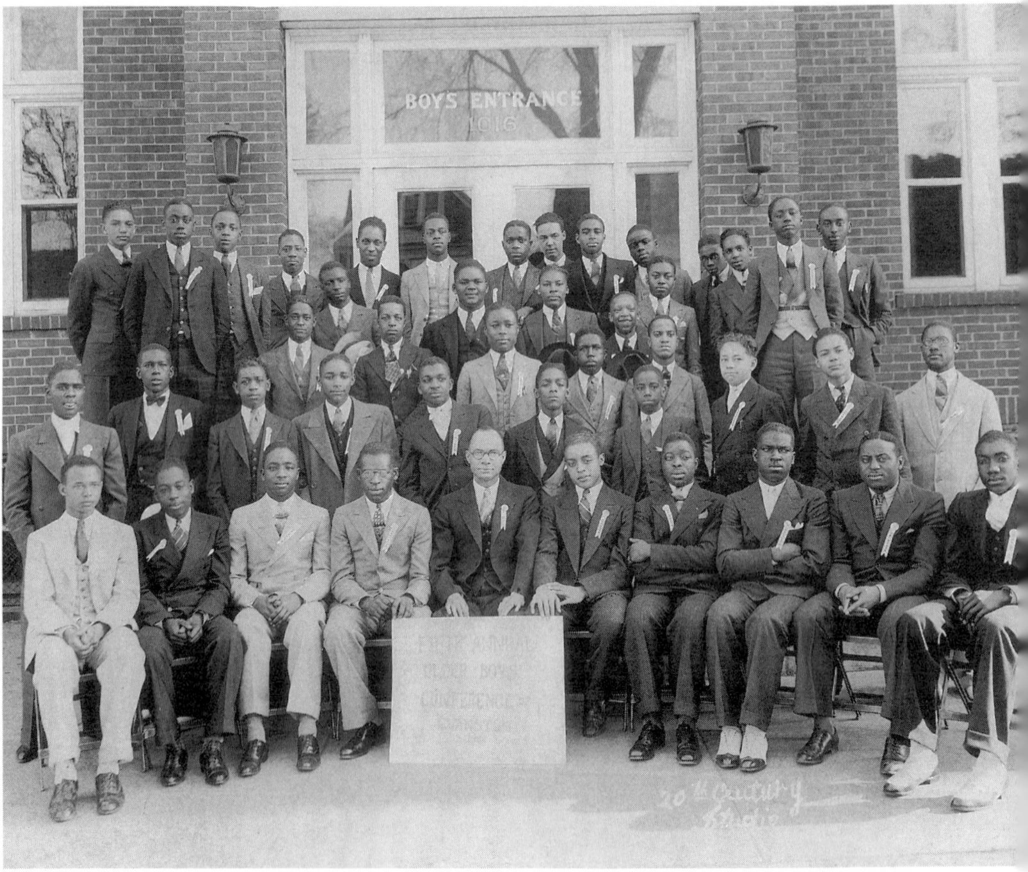
BOYS ENTRANCE
1016

Appendix C

Community Hospital of Evanston

The following material is taken from the Fleetwood-Jourdain Art Guild Publication, "The Shaping of Black Evanston," January 15, 1996.

Community Hospital of Evanston began its life as the Evanston Sanitarium and Training School in 1914. During this time African-Americans were not admitted on the medical staffs of the existing hospitals on the North Shore. Drs. Isabella Garnett Butler and Arthur Butler, African-Americans living in Evanston, had completed their medical degrees and set up practices. However, they needed a place where they could admit and treat their patients.

Isabella Garnett was born in Evanston and finished her medical education at the College of Physicians and Surgeons (now the University of Illinois College of Medicine) in 1901.

Arthur Butler graduated from Northwestern University Medical school in 1909.

The couple converted their home at 1918 Asbury Avenue in Evanston into a sanitarium and moved into a smaller house on the back lot. Even though Dr. Butler died in 1924, Dr. Garnett continued to run the institution at that location until it was moved to a larger building in 1930.

Meanwhile, women of the First Methodist Church in Evanston formed a group in 1924, which they named the Interracial Cooperative Council. Within the council, they formed the Booker T. Washington Association, to study the health needs of "colored" people of Evanston on the North Shore.

The name was changed in 1927 to the Community Hospital Association of Evanston. Even though the study indicated the need for a larger facility, contributions were not large during the Depression. Therefore, they rented and moved to the Dr. Penn House at 2026 Brown Avenue on December 7, 1930.

When Anna Shuman Eliot died in 1936, she left the hospital $50,000, and the board bought the building. Dr. Garnett was the superintendent for many years and worked with the hospital until her death in 1948. In the meantime, Dr. Elizabeth Hill, another African-American

Evanstonian, had completed her medical education at the University of Illinois Medical School and joined the staff at CHE in 1931. She became chief of staff in 1943 and served for many years.

Since the "basement surgery" necessitated by the existing facilities was not acceptable, the hospital needed a new building. In 1951 government funds were secured and this sparked a controversy in the community. Some people thought that building a new facility would perpetuate segregation, but Dr. Hill maintained that the sick couldn't wait fifteen years for Evanston hospitals to be integrated. The new building was opened on October 5, 1952 amid much fanfare and celebration.

The staff and board of directors always had people from many races and countries. In 1958, James Neal became the first African-American hospital administrator. There was always ongoing support from Evanston, and other North Shore communities contributed charitable funds over the years.

In 1939, Dr. Hill had formed the Woman's Auxiliary, which fostered community outreach, served as the main fund-raising arm, and provided invaluable services. The women did sewing, and candy stripers served patients and helped the Garden Teas. These teas were started in 1949 and continued to be the major fund-raising event.

Dr. Warren Spencer, a long time staff physician, was admitted to the staff at St. Francis Hospital in Evanston in 1963, and with the civil rights movement, the availability of health care for African-Americans began to change. Larger hospitals evolved to sustain the expensive new technology and small hospitals like CHE had difficulties trying to compete. In the 1970s there were major problems for CHE, including lawsuits against the Board of Directors by Dr. Spencer and an alternative group who questioned the board's authority. Evanston Hospital, Northwestern University, and CHE formed a tripartite group to study and initiate cooperation. They explored a viable and independent use for CHE. In 1973, three CHE doctors were finally admitted to the Evanston Hospital staff.

Early in the 1980s, a Chicago newspaper exposed an alleged fraud, after which the hospital lost its accreditation and the doors were then closed on June 9, 1980.

Appendix D

Alpha Kappa Alpha Sorority

This article was taken from the UNITY publication, June 25, 1995.

Alpha Kappa Alpha Sorority, Inc., the first African-American sorority, was founded at Howard University In 1908, Delta Chi Omega, the Evanston alumnae chapter was chartered on June 28, 1948. One mission of Alpha Kappa Alpha Sorority, Inc., stated in the preamble to its constitution, is " to cultivate and encourage high scholastic standards." Criteria for scholarships are grade point average, financial need, interview, self-description, extracurricular/community involvement, and recommendations. The chapter implements this mandate by granting scholarships each year.

1. Academic Award Evanston Township High School
To a graduating African-American female senior pursuing higher education, $1,000 award to be continued as $500 through graduation if GPA of 2.5 (C+) or more is maintained.

2. Achievement Award Suburban/St. Scholastica
Given to graduating African-American female senior(s) pursuing higher education, $500 or more. Winners are eligible for the Lucile Roberts Continuing Award for remaining college years.

3. Special Recognition Achievement Award
To a graduating African-American female senior(s) whose academic and extracurricular activities warrant recognition. Winners eligible for the Lucile Roberts Continuing Award for remaining college years.

4. Lucile Roberts Continuing Award
Named for the first chapter president, this award of $500 is given to young women who previously received an Achievement or Special Recognition Award, a GPA of 2.5 (C+) is required.

5. Dr. Elizabeth Webb Hill Scholarship Award
Named for chapter member who was a founding member of the Community Hospital of Evanston. A $500 award is given to one member of the undergraduate chapters at Northwestern University, National-Louis University, or Kendall College.

6. Helen Cromer Cooper Beginnings Award
Named for the chapter's golden member, $500 award given to a teen parent who is pursuing higher education.

Nationally, the Alpha Kappa Alpha Educational Advancement Foundation annually awards Merit Awards for students who have excelled academically and show evidence of leadership through participation in community or college service. Each of these students receives $1,000.

Unmet Financial Assistance Scholarships are awarded to students who, in addition to good academic standing, need financial assistance to complete a particular program of study. These awards range from $500 to $1,500 and are typically given to individuals who have endured great hardship to achieve their education goals. Applications may be made to the Educational Advancement Foundation, 5656 South Stony Island Avenue, Chicago, Illinois 60637, Attention: Mrs. Doris Parker, Executive Secretary.

The article below was taken from Unity Publication June 25, 1995.

Delta Sigma Theta, Inc.
A Public Service Sorority Evanston
North Shore Alumnae Chapter
Robin Richmond-Cross, President

Delta Sigma Theta, Inc. was the first black sorority to establish a chapter In Evanston. The charter was issued on January 20, 1948 to Gamma omicron Chapter, a mixed chapter of undergraduate and graduate members. In late 1974 and early 1975, the Delta Grand Chapter disbanded the remaining mixed chapters, nationwide, and established an independent joint undergraduate chapter at Northwestern University/National-Louis University. On February 9, 1975 Gamma Omicron was rechartered as Evanston-North Shore Alumnae Chapter, for graduate members only.

The principal purposes and aims of this public service sorority are to establish, maintain, and encourage high cultural, intellectual, and moral standards among its members; to engage in public service programs; and to promote and encourage achievement in education by granting scholarships to high school graduates from ETHS. A limited number of scholarships are made available to students from other North Shore area high schools. Previous recipients are also eligible to reapply. In 1988 the local chapter designated one of its scholarships, The Billie Chiles Memorial Scholarship, in honor of our deceased soror who was a charter member and who served as president for many years.

Delta Sigma Theta was founded at Howard University, Washington, D.C. in 1913. Thirteen founding members wanted to emphasize civic involvement for black women. As a result, one of their earliest records of involvement was participation as suffragettes in the campaign for women's voting rights.

The sorority continues to encourage fully the notion of pride, leadership, and family stability among all African-American women. In every aspect of their lives.

Appendix E

The History of the North Shore Illinois Links

by Beulah Avery - April 1995
Additional Historical Tidbits - Carmelia Hill - January 1996

On November 19, 1972, twenty-six ladies joined the Chain of Friendship of the Links, Inc. to give service in various communities along the North Shore of Illinois, north of the city of Chicago. Link Anna Julian*, Chapter Establishment Officer, was ably assisted by Link Dorothy Harrison and other members of the Chicago Chapter of Links, Inc. in the establishment of The North Shore Illinois Chapter. Link Helen Edmond* was National President and Link Willie Glanton was area director. Georgia Williams and Vivian McMillan were organizers of the chapter and helped the Chicago Chapter identify members of the North Shore who met certain criteria. The North Shore Illinois Chapter will always have fond memories of those who were instrumental in establishing it.

Of the original twenty-six members, five are still **active** in the North Shore Chapter: Carmelia Hill, Eleanor Hill, Vivian McMillan, Alice Robinson, and Gladys Turner; four are **active alumnae**: Beulah Avery, Helen Cooper, Hazel Huggins, and Christine Loving. Etta Moten Barnett is in a category by herself. She was classified as **honorary**, then **active**, then **active alumnae**. Nine transferred out to towns closer to their homes or new jobs, or their husbands' new locations: Madeline Coleman, Ruth Emmons, Mary LaNier, Majorie Mims, Lucia Peele, Beulah Stamps, Joan Wallace, Georgia Williams and Ruth "Teena" Williams; four **resigned**: Patricia Atherton, Delores Cross, Janie Hurd, and Frankie Webb; three are **deceased**: Audrey Fountain*, Ollie Matthews*, and Josephine Robinson*; one with **address unknown**: Anna Reid.

The eight chapter presidents (in their proper order) are Georgia Williams, Vivian McMillan, Beulah Avery, Gladys Turner, Audrey Fountain, Doris Yancy, Yvonne Sharpe, and Alice Robinson. Under their guidance, the chapter has moved steadily forward and has worked with other organizations to honor those who have made unusual accomplishments at the local level; Connecting Link Joseph Hill, the first black superintendent of schools in Evanston; Margaret Labat, the first black women superintendent in Evanston; also, important speakers have been introduced to the community via open meetings: Barbara Bowman, early childhood educator; Harry Porterfield of TV fame; the late Link JoAhn Brown-Nash*, nationally known entrepreneur; Link Amanda Rudd, Commissioner of Libraries of the City of Chicago; Link Ethel Payne*; well-known columnist—just to name a few.

It was a delight to entertain Michael Morgan, nationally known Symphony Conductor, after the opening night's performance and also the cast of *Porgy and Bess* after opening night's performance in Chicago. The cast graciously accepted the courtesies bestowed upon it, but seemed far more delighted to meet North Shore's own Etta who was the first "Bess" of *Porgy and Bess*.

Several members who contributed to the history of this chapter at area and national levels should also be noted:

1. Beulah Avery: co-chair of Cluster Chapters who hosted the National Assembly in Chicago in 1978; National Rules Committee; Area Nominating Committee; Co-organizer of the Etta Moten Travel group.

2. Etta Moten Barnett: NGO Representative of Links at the United Nations; Leader of Links to International Decade of Women in 1985 in East Mica; National Chairman of International Trends and Services; Recipient of many honors including the EMB Scholarship through travel to many countries in South America, the Far East and Europe.

3. Mary Casselberry: Area Nominating Committee Chair; Presenter at Area Art Workshop; Illinois State Coordinator for Links Foundation.

4. Helen Cromer Cooper: Area Secretary.

5. Carmelia Hill: National Scholarship Committee; National Timekeepers Committee; Area Task Force Worker for nine chapters; Area Evaluation Committee; presenter at Area Bylaws Workshop; Chair of Etta Moten Scholarship Travel Group.

Conversations with Blacks in Evanston, Illinois • 305

6. Vivian McMillan: Co-organizer of North Shore Illinois Chapter; National Chapter Committee; Area Archivist; National Archivist; Co-organizer of Etta Moten Barnett Travel Group.

7. Thera Ramos and Edna Smith: Presenters at Area and National Workshops on Outstanding Annual Health Fair since 1978 for which prizes were won.

8. Alice Robinson: Area Director of the Arts; Benefactor of many Transportation Services locally for chapter activities as well as for area-wide and national participation.

9. Josephine Robinson: First donor to contribute over $5,000 to purchase National Headquarters building in Washington, D.C. Her picture hangs in National Headquarters today.

There were always proportionately more Links and Connecting Links from the North Shore Chapter (excluding the host chapters) who attended National and Area meetings to meet and greet Links from everywhere. "The true meaning of the word Friendship" is enhanced by attending area and national meetings.

Some of the many organizations that benefited from the chapter's financial aid are: NAACP Million Dollar Campaign, NAACP Legal Defense Fund, NAACP Life Membership, NAACP Golden Heritage Fund, National Achievement Scholarship for Outstanding Negro Students (Connecting Link Lemmon McMillan piloted this program.), Center on Deafness, Park School for the Handicapped, Mississippi Crisis, African Water Wells every year, Family Focus Community Center, Gloria Bond Clunie's Drama group of Jr. High Students, United Negro College Fund, Du Sable Museum, Unity Scholarship Fund, Etta Moten Barnett Scholarship Fund, Lake County Head Start, Ethiopian Famine Relief, UNICEF Projects, Artists' Showcase in Lake Forest, Ethnic Art Fair on the Lake, Operation Big Vote, and others.

As new members were inducted (Shirley Mines was the first inductee) or transferred into the chapter (Thera Ramos and Ethel Payne were the first two to transfer in) the true spirit of the twenty-six continued. The Links took care of business, learned from others, exchanged ideas and had lots of fun, too. The fun started when they boarded a Robinson Coach going to some meeting—somewhere. The

Chapter Delegate stayed in the suite that doubled as the chapter hospitality room which Connecting Links kept well stocked and hospitable.

And today, the dynamic leaders and followers, young executives, business women, professionals, doers, dreamers, drivers, dazzlers, will keep the North Shore Chapter in high esteem in Linkdom. The four Facet Chairs are finding advantages of high-tech umbrella programs in collaboration with other groups in the community and including all members of the chapter.

Friendship, LEADERSHIP, COMMITMENT and SERVICE along with other key values are always foremost in the undertakings of the North Shore Illinois Chapter in order to positively affect the quality of lives of others. The now forty-seven members are continually committed to service—QUALITY SERVICE - THE MEASURE OF OUR SUCCESS (the chapter motto).

*deceased

The Dunbar Woman's Club.
Organized Feb. 19, 1911.
Bank Book — City National
No 31569
Order of meeting

= Call to order
= Singing — Prayer — Quotation —
= Roll call of officers —
 = Reading of minutes —
5 = Report of sick and philantropic com.
 = Report of any un mentioned sick
 = Applications for membership —
 = Balloting for members —
 = Communications or bill —
 = Report of standing com —
 = " " special " —
2 = Unfinished business —
3 = New business —
4 = Financial roll — paying of dues —
5 = Remarks for good of club —
 = Program —
7 = Adjournment —
Quarterly dues to be ped — 1.00
Yearly Budget paid in March — 5.00

Sept
Dec
May
July

10. Standing Com.

1 Sick Com { Payne, Philmon, Molton, Noah, Bethel-Scott

2 Printing { Currey, Fletcher, Wainright

3 School { Collier-Johnson, Hadley, E. Cannon, Barton, Smggs

✓ 4 Old Folks Home { Esther Bryant, Erving, Green, Finley, Payne

✓ Courtesy { Lillian Cannon, Bailey, Houser, Matney

Financial { Davis, Penn, Bryant

✓ Building { Bryant, Penn, Floyd, Hadley, Keen

Auditing { Ethel Cau..., Esther Edwa..., Effie Settle

✓ Membership { Collier John..., Addie Scott, Lydia Dav...

Banking — Esther Bry..., Loretta St..., Evelyn Kee...

Special Com
1 Old Folks Home
2 Building —
3 Courtesy Banking
4 Membership
5 Bazaar —

p. 339

Program 1931 – 32

Sept. Opening Party – President has in charge
Oct. – Household ec – Addie Scott – Lillian Clinton – [illegible]
Nov. – Art Literature Music = Buck Roy – Edwards – Jara Moore – Clerbin Moore
Dec. – Philanthropic – Cotton Dobson – Green – Ashmore – Noah
Jan. = Civic – Russell – Taylor – Kincaid – Houser
Feb. = Historic = Edwards – Buck Roy – Brockett – [illegible] Bryant
Mar. – Floyd – Currey – Berry – Estelle Johnson – Mrs. Young – Madeay Morrell – Ellen Johnson
April = Spring Luncheon – Nanser – Stewart – Lunn – [illegible]
April = Bazaar – Esther Bryant – Twiggs – Keene – Branch – Floyd – Houser – Ethel & Lillian Canning – [illegible] – Golden Moore – Effie Settler – Miss Currey – [illegible] – Mrs Molton – Breckenridge – P. Ketchum Dot – Molton – Settler
May – Child Welfare – Loretta Stewart – Edwards – Estelle Johnson
June – Closing Party – Thurman – Bailey – Keene – Golden – [illegible] – Bryant – Molton – Martin – Lillian Can[illegible]

Delegates to City Fed. { Keene, Floyd, Payne, Davis

Thur Sept 11 1930

Call meeting at the home of the Ed. Board Chairman Mrs Marie Floyd.

Report of "Privilege" Committee

To the President, officers and members of the Dunbar Womans Club. We your committee submit the following report -

We recommend that the club continue holding meetings at the "Y" until we hear from the Ex. Com. of the "Y." We further recommend that all indebtedness be paid before change of meeting place, This to place the club on a higher business basis

Julia Hadley
Marie Floyd
Anna Fletcher
Loretta Stewart

Sept 23 1930
Dunbar Womans Club
Dear Friends,

The Com. has requested me to inform you of the following prices for rentals and use of our kitchen facilities -

1/ For afternoon teas, $ to use of dishes silver tables & room for meet-

p. 341

30

$5.00 No meals to be prepared or served

$10.00 Same facilities for night, 8 to 11
No meals to be prepared or served

3 For facilities for cooking dinners or serving meals at which a charge is made by Dunbar to other people & purposes of raising money the rental is $25.00

4 Payments of Rents
One half of rental fee must be paid upon application for use the balance when rooms are open In every case the rent is due in advance —

5 These regulations are effective at   and will continue until further notice of changes has been given

Very sincerely
P. J. Houser

Miss Sarah Gurrey
Act. Sec. Dunbar Woman[?]

p. 342

The following material was taken from a Unity publication, June 25, 1995

UNITY History

Women don't just get together and gossip, but women do often get together and dream of concepts such as UNITY. So it was when two friends, C. Louise Brown (Alpha Kappa Alpha) and Yvonne Davis (Delta Sigma Theta) made a firm commitment to each other to see the idea come to fruition. One year later, Delta Sigma Theta's Evanston North Shore Chapter sent out the call to at least a dozen other black community groups, who gave scholarships to young people. Alpha Kappa Alpha, Ione S. Browne, Kappa Alpha Psi, and NAACP answered the call to unity and the first Community Scholarship Tea was held in July of 1985 at Second Baptist Church. The scholarship chairpersons from the five groups were the committee. These five were extremely proud and their excitement spilled over into the following year when an additional thirteen organizations enthusiastically joined the ranks and followed the leadership of the original five. Helen Cromer (Alpha Kappa Alpha) bridged the gap between our past and present and told us of a time, more than twenty years ago, when several black organizations had for several years held the same type of scholarship tea. Our group was elated to be revitalizing a portion of our community's history.

During the 1986 planning, Charlene Jones (NAACP) arrived at one meeting with a meticulously hand-lettered logo for the group to be called UNITY. Her idea and design captured the essence of what we had felt, and UNITY was born without a dissenting voice. Charlene's design has been computerized and is the permanent and proud symbol of black community organizations working together toward a unifying experience. It appears today on our program book cover. Efforts such as hers are typical among the group's representatives. In other words, UNITY works because we want it to.

We are extremely grateful to every individual, organization, and business who supported our preparation efforts.

Thank you very much,
Yvonne Davis

Twentieth Century Golf Club Evanston Illinois

On April 4, 1948 a group of approximately one hundred people of color headed by a dentist, Dr. Joseph Howard, gathered together to form a golf club which was ultimately called Twentieth Century Golf Club.

The initial meeting was held at the Emerson Street, YMCA, Room D. Dr. Howard acted as president and Thomas McNeal acted as secretary until the election of officers, which was accomplished that evening.

The following persons were elected:

Joseph Howard	President
Charles Fisher	Vice-President
Ms. Willie Higgins	Secretary
Charles Tarkington	Treasurer
Augustus Watts	Chairman, Rules Committee
Thomas Butler	Sergeant At Arms

Thirteen names for the club were submitted for consideration, with the official name to hopefully be The Evanston Golf Club. Two other persons were elected to the roster of officers for positions considered to be of importance for a fledgling club, i.e. Eugene Beck Chairman, Arrangements Committee Charles Jones Club Reporter

$4.70 was raised at this meeting to/pay for an advertisement in the *Newsette Newspaper*. No fees were set for joining or dues at this meeting. The meeting was adjourned and 4/19/48 was scheduled for the next one to be held at the YMCA.

On April 19, 1948 the meeting was held at the Subway Lounge in the lower level of the Masonic Temple on Emerson Street, instead of the YMCA. The following people were selected to form a committee to draw up a constitution and by-laws:

Thomas Butler Chairman	Jack Bonner
Ms. Willie Higgins (Chief "Go For")	Sydney Callendar
Michel Laurent	Cornell Cromer
Ms. Evelyn Peak Charles Fisher	Tennis Sanders

Instructions: Clifton Adams, Lead Instructor.

Donations for instructions was suggested. The donations were to be given to Mr. Hummons at the Y and instructions were to be available every Monday at 8:00 P.M. until further notice. $2.00 per month per participant in group instructions with private instruction fees to be set by Mr. Adams and the person seeking instructions was the suggested plan. The fees were to be paid the first night of instruction.

Joining fees and dues: $1.00 joining; $.50 monthly for dues was set as the initial requirements at this meeting.

Tournament Committee: Charles Tarkington, Chairman, Michel Laurent, Charles Fisher, Mr. Watt, and Eugene Beck

Meetings: Every Monday at 9:00 P.M. after instructions, until the group was better organized. Meetings were to be held at the YMCA in Room D.

4/26/48   The secretary was authorized to draw money from the treasury for stationery and various other expenses pertaining to that office. Larger expenses were to be voted upon. The Constitution & By-Laws were presented, corrected (finally approved) and accepted as corrected. New members were enrolled. The first tournament was to be held approximately in the middle of August 1948. Charles Jones volunteered to become the second golf instructor, along with Mr. Adams.

5/3/48   President & Vice Pres. absent, so Secretary conducted the meeting (a pattern that was followed many times down through the years). First tournament was to be a closed tournament because of the inexperience of some of the members who would only create problems for the more experienced golfers. Possible tournament site was the golf course called "Way Side." Dr. Tarkington was to investigate for an optional site in the vicinity of Evanston. Laura Fleetwood suggested that the women needed more lessons in the fundamentals of the game. (A-MEN, however, they did not mention that there was also a LOT OF MEN "HACKERS"). Charles Fisher suggested that at the following Monday, at the meeting, (THE BIG, STRONG) experienced men let the women know when they were going to golf course and issue an invitation to those who wished to play (golf - that is!). Michel Laurent, (one of the most undisciplined, irrational, and profane males in the group) suggested that several more MEN join in instructing the women so that the women would at least be able to HOLD THEIR OWN before going out on the golf course (probably in the field of PROFANITY).

Many more suggestions were made, and since most of the men were married, they tried to mollify the ladies by volunteering to car pool on Sundays, volunteering to take (those desiring to learn how to hit the ball) anyone out to the Driving Range to practice, and offering a prize to the most promising lady golfer in order to keep the ladies' interest alive. (That was using the "old noggin.")

Since everyone had not paid their $1.00 joining fee, it was suggested that these people be notified to pay up by 5/17/48 or they would not be included as Charter Members in the application to the State of Illinois. It was also agreed that once a month the group would meet at the Subway Lounge and have movies and refreshments. It was later agreed to secure a SERIES OF SIX FILMS TO BE SHOWN AT REGULAR MEETINGS by "kittying up" the fee of $8.00 for the series. (Try to get that now.)

Dr. Tarkington, Tournament Director, informed the group that the tournament could be held at Northwestern Golf Course (now Chick Evans Golf Course) on a "first come, first served basis," and the course could not be closed to accommodate the tournament players.

Twentieth Century G.C. was invited to join Central States Golfers Association which included Illinois, Colorado, Nebraska, Iowa, Missouri, Ohio, and several other states. Midwest Golfers' Association also invited the club to join with them. That association included Illinois, Michigan, Ohio, Indiana, and a few other states.

A new name was selected for the golf club, since the name of "The Evanston Golf Club" had already been taken by another group some time prior to 1948. The group settled on the name of Twentieth Century Golf Club, not 20th as so many people chose to call it. The spelling seemed more impressive than the numeral for the purpose of the charter.

In June, Messrs Cox, Jones, and Laurent were appointed to investigate the possibility of having the August tournament at either Bunker Hill Golf Course, Way Side, or Northwestern Golf Course. The joining fee for the club was increased to $2.00, and annual dues were to be $12.00. (Oh, joy!)

The first tournament was to be held at Northwestern Golf Course. 8/14/ & 8/15 were to be qualifying days with the playoffs on 8/17/48. Entertainment and presentation of the trophies to be on the final date. Thomas Butler would be the entertainment chairman, and Evelyn Peak the photographer. The Entertainment Committee consisted of Percy McCullough, Harriette Brown, Lucille Simpson, Sydney Callendar, Lucille Roberts, and Priscilla Taylor.

The following new members were accepted 6/22/48: Glenna Allen, Grace Ubanks, Dorothy Hands, Juanita Jones, Spurgeon Pringle, Frederick Ivester, Sam Mitchell.

Ms. Peak submitted a design for the Corporate Seal. The first souvenir program was put together by Thomas Butler with pictures of Northwestern's Club House and Golf Club members. Mr. Twiggs designed the first membership card and a metal seal was to be obtained for all official business. A cocktail party was held at the Subway Lounge on 7/9/48 to raise funds for the tournament.

In July the secretary was leaving town and Evelyn Peak was appointed secretary, with her sister, Lucille Simpson as assistant. (Guess who did all the work!)

New members accepted into the club: Lucille Thomas (Kenilworth), Rev. & Mrs. C.F. Stewart (Detroit), Sue Higginbotthom, Alberta Prather, Wilton Jennings, John Dixon, Charles Cannon, Clifton Adams was dropped from the Board of Directors for failure to attend four consecutive meetings (pretty strict - huh?). A total of $101.45 was turned over to the president in order to open the first bank account for the club. (Hot dog, off and running!!! Yow!)

Meetings were changed from every Monday to the first Monday of the month. $25 contribution for a group membership was made to the Y, which would entitle the club to a Social Membership. Club membership cards were distributed to members who were three months or less in arrears with their dues. The club stationery would not bear the names of the officers, making it unnecessary to change stationery every year after each election.

The officers for 1949 were:

Joe Howard, President; Charles Jones, Vice President; Evelyn Peak, Secretary; Lucille Simpson, Corresponding Secretary; Charles Tarkington, Treasurer

A Sick Committee was appointed and authorized to spend $10.00 for an illness and $5.00 for the death of a member. Appointed were:

Laura Fleetwood, Jack Bonner, and Vivian Allen.

The 1949 Tournament was to be held at Bunker Hill Golf Course. The Souvenir program pages were to be divided into sections and sold for $5.00 each. Green fees were to be $5.00 for men, $3.00 for women. (At that time, "seniors" was not in our vocabulary.) Mrs. Graves was appointed to write a series of articles for the *Chicago Defender*, National Edition re the Club and upcoming tournaments. Any member wishing to play in the 1949 tournament must be paid up in dues through August in order to be eligible. Each member was to be responsible for securing ads, which were to be in by July fifth. Messers. Tom McNeal and Walter Powers were to select the trophies, fifteen in all, to be displayed at Harry Brown's Beauty Shop. Pat Ball, Golf Pro, would run the tournament. A copy of the program was to be mailed to each sponsor.

In September, the club was asked to host the CSGA Tournament in 1950. The discussion was tabled until a later date. The club joined United Golfers' Association, a group of Negro golf clubs organized from all the states who had joined Central States Golfers' Association., Eastern Golfers' Association, and/or Midwest Golfers' Association. It was also decided to hold an election of officers after each tournament. Meetings were changed from Mondays to Wednesdays and joining fee for the balance of 1949 to be increased to $4.00 and doubled each year thereafter.

In October 1949 it was decided that any person who had dropped out of the club and wished to rejoin would have to pay all back dues. If a member allowed dues to lapse for a year, that person would be dropped from the roster after being notified and who had not responded to the notice. The changes were to become amendments to the constitution.

In November 1949, it was decided not to hold an election after the 1950 tournament, and the $4.00 joining fee would be extended until the 1950 tournament and then doubled each year thereafter. Meetings had been changed from the Y or Subway Lounge to be held at the home of a different member each month.

Mr. McCullough had made arrangements for and secured twelve ID cards for admittance to the Winnetka Community House Bowling Alley for Saturday nights bowling for those wishing to participate.

In January 1950, Dr. Howard and Tom Mc Neal were to represent Twentieth Century G.C. They were to request our 1950 tournament date to follow the date of the Windy City Golf Club Tournament. (Because the club had joined all these different associations, there was not such thing as having an independent tournament. All dates had to be cleared through U.G.A., so as not to interfere with any other tournament being held by C.S.G.A., E.G.A, or M.G.A member clubs.) Dr. Howard reported in March that U.G.A. had scheduled tournaments for every week from June through September 1950. Twentieth Century's date was for two days before Labor Day. Annual fee to U.G.A. would be $1.00 per member or a minimum of $25.00 if less than twenty-five members and a maximum of $100 for clubs with membership of one hundred. (Huh??) Dr. Howard had been appointed to the U.G.A. Tournament Committee. Fleetwood, Tarkington, and McCullough were appointed to a committee to create interest of delinquent members in the Club's activities.

New member in February 1950: Tennis Sanders

In June 1950, $50.00 for full coverage of the upcoming tournament in September was set aside for the *Pittsburgh Courier*. All members were requested to go to the Northwestern Golf Course for group and individual pictures. It was decided to hold meetings at Dr. Howard's office every Monday at 9:00 P.M. until after the tournament. Dr. Howard reported that the club will be unable to secure a course for the weekend tournament. The date was for August 30th and 31st. A closed tournament was scheduled for July 9th at Northwestern Golf Course- open only to members in good standing. The open tournament scheduled to be held at Bunker Hill Golf Course could not be held on the dates requested. Northwestern Golf Course to be contacted.

7/6/60   Names of new members submitted were: Mr. Hammond, Chicago Heights; Cecil Watts, LaGrange; reinstatement, Joe Curry, Evanston; Wendell Carpenter, Glencoe.

At the July 10th meeting $25.00 was given to Ms. Higgins for the purpose of securing four trophies for the closed tournament (members only), one trophy for each flight. Dr. Howard was authorized to order entry blanks for the open tournament ,and a $200.00 total limit was for the trophy.

The total cost of the trophies for the two tournaments eventually cost only $267.00 including engraving. (How's that for economy?)

On July 16 several of our members played on the Glencoe Golf Course (not one of the courses welcomed Negroes) where some persons proceeded to become quite and completely obnoxious causing embarrassment to the Twentieth Century officials and Glencoe Golf

Conversations with Blacks in Evanston, Illinois • 319

Course. Dr. Howard had contacted the course officials who later agreed to allow Negroes to use the course.

At the Central States Tournament and Meeting, Thomas McNeal was elected president of U.G.A. (United Golfers Association), a real honor. Several Windy City members had claimed membership in Twentieth because Windy City was extinct, and in order to play in the C.S.G.A. Tournament, they had to belong to a club that was a member of U.G.A. Rockford was willing to join with Chicago in hosting the 18th Annual C.S.G.A. Tournament; however, the Chicago group left the bidding for the tournament to Twentieth Century, who agreed to host the tournament and ruled out Rockford as a co-host. McNeal was appointed chairman of the C.S.G.A. Tournament Committee with the power to appoint any person he wanted to work with him, and all plans were to be cleared through him and his committee. Dr. Howard and Aaron Hammond were to work with him on the committee with powers to designate any person to any particular job to be done (especially the tough ones, like housing accommodations, since Negroes were not welcomed at the Orrington and had to stay at the colored Y or someone's home (Oh, delightful!) in Evanston, during the years before the advent o of Holiday Inn, after which we could at least get some kind of accommodations.

Wendell Carpenter and Fred Hunter were approved for membership at the meeting 8/28/50. Plans for an open tournament in 1950 were finalized and a set of rules for all players was drawn up. No person, regardless of his status with the club (financial or unfinancial) would be barred from playing in the OPEN TOURNAMENT (GTM - Get the Money!). Justus Jackson was also invited to play in the upcoming tournament, after which his application for membership would again be considered.

The tournament report given on 9/18/50 showed that sixty-five people had played, twelve women, five seniors (men over fifty years old admittedly), and forty-eight men. (There must have been a "gender" question back then, for you were either a MAN or a WOMAN. Seniors must have been considered WHATSIS. The club cleared the whole sum of $370.23 after expenses.

9/25/50 meeting and election of officers (by secret ballot yet).
Dr. Howard - President.   Tom McNeal - Vice President
Ms. Willie Higgins - Secretary Leslie Pollard - Corres. Secretary
Jack Bonner - Sergeant At Arms Harry Brown - Treasurer

Total funds were turned over to the treasurer in the amount of $893.84 (bank balance, cash, and checks). New books for the treasurer, minutes, and dues were to be purchased by the secretary.

Down through the years from 1950 throughout November 2, 1987 when the club was dissolved, there had been many changes in officers, membership, and activities too numerous to mention here. To wit: In June 1962, Twentieth Century G.C., under the presidency of Harry Brown, purchased the frame building at 1811 Church Street. A basement addition was made and used as a club room, with the first and second floors rented out as residential rental property. Because the Twentieth was tax exempt under Code Section 501 (c)(3), no federal tax was due on any income relating to the golf club, and because the club never had income (gift or investment, etc.) in excess of $5,000, the requirement to file Form 990 was discontinued in the late 1960s or early 1970s (for which the secretary was most grateful).

Because many of the membership had decided to no longer be a part of the golf club because of the purchase of 1811 Church St. (which they objected to), the persons who remained as members formed a Holiday Association which was incorporated by the State of Illinois on June 11, 1962 under the name of 20th Century Golfers' Holding Association, a separate entity from Twentieth Century Golf Club, and shares were issued to these remaining persons. Anyone who wished to join the golf club could do so at any time. However, they would be members only of the golf club and not of the holders association.

At the dissolution of the golf club, November 2, 1987, the treasurer of the Twentieth Century Golf Club contained $15,148.35 which was distributed (over the objections of the then president, Harriette Brown Powell and some of the members) by the secretary, Willie Higgins and the treasurer, Sydney Callendar, to each of the club members according to their length of their membership and the amount they paid in from the date of joining.

A donation of $1,000 was made to the United Negro College Fund. No one refused to accept their distributive share, and although each had the opportunity to donate their share of the distribution to the United Negro College Fund, no one did so. (So much for charitable giving - ha!) In fact, several of the recipients thanked the secretary for the foresight of tying up the funds and making the type of distribution she had made.

After the dissolution of the Golf Club, and because most of the members of the holding association were deceased or had moved away from Evanston, the holding association was dissolved on June 15, 1989, and the property at 1811 Church Street was sold to Clifford Wilson, President of the Mt. Pisgah Pentecostal Faith Church for approximately $50,000, less the cost of the sale on 8/8/89. The proceeds from this sale were distributed to the remaining members or their beneficiaries of the holding association.

Original members of the Golf Club who are known to be still living as of November 1995 are Rachel Graves, Willie Higgins, and Leslie Pollard Keeling, and possibly, Charles Jones, Michel Laurent, and Thomas McNeal. Of course, there are surviving members who joined in the years after 1948 through 1962, these are not considered to be original members, those who joined in April or May of 1948.

Submitted by
Ms. Willie Higgins,
Secretary

Appendix F

HOW TO APPLY FOR SCHOLARSHIPS IN THE AFRICAN AMERICAN COMMUNITY

ORGANIZATION	SCHOLARSHIP CHAIRPERSON	ADDRESS	WHO MAY APPLY	WHERE TO OBTAIN	WHEN TO APPLY	GPA AND OTHER REQUIREMENTS
ALPHA KAPPA ALPHA SORORITY	Donna Richardson	P.O. Box 5112 Evanston, IL 60201	African American seniors accepted in a 4-year college or university. FEMALE ONLY; special grant for teen parent accepted in any post high school institution including trade and business school; and continuing under-graduates.	ETHS Counselors or Scholarship Chairperson	Feb. to mid-April	Upper 1/2 of class
BLACK NURSES FORUM OF THE NORTHSHORE	Emma Johnson	P.O. Box 1254 Evanston, IL 60201-204	Any African American graduating senior from ETHS who will pursue nursing education towards becoming a registered nurse.	ETHS Counselors	April 1 - Return to Counselor	2.5 minimum GPA; must demonstrate good moral character and compassion for mankind; must relate strong aspiration towards becoming a registered nurse through academic preparation and curriculum.
IONE S. BROWN MEMORIAL SCHOLARSHIP- SECOND BAPTIST CHURCH		Second Baptist Church 1717 Benson Avenue Evanston, IL 60201	SECOND BAPTIST MEMBERS - Graduating high school seniors, college undergraduates; trade and business schools will be considered.	Second Baptist Church Office Mon. - Fri. 9 am. - 5 pm. Sun. following worship.	March 1	Active participation at Second Baptist; minimum 2.5 or evidence of acceptance at a college. Re-apps need letter of "good standing" from college or university
CHESSMEN, INC.	Aaron Horne	P.O. Box 1265 Evanston, IL 60204	Graduating high school MALE/FEMALE; book scholarships also available.	North Shore area Senior Counselors	March 15 to May 1	Strong academics; citizenship; financial need.

324 • Williams

ORGANIZATION	SCHOLARSHIP CHAIRPERSON	ADDRESS	WHO MAY APPLY	WHERE TO OBTAIN	WHEN TO APPLY	GPA AND OTHER REQUIREMENTS
DELTA SIGMA THETA SORORITY, INC.	Chairman Scholarship Committee	P.O. Box 618 Evanston, IL 60204	Graduating high school senior planning to attend an accredited college/university, or an undergraduate student who is a past recipient of a scholarship from Delta Sigma Theta, ENSA Chapter.		Jan. 1 thru April 1	Minimum GPA of 2.0 on 4.0 grading scale; resident of Evanston-North Shore community.
DISTINCTIVE LADIES OF THE NORTH SHORE	Brenda Wilson	9038 Lincolnwood Skokie, IL 60203	Graduating high school seniors - ETHS and North Shore MALE/FEMALE (based on financial need).	Scholarship Chairman	Feb. 1 to May 1	2.0 minimum GPA.
EBENEZER A.M.E. CHURCH	Scholarship Chairman	Ebenezer A.M.E. Church 1109 Emerson Street Evanston, IL 60201	Graduating high school seniors; EBENEZER MEMBERS	Ebenezer Church	Feb. to May 1	Active church participation and accepted in a college.
THE EVANSTON BROS. (Int'l Assn. of Black Professional Fire Fighters I.A.B.P.F.F.S.)	Joseph Burton	P.O. Box 6200 Evanston, IL 60202	Male/Female graduating African-American	Scholarship Chairman	Jan. to May 1	Active church participants accepted to a 4-year college or university.
EVANSTON DRUM & BUGLE CORPS.	Allen "Bo" Price	Fleetwood-Jourdain Center Evanston, IL 60201	Graduating high school seniors; MALE/FEMALE; Drum and Bugle Corps and/or FJ Theater participant; exhibition of leadership.	Merrie Smith Fleetwood-Jourdain Community Center	Jan. 1 to Feb. 28	2.5 minimum GPA.
FRIENDSHIP BAPTIST CHURCH	Herman Walker	Friendship Baptist Church 2201 Foster St. Evanston, IL 60201	Graduating high school seniors - MEMBER OF FRIENDSHIP BAPTIST CHURCH	Church Office	March 1 to May 1	Active in service to Friendship Baptist Church.
TRUDY FULLER SCHOLARSHIP	Priscilla Giles	1829 Ashland Avenue Evanston, IL 60201	Graduating high school students; MALE/FEMALE (ETHS ONLY)	Scholarship Chairman	Feb. 1 to April 30	Interest in working with children; acceptance at an accredited 4-year college or university. Active in community.

ORGANIZATION	SCHOLARSHIP CHAIRPERSON	ADDRESS	WHO MAY APPLY	WHERE TO OBTAIN	WHEN TO APPLY	GPA AND OTHER REQUIREMENTS
FREDERICK E. GREEN MEMORIAL AWARD	Ann Green	P.O. Box 1564 Evanston, IL 60204	Graduating high school seniors intending to major in math/applied sciences.	ETHS Senior Counselors	April 1 to May 1	Evidence of academic potential; community involvement/motivation. Acceptance at 4-year accredited college or university.
HILL-PEARRY SCHOLARSHIP	Delores Holmes	Family Focus Our Place 2010 Dewey Avenue Evanston, IL 60201	Graduating ETHS Seniors and college undergraduates.	Family Focus Our Place	April 1 to May 1	Demonstrated ability to overcome adversity; social awareness and community involvement. Minimum 2.5 GPA.
HILL/SMALL MEMORIAL SCHOLARSHIP	Sandra Hill	4 Martha Lane Evanston, IL 60201	African American MALES, ETHS graduating senior who plans to attend 4-year college (can renew for sophomore year)	ETHS Counselors	by April 1	Minimum 2.0 GPA (most improved from Freshman year)
JACK & JILL OF AMERICA - NORTHSHORE CHAPTER	Debbie Sampson	Debbie Sampson 27 Chestnut Terrace Buffalo Grove, IL 60089	Graduating High School Seniors	High School Counselors or Scholarship Chairperson	Jan. 15 to April 15	2.0 GPA; extracurricular involvement; financial need.
KAPRA ALPHA PSI FRATERNITY	Henry Young	8922 Ewing Skokie, IL 60203	Graduating high school seniors (ETHS) AFRICAN AMERICAN MALES ONLY	ETHS Senior Counselors	Jan. 15 to April 30	Upper 50% academic scholastic achievement; co-curricular activity participation and financial need.
MT. ZION HAROLD BELL SCHOLARSHIP		Mt. Zion Baptist Church 1113 Clark Street Evanston, IL 60201	Graduating high school seniors, MT. ZION CHURCH MEMBERS ONLY	Church Office	Jan. 1 to May 1	Active in service to Mt. Zion Baptist Church.
NATIONAL ASSN. FOR THE ADVANCEMENT OF COLORED PEOPLE (NAACP)	Scholarship Chairman	NAACP 2010 Dewey Avenue Evanston, IL 60201	ETHS Graduating high school seniors; college undergraduates.	2010 Dewey Avenue Evanston, IL	Jan. 1 to May 1	2.5 minimum GPA; financial need; c ndale.

ORGANIZATION	SCHOLARSHIP CHAIRPERSON	ADDRESS	WHO MAY APPLY	WHERE TO OBTAIN	WHEN TO APPLY	GPA AND OTHER REQUIREMENTS
NORTH SHORE ILLINOIS CHAPTER THE LINKS, INC.	Helen Cromer Cooper	1510 Pitner Avenue Evanston, IL 60201	Graduating high school senior, MALE/FEMALE. Continuing award evaluated each year through Junior year, to awardees who maintain a 2.8 average.	Helen Cromer Cooper	May 1	Highly motivated, community involved; extra-curricular participant with 2.8 minimum GPA.
BETTY BURNS PADEN/ALVIN PADEN INCENTIVE AWARD	Tina Paden	1122 Emerson Street Evanston, IL 60201	Financial need, evidence of academic potential. Community activities or employment.	Law Office of Betty Burns Paden 1122 Emerson Evanston, IL 60201	Jan. 1 to May 1	Strong academic record; citizenship; financial need; highly motivated.
SLOAN-WHITNEY MEMORIAL SCHOLARSHIP	Eleanor Whitney	1005 Ridge Avenue Evanston, IL 60202	ETHS graduating high school seniors	Eleanor Whitney 1005 Ridge Avenue Evanston, IL 60202	March 1 to April 30	Minimum 2.5 GPA.
SPRINGFIELD M.B. CHURCH	Karen Underwood	Springfield M.B. Church 1801 Emerson Street Evanston, IL 60201	SPRINGFIELD MEMBERS ONLY - Graduating high school student or college or university undergraduate.	Church Office	March 1 to April 30	2.0 minimum GPA; active church participant; financial need.
YOUTH BACKERS SCHOLARSHIP CLUB	Denelda Green	Youth Backers Scholarship P.O. Box 1029 Evanston, IL 60204	Graduating seniors and college undergraduates	Youth Backers Scholarship P.O. Box 1029 Evanston, IL 60204	Feb. 1 - April 15	2.5 minimum GPA; financial need.

1995 SCHOLARSHIP AWARD RECIPIENTS

STUDENT	HIGH SCHOOL/UNIVERSITY	MAJOR ACTIVITIES	AWARDING ORGANIZATION(S)
Barnes, Jennifer	University of Illinois at Chicago	Dean's List - 3.25 GPA; Gospel Choir; Volunteer - Illinois Children Rehabilitation and Education Center; African American Academic network; Excellence Award. Major: Physical Therapy.	Alpha Kappa Alpha Sorority
Bata, Tanisha	Evanston Township High School	Foster Reading Center Tutor; Fairy Tales Trail Volunteer; Volunteer - Kohl Children's Museum; Honors Award; Math Award; Spanish Award. Plans to attend Cornell College.	Delta Sigma Theta Sorority, Inc.
Booker, Caton	Carleton College	Black Student Union; 2.2 GPA; Actress - theater production "Five Minute Shorts" and "Ohio Guide to Chess"; Tutor - English As A Second Language. Major: Sociology.	Alpha Kappa Alpha Sorority, Inc.
Brathwaite, Arusha	Evanston Township High School	Honor Society; Girl's Basketball Team Manager; Secretary of North Shore Usher Board National League. Plans to attend Pace University.	Delta Sigma Theta Sorority, Inc.
Brown, Coyzen	Evanston Township High School	Honor Roll; 3.12 GPA; Volunteer at St. Francis Hospital; Library Volunteer; English Award.	Chessmen Club of The North Shore
Brown, Melissa	University of Illinois - Urbana	African American Homecoming Committee; Snyder Hall Floor Council; NAACP; Caribbean (Caribbean Students United). Major: Pre-Med.	Alpha Kappa Alpha Sorority, Inc.
Cole, Letitia S.	Alabama A&M University	Dean's List - 3.0 GPA; Volunteer Tutor; Volunteer Voter Registrar; member Alpha Kappa Alpha Sorority; Accounting Club. Major: Accounting.	Alpha Kappa Alpha Sorority, Inc. Iona S. Brown Memorial Scholarship
Crane, Heather	Evanston Township High School	Honor Roll; African History Award; U.S. History Award; Creative Writing Award. Plans to attend North Carolina State University.	Chessmen Club of the North Shore
Cummings, Dreama	Clark-Atlanta University	Former youth coordinator - Youth Action Ministry. Major: Education.	Iona S. Brown Memorial Scholarship
Deale, Lorraine	Northwestern University	Academic Achiever; Honor Award - African American Student Affairs; Sp... ng of Sex. Major: Anthropology.	Alpha Kappa Alpha Sorority, Inc.

1995 SCHOLARSHIP AWARD RECIPIENTS

STUDENT	HIGH SCHOOL/UNIVERSITY	MAJOR ACTIVITIES	AWARDING ORGANIZATION(S)
Demus, Daniel	Hoffman Estates High School	National Honor Society; Vice President - Human Relations; Sports Editor; Peer Mediation; A.P. Scholar Award; Who's Who Among American High School Students.	Northshore Chapter of Jack & Jill
Ellis, Maery A.	Evanston Township High School	National Honor Society; Illinois State Scholar; National Achievement Finalist; 4.32 GPA; co-captain Varsity basketball; North Evanston Mother's Club Award.	Chaemen Club of the North Shore; Delta Sigma Theta Sorority, Inc.; North Shore Illinois Chapter, The Links, Inc.
Frazier, Micah	Roosevelt University	Major: Music	Kappa Alpha Psi Fraternity
Frazier, Patrice	Illinois State University	Resident Hall Leader; Mentor. Major: Political Science.	Ione S. Brown Memorial Scholarship
Guerrier, Joseph	Evanston Township High School	National Honor Society; 3.10 GPA; Scholar Athlete Award; Volunteer - Soup Kitchen. Plans to attend one of the following: Univ. of Illinois, Univ. of Arizona, Univ. of Miami or Georgia Tech.	Chaemen Club of the North Shore
Gurley, Mary	Evanston Township High School	National Honor Society; Student Council; Debate Team; Cheerleader; Hospital Volunteer. Plans to attend Fashion Institute of Design and Merchandising.	Delta Sigma Theta Sorority, Inc.
Hemphill, Denisha	Evanston Township High School	Senior Class President; National Honor Society; Homecoming Queen; Voices of Faith Youth Choir; Hospital Volunteer. Plans to attend Ohio State University.	Delta Sigma Theta Sorority, Inc.
Howard, Stephanie V.	Evanston Township High School	Student Council; Top Teens of America; member of Ebenezer A.M.E. Church; President of Youth Choir; Youth Usher Board; Summer Literary Program; speaker at Ebenezer A.M.E. banquet honoring Bishop to South Africa. Plans to attend Illinois State University.	Delta Sigma Theta Sorority, Inc.; Derivative Ladies of The North Shore
Hynes, Maeie	University of Illinois - Urbana	Fellowship program for study abroad. Major: International Business.	Alpha Kappa Alpha Sorority, Inc.
Jackson, Tamaka J.	Evanston Township High School	Student Council, Community Service Club; Foster Reading Center Tutor; Treasurer of Church Choir; Church Youth Group. Plans to attend Clark-Atlanta University - Major: Civil Engineering.	Alpha Kappa Alpha Sorority, Inc.; Chaemen Club of the North Shore; Delta Sigma Theta Sorority, Inc.

1995 SCHOLARSHIP AWARD RECIPIENTS

STUDENT	HIGH SCHOOL/UNIVERSITY	MAJOR ACTIVITIES	AWARDING ORGANIZATION(S)
Jacobs, Lorenzo	Evanston Township High School	National Honor Society; Honor Roll; 2.96 GPA; Church Youth Group; Evanston Summer Youth Program; Presbyterian-Home Volunteer. Plans to attend University of Illinois - Urbana.	Chessmen Club of the North Shore
Jennings, Amanda C.	Xavier University, New Orleans	Girl Scout Troop Leader in New Orleans; Represented Xavier in Honda All-Star Quiz Bowl - placed 2nd; accepted to serve on 1995-96 Peer Dean's Association.	North Shore Illinois Chapter, The Links, Inc.
Jennings, Tasha	Waukegan High School	P.I.C. Outstanding Achievement Award; Cheerleader; S.T.E.P. Award for Outstanding Performance in Class.	Northshore Chapter of Jack & Jill
Johnson, Brian	Evanston Township High School		Frederick E. Green Memorial Scholarship
Johnson, Lisa D.	University of Chicago	President - Residential hall; Secretary - The U. of Chicago Debate Society; Publicity Officer - Black United Front; Volunteer - Rape Prevention Resource Center; United Protestant Campus Ministries.	North Shore Illinois Chapter, The Links, Inc.
Juden, Linda	Evanston Township High School	Freshman Track; Cheerleader; Manager of ESANDE School Dance Troupe; Community Service Club - Habitat for Humanity Project. Plans to attend University of Illinois.	Delta Sigma Theta Sorority, Inc.
Kelley, Diana C.	Evanston Township High School	Student Council; Pompon Squad; National Honor Society; 3.81 GPA; VP mentor for freshmen students; Career Pathways Committee; 3.81 GPA. Plans to attend Northwestern University. Major: Education.	Alpha Kappa Alpha Sorority, Inc. Chessmen Club of the North Shore
King, Lakeisha	Evanston Township High School	Honor Roll; Honorable Mention in State Writing Contest; Senior Band Member; Biology Award; Business Education Award; Work Study - 4 yrs.; Church Choir. Plans to attend University of Illinois.	Delta Sigma Theta Sorority, Inc. Sloan-Whitney Memorial Scholarship
Maddox, Ginger	Evanston Township High School	Most Likely to Succeed Award. Plans to attend Florida A&M University.	Delta Sigma Theta Sorority, Inc.

1995 SCHOLARSHIP AWARD RECIPIENTS

STUDENT	HIGH SCHOOL/UNIVERSITY	MAJOR ACTIVITIES	AWARDING ORGANIZATION(S)
Massey, Joy T.	Zion Benton High School	Harambee Academic Queen and President; Excellence in Mathematics Award; 3.95 GPA; Who's Who of American High School Students; Martin Luther King Oratorical Award; Secretary, Chapter of National Honor Society.	North Shore Illinois Chapter, The Links, Inc.
McNeal, Andrea	St. Scholastica High School	Blue Key Club; 3.40 GPA; Sisters Working for African American Awareness; Senior Honor Assembly; Big/Little Sister Steering Committee; Prom Committee. Plans to attend University of Illinois - Chicago. Major: Chemical Engineering.	Alpha Kappa Alpha Sorority, Inc.
Medard, Cassandra	Oakton Community College	Youth Mentor; Dancer; former youth coordinator of Youth Action Ministry. Transfer student from Oakton Community College. Plans to attend Clark-Atlanta University.	Ione S. Brown Memorial Scholarship
Morgan, Keryn	Evanston Township High School	Community Service Club; Honor Roll; 3.16 GPA; church activities. Plans to attend San Francisco State University. Major: Forensic Science.	Alpha Kappa Alpha Sorority, Inc.
Murray, Seaheen	Regina Dominican	National Honor Society; Youth Council; Peer Helper; Orchestra; Tri-M Music Honor Society; Class Council Representative. Plans to attend University of Rochester. Major: Biological Sciences.	Alpha Kappa Alpha Sorority, Inc.
Powell, Sonya	Fisk University	Former coordinator of Youth Action Ministry; member of Delta Sigma Theta Sorority. Major: Pre-Med.	Ione S. Brown Memorial Scholarship
Pusto, Quiana M.	Evanston Township High School	Member Mt. Zion M.B. Church; Cheerleader; Track. Plans to attend Oakton Community College.	Evanston Bowling Senate
Roberts, Nahed	Illinois State University	Essence Magazine Intern; Black Writers Forum; Teaching Assistant; member of Alpha Kappa Alpha Sorority. Major: Mass Communications.	Alpha Kappa Alpha Sorority, Inc. Ione S. Brown Memorial Scholarship
Scott, Jule	Niles Township High School	Track; Soccer; Project Lead (Mentor Group); Youth Action Ministry; Volunteer - Soup Kitchen. Plans to attend Spelman College.	Ione S. Brown Memorial Scholarship

Conversations with Blacks in Evanston, Illinois • 331

Appendix G

Evanston, Illinois
February 22, 1995

I am capsulizing what William Benjamin Snell did in his space and time. To use an old Chinese proverb, "one picture is worth a thousand words."

Sergeant William Benjamin Snell, a native of South Carolina, was born in 1919 to proud parents, Mr. and Mrs. Snell.

Nina Rosemary Thompson of Evanston, and he, were joined in holy matrimony on February 11, 1942 in Jacksonville, Florida.

Prior to his Army enlistment on February 14, 1941, he had a brilliant future in pugilism as a heavy weight. Having been employed by the Brown Bombers trainer, Jack Blackburn, he was Lewis' sparing partner in preparation for the Sergeant Joe Louis versus Bob Pastor fight.

His splendid physique attracted the attention of the artist Katherine Lord. He modeled frequently for her, the Art Institute of Chicago, and other artists in various studios in Evanston and the near North Side.

While in the Army he participated in sports, and was involved in breaking a precedent in the South where there had never been a public bout between an African-American and a white boxer. "William B. Snell, in collaboration with Tommy Gomez, worked for the interest of the public in tearing that barrier down . . ." declared the late Sergeant Bill Henderson of the 603rd Ordinance, Camp Blanding, Florida

The Evanston Historical Society reported that William Benjamin Snell (of the 603rd Ordinance) was Evanston's first African-American soldier to give his life in the line of duty in the North African campaign on March 25, 1943.

The Tech Sergeant William Benjamin Snell Post No. 7186 of the Veterans of Foreign Wars received its charter in 1946 to honor his memory.

Researched and submitted by the Sergeant William Benjamin Snell Post Auxiliary Historian, Elsie L Liddell.

Snell Post History

Early in 1946, Albert Jones from the Shannon Taylor VFW Post of Chicago visited several churches in Evanston with the intention of organizing a VFW Post. Jones left literature on the churches' bulletin boards. One of the churches Jones visited was the Second Baptist Church where Dorothy Handcock carried a leaflet home to her husband, Robert Handcock. From this began the organization of Snell Post.

The first meeting was attended by four World War II veterans: Tom Edelin, Robert Handcock, Alex Richards, and John R. Walker. They met with Albert Jones, who explained the function of the Veterans of Foreign Wars. This meeting was held at the Emerson Street Y.M.C.A.

There were several meetings held at this site. Several future members met with Jones. Sam Mitchell, the first commander of Snell Post, and Albert "Jack" Price, Snell's second commander.

Among them, Alex Richards was the first member paying his dues of $5.00, and Robert Handcock was the second member to pay. Albert Jones asked the members to name the Post, and it was decided to name the Post after the first African American from Evanston to give his life in Oran. North Africa during World War II in the service of his country. After getting permission from his widow and mother, the Sergeant William B. Snell Post #7186 Veterans of Foreign Wars was organized and instituted by Comrade Albert Jones on April 27, 1946 at the Emerson Street Y.M.C.A. The Post began with thirty-nine members, who are listed on another page.

For the first few years, the Post met at the Emerson Street Y.M.C.A. and then met at the Masonic Temple for a while, returning to the Y.M.C.A. and meeting there until 1967, when the Emerson Street Y was sold. From 1967 until about 1985, Post meetings were held at Union Hall. Then meetings were moved to the Fleetwood Jourdain Center. The Post now meets at Family Focus the third Tuesday of every month.

In the early 1950s, Snell Post sponsored its first pre-Easter and pre-Thanksgiving dances at the Bunker Hill VFW Post in Niles. Dances were later held in downtown hotel ballrooms, such as the Hilton, Palmer House, Sherman, Drake, and others. The dances usually drew capacity crowds to enjoy some of the big name bands of the 1950s. Funds raised at these functions were used to help needy veterans and their families. Snell Post contributed funds to Thanksgiving and Christmas baskets and monies to needy families to the VFW National Home at Eaton Rapid, Michigan, to summer and after school programs at Fleetwood Jourdain Center to sponsorship of outings for hospitalized veterans, and to many other community activities. The Post also sponsored the voice of Democracy Program of Evanston Township High School, the Famous Drill Team, and the Drum & Bugle Corps, under the leadership of Allen "Bo" Price more than forty years. The 1992 Voice of Democracy first place winner in district and state and a contender at the national level was Aliya Esmail, a junior from Evanston Township High School. You can read more about this under Youth Activities.

Snell has participated in many district, state, and national conventions. From Snell Post, many comrades have been elected or appointed to national, state, and district offices. Commander Leroy Davis, the 1995 to 1996 Fourth District Commander is from Snell Post. Art Nelson is the department representative at North Chicago VA Hospital, and Allen "Bo" Price is Assistant National Parade Marshall. Bo also received the prestigious Carl Rosenbaum Traveling Trophy as outstanding 1989 Illinois Post Service Officer.

There have been many awards and citations given to this Post over the last fifty years, and many dedicated comrades have carried on their obligations to this Post for fifty years. To those comrades we give honor and tribute for such dedication. To the public who has supported us over these fifty years, we give many many thanks for your support. We have tried to give as much back to the Evanston community and beyond. How can we thank our Auxiliary 1947-1996 for their support and dedication of all our endeavors. They have been essential to the success of this Post, and without them we would not have been able to achieve so many of our projects. What a job well-done! Again, many thanks to Snell Post's auxiliary.

As we celebrate our fiftieth anniversary, we dedicate this souvenir booklet to the memory of those fallen comrades and to those who remember.

50th Anniversary Chairman
John R. Frazier

50th Anniversary Committee
Leroy Davis, Marion "Vet" Johnson, Furman Sizemore, Byron Wilson, Robert Handcock, Ladrew Warren, Art Nelson, Ken Wideman

Snell Post Commanders

*Sam Mitchell	1946-1947
Albert "Jack" Price	1947-1951
James Brown, Jr.	1951-1952
James Petway	1952-1954
Albert "Jack" Price	1954-1955
Byron Wilson, Jr.	1955-1957
*James Avery	1957-1958
William Marion	1958-1960
Allen "Bo' Price	1960-1962
Johnny Butler	1962-1963
Ladrew Warren	1963-1964
Wallace Galbreath	1964-1966
John R. Frazier.	1971-1973
James Brown	1968-1969
*Ponce D. Lewis	1969-1971
John R. Frazier	1971-1973
*James Douglas	1973-1975
*James Thurman	1975-1977
Arthur Nelson	1977-1978
*Ponce D. Lewis	1978-1979
Willis R. Lawrence, Jr.	1987-1988
*Loyal Williams	1981-1983
Allen "Bo" Price	1983-1996
Arthur Nelson	1986-1987
Willis R. Lawrence, Jr.	1979-1981
Arthur Nelson	1988-1990
Leroy Davis	1990-1993
Furman Sizemore	1993-1994
Arthur Nelson	1994-1996

*deceased

Youth Programs

The Drill Team was organized in 1947 under the direction of Allen "Bo" Price. The Drill Team practiced out of the Foster Center and the Emerson Street Y.M.C.A. Original members were Richard "Sonny" Matthews, William "Billy" Johnson, Frank Reed, and Raymond Bell. This fine group of Evanston men and women won many championships. Our first state championship was won in Springfield, Illinois, and one of the fellows sat on the trophy and broke it. After that the Drill Team won fourteen VFW State Championships. In 1957, the Drill Team won their first VFW National Championship in Miami, Florida. We were also the only blacks to compete and win the national competition. The VFW Drill Team won eight additional national championships. In 1969, the Gay Blades Drum and Bugle Corps was formed and represented the Snell Post in many parades and contests in the midwest.

At the Milwaukee, Wisconsin, National Open contest, they won six times. Veterans Day at the Illinois State Fair gifted us with ten victories. The Corps performed at a Harlem Globetrotter's half-time show it the Chicago Stadium, appeared at the Chicago Cardinal Football game at half-time and also appeared at the Rock Island Railroad Centennial. In 1963, they performed on NBC-TV, Channel 5, for the 100th Anniversary of the Emancipation Proclamation.

In 1978, Allen "Bo" Price answered a call from his community and the City of Evanston officials to organize an instrumental corps, which was later named the Pride of Evanston Drum and Bugle Corps. The Corps is funded by the City of Evanston and has received support from the local VFW as well as the National VFW. This support has enabled the Corps to attend and participate in many VFW National competitions. The Corps was designed to teach children and youth the basic fundamentals of music, discipline, team work, presentation and performance standards. The Corps has served over 2,000 children and youth since its inception, and has performed in over 320 parades. The Corps is a well established program and is highly recognized throughout the state of Illinois and nationally. They have made guest performances and appearances in Texas, Tennessee, Wisconsin, Minnesota and Missouri. They have also received many awards and honors for their presentation and style.

The Snell Post also supports the Fleetwood-Jourdain High School Basketball Program. A team named for the Post has won two championships over the past four years. The Post has also contributed to the Fleetwood-Jourdain Summer Playground, the After School programs and the Fleetwood-Jourdain Art Guild.

I would like to thank the Snell Post for allowing us the opportunity to represent them. Special thanks is also extended to the members who hauled us around and whose cars we tore up. It was nothing like picking up the phone and hollering, "Help, I need transportation." The Post members always came through with flying colors. If it were not for the Post many of the youngsters would not have had the opportunity of traveling through these United States of America (Miami, Los Angeles, Detroit, Cleveland, Minneapolis, St. Louis, Dallas and New Orleans).

I'm now beginning to experience brain cramps; therefore, if I missed anything at our rap session and anniversary dinner, please let me know.

Special thanks to my wife, Wilhelmenia, who has put up with me, and all my 2,000 children, for all these forty-seven years.

I'll never forget this Post, the members of the Fourth District, the Department of Illinois, and the City of Evanston for all of their support over the past fifty years.

I'd like to take this opportunity to thank the thousands of parents for trusting me with their most precious possessions-Your Children!

Allen "Bo" Price
Past Post

Ladies Auxiliary Veterans of Foreign Wars of the U.S.

Be It Known That Tech. Sgt. William Snell Auxiliary to Post No. 7156 stationed at Evanston, Illinois has been organized and duly instituted with 17 members.

In Witness Whereof, we have hereunto set our hands and seal this 20th day of April 1947.

Snell Auxiliary Past Presidents

Wilhelmenia Strong	1947-1948
Anna Belle Frazier	1948-1951
*Bernice Freeman Brooks	1951-1953
Anna Belle Frazier	1953-1955
*Annamelia Davis	1955-1957
Lois Johnson	1957-1960
Wilhelmenia Price	1960-1963
*Louise Brown	1963-1966
*Dolly Payne	1966-1967
Kathryn Sibert	1967-1969
Idell Silliams	1969-1971
*Louise Watson	1971-1973
Beverly Thurman	1973-1975
*Emma McClain	1975-1977
Berthene Hudsorn	1977-1979
Lena Johnson	1979-1981
*Rosary Galbreath	1981-1983
*Inez DeVaul	1983-1985
Sharon Malcolm	1985-1987
Louie Calvey	1987-1988
Emma Gaston	1988-1989
Wilhelmenia Price	1989-1991
Katherine Bridges	1991-1992
Nancy Adams	1992-1994
Katherine Bridges	1994-1995
Audrey Steele	1995-

*deceased

Appendix H

History of the Alpha Phi Alpha Fraternity, Inc.

During the school year 1905-1906 at Cornell University, Ithaca, New York, a group of black male students, in order to enhance their social and academic life, decided to organize a social and literary association. They were strongly motivated to do this because, due to the limited financial resources and rigid color line drawn at the university, it would have been difficult to compete with the other students socially or academically.

Their first meetings were as a social and literary group and provided them with many "good times." Also, they enhanced their academic performance by placing copies of examination questions in the hands of members of the group, thereby enabling them to prepare for future examinations. This resulted in good performances in the examinations by the members.

During the year 1906-1907 members of the social-literary group organized as Alpha Phi Alpha Society on October 23, 1906. They decided to become a fraternity on December 4, 1906 and became Alpha Phi Alpha Fraternity.

Since this was the first chapter of the fraternity, it was called Alpha chapter.

The founders of Alpha Phi Alpha Fraternity are spoken of with deep reverence and are known as "Jewels." They are as follows:

George B. Kelley	Civil Engineer
Henry A. Callis	Physician
Charles H. Chapman	Teacher
Nathaniel A. Murray	Teacher
Vertner W. Tandy	Secretary of the Office of Committee, on Appropriations of the U.S. Senate
Eugene Kinckle Jones	Executive Secretary of the National Urban League
Robert H. Ogle	Secretary of the Office of Committee, on Appropriations of the U.S. Senate

As the result of an expansion program, undergraduate and graduate chapters were formed at colleges and universities throughout the country.

In Evanston, Illinois, Alpha Mu chapter was formed at Northwestern University as the undergraduate chapter, in 1922.

Graduate brothers of A Phi A, residing in Evanston, were aware of an undergraduate chapter, Alpha Mu, with a charter for Northwestern University, and were also aware that the chapter was inactive, primarily because brothers had graduated and had not left behind a nucleus to perpetuate the chapter. Thus, in 1953-1955 the graduate brothers, in their effort to revive Alpha Mu, took out the name of associate members in Alpha Mu.

During this period, the graduate brothers held initiations and revived the chapter, so that in 1956 Alpha Mu was strong enough to stand alone. On March 25, 1956 Zeta Xi Lambda was chartered as the graduate chapter.

Zeta Xi Lambda continues to advise, support, and work with Alpha Mu in all programs and activities.

Founding officers and Members of Zeta Xi Lambda

Officers

President	Roscoe L. Barrett
Vice-President	Charles M. Smith
Secretary	Theordore M. Harding
Treasurer	William B. Martin

Members

Scott Harper	Nathanael Hawk
James L. Patrick	Joseph Swafford
Arnold F. Winfield	Prentice H. Winfield

Since it was organized in 1956, the Zeta Xi Lambda chapter has placed equal emphasis on business and recreation.

The first part of our meetings is usually devoted to participating in the affairs and concerns of the Evanston community, such as improvement in the academic progress of the children, reduction of delinquency, care for senior citizens and families of deceased members of the fraternity, a scholarship program which makes an annual award to a black male high school graduate who plans to attend college. This award is called the Dr. Martin Luther King, Jr. Award.

After the local business has been completed, we consider the requirements of the national organization and make an effort to comply with those responsibilities. Then we play cards and enjoy refreshments.

The chapter is in need of more new members because many of the older members are not able to participate as they used to. Also, many of our brothers have moved away. Fortunately, we have been able to initiate several college graduates who are interested in Alpha Phi Alpha.

One program we still try to maintain is the Dr. Martin Luther King, Jr. Award. Some features of this program are described in the following materials.

Dr. Martin Luther King Jr. Award

The Zeta Xi Lambda Chapter of the Alpha Phi Alpha Fraternity, Inc., Evanston, Illinois, in memory of our outstanding brother, Dr. Martin Luther King, Jr., makes an annual award in his name to the black male graduate of Evanston Township High School, who, in the opinion of the chapter, best meets the following requirements:

a. He must have a grade average of 2.5 or better at the time of graduation.

b. He must have been accepted at an accredited college or university for the next fall term.

c. He must have worked steadily for pay or participated in extracurricular activities during his high school career.

This award will be in the amount of three hundred dollars for each of four successive years the recipient remains in college and maintains a C or better average.

To apply for this award, applicants must complete the attached form. Applications will be reviewed by the Zeta Xi Lambda Chapter, and winners will be announced through the high school office

The chapter has made this award since 1975.

EVANSTON TOWNSHIP HIGH SCHOOL
1600 DODGE AVENUE · EVANSTON ILLINOIS 60204

October 25, 1988

Mr. George Williams
1115 S. Plymouth Ct. #201
Chicago, IL 60605

RE: DR. MARTIN L. KING FR. AWARD

Dear Mr. Williams:

Enclosed is the enrollment verification form for the following student with regard to the above scholarship:

    1988 Recipient - Jeffrey E. Smith

You may proceed to process the check for Jeffrey E. Smith. If you have any questions regarding this, don't hesitate to contact me at 492-5931. Thank you.

Sincerely,

Manuel L. Isquierdo
Associate Principal
for Student Services

MLI:gg

encl.

mr George William
1115 S Plymouth
 # 20
Chicago IL 60605

SEP 23 1988

EVANSTON TOWNSHIP HIGH SCHOOL
1600 DODGE AVENUE   EVANSTON ILLINOIS 60204

May 25, 1988

Dear Award Recipient **JEFF SMITH**

In order to receive your financial award please present the form/letter below to the registrar of your college, university, vocational school within thirty (30) days of enrollment.

Best wishes for an academically rewarding year!

ETHS SCHOLARSHIP COMMITTEE

TO BE COMPLETED BY SCHOOL OFFICIAL

TO: Dr. James E. Phillips, Assistant Superintendent
Evanston Township High School
1600 Dodge Ave.
Evanston, IL 60204

DT: NORTHWESTERN UNIVERSITY
OFFICE OF FINANCIAL AID
1801 HINMAN - 2nd FLOOR
EVANSTON, IL 60201

FR: _____
Name of college/university/school

_____
Address

_____
City/State/Zip

This is to verify the enrollment of **Jeffrey E. Smith**
(Name of Student)
for the school year **1988-89**. It is understood that he/she has received the **Dr. Martin L. King Jr. Award**
(Name of ETHS Award/Scholarship)
in the amount of **$300.00**.

In order that these monies may be applied towards his/her tuition and/or fees, please forward to our school official as indicated below.

Barbara Fleury
(Signature of School Official)

Official School Seal

p. 374

Letters of Gratitude from Two Award Winners

Jean Denis — 1975 recipient,
graduated from the University
of Indiana, Bloomington, Indiana

I don't think one can feel as proud as I do today, when I discovered that I was selected as the winner of this year's Martin Luther King, Jr. Award.

I am proud, because this award reflects the way that I was brought up by my parents. Now, the rest of the community is discovering it, and they are honoring them for it.

I am proud, because some of the financial burden will be lighter, which will make it easier on everybody.

Finally, I would like to thank you and the men of the Alpha Phi Alpha Fraternity (Zeta Xi Lambda Chapter) for giving my family and me this great honor. Thank you very much, and God Bless you.

Sincerely,

Jean Denis

David Taylor — 1982 recipient,
graduated from the University
of Illinois, Urbana, Illinois

Just a note of thanks to let you know that I received your check, and I am very grateful to you and the Alphas for your support.

The money was very timely, in that I needed to buy my books for the semester, and I was finally able to do just that with your aid.

Once, again I would like to give my sincere thanks to you and the entire organization for your continued support.

Sincerely,

David M. Taylor

Report from the 57th Anniversary Convention of the Alpha Phi Alpha Fraternity, Inc.

Boston, Massachusetts, August 16-23, 1963

To: Members of the Zeta Xi Lambda chapter of Alpha Phi Alpha Fraternity, Inc., Evanston, IL.

From: George W. Williams, delegate

Dear Brothers in Alpha:

It gives me great pleasure to bring to you a report of the important proceedings of our 57th Anniversary General Convention. Some of the details of the program will be omitted in this report because they have already been brought to your attention in a previous edition of the *Sphinx* magazine. However, the highlights and general impressions of the convention are presented here in the hope that they will be of interest to you.

My wife, Betty, and I arrived in Boston Friday, August 16, and registered at the Statler-Hotel, headquarters of the convention. Registration had begun earlier on this day, but had closed when we arrived. We were in time, however, for a get-acquainted dance that evening in the hotel. At this time, we had the pleasure of meeting many Alpha men and their wives who had come from various parts of the country.

Our registration was completed Saturday morning. We were given kits for ourselves and wives, containing material such as programs, badges, announcements, and tickets which were necessary for full participation in the convention. Also, at this time, each delegate was given a designated seat, which was to be his during the convention.

In as much as no business was scheduled for Saturday, other than registration, most of the brothers took this opportunity to enjoy the sights of historical Boston. We were able to take a bus tour of the educational institutions of the city. These included the campuses of Harvard and Radcliffe, the mother church of Christian Scientists, and the home of Henry Wadsworth Longfellow.

On Sunday an important pre-convention meeting was held, open to the public, at Fenueil Hall. At this time, an address was given by Brother Edward W. Brooke, Attorney General of Massachusetts. It was very inspiring to see and hear a young man of such great ability, particularly since Brother Brooke holds the highest state office held by any other Negro in the country.

The awards committee of the convention presented a plaque to Brother Brooke in recognition of his outstanding achievements. Also, on this day, a reception was held at the Freedom House, where delegates and their wives were able to meet the members and wives of the host chapter.

The 57th General Convention met in its first session Monday, August 19, 1963. I am not sure if it is a tradition, but the meeting was one hour late. The brothers seemed to take this delay in stride, so I assume that it is not a custom to rush into the first session.

Nine items of business were scheduled for this first session, but after the first item, invocation, the meeting became bogged down by the introduction of unscheduled matters. The manner in which delegates were seated was questioned by some of the brothers, and the controversy was eventually resolved by requiring each brother to show his credentials before he could be seated as a delegate. This procedure voided the seating arrangement which had been previously established. Following the seating of delegates, the convention was given the tone it was to follow until the last day by a report from Brother Belford Lawson of Washington, D.C. It concerned the March on Washington, D.C. to be held on August 28, 1963. He urged that Alpha Phi Alpha be in this march and led by the national officers of the fraternity. No other business was considered this morning, except how Alpha Phi Alpha could best contribute to the fight for civil rights.

The second session of the convention, held in the afternoon of the same day, began with greetings from the vice president of Alpha Kappa Alpha Sorority, NAACP, and others wishing the convention a success. General President, Winston Cole Sr. gave an address in which he said that in order for the fraternity to function at its best, it must know itself. He urged Alpha men to look to the future great men, rather than dwell on the past great. He further stated his belief that Alpha men must close ranks and join the fight for civil rights. He suggested that each chapter join hands with the NAACP, and he cited the history of cooperation between Alpha Phi Alpha and NAACP.

Following Brother Cole's address, a plaque was presented to Jewel Brother Dr. Henry A. Callis, which was accepted by Dr. Winters, due to Brother Callis' inability to attend the convention. The remaining time of this session was taken by brothers who had certain grievances to express. One, in particular, was a complaint about the selection of the same men, year after year, to work on the committees. This question was of great interest to me because it appeared that, since the committees were all formed before the General Convention began, a new delegate would never be able to have a part in the important deliberations of the convention. Later, I was to discover that, due to the manner in which the committeemen were appointed, not only were new delegates left out, but also many men who had been attending General Conventions for from ten to twenty years could not get on a committee without much difficulty.

The fraternity recognizes that certain injustices exist, and in order to eliminate them as much as possible, has established a committee to consider the reorganization of the internal structure.

An inspiring memorial service was held for departed brothers and their induction into Omega Chapter. The service was led by the chaplain, Brother Reverend Clinton Hoggard.

Following reports from the general officers and committee chairmen, this session was adjourned. All reports were written and are available for inspection by members of our chapter.

The third session was opened Tuesday morning with a continuation of the reading and acceptance of committee reports. At twelve o'clock this session was adjourned, in order to permit the members of Alpha Phi Alpha to participate in an historical commemoration, and, at the same time, aid a local group in its fight to eliminate segregation in the schools in Boston.

Brother Frank Morris, chairman of the committee on Emancipation Proclamation, is a resident of Boston and active in the civil rights struggle here. He recommended to the fraternity that some moral support should be given to those who are picketing the Boston School Committee Building, in protest of what they considered defacto segregation in the schools. As a result of his recommendation, it was decided that the members of the convention would assemble in a column of two's in front of the hotel, march to the scene of the picketing, swing by them in a gesture of support, and continue to the nearby Boston Commons, where we would assemble in front of a memorial commemorating the All Negro 54th and 55th Massachusetts Regiments of the Civil War.*

Here, Brother Dr. Charles Wesley, the fraternity's historian, gave an inspiring speech about Negro freedom in this country and recited a brief history of the Negro regiments. Following this moving speech, the brothers sang two verses of the Alpha Hymn. This occasion aroused the emotions of the brothers to the extent that several could be seen weeping unashamedly. Truly, every one who participated in this demonstration was proud of Alpha Phi Alpha's contribution the cause of freedom

Following this demonstration, the members of the convention returned to the hotel in just as orderly a manner as when they left.

The afternoon session was devoted to seminars. Members had their choice of two of six topics:

a. Human Relations and Civil Rights
b. Diplomatic Service and Other Government Careers
c. The impact of Africa and Other Nations on the American Scene
d. The Equal Employment Program in Federal Services
e. The Peace Corps
f. Higher Education

Your delegate attended two seminars: Diplomatic Services and other Government Careers, and The Peace Corps.

The seminars were something new to the convention. Due to the able coordinating of Brother John Bowen, the sessions were expertly conducted and were thoroughly enjoyed by all who attended. It was agreed by the members of the convention that such seminars become a part of future conventions.

The fourth and fifth sessions were held Wednesday morning and afternoon. These sessions were devoted to the presentation and acceptance of reports from committee chairmen, and the nomination and election of national officers whose terms had expired. All of the five vice presidents and assistant vice presidents were elected by nomination, because of lack of opposition. The offices of general counsel and education director were the only elected offices voted on by the

---

*The motion picture *Glory*, which starred Denzel Washington, was based on the performance in the Civil War of the 54th and 55th Massachusetts Regiments.

general body. As a result of votes cast, Brother Ritchie was elected education director. The office of general president will be voted on by mail in December. Brother T. Winston Cole was nominated to succeed himself, and Brother Lionel H. Newsome was named his opponent. The Elections Committee recommended that one half of the ballots show Brother Cole's name first, and one half show Brother Newsome's name in the first position. This recommendation was accepted by the convention.

This sums up the essentials of the business of the convention. The social affairs, however, were not without inspiration, as well as pleasure.

For example, an undergraduate luncheon was sponsored by the five assistant vice presidents, all undergraduates. We were fortunate enough to hear an address by Brother Hamilton Holmes*, Assistant to the Vice President. Brother Holmes is familiar to most of you as a result of publicity he received upon his admittance in June to the University of Georgia. He was graduated from this university and will enter Emory Medical School in the Fall of 1963. It was a pleasure to meet Brother Holmes, for he is a very capable and modest young man.

The concluding affair was the formal banquet and dance Wednesday night. This affair must have been attended by at least four hundred people. The banquet was addressed by Brother Franklin H. Williams, an extremely able attorney and speaker, who now holds the position of Director of Private and International Cooperation of the United States Peace Corps. The banquet ended with the singing of the Alpha Hymn and saying the prayer, led by the chaplain. Dancing followed.

Although this was my first experience as a delegate to a General Convention, I believe I can make the following observations.

1. Undergraduate chapters want to be considered more seriously and desire a more important role in the convention.
2. Brothers are demanding a more democratic method of selecting committee members.
3. More chapters should be represented at General Conventions, otherwise, there will be no alternative but to elect the national officers from a small and non-representative group.

*Brother Dr. Hamilton "Hamp" Holmes graduated from Emory Medical School and served his community well. He was head of orthopedic surgery at Grady Memorial Hospital and a professor at the Emory School of Medicine. Sadly, his obituary appeared in the 1996 Spring issue of *Sphinx* magazine.

Post Convention Activities

At the close of the convention, Betty and I drove our new red Ford Galaxy convertible from Boston to Woods Hole, Massachusetts. There we took the Ferry to Martha's Vineyard, and drove to Oak Bluffs to visit Betty's father who has a cottage there. Her father is a charter member of Tau chapter of Alpha Phi Alpha, located at the University of Illinois. He also was a founder of a chapter in Monrovia, Liberia. He was on leave from his duties as auditor of the European embassies of the Liberian government. His headquarters are in Paris France.

He welcomed us and many of his Alpha Phi Alpha brothers who had attended the Convention in Boston and had come to Martha's Vineyard for fun and relaxation. It was a pleasure to join this group while we watched the exciting March on Washington of 1963 on TV.

I sincerely appreciate the opportunity to represent the Zeta Xi Lambda Chapter of Alpha Phi Alpha in this 57th General Convention, and I hope this report will inspire the chapter to send delegates to future conventions.

Appendix I

Shaw, Clifford R., *The Jack-Roller*, University of Chicago Press

The Jack-Roller is a detailed case study of a young male delinquent. It has been published as part of the program of sociological research at the Institute for Juvenile Research and Behavior Research Fund. Its purpose is to illustrate the use of "own story" material in the study and treatment of the delinquent child.

The delinquent's "own story" is his life history record, an account of his experiences, written as an autobiography, as a diary, or presented in the course of a series of interviews.

Mr. Shaw considers it extremely desirable that the "own story" be developed as an integral part of the total case history. This would include the usual family history, the medical, psychiatric, and psychological findings, the official record of arrest, offenses, and commitments, the description of play-group relationships and any other verifiable material which may throw light upon the personality and actual experiences of the delinquent in question.

The author said that the "own story" reveals useful information concerning the following aspects of delinquent conduct:

1. The point of view of the delinquent.
2. The social and cultural situation to which the delinquent is responsive.
3. The sequence of past experiences and situations in the life of the delinquent.

The use of this information is considered valuable in the diagnosis and treatment of cases of delinquency by affording a basis for devising a plan of treatment which suits the attitudes, interests, and personality of the child. The author considers the life history information of further value in affording a basis for the discovery of causal factors involved in the development of delinquent behavior patterns.

The story of Stanley can be evaluated in the area of the three aspects of delinquent conduct.

I. The point of view of the delinquent.

This is important, because it reveals the child's feelings of inferiority and superiority, his worries and fears, his ideals and philosophy of life, his antagonisms and mental conflicts, his prejudices and rationalizations. Stanley's attitude is revealed by his interpretation of the following situations:

Hope: Stanley was of the opinion that life is guided by fate, even before birth. He considers himself handicapped by a "no good, ignorant and selfish" stepmother. Stanley resented his stepmother's neglect and his own father's refusal to interfere, so he left home to escape this situation.

School: Stanley did not like school and often played hookey. He considered school dull and preferred to roam and be carefree. Stanley liked to read, however, preferring such books as Horatio Alger, James Oliver Curwood, and Zane Grey. No doubt this reading contributed to his desire for adventure.

Neighborhood: Stanley's first close companions were his stepbrother, William, and a friend, Tony. They were older than he and gained his admiration for their ability to steal. This was not surprising, because stealing in the neighborhood was common practice among the children and approved by some of the parents. All boys did it. Fellows who "had done time" were big shots and looked up to. They gave the little fellows tips on how to get by and pull off big jobs.

Correctional Institutions: Stanley's first impression of the detention home was good. Clean sheets, clothes, good meals, baths made him want to stay and never go home. Strict discipline here was hard for Stanley to take. He did much day dreaming. His dreams seemed to enable him to withstand the discipline.

At St. Charles the discipline was worse. Beatings, imposed silence, and loneliness were almost more than Stanley could bear. Stanley hated boy leaders and other officials. He learned well the code of the inmates, "Stick together against boy leaders and officials." Here Stanley pitied himself because he was little and couldn't defend himself against bigger boys.

In spite of beatings at St. Charles, Stanley had no intention of reforming. He only wanted to get ahead as a criminal.

Stanley's experiences at Pontiac changed his outlook somewhat. When his hair was shaved and he was given a number and prison uniform and cell he felt like a criminal for the first time. Because of his size he was called "midget" by older prisoners. He enjoyed their pity. He also indulged in self pity.

Employment: Stanley's work record, which began at twelve years of age, was poor. He held many jobs, but for short durations, primarily because of his rejection of authority or some personality conflict with other employees.

Underworld: Stanley was attracted to crowds of people on West Madison and South State Streets. He talked of his problems with others there. He felt the people there understood him. His pals were pickpockets, panhandlers, petty thieves, and jack-rollers. Stanley was impressed by Italian gamblers, and he aspired to climb the underworld social ladder higher than jack-roller.

II. Social and Cultural Situation to Which the Delinquent Is Responsive.

Stanley's mother died when he was four, leaving him and an older brother and younger brother. His father subsequently married a widow who had seven children of her own. There was constant conflict in the family due to the stepmother's apparent favoring of her children over her stepchildren, and the mother's abuse by the father who habitually came home drunk.

When Stanley was seven, it was recommended that he be placed in a foster home. This recommendation was not followed and Stanley's delinquency continued.

Stanley became a member of a boys gang at the age of seven. These boys had a long tradition of petty stealing, burglary, and sex practices. Stanley received his first experiences in delinquency with this gang.

In Stanley's neighborhood the population was mostly Polish with 52.1 percent foreign born. In many families the emotional conflict between parents and native born children resulted in problems of parental control.

Stanley was so influenced by this background that when he was placed in a more wholesome environment the strain was too great for him. This was illustrated when, upon his release from St. Charles, Stanley went to live with the vice president of the firm for which he worked. The home was upper class, and he was well cared for. But Stanley longed for his old neighborhood and old pals.

Also, keeping good manners was too much for him. Other attempts to get Stanley away from his old environment failed, also, because he could not resist the urge to return to people whom he felt understood him.

III. The Sequences of Past Experiences and Situations in the Life of the Delinquent.

Stanley's delinquent behavior can be attributed to a sequence of past experiences. Some of these are:
1. Lack of love and consideration by his parents.
2. His childhood neighborhood in which there was a tradition of crime.
3. His membership in a boys gang at the age of seven.
4. His periods of confinement in correctional institutions where he came in contact with older, more experienced criminals from whom he learned and accepted their code of criminality.
5. His rejection by society when they discovered his criminal background.

Mr. Shaw, the author, made use of the information obtained by "Stanley's Own Story" to determine the best treatment for him. Consequently, the following program was decided upon.
1. Put Stanley in a new social situation and adapt treatment to his particular attitudes and personality.
   a. Secure foster home in nondelinquent community where relationships were sympathetic and informal.
   b. Avoid formal methods of control.
   c. Guard against behavior which would be construed by Stanley as personal discrimination on grounds of his inferior social status and delinquent record.
2. Vocational Guidance
   a. Stanley's most favorable reactions occurred in positions which gave him a sense of superiority and in which he was not under the direct control of a person of superior rank.
   b. Given a job as salesman to which he adjusted.
3. Assist Stanley in making contacts with groups of young people of his age in the vicinity of his new home.

During the first two years of the period of treatment, personal contact with him was had at least once a week.

This method of treatment resulted in Stanley's adjustment to a profitable occupation, desire for more education, and a reevaluation of ideals. Also, his contact with a girl whom he later married was a powerful factor in his rehabilitation.

The boy's "own story" method of obtaining information to aid in prescribing treatment for a delinquent was successful in this case. I believe this is partly due to the subject boy's ability to relate his experiences in a manner which would be superior to that of the average delinquent. Stanley's love of reading was an aid to him in describing his attitudes, conflicts, and situations. Such an attempt from a delinquent less articulate would perhaps be less successful.

Mr. Shaw said, "The permanent significance of the case of Stanley is in its contribution to the fund of scientific knowledge."

There is no doubt that this study is a definite contribution and with the perfection of technique, it could be a valuable aid in the treatment of the delinquent.

The following is an excerpt taken from *Gang Delinquency and Delinquent Subcultures*, edited by James F. Short Jr., Washington State University, published by Harper and Row.

Juvenile Delinquency: A Group Tradition
by Clifford Shaw

p. 82

"Delinquency is very often regarded by the general public as an expression of 'innate perversity,' 'inherent viciousness,' or 'willful disobedience.' Despite rather widespread acceptance of this belief, there is considerable evidence to substantiate the assumption that the wishes and desires underlying the delinquent boy's participation in the unlawful practices of his group are essentially not unlike those of member groups whose activities meet conventional social approval."

p. 83

"The member of a delinquent group may achieve **recognition** and derive a feeling of superiority by displaying courage in committing a daring crime, by refusing to divulge to the police the identity of his confederates in delinquency, or by virtue of the fact that he has a long record of delinquency or has served a period of incarceration in a correctional institution.

"The boy in a conventional group may achieve similar satisfaction by receiving honors for scholastic achievement, excelling in sports, or by virtue of the fact that his family has prestige and prominence in the community.

This being the case, it appears that the important challenge to the community is to provide legitimate activities and programs in which the underprivileged youths can excel and receive the proper recognition they crave."

This is the challenge that faces Evanston and many other communities today.